Policing European Metropolises is an excellent international comparative study on the politics, governance and practices of security in large cities in nine different European countries. The contributions by distinguished scholars show convincingly that globalization does not only result in convergence, but also in new forms of divergence in policing and security politics. The authors strongly argue that the impact of globalization on security can only be understood by looking at the local level. The study provides a lot of food for thought and for new debate about policing and security in a world of cities.

Jan Terpstra, *Professor of Criminology, Radboud University Nijmegen, the Netherlands*

This path-breaking project documents how local policing policies play out across 22 cities in nine nations. While powerful national and global forces push some metropolitan areas toward standardized responses to common problems, in other places local political and social realities have spawned unique approaches to the issues of terrorism, fiscal austerity, mass migration, emergent nationalism, youth delinquency and adult crime. In its scope and rigor, there has never been anything to match this powerful analysis.

Wesley G. Skogan, *Professor of Political Science and Faculty Fellow of the Institute for Policy Research, Northwestern University, USA*

Mega-cities now dominate world geographies. Tied to shifting demographics, globalization and urbanization, mega-cities have grown in complexity, now representing the highest concentration of peoples across the world. Understanding how such complexities are made secure and safe, by the police and others, is a new intellectual frontier. *Policing European Metropolises* is a significant intellectual and grounded theoretical contribution to understanding such complexities and expanding theories of Metropolitan Police Governance. A must read in a globalized world.

Jack R. Greene, *Professor in the School of Criminology and Criminal Justice, Northeastern University, USA*

Policing European Metropolises

Understanding the politics of security in city-regions is increasingly important for the study of contemporary policing. This book argues that national and international governing arrangements are being outflanked by various transnational threats, including the cross-border terrorism of the attacks on Paris in 2015 and Brussels in 2016; trafficking in people, narcotics and armaments; cybercrime; the deregulation of global financial services; and environmental crime.

Metropolises are the focal points of the transnational networks through which policing problems are exported and imported across national borders, as they provide much of the demand for illicit markets and are the principal engines generating other policing challenges including political protest and civil unrest. This edited collection examines whether and how governing arrangements rooted in older systems of national sovereignty are adapting to these transnational challenges, and considers problems of and for policing in city-regions in the European Union and its single market.

Bringing together experts from across the continent, *Policing European Metropolises* develops a political sociology of urban policing in Europe and a unique methodology for comparing the experiences of different metropolises in the same country. This book will be of value to police researchers in Europe and abroad, as well as postgraduate students with an interest in policing and urban policy.

Elke Devroe is Associate Professor at the Institute of Security and Global Affairs, University of Leiden, the Netherlands.

Adam Edwards is Reader in Politics and Criminology at the School of Social Sciences, Cardiff University, UK.

Paul Ponsaers is Emeritus Professor at the Department of Penal Law and Criminology, University of Ghent, Belgium.

Routledge Studies in Crime, Security and Justice

Edited by
Adam Edwards, Cardiff University
Gordon Hughes, Cardiff University
Reece Walters, Queensland University of Technology

Contemporary social scientific scholarship is being transformed by the challenges associated with the changing nature of, and responses to, questions of crime, security and justice across the globe. Traditional disciplinary boundaries in the social sciences are being disturbed and at times broken down by the emerging scholarly analysis of both the increasing merging of issues of 'crime' and 'security' and the unsettling of traditional notions of justice, rights and due process in an international political and cultural climate seemingly saturated by, and obsessed with, fear, insecurity and risk. This series showcases contemporary research studies, edited collections and works of original intellectual synthesis that contribute to this new body of scholarship both within the field of study of criminology and beyond to its connections with debates in the social sciences more broadly.

Policing European Metropolises
The Politics of Security in City-Regions
Edited by Elke Devroe, Adam Edwards and Paul Ponsaers

Policing European Metropolises

The Politics of Security in City-Regions

Edited by
Elke Devroe, Adam Edwards and
Paul Ponsaers

LONDON AND NEW YORK

First published 2017
by Routledge
2 Park Square, Milton Park, Abingdon, Oxon OX14 4RN

and by Routledge
711 Third Avenue, New York, NY 10017

Routledge is an imprint of the Taylor & Francis Group, an informa business

© 2017 Elke Devroe, Adam Edwards and Paul Ponsaers

The right of the editors to be identified as the authors of the editorial material, and of the authors for their individual chapters, has been asserted in accordance with sections 77 and 78 of the Copyright, Designs and Patents Act 1988.

All rights reserved. No part of this book may be reprinted or reproduced or utilised in any form or by any electronic, mechanical, or other means, now known or hereafter invented, including photocopying and recording, or in any information storage or retrieval system, without permission in writing from the publishers.

Trademark notice: Product or corporate names may be trademarks or registered trademarks, and are used only for identification and explanation without intent to infringe.

British Library Cataloguing in Publication Data
A catalogue record for this book is available from the British Library

Library of Congress Cataloging in Publication Data
A catalog record for this book has been requested

ISBN: 978-1-138-95155-6 (hbk)
ISBN: 978-1-315-66813-0 (ebk)

Typeset in Goudy
by Taylor & Francis Books

Printed and bound by CPI Group (UK) Ltd, Croydon, CR0 4YY

Contents

List of illustrations ix
List of contributors xi

PART I
Introduction 1

1 Processes of convergence and divergence in the policy formulation of policing strategies for European metropolises 3
ELKE DEVROE, ADAM EDWARDS AND PAUL PONSAERS

2 European national police systems and metropolitan realities 23
ELKE DEVROE AND PAUL PONSAERS

PART II
Convergence: The dominance of national states in agenda setting 75

3 France: Governing metropolises: The false pretences of metropolisation 77
JACQUES DE MAILLARD AND CHRISTIAN MOUHANNA

4 Portugal: Urban security governance in Portugal: Key elements and challenges 95
CARLA CARDOSO AND JOSEFINA CASTRO

5 Finland: Policing regimes in transition in the Nordic countries: Some critical notes from the Nordic reality 121
SIRPA VIRTA AND JARI TAPONEN

6   Slovenia: Metropolitan policing in post-socialist countries:
    The case of Slovenia   144
    MAJA MODIC, BRANKO LOBNIKAR, BERNARDA TOMINC, ANDREJ SOTLAR
    AND GORAZD MEŠKO

PART III
Divergence: active city-regions pursuing their own policing agendas 165

7.1 Italy: Urban policing in Italy: Some reflections from a
     comparative perspective   167
     ROSSELLA SELMINI

7.2 Italy: Policing and urban control in Rome and Milan: A view
     from the southern edge of Europe   182
     MARCO CALARESU AND ROSSELLA SELMINI

8   Britain: Metropolitan policing agendas in Britain: Divergent
     tendencies in a fragmenting state?   201
     ADAM EDWARDS, SOPHIE CHAMBERS, NICK FYFE AND ALISTAIR HENRY

9   Germany: Policing metropolises in a system of cooperative
     federalism: Berlin as the German capital and a city-state
     compared to Cologne as the biggest city in North
     Rhine-Westphalia   229
     HARTMUT ADEN AND BERNHARD FREVEL

10   Belgium: Governance of security in Antwerp and Brussels:
     Two of a kind?   249
     EVELIEN DE PAUW AND MARLEEN EASTON

11   The Netherlands: Local strategies for glocal challenges:
     Comparing policing agendas in Amsterdam and Rotterdam   268
     RUTH PRINS AND ELKE DEVROE

PART IV
Conclusion 301

12   The European world of metropolitan policing: Interpreting
     patterns of governance, policy and politics   303
     ADAM EDWARDS, ELKE DEVROE AND PAUL PONSAERS

     Index   332

List of illustrations

Figures

1.1	Sampling logic of embedded cases for PEMP_2	9
1.2	Conceptual frameworks for comparing the formulation of public policing strategies in European metropolises	10
1.3	Multiple, intersecting, internal security fields in Europe	13
2.1	Essential characteristics of police systems	26
2.2	Typology of police systems, according to the number of forces and types of police	26
2.3	The French police system	30
2.4	The Italian police system	33
2.5	The Portuguese police system	36
2.6	The Spanish constitutional layers and their police forces	38
2.7	The police system in England and Wales	43
2.8	The police system in the German Federal Republic	45
2.9	The police system in Switzerland	47
2.10	The police system in Belgium	49
2.11	The police system in Denmark	53
2.12	The police system in the Netherlands	55
2.13	The police system in Northern Ireland	58
2.14	The police system in Scotland	60
2.15	Police capacity per 100,000 inhabitants in the countries under study, 2011	61
2.16	Police capacity per 100,000 inhabitants according to the typology	62
4.1	Total number of police officers and private security guards in Portugal in the last decade	104
9.1	Reduced organisational chart of the Berlin Police	236
9.2	Structure of the Police in North Rhine-Westphalia	239
9.3	Reduced organisational chart of the Cologne Police	239
10.1	Comparison of agenda setting in Antwerp and Brussels, 2016	261

x List of illustrations

Tables

3.1	Compared staffing levels of security forces	83
5.1	Range of tasks for the police in the Nordic countries	126
6.1	Number of reported crimes in the period 2010–14 in Ljubljana and Maribor compared to Slovenia	154
9.1	Facts and figures (Berlin, Cologne)	233
12.1	Diagnostic tool of metropolitan policing dispositions: orientations, populations and objectives	307

Contributors

Hartmut Aden is Professor of German and European Public Law at the Berlin School of Economics and Law and a member of the Research Institute for Private and Public Security Berlin (FÖPS). He studied law and social sciences (especially political and administrative science) in Göttingen, Hanover and Paris.

Marco Calaresu earned a PhD in Political Science at the Istituto Italiano di Scienze Umane – Scuola Normale Superiore (Florence-Pisa, Italy). He was Visiting Researcher at the International Business School of Jönköping, and Visiting Scholar at New York University. He is currently a Post-doctoral Research Fellow at University of Sassari. His research interests include security policies, the quality of democracy, and urban change.

Carla Cardoso has a PhD in Biomedical Sciences, University of Porto. She is Professor at the School of Criminology, Faculty of Law, University of Porto. Her main research interests and publications are on experimental and biosocial criminology, fear of crime, security and crime prevention.

Josefina Castro has a master's degree in Criminology from the University of Porto. She is sub-director and invited Assistant Professor at the School of Criminology, Faculty of Law, University of Porto. Her research interests and publications are on juvenile justice and delinquency, security and crime prevention.

Sophie Chambers is a PhD researcher at Cardiff University, within the School of Social Sciences, and School of Law and Politics. Her principal research interest is the governance of policing in England and Wales, particularly in times of legislative reform of policing.

Jacques de Maillard is Professor of Political Science at the University of Versailles – Saint-Quentin, and Deputy Director of CESDIP (Le Centre de recherche sociologique sur le droit et les institutions pénales). He works on police reform and the local governance of public security, topics on which he is widely published.

Evelien De Pauw is a criminologist and PhD candidate at the research group 'Governing & Policing Security' located at the Faculty of Economics & Business Administration, Ghent University, Belgium. Furthermore Lecturer and Researcher at VIVES University College, Kortrijk, Belgium. She is head of the research group on safety and security. The main topics of her research field are policing, internal safety and security, crisis management, and technology and innovation.

Elke Devroe has a doctoral degree in Criminology. She is Associate Professor at the University of Leiden, Campus The Hague (Netherlands) at the Institute of Security and Global Affairs. Her main fields of interest are prevention and maintenance of urban crime and social disorder in the public domain.

Marleen Easton is Professor and Director of the research group 'Governing & Policing Security' located at the Faculty of Economics and Business Administration, Ghent University, Belgium. Her main topics of research are governance and management in the field of security.

Adam Edwards is a Reader in Politics and Criminology in Cardiff University School of Social Sciences. He is a founding member of the Policing European Metropolises Project and prior to that he directed the European Society of Criminology's working groups on 'Crime, Science and Politics' (2009–11) and the 'Governance of Public Safety' (2003–09). He is currently Regional Editor of the *European Journal of Policing Studies*. His principal research interest is in liberal democratic modes of governance and their security implications.

Bernhard Frevel studied Pedagogy, Sociology and Political Science in Siegen, Cologne and Hagen. He is Professor of Social Sciences at the University of Applied Sciences for Public Administration of North Rhine-Westphalia and Associate Professor for Political Science at the University of Münster.

Nick Fyfe is Director of the Scottish Institute for Policing Research, Professor in the School of the Environment at the University of Dundee and co-chair of the Policing Working Group of the European Society of Criminology. The main focus of his research at present is police reform. He co-edited (with Jan Terpstra and Pieter Tops) *Centralizing Forces: Comparative Perspectives on Contemporary Police Reform in Northern and Western Europe* (Eleven Publishing, 2013) and is currently directing a four-year evaluation of police and fire service reform in Scotland funded by the Scottish Government.

Alistair Henry is Associate Director of the Scottish Institute for Policing Research, Lecturer in Criminology in the School of Law at the University of Edinburgh, and co-chair of the Policing Working Group of the

European Society of Criminology. His current research interests include police governance and accountability, community safety and partnership working, academic-practitioner research collaborations, and reflexivity in criminal justice research.

Branko Lobnikar, PhD, is Associate Professor of Security Management, Head of the Chair of Policing and Security Studies at the Faculty of Criminal Justice and Security, University of Maribor, Slovenia. His areas of expertise comprise policing, human resource management, and deviant behaviour within organisations.

Gorazd Meško, PhD, is Professor of Criminology at the Faculty of Criminal Justice and Security, University of Maribor, Slovenia. His current research interests include crime prevention, provision of safety/security, and legitimacy of policing and criminal justice.

Maja Modic, PhD, is Assistant Professor of Security Studies at the Faculty of Criminal Justice and Security, University of Maribor, Slovenia. Her current research interests include policing, police-residents relationships and legitimacy of policing.

Christian Mouhanna is a sociologist and researcher at the National Centre for Scientific Research, France, working on police organisations, security policies, and relationships between police forces and population.

Paul Ponsaers graduated in Sociology and has a doctoral degree in Criminology. He was Departmental Head of the Police Policy Support Unit. From 1998 to 2012, Paul was working as Senior Professor at Ghent University, Belgium, in the Department of Penal Law and Criminology. Today he is Emeritus Professor. He is an active author in the domains of policing, security policy, and financial and economic crime.

Ruth Prins is PhD and Assistant Professor at Leiden University, the Netherlands. Ruth is employed as an Assistant Professor at the Institute of Public Administration at Leiden University, Campus The Hague. Her research focuses on public safety governance, policing, local government, policy dynamics, agenda setting and framing. Ruth has published on integrated safety policies, community policing and the role of Dutch mayors in tackling new threats to local order and public safety.

Rossella Selmini has a PhD in Social and Political Science from the European University Institute (Florence, Italy). While teaching in several Italian universities, she was also, for many years, the director of a government department in Emilia Romagna working on research, crime prevention programmes and coordination of municipal police. Since 2012 she has been Associate Professor of Criminology in the Department of Sociology, University of Minnesota.

Andrej Sotlar, PhD, is Associate Professor in Security Studies at the Faculty of Criminal Justice and Security, University of Maribor, Slovenia. His main research fields of interest are: the structure of national security systems; security policy-making process; intelligence and security services; private security and the relationship between public and private security/ policing providers; and terrorism.

Jari Taponen is Chief Inspector of the Helsinki Police Department and a PhD student at University of Tampere, Finland.

Bernarda Tominc, BA, is Lecturer in the Faculty of Criminal Justice and Security, University of Maribor, Slovenia. Her research interests include international political and security integration, national security systems, and security threats in contemporary society.

Sirpa Virta is Professor of Policing and Police Management in the School of Management, University of Tampere, Adjunct Professor, Department of Leadership and Military Pedagogy, Defence University, Helsinki, and Head of the Nordic Centre of Excellence NordSTEVA (Nordic Centre of Security Technologies and Societal Values), at University of Tampere.

Part I

Introduction

Chapter 1

Processes of convergence and divergence in the policy formulation of policing strategies for European metropolises

Elke Devroe, Adam Edwards and Paul Ponsaers

This edited collection forms part of a broader, ongoing research project, the 'Policing European Metropolises Project' (PEMP). The Project has its origins in a network of researchers interested in the significance of sub-national policing for understanding processes of convergence and divergence in policing across Europe. The Project commenced in 2013 and reported the findings of its first phase (PEMP_1) in a special issue of the *European Journal of Policing Studies* (Ponsaers et al., 2014). The initial aim of the Project was to address the question:

> To what extent is a local police still present in European metropolises and how is this reality linked with other actors in the security field?
> (Ponsaers et al., 2014: 4)

This question was defined in relation to current debates in policy discourse and social science about the relationship of sub-national, specifically metropolitan, policing to developments in the European 'internal security field' (Bigo & Guild, 2005). This includes developments in supra-national policing policy, including the European Union's (EU) objective of creating a Union-wide 'Area of Freedom, Security and Justice' (AFSJ), transnational policing arrangements, such as the Schengen Agreement, and the continued importance of national policing strategies given the variegated historical experiences of European countries, for example those in transition from former Soviet regimes in Eastern and Central Europe or Latin countries in transition from former dictatorship.

In questioning any continued 'local reality' of policing, the Project seeks to distinguish itself from theories of convergence in European policing as a consequence of, for example, 'Europeanisation' (Bigo & Guild, 2005), 'securitisation' (Waever, 1995; Hallsworth & Lea, 2011), 'responsibilisation' (Garland, 2001), 'neo-liberalisation' (Wacquant, 2001) the formation of a 'transnational state' (Bowling & Sheptycki, 2012) or the promotion of 'plural policing' (Jones & Newburn, 2006).

Rather, the Project acknowledges these 'tendencies' but seeks to identify their uneven impact and the adaptation of local policing to alleged master narratives of policing change. In turn, this interest in divergence has been stimulated by arguments about the particular importance of metropolises in the constitution of 'global' security threats and policing responses. These arguments reflect wider debates in social science about 'glocalisation' or the idea that, as a consequence of the greater mobility of capital, labour, goods and services across national borders, it is powerful metropolises or, in the argot of public policy, 'city-regions', that become a key focus of comparative social research. They become the principal centres of power through which globalisation is accomplished as they project their political, economic and cultural powers onto other, less powerful, localities, circumventing if not subordinating nation-state authorities. This is akin to the concept of an evolving 'world urban system' (King, 1997) in which national states represent only one centre of authority within other circuits of power (Clegg, 1989; Edwards et al., this volume). In these terms, certain metropolises become the key nodal points (Castells, 1996) or 'command centres' (Sassen, 2001) in more networked and globally integrated social relations whilst other metropolises have to adapt to these forces with minimal protection from national authorities. In a further development of this argument it is suggested that national governing programmes are often subordinated to, and increasingly oriented around, the interests of powerful city-regions (Scott, 2012).

A key implication of these broader debates is a need for comparative research capable of understanding the role of metropolitan authorities in driving policing change and whether this role enables a greater diversity in policing policies, generating opportunities for comparing and contrasting rival approaches and their outcomes, or whether the involvement of metropolitan authorities in transnational networks creates tendencies toward policy convergence (Pollitt, 2001). An important corollary of this research aim is to identify the political agency and discretion available to metropolises to define and accomplish their own policing agendas and to question what the role of social science can be in constituting such agendas. However, in pursuing these research aims, it is necessary to address major challenges of translation in cross-cultural analysis: linguistic, conceptual and disciplinary. These challenges can be elaborated through reference to developments in policy and social scientific discourse about public policing in Europe.

I The changing policy and social scientific discourse on public policing in Europe

Public policy-makers in the institutions of the European Union itself have argued that the AFSJ marks a major turning point in the reorganisation of policing amongst member states of the Union, regarding it as an inevitable and inexorable consequence of the 'four freedoms' constituting the Union (freedom of movement of goods, workers, services and capital).

Realising these four freedoms creates, at one and the same time, an 'internal security field' within the borders of the Union and the necessity of 'external border control'. In these terms, the EU has claimed a competence for issues of home affairs and (criminal) justice, hitherto regarded as the sole preserve, indeed core constitutive element, of national sovereignty. The 'Europeanisation' of policing can be traced in the multi-annual programmes for AFSJ which commenced with the Tampere programme (1999–2004) and then the Hague (2005–10) and Stockholm (2010–15) programmes, and which has culminated in the current New Security Agenda for Europe, agreed in 2015 (European Commission, 2015). The Tampere programme further justified the increasing competence of the EU in issues of home affairs and justice, including the establishment of Union-wide policing (Europol) and justice (Eurojust) agencies, through reference to perceived 'threats' to the shared internal security of member states, specifically 'transnational organised crime' and 'illegal immigration'.

Subsequently, the 9/11 attack on the United States and the bombing of the public transport system in Madrid in 2004 promoted the concern with transnational terrorism as another major threat and consequently the priority accorded to counter-terrorism in the Hague programme. Finally, the Stockholm programme extended the competence of the EU even further into the realms of volume crime prevention and issues of social integration, variously referred to as 'urban security' (e.g. 'citta sicura'), integral security (e.g. 'integrale veiligheid') and, in the Anglophone world, 'community safety'.

In turn, this evolving Europeanisation of public policy discourse about home affairs and justice has been accompanied by a criticism of the limits to the capacity of nation-states to effectively respond to transnational threats emanating from within the Union, as a consequence of the four freedoms, and from without, including the post-Cold War liberalisation of the mobility of capital, labour, goods and services and the advent of transnational terrorism in reaction to the foreign policy commitments of European states in the Middle East. This policy discourse also has an affinity with arguments about glocalisation as the uneven impact of transnational threats, on certain metropolises and not others, is increasingly recognised. Indeed it is precisely because transnational threats have this uneven impact but circumvent the capacity of nation-states to effectively protect localities in their own national jurisdiction, that the EU has claimed an increasing competence in home affairs. The conclusion of this policy discourse for research is that understanding, and acting upon, problems of internal security needs to take metropolises as basic units of analysis.

One response to this policy discourse within policing studies has been to identify the emergence of a 'transnational state system' (Bowling & Sheptycki, 2012) that is compensating for, and in turn challenging, national state sovereignty in matters of home affairs. A complementary argument is that policing research needs to investigate how transnational networks are constituted by powerful local actors as well as by transnational institutions (for example the Schengen Area). This line of argument emerged out of PEMP_1 (Ponsaers et al., 2014; Edwards et al., this volume).

However, theses on the withering of nation-state power have been challenged for ignoring the continued resilience, if not primacy, of nation-states and of inter-national relations in shaping home affairs, including those within the internal security field of the EU (Stenson, 2008; Lea & Stenson, 2007). Critics note the resurgence of popular nationalist movements both within the electorates of member states, notably the 'Brexit' referendum in the UK in favour of leaving the EU (see Edwards et al., this volume) and in elections to the European Parliament. They also note the resurgence of nationalist conflicts on the Eastern borders of the Union, most notably in the Ukraine and in the Baltics. Critics of the 'transnationalisation thesis' also note the emergence of national 'security state' formations (Hallsworth & Lea, 2011), which in the first two decades of the 21st century have enhanced their intrusive powers of surveillance, detention without arrest and prosecutorial powers, including reversals in the burden of proof (as in the power to seize assets obtained by criminal means). From this perspective, far from withering, the nation-state is becoming an even more assertive actor subject to less democratic oversight, scrutiny and legal constraint.

2 Translating the policing of European metropolises

Investigating these competing policy and social scientific claims about the relative power of national, supra-national, trans-national and sub-national authorities to determine policing agendas implies a programme of comparative research. As noted in the introduction, however, such programmes encounter significant problems of translation which need to be addressed if European social scientists wish to avoid talking at, or past, rather than with one another.

Most obviously there is the linguistic challenge of translating the meaning of apparently similar concepts that actually signify quite divergent practices. For example, the connotation of 'policing' in some European contexts with the public policies formulated and implemented by state police actors and, in others, with strategies undertaken by a multiplicity of state, commercial and voluntary actors working 'in partnership' to address issues of crime, public order and social integration. Underpinning such linguistic differences is the further challenge of translating the meanings 'in use' of policing, both in public policy and social scientific discourse. For example, the use of policy constructs like 'community policing' or 'urban security' to signify a broad range of interventions against crime and civil unrest that can include social and economic policies to promote social integration (e.g. work with young people, families, employment and training and so forth), as well as the more conventional focus on criminal justice policy responses. A key implication of this broader translation of policing problems is precisely the necessary involvement of agencies beyond nationally constituted criminal justice systems to include other actors at the sub-national level, given the perceived importance of intervening at the level of the metropolis and at the sub-metropolitan level of 'neighbourhoods' which are the contexts in which problems of security are actually experienced. In turn, the use of social scientific constructs, such as 'securitisation' and 'responsibilisation', to interpret and criticise policy constructs presents a further problem of translation, that of the 'double hermeneutic', in which social scientists have to interpret the interpretations of their research subjects, a problem that exists in any social context but which is accentuated in the cross-cultural contexts of 'Europe'.

A final, yet further, aspect of these problems of translation is the communication amongst social scientists from different disciplines in placing their interpretations on the interpretations of their research subjects. In an earlier account of this problem, the policing researcher, Robert Reiner (1988), identified a 'parallel blindness' between the research programmes of criminology and political science which echoed David Matza's (1969: 143–144) broader criticism of positivist criminology, 'which achieved the seemingly impossible, divorcing crime from the state'. The parallel quality of this blindness can still be detected in tendencies to divorce substantive security 'problems' from the social reaction to them. In effect, what persists in criminology on the one hand, and political sociology on the other, is a treatment of security problems as if they are either the artefacts of policing and governing rationalities (a form of extreme constructionism) or as if they exist independently of these rationalities (the positivist 'sensing' of crime).

In this regard the emerging inter-disciplinary subject of 'security studies' presents an opportunity to understand policing as an emergent product of interactions between 'problems' and 'responses' (Balzacq & Dunn Cavelty, 2016). Recognising this emergent quality of policing implies an analytical concern with political competition, which includes but is not reducible to governing rationalities or 'governmentalities' (Foucault, 1991; Rose, 2000) and consequently requires an understanding of other policing dispositions, how they are facilitated by technologies of production and discipline but also how these are apprehended or neglected and then acted on by competing policing actors (Clegg, 1989; Edwards, 2016). In short, policing research needs to be located in an explicit analytic of power.

A fundamental proposition of the PEMP is that these linguistic, conceptual and disciplinary problems of translation necessitate a collaborative approach to cross-national and inter-disciplinary research. More provocatively, it can be argued that these problems of translation are not specific to the analysis of policing but are constitutive of social science in Europe (Bourdieu, 1998), including a distinctively 'European' criminology (Smith,

2004). The implication of this collaborative approach is that research strategy needs to be accomplished through a series of sequential phases of discussion and criticism in which the meanings of policing across different European contexts can be established through dialogue and deliberation rather than treated as given. Technically, this research strategy can be depicted as 'inductive – adaptive', where theoretical propositions enabling comparative social scientists to criticise, not just reiterate, constructs in policing policy and research emerge out of initial phases of conceptual clarification and description and are then revised, 'adapted', in the light of empirical investigation. In these terms, the first phase of PEMP sought to establish the existence of metropolitan policing strategies as objects of policing politics and governance that are distinct from, and cannot be reduced to, policing policies formulated elsewhere, in, above or beneath the nation-state. The key insight of the first phase of the Project is that such strategies do exist, for example in the 'Axis Plan' for Barcelona (Recasens i Brunet & Ponsaers, 2014) and the 'Police and Crime Plan' for London (Edwards & Prins, 2014), although their relationship to national and supra-national strategies affecting the policing in these and other metropolises is less clear. In response to the presentation of this key insight, along with other findings from PEMP_1, at the annual meeting of the European Society of Criminology in Prague in September 2014, a number of constructive criticisms were made which have driven the second phase of the Project, whose findings are reported in this volume. These criticisms can be distinguished in terms of the empirical, methodological and conceptual aspects of the Project.

The multiple but holistic case study design adopted for the first phase of the Project, in which policing in one city per country was investigated, stimulated discussion about the need for further research capable of clarifying the grounds for demonstrating the specifically *metropolitan*, rather than *national*, effect on sub-national policing strategies. To this end, PEMP_2 has adopted a multiple-embedded case study design in which the multiplicity of national contexts has been expanded, beyond the original five (England and Wales, Bulgaria, Germany, France and Spain), to include Italy, the Netherlands, Belgium, Great Britain (England, Wales and Scotland), Finland, Slovenia, Portugal, Germany and France, and the units of analysis within these cases extended to include an *intra*-national comparison of policing in at least two metropolises.

To this end, PEMP_1 adopted a more inductive approach seeking to build a cross-national research network that accommodated the breadth of empirical and conceptual interests in policing at the metropolitan level rather than an overly directive approach driven by a particular theoretical approach or thesis. Rather, the intention of PEMP_1 was to explore whether it was possible to reach a consensus about the appropriate empirical and conceptual approach to comparison, not least to recognise genuine variegation in policing strategies across these different contexts, for example the

Policy formulation of metropolitan policing strategies in Europe 9

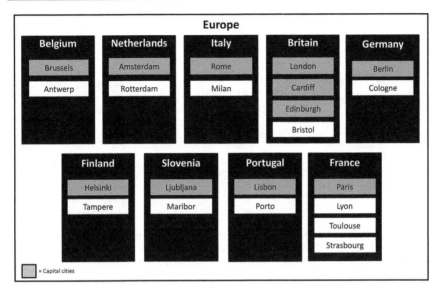

Figure 1.1 Sampling logic of embedded cases for PEMP_2

reduction of metropolitan policing to national police strategy. As such, this inductive approach necessarily under-conceptualised the units of comparative analysis but generated a rich repertoire of suggestions for further research.

3 Comparing the formulation of public policing strategies in European metropolises: a conceptual framework

These parameters can be summarised through reference to the methodological arguments of the Polish sociologist Piotr Sztompka (1990), in terms of 'the scope of applicability, objects and predicates' of comparative analysis (see Figure 1.2). As implied in the background discussion of PEMP_1 and its reception, the scope of applicability is metropolises within member states of the European Union since the advent of the multi-annual programmes for AFSJ and, in particular, the period of the Stockholm programme and the extension of the EU's interest in matters of urban security.[1] This, of course, is not to ignore the significance of earlier periods of policy-making about policing strategies where they clarify continuities and key policy shifts in particular national and metropolitan contexts (for example, the shift from community safety back to narrower police-centred strategies in Italy post-2008 financial crisis and the onset of 'austerity', Selmini, this volume).

The first phase of the Project also reflected a broader ambiguity and argument over the relationship between 'police', 'policing' and various 'social integration' strategies (variously translated as 'community safety', 'integral

	Foci of Comparison		
	Scope of Applicability	Scope of Objects	Scope of Predicates
Logic of Comparison — Seeking Convergence	Europe	Public Policy Formulation	P1. Standing Conditions P2. Dispositions P3. Facilitative Powers
Seeking Divergence	Metropolises	Strategic Plans	P1. Means and Resources P2. Rules Fixing Relations of Meaning and Membership P3. Innovation in Techniques of Discipline and Production

Figure 1.2 Conceptual frameworks for comparing the formulation of public policing strategies in European metropolises
(Adapted from Sztompka, 1990; Clegg, 1989; Edwards & Hughes, 2005)

security' and 'urban security') (Edwards et al., 2013), as either objects or predicates of comparison. Of course, this is not particular to PEMP but is an ongoing dispute within the contemporary sociology of policing, reflecting an interest in the phenomenon of 'plural policing' and a broadening of the scope of objects of comparative analysis to include commercial and voluntary, formal and informal, actors and the distinction between policing as a process (which can be undertaken by a multiplicity of actors beyond the state police) and 'police' as a very particular apparatus or modern institution (Jones & Newburn, 2006; Reiner, 2010; Crawford, 2008; Loader, 2000; Terpstra, 2012; Devroe, 2015; Devroe & Terpstra, 2015; Prins et al., 2012). More recently a further dimension of analysis has been introduced through the distinction between 'strategic' and 'operational' policing, with the former referring to the role of elected and appointed decision makers in setting the medium-term (four- to five-year plans covering terms of office) and overall direction and priorities for policing across various territories and the latter referring to the mundane, everyday and operational, tactical decisions made by those policing actors with responsibility for implementation. This broader debate over 'plural policing' exacerbates the problem of translating concepts for comparative research and increases the risk of researchers adopting empirical foci that are not actually compatible.

To address this translation problem, the second phase of the Project delimits the scope of objects to the formulation of public policies for policing European metropolises which, in particular cases, are signalled by the formulation of medium-term 'strategic plans' that run concurrently with elected terms of office (for example, the four-year term of office for the elected mayor of London). In these terms the comparative work undertaken for the second phase of the Project delimits the objects of analysis to 'public' (not commercial, involuntary or informal, etc.) policing, 'policy formulation' (not implementation or outcomes) that is 'strategic' and concerned with medium-term planning and agenda setting (not operational policing). This is not to deny the significance of these other parameters of comparative policing research, some of which will form a focus for research in subsequent phases of the PEMP, especially phases considering policing metropolises 'in action'. Rather, it is to ensure there is a compatibility between the foci of comparison in the various case studies of metropolitan policing considered in this volume and to privilege, in the first instance, a concern with the capacity of metropolitan authorities to set their own policing agendas.

Having established the scope of objects for comparison in contributions to the second phase of the Project, Figure 1.2 draws upon theories of power in social science, in particular Clegg's (1989) 'circuits of power' framework, to distinguish the kinds of power that can produce or inhibit metropolitan policing strategies – that is, the 'predicates' of public policy formulation in this field. These predicates, initially developed in Edwards and Hughes (2005), can be distinguished in terms of the 'standing conditions', which policy actors necessarily inhabit and which enable or constrain their capacity to advance particular policing agendas (for example, the constitutional-legal powers that particular actors have to make or contest policing strategies, the financial resources and organisational resources available to them, and the kinds of intelligence and 'data' that can inform or contest policing agendas); the 'dispositions' that characterise these agendas and the strategic direction that policy actors wish to set (for example, the pursuit of criminal justice and risk management or restorative and social justice policing goals); and the 'facilitative powers', the technologies of production and discipline, which can disrupt or help consolidate particular policing strategies, for example, economic crises, such as the 2008 financial crisis and subsequent sovereign debt crises affecting a number of European countries, the migration crisis, within and from without the European Union, or the impact of innovations in digital technologies facilitating 'smart policing', etc. (Edwards, 2016).

Defining and differentiating these objects and predicates of comparison for the second phase of the Project was the remit of papers presented at the annual meeting of the European Society of Criminology in Porto in September 2015. In these terms the main aim of the second phase of the Project is to question: What processes of convergence and divergence exist in the policy formulation of policing strategies for European metropolises and how can these be explained?

4 Comparing metropolitan policing strategies in the context of multiple internal security fields: a conceptual framework

Whilst an emphasis on metropolitan policing strategies helps to better clarify the scope of comparative analysis, providing a logic for better identifying, characterising and explaining any processes of convergence and divergence, there is a danger of presuming that metropolitan-level strategies exist across all of the metropolises that are of interest. However, this would be to reduce the complex reality of continuity and change in sub-national policing in ways that obscure the ongoing importance of national authorities, indeed their centrality to the formulation of policing strategies for cities in particular countries, as well as other centres of power in the supra-national and transnational contexts of metropolitan policing. As discussed in greater detail through the various contributions to Part II of the book, these strategies inhabit a multiplicity of internal security fields rather than a (singular) European internal security field as presumed in the first phase of the Project. Rather, findings from the first phase of the Project implied the existence of a number of contexts which policing strategists in particular metropolises can inhabit and which are envisaged here in Figure 1.3.

This conceptual framework is informed by Bourdieu's (1977, 1990) concept of 'semi-autonomous fields'. For Bourdieu fields are systems of objective relations between positions that are constituted by various species of capital or power. Positions in a field are occupied by actors and are interrelated. Fields are characterised by asymmetric power relations, as a structured social space, with its own rules, schemes of dominance, subordination and legitimate opinions which are, in turn, 'relatively autonomous' of the broader social structure. The principal implication is that the formulation of policing strategies is an emergent outcome of influences from a number of discrete but interrelated internal security fields. Rather than there being a, singular, 'internal security field' (see Bigo, 2000), the implication of research undertaken for PEMP_2 is that there are a multiplicity of semi-autonomous fields of policing, which encompass competing objects of 'freedom, security and justice'. It is precisely in questioning how these are configured in particular metropolises but not others that explanatory theories about divergence and convergence in policing at the sub-national level in Europe can be built.

Apropos the scope of applicable comparisons, all metropolises inhabit a national security field, all the metropolises considered in PEMP_2 also inhabit the EU's AFSJ and are subject to its multi-annual programmes (although this could alter in future phases of the Project if non-EU metropolises are included or in the event that metropolises currently in the EU exit, such as those in the UK post-Brexit referendum), and all metropolises inhabit the global context of, for example, the internet and deregulated financial services. Within these national and supra-national contexts, however, there is an important variegation in the particular transnational contexts inhabited by some metropolises but not others. For example, not all metropolises in the EU inhabit the transnational context of the Schengen Agreement (e.g. the British cities of Bristol, Cardiff, Edinburgh and London), or inhabit various informal policy networks amongst, for example, metropolitan authorities in the Nordic states (see Virta and Taponen, this volume)

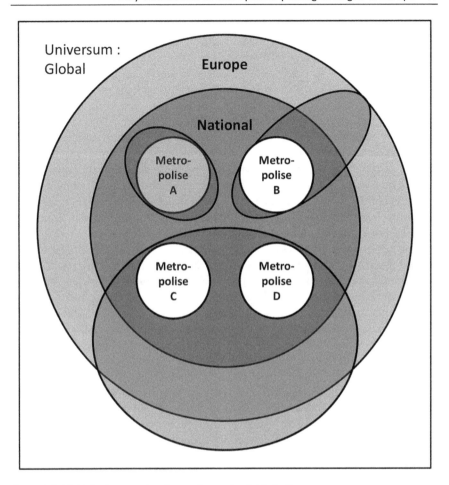

Figure 1.3 Multiple, intersecting, internal security fields in Europe

or amongst Southern European countries (see Recasens et al., 2013). The proposition is that the particular insertion of metropolises within these overlapping security fields helps to identify, characterise and explain significant divergences in policing strategy.

Conceptualising the comparison of policing strategies in this way also recognises the variegated insertion of metropolises within a 'world urban system' (King, 1996), which, in addition to their location within the European security field, shapes the particular opportunities for, and threats to, freedom, security and justice that specific metropolises export and import. For example, London imports particular security threats as a consequence of its status as a capital city involved in foreign policy networks and as its status as a centre of global financial services (see Edwards & Prins, 2014;

Edwards et al., this volume). Similarly, as horrifically witnessed on Friday 13 November 2015, Paris imports major security threats as a consequence of its insertion in the global struggle against supporters of Islamic State. To this end, our 'internal security fields' heuristic alerts comparativists to the insights that can be gleaned from the cross-national comparison of similar kinds of metropolis. In this example, comparisons between London and Paris are liable to yield insights into processes of divergence and convergence in policing strategies within metropolises experiencing comparable problems.

Heuristics are not, however, explanations and so a final ambition of PEMP_2 is to stimulate argument over the possible causes of divergence and convergence in the formulation of policing strategies. As such, the ambition of the second phase of the Project is to advance more explicit analytical reflections on the formulation of policing strategies in particular metropolises. To stimulate this kind of theory building, contributions to the book draw upon broader 'circuits of power' (Clegg, 1989) in social science to distinguish the causal power of particular policing strategists (chief police officers, elected mayors, ministers of the interior, etc.) and the various 'standing conditions' (the constitutional-legal mandates, financial resources, organisational forms, political scandals and intelligence) in which this causal power is exercised from other kinds of power that may also help to characterise and explain the policing strategies formulated by these actors. In these terms it is possible to distinguish further the 'dispositional' power that establishes the meaning of, and membership in, policing strategies oriented around 'criminal justice' agendas and/or those of 'risk management', 'restorative justice' or 'social justice' to name some familiar, if not exhaustive, policing dispositions. Finally, processes of divergence and convergence might be conceptualised in terms of the 'facilitative' power that enables the constitution and reproduction of certain policing dispositions whilst disabling and discrediting others. For example, we might reflect on the impact of terrorist atrocities, such as the Paris attacks on 13 November 2015, on the consolidation or disruption of criminal justice dispositions.

In limiting the object of comparison in PEMP_2 to policy formulation, it is acknowledged that we cannot impute much about the actual practise and outcomes of policing strategies 'in action' (Latour, 1987, 1986). This implies a further phase of research capable of examining any 'implementation gap' between policy in formulation and policy in action through more ethnographic research methods. Although this is beyond the scope of the current volume, this is an ambition for subsequent phases of the Project.

5 Organisation of the book

The book is divided into four parts. The first introductory part (Part I) contains this introduction, 'Processes of convergence and divergence in the policy formulation of policing strategies for European metropolises', written by Elke Devroe, Adam Edwards and Paul Ponsaers (Chapter 1), in which we elaborate and exemplify our suggested conceptual framework for comparison, which understands metropolitan policing strategies as the outcome of influences from multiple, intersecting, 'fields of internal security'.

Part I also contains a second chapter, 'European national police systems and metropolitan realities', written by Elke Devroe and Paul Ponsaers (Chapter 2). They consider the continued significance of the national contexts of metropolitan policing, which are often neglected in accounts of transnational and supra-national internal security fields. The chapter develops a typology of national policing systems, distinguishing between historically diverse police systems, territorially divided police systems and unified national systems. As such, the chapter considers the alignment of national policing systems with the political constitution of different European nation-states, as a means of questioning the particular significance and institutional effects of federal and unitary polities for metropolitan policing strategies.

In Part II, 'Convergence: the dominance of national states in agenda setting', we focus on those national realities that clearly dominate the formulation of metropolitan policing agendas. Originally we thought that this part should look at *transnational* policing issues, including regional relations (e.g. policing agreements amongst Scandinavian countries, or the distinctiveness of metropolitan policing in Eastern and Central Europe in countries still experiencing the legacy of communist regimes, or of metropolitan policing in societies still experiencing the legacy of dictatorship as in Portugal and Spain). As we received contributions to this part, it became apparent that variation amongst the politics and policy agendas of policing in the metropolises under study was negligible because of the apparent dominant position of national state agendas and the inability of metropolises to pursue their own policing agendas through distinctive city-regional policies.

The first country considered in this part is France, the chapter entitled 'Governing metropolises: the false pretences of metropolisation', written by Jacques de Maillard and Christian Mouhanna (Chapter 3). The authors are analysing the efforts of the local governance of four metropolises (Paris, Lyons, Toulouse and Strasbourg), to develop a policing agenda that is divergent from the national one. Starting from the 1983 Bonnemaison report, de Maillard and Mouhanna illustrate the limits of local governance in the field of security and the manoeuvring of central authorities to maintain their dominant position in this area.

Next Carla Cardoso and Josefina Castro discuss the interaction of internal security fields in the context of Portuguese metropolises (Lisbon and Porto) since the transition from Salazar's dictatorship to a liberal democratic polity. In their chapter, 'Urban security governance in Portugal: key-elements and challenges' (Chapter 4), Cardoso and Castro argue that the strategic power of the Portuguese nation-state in formulating policing policy has been maintained in ways that continue to restrict the discretion of Portuguese metropolises to formulate their own policing strategies. Although the strategic power of the Portuguese nation-state has been maintained, they identify three distinctive periods of the liberal democratic state in which the disposition of policing has altered. Finally they characterise the current dominant national policing strategy, since 2010, as one struggling to adapt to conditions of austerity.

In 'Policing regimes in transition in the Nordic countries (some critical notes from the Nordic reality)', Sirpa Virta and Jari Taponen (Chapter 5) explore the interaction of national, supra-national and transnational internal security fields in the particular context of Nordic metropolises. In the first instance, these metropolises inhabit unitary nation-states with powerful central authorities that in the immediate post-war period were concerned to maintain social democratic welfare states. In the second instance, these nation-states established formal and informal international agreements for internal security. The authors argue that this combination of strong nation-states engaged in international agreements has reduced the discretion available to metropolises to formulate their own distinctive policing strategies and acted as a major driver of convergence in policing dispositions amongst Nordic metropolises. Whilst the strength of this international internal security field continues, Virta and Taponen argue it is currently undergoing a process of transition from a social democratic to a neo-liberal disposition as Nordic states struggle to adapt to the impact of the increased freedom of movement for capital, labour, goods and services across national borders.

In Chapter 6, 'Metropolitan policing in post-Soviet countries: the case of Slovenian convergence and diversity in policing post-socialist countries', Maja Modic, Branko Lobnikar, Bernarda Tominc, Andrej Sotlar and Gorazd Meško discuss the interaction of national, supra-national and transnational internal security fields in the particular context of Central and Eastern European metropolises. The distinctiveness of this context is the shared history of experiencing policing in transition to liberal democracies from former communist political systems. The provision of security is to a large extent under state patronage in both the metropolises under study (Ljubljana and Maribor). The legislative regulation for all institutions of policing contributes to very few differences in both analysed cities, and mayors do not have much of an impact on the agenda of the centralised state police. Furthermore, the national law on local police does not allow municipalities to have full autonomy with regard to the functioning of municipal warden services in these metropolises.

Part III, 'Divergence: active city-regions pursuing their own policing agendas', includes contributions that distinguish metropolitan-specific effects on policing from national effects. Here metropolises are actively encouraged to pursue their own policing agendas through city-regional policies.

Chapter 7 is built on two contributions from Italy: first, 'Urban policing in Italy: some reflections from a comparative perspective', written by

Rossella Selmini; and second, 'Policing and urban control in Rome and Milan: a view from the southern edge of Europe', written by Marco Calaresu and Rossella Selmini. The authors consider the interaction of internal security fields in the context of Italian metropolises (Rome and Milan), in which the nation-state has had the constitutional mandate for formulating policing strategy but has struggled to project this strategic power over metropolitan authorities which, as a consequence, have significant discretion to formulate their own policing agendas. The authors observe an asymmetric relationship between a weak national state and relatively autonomous local states. They depict the current period as one in which those metropolises that did adopt local urban security strategies encompassing social and economic policy responses to problems of routine, volume, crime and civil unrest have now withdrawn from these, not least under the pressure of the post-2008 financial crisis and subsequent sovereign debt problems experienced by Italy and other Southern European states. As a result, there has been a re-emphasis on a national policing agenda prioritising criminal justice and risk management but the capacity to advance this agenda remains open to doubt with the possible consequence of policy vacuums and policy drift. Nevertheless, Milan was able to develop a more socially inclusive approach and a less 'law and order'-oriented policing style during Mayor Pisapia's administration, demonstrating a remarkable capacity to resist the punitive and exclusionary rationalities characterising the national agenda for metropolitan policing in Italy.

In their discussion of 'Metropolitan policing agendas in Britain: divergent tendencies in a fragmenting state?' (Chapter 8), Adam Edwards, Sophie Chambers, Nick Fyfe and Alistair Henry consider the implications of major constitutional reforms for the politics of metropolitan policing in Britain. They identify two recent periods of reform, both aimed at maintaining the integrity of the United Kingdom and its membership of the EU. First, the period under the UK administrations of New Labour (1997–2010), of agreements to devolve powers from the UK government to the Scottish Parliament and to assemblies in Wales and Northern Ireland. Second, the period of 'secessionist referenda' covering the UK coalition government of Conservatives and Liberal Democrats (2010–15) and the election of the Conservative UK government in May 2015. This latter period included a narrow loss of the referendum on Scottish independence from the UK by the secessionists in September 2014 but a rekindling of the Scottish independence movement following the shock victory, in June 2016, of the Leave campaign in the UK referendum on membership of the European Union. It is argued that this 'Brexit' vote has compounded other tendencies toward the fragmentation of metropolitan governance in the UK, including the 'new localism' of devolving responsibilities for both setting and funding policing agendas, in conditions of austere public expenditure settlements, to regional actors in England and Wales, in particular the recently established

Police and Crime Commissioners (PCCs), and to municipal authorities working 'in partnership' with the PCCs to deliver agendas for safer and cohesive communities.

In 'Policing metropolises in a system of cooperative federalism: Berlin as the German capital and a city-state compared to Cologne as the biggest city in North Rhine-Westphalia' (Chapter 9), Hartmut Aden and Bernhard Frevel discuss the situation in Germany. The 16 German states enjoy a high level of autonomy. The Berlin police system has had to deal with a completely new political and administrative context since the 1990s, as a consequence of reunification. Consequently, in the city-state of Berlin, the police and local government are more closely dependant on each other, while both belong to the same government and the political steering of the policy agenda is more direct. By contrast, in Cologne, the police are an independent authority belonging to the state of North Rhine-Westphalia, disconnected from local governance. However, the authors show that in spite of these differences in dispositions, the German political system leads to convergence in agenda setting in both cities, because of the strong tradition of 'cooperative federalism', the dominance of cooperation with non-governmental organisations and other actors outside the security sector, and the fact that sharing responsibilities between state and civil society seems to be a core element of the 'activating state' in Germany. This 'path dependency' towards a 'cooperative federalism' is underpinned by the more profound commitment to 'Rechtstaat', the legal state, and an antipathy to pre-judicial and extra-judicial security strategies.

Evelien De Pauw and Marleen Easton's contribution, 'Governance of security in Antwerp and Brussels: two of a kind?', considers metropolitan policing in Belgium (Chapter 10). The authors argue that notwithstanding federal government attempts to steer metropolitan policing, there are significant opportunities for the exercise of local discretion. In Brussels and Antwerp we observe a complex mixture of local and national police forces, steered by different policy agendas – especially in Brussels, where there is a complex admixture of local and national police forces, functioning according to different policy agendas on the territory of the same metropolitan area. This complexity is, in turn, a consequence of the broader attempt to maintain the integrity of the Belgian state by accommodating the competing regional and linguistic interests of Flanders and Wallonia in the government of the capital. The ongoing interference from the regions on the one hand, and the strong autonomy of the municipalities on the other, are simultaneously causing a greater 'divergence' in policing agendas. Local politics has a huge impact on local security plans and can differ widely from national policy. This raises the question of whether or not we are dealing with 'urban republics' where the mayor's political affiliation determines security policy. Politics in Brussels and Antwerp seems to be largely characterised by the competition of power between the national state and municipal authorities.

The recent increase in the terrorism threat to level three (serious) and to level four (very serious) in Belgium and Brussels, following the attack on Brussels airport in March 2016 and the use of the municipality of Molenbeek in Brussels as a base by those involved in the attacks on Paris the previous November, have provoked a major debate about the need to reconcile competing national and municipal agendas for metropolitan policing.

In 'Local strategies for glocal challenges: comparing policing agendas in Amsterdam and Rotterdam', Ruth Prins and Elke Devroe (Chapter 11) analyse the politics of policing, with a specific focus on policing agendas in the two largest cities in the Netherlands. Both Amsterdam and Rotterdam are considered metropolises facing 'glocal' challenges related to multicultural populations in urban areas, social inequalities in terms of household income, international harbours, crime and disorder. In order to get an understanding of the tendencies towards divergence and convergence in urban policing in these city-regions, the authors sketch the general trends in policing in the Netherlands. They discuss the national, regional and local constitutional arrangements and discretionary powers entailed in public police management in these cities. Prins and Devroe compare and contrast policing agendas in Amsterdam and Rotterdam and conclude with an account of the possible explanations for convergence and divergence in the politics of policing in these metropolises. In turn, these are related to the political 'circuits of power' of the municipal ruling coalitions in these two cities and in the wider institutional environment they inhabit.

Part IV concludes this volume with Chapter 12, 'The European world of metropolitan policing: interpreting patterns of governance, policy and politics', written by Adam Edwards, Elke Devroe and Paul Ponsaers. This chapter elicits theoretical propositions from contributions in Parts II and III of the book, which are capable of explaining processes of convergence and divergence in metropolitan policing.

Note

1 See the special issue of the *European Journal of Policing Studies*, volume 2, issue 1, 2014 (Ponsaers et al., 2014; Aden & De Pauw, 2014; Devroe & Petrov, 2014; Edwards & Prins, 2014; Mouhanna & Easton, 2014; Recasens i Brunet & Ponsaers, 2014); see also the special issue of *European Journal of Criminology*, volume 10, issue 3, 2013 (Virta, 2013; Edwards & Hughes, 2013; Edwards et al., 2013; Meško et al., 2013; Recasens, 2013; Gilling et al., 2013; Devroe, 2013; Frevel, 2013; Xenakis & Cheliotis, 2013).

Bibliography

Aden, H., De Pauw, E. (2014) 'Policing Berlin. From separation by the "iron curtain" to the new German capital and a globalised city', *European Journal of Policing Studies*, 2(1): 355–371.

Balzacq, T., Dunn Cavelty, M. (eds) (2016) *Routledge Handbook of Security Studies*, London: Routledge.
Bigo, D. (2000) 'When two become one: Internal and external securitizations in Europe', in Morten Kelstrup and Michael C. Williams (eds), *International Relations Theory and the Politics of European Integration*, London: Routledge.
Bigo, D., Guild, E. (2005) *Controlling Frontiers: Free Movement into and within Europe*, Aldershot: Ashgate Publishing.
Bowling, B., Sheptycki, J. (2012) *Global Policing*, London: Sage.
Bourdieu, P. (1977) *Outline of a Theory of Practice*, Cambridge: Cambridge University Press.
Bourdieu, P. (1990) *The Logic of Practice*, Cambridge: Polity Press.
Bourdieu, P. (1998) *Acts of Resistance: Against the New Myths of Our Times*, Cambridge: Polity.
Castells, M. (1996) *The Rise of the Network Society*, Cambridge: Blackwell.
Clegg, S. (1989) *Frameworks of Power*, London: Sage.
Crawford, A. (2008) 'The pattern of policing in the UK: Policing beyond the police', in T. Newburn (ed.), *The Handbook of Policing*, Cullompton: Willan.
Devroe, E. (2013) 'Local political leadership and the governance of urban security in Belgium and the Netherlands', *European Journal of Criminology*, 10(3): 314–325.
Devroe, E. (2015) 'Purple vests. The origins of plural policing in Belgium', *European Journal of Policing Studies*, 2(3): 304–325.
Devroe, E., Petrov, M. (2014) 'Policing Sofia. From centralisation to decentralisation', *European Journal of Policing Studies*, 2(1): 30–60.
Devroe, E., Terpstra, J. (2015) 'Plural policing in Western Europe: A comparison', *European Journal of Policing Studies*, 2(3): 235–245.
Edwards, A. (2016) 'Multi-centred governance and circuits of power in liberal modes of security', *Global Crime*, 17(3–4): 240–263.
Edwards, A., Hughes, G. (2005) 'Comparing the governance of safety in Europe: A geo-historical approach', *Theoretical Criminology*, 9(3): 345–363.
Edwards, A., Hughes, G. (2013) 'Comparative European criminology and the question of urban security', *European Journal of Criminology*, 10(3): 257–259.
Edwards, A., Hughes, G., Lord, N. (2013) 'Urban security in Europe: Translating a concept in public criminology', *European Journal of Criminology*, 10(3): 260–283.
Edwards, A., Prins, R. (2014) 'Policing and crime in contemporary London: Towards a developmental agenda?', *European Journal of Policing Studies*, 2(2): 63–93.
European Commission (2015) *Communication from the Commission to the European Parliament, the Council, the European Economic and Social Committee and the Committee of the Regions: The European Agenda on Security*, Strasbourg, 28.4.2015, COM (2015) 185 final.
Foucault, M. (1991) 'Governmentality', in G. Burchell, C. Gordon, P. Miller (eds), *The Foucault Effect: Studies in Governmentality*, Chicago, IL: Chicago University Press.
Frevel, B. (2013) 'Managing urban safety and security in Germany: Institutional responsibility and individual competence', *European Journal of Criminology*, 10(3): 354–367.
Garland, D. (2001) *The Culture of Control. Crime and Social Order in Contemporary Society*, Oxford: Oxford University Press.
Gilling, D., Hughes, G., Bowden, M., Edwards, A., Henry, A., Topping, J. (2013) 'Powers, liabilities and expertise in community safety: Comparative lessons for

"urban security" from the United Kingdom and the Republic of Ireland', *European Journal of Criminology*, 10(3): 326–340.

Hallsworth, S., Lea, J. (2011) 'Reconstructing Leviathan: Emerging contours of the security state', *Theoretical Criminology*, 15(2): 141–157.

Jones, T., Newburn, T. (eds) (2006) *Plural Policing: A Comparative Perspective*, London: Routledge.

King, A. (ed.) (1996) *Re-presenting the City*, London: Macmillan.

King, A. (1997) *Culture, Globalization and the World-System, Contemporary Conditions for the Representation of Identity*, Minneapolis: University of Minnesota Press.

Latour, B. (1986) 'The Powers of Association', in J. Law (ed.), *Power, Action and Belief*, London: Routledge and Kegan Paul.

Latour, B. (1987) *Science in Action. How to Follow Scientists and Engineers through Society*, Cambridge, MA: Harvard University Press.

Lea, J., Stenson, K. (2007) 'Security, sovereignty, and non-state governance from below', *Canadian Journal of Law and Society*, 22(2): 9–27.

Loader, I. (2000) 'Plural policing and democratic governance', *Social & Legal Studies*, 9(3): 323–345.

Matza, D. (1969) *Becoming Deviant*, Englewood Cliffs, NJ: Prentice Hall.

Meško, G., Tominc, B., Sotlar, A. (2013) 'Urban security management in the capitals of the former Yugoslav republics', *European Journal of Criminology*, 10(3): 284–296.

Mouhanna, Ch., Easton, M. (2014) 'Policing Paris. "Out of" or "still in" Napoleonic time?', *European Journal of Policing Studies*, 2(1): 94–109.

Pollitt, C. (2001) 'Clarifying convergence: Striking similarities and durable differences in public management reform', *Public Management Review*, 4(1): 471–492.

Ponsaers, P., Edwards, A., Verhage, A., Recasens i Brunet, A. (eds) (2014) *European Journal of Policing Studies*, Special Issue Policing European Metropolises, Antwerpen/Apeldoorn: Maklu, 2(1).

Prins, R., Cachet, L., Ponsaers, P., Hughes, G. (2012) 'Fragmentation and interconnection in public safety governance in the Netherlands, Belgium and England', in M. Fenger, V. Bekkers (eds), *Beyond Fragmentation and Interconnectivity*, Amsterdam: IOS Press, 19–43.

Recasens, A., Cardoso, C., Castro, J., Nobili, G. (2013) 'Urban security in Southern Europe', *European Journal of Criminology*, 10(3): 368–382.

Recasens i Brunet, A., Ponsaers, P. (2014) 'Policing Barcelona', *European Journal of Policing Studies*, 2(1): 452–470.

Reiner, R. (1988) 'British criminology and the state', *British Journal of Criminology*, 28(2): 138–158.

Reiner, R. (2010) *The Politics of the Police*, Oxford: Oxford University Press.

Rose, N. (2000) 'Governing liberty', in R. Ericsson, N. Steher (eds), *Governing Modern Societies*, Toronto: Toronto University Press.

Sassen, S. (2001) *The Global City: New York, London, Tokyo*, Princeton, NJ: Princeton University Press.

Scott, A. (2012) *A World in Emergence. Cities and Regions in the 21st Century*, Cheltenham: Edward Elgar.

Smith, D. (2004) 'Editorial: Criminology and the wider Europe', *European Journal of Criminology*, 1(1): 5–15.

Stenson, K. (2008) 'Surveillance and sovereignty', in M. Deflem (ed.), *Surveillance and Governance, Sociology of Crime, Law and Deviance. Volume 10*, London: Emerald, 281–303.

Sztompka, P. (1990) 'Conceptual frameworks in comparative inquiry: Divergent or convergent?', in M. Albrow, E. King, *Globalization, Knowledge and Society: Readings from International Sociology*, London: Sage.

Terpstra, J. (2012) 'The warning and advisory task of the police: Forging a link between police information and multi-agency partnerships', *Policing: A Journal of Policy and Practice*, 6(1): 67–75.

Virta, S. (2013) 'Governing urban security in Finland: Towards the European model', *European Journal of Criminology*, 10(3): 341–353.

Wacquant, L. (2001) 'The penalisation of poverty and the rise of neo-liberalism', *European Journal of Criminal Policy and Research*, 9(4): 401–412.

Waever, O. (1995) 'Securitization and desecuritization', in R. Lipschutz (ed.), *On Security*, New York: Columbia University Press, 46–86.

Xenakis, S., Cheliotis, L. (2013) 'Spaces of contestation: Challenges, actors and expertise in the management of urban security in Greece', *European Journal of Criminology*, 10(3): 297–313.

Chapter 2

European national police systems and metropolitan realities

Elke Devroe and Paul Ponsaers

> 'They [the police] symbolize as well the continuity and integrity of the society by their visibility and attachment to traditional values [...] Their actions underscore and implement the intentions of the state – they are Leviathan enacted. The modern police as a rational, bureaucratic force stand ready to enforce the law with the ultimate sanction, violence.' Furthermore: 'The police role conveys a sense of sacredness or awesome power that lies at the root of political order, and authority, the claims a state makes upon its people for deference to rules, laws and norms.'
>
> (Manning, 1997: 20–21)

I Introduction

By including this chapter in the volume we want to avoid that each of the contributors has to explain the broad national policing context and the standing conditions in their chapters, while it is precisely the intention to focus on differences in metropolitan policing. In other words, the ambition of this publication is *cross*-national, even *trans*national, comparison.[1] However, the endeavour is also *intra*-national. It was the merit of Wesley Skogan to suggest[2] to compare in each country two or more major cities in one and the same country, trying to discover to what extent policing in these cities differs from each other. The underlying assumption is that differences in policing in metropolises in the same nation-state reflects the elbowroom of metropolitan areas to develop their own policing policy, in spite of one and the same national context. We assume that the reverse is also probable, more precisely that the absence of prominent metropolitan differences in one and the same country mirrors largely the dominance of a national security policy. Therefore it is necessary to include this chapter in the volume.

Politics in European metropolises is largely characterised by the competition of power between the nation-state and metropolitan governance.[3] In the majority of European countries the state police are still considered as the formal guardian (or the relic of a vanished age) of sovereignty on the national territory and the visible expression of state power.

It seems that European nation-states consider police matters still as *their* property and that national governments conceive *their* police system as one of the national symbols of their existence. Police are considered as the visible presence of the state in public space.

In this chapter we present a typology of different national police systems, useful for the interpretation of a metropolitan reading of policing realities within different national contexts. Given this general framework, we tried to build this typology on the question of (historical) national dominance or regional autonomy in policing.

2 An analytical tool for the Policing European Metropolises Project

In this chapter, we develop a comprehensive framework, based on working definitions of essential characteristics of different national police systems. The analysis is developed at the level of police systems, *not* at the level of police forces. Underneath we develop and define the central notions used.

2.1 Police versus policing

In this chapter we are dealing with the public *police apparatus*. Etymologically the word *police* comes from Latin *politia*, which is the Latinisation of the Greek *politeia*, 'citizenship, administration, civil polity'. This is derived from *polis*, 'city'. A police force is a constituted body of persons empowered by the state to enforce the law. The term is commonly associated with police services of a sovereign state that are authorised to exercise the police power of that state within a defined legal or territorial area of responsibility. In other words, the notion police refers to an organisational principle.

A *police function* is a generic term for a domain of activity of the police, e.g. maintenance of public order, law enforcement, criminal investigation, surveillance, beat policing, prevention of crime, etc. As mentioned in the introduction, the notion '*policing*' is often used to refer to the activity of a complex network of formal and informal public and private partners, mostly identified with the notion of plural policing (Terpstra et al., 2013; Loader, 2000; Loader & Walker, 2001; Jones & Newburn, 2006b), contributing to certain police functions (*assemblages* of police forces with city guards, special investigation officers, parking controllers, environmental functionaries, social inspectors ...; intelligence agencies; private commercial agencies; citizens' initiatives, Neighbourhood Watch programmes ...) (Bayley & Shearing, 1996, 2001; Crawford, et al. 2005, Jones & Newburn, 2006a; Loader, 2000).

In this chapter we limit ourselves, for reasons of feasibility, to public police forces, not including the *assemblages* made with external agencies, but to the core apparatus of the public ('dark blue') police itself. It is clear that this limitation is only for the sake of this chapter. In other words, we are dealing here with the 'predicates' of public policy formulation in this field. These predicates can be distinguished in terms of the 'standing conditions'.

2.2 National police system: hierarchically integrated?

As a working definition we use the notion *'national police system'*, referring to the complex of different constituted bodies that are considered as public police in a particular country, empowered by a specific nation-state. As a consequence of this definition, we focus upon those agencies with competences legally defined by a national legislator, more precisely those competences that are linked to the use of the monopoly of legal and legitimate violence. Notwithstanding the reality of international and European agencies directed towards police cooperation (e.g. Interpol, Europol, Frontex, etc.), the operational police work is still largely defined within national boundaries. This is precisely the reason why we use the notion *'national police system'*.[4] Within one police system, hierarchical lines between different forces can be *integrated*, or can function *autonomously*.

We consider *police systems* as empirical realities, apart from the notion *'police models'* (Ponsaers, 2001). Police models are underlying police philosophies, ways to think about police, often used for strategic reasons. Police models (e.g. 'military-bureaucratic policing', 'crime fighting policing', 'community policing', 'problem-oriented/solving policing', 'restorative policing', etc.) express different prescriptive points of view on the way the police *should act*. In other words, police models give a normative direction to the police, while the study of police systems refers to the empirical substrate in which police forces *are* acting.

Research on police models deals with *cultural* aspects, while studying police systems deals with *structural* aspects. Within a certain police system, often different police models compete, while one is mostly dominant in a specific timeframe and specific territory. A combined interpretation of both aspects seems the most productive to us for an exhaustive and useful analysis.

2.3 Police forces: functionally or geographically integrated?

A police force executes mostly different *police functions* at the same time. A force that executes a broad range of these police functions has integrated competences, or better is *generic* in nature. Nevertheless, a force can also have *specialised* competences in one or a few specific functions, e.g. a criminal police force, or a gendarmerie, which is mostly a military unit specialised in maintenance of public order.

In complex police systems, police forces often reflect differences in geographical scope. Some forces are considered as national or federal forces, others are limited to provincial or regional level, or even to metropolitan or municipal level. From this point of view, police forces within one police system can have different geographical competences. Some forces have *national* competences, others have *limited* territorial competences. Often a police system is characterised by a tension between central and local decision-making authorities.

2.4 One/different force(s), one/different type(s) of force(s)?

Different *police forces* within one police system can have different training and educational programmes, salary scales and grades; they can have different controlling bodies, or different databases, different regulations, different labour unions, etc. In other words, different police forces can represent different *types of police*. In most cases, this patchwork format of a police system is the result of long historical developments. Therefore we call these '*historical diverse police systems*'. Sometimes this kind of police system contains autonomous 'functional police' forces.

In spite of the fact that one police system includes different forces, it is possible that all these forces have the same design and format. Mostly this is the case in police systems that are based on territorial (local or supra-local) division of labour in Europe. In this kind of police system, each force is constituted with the same type of police. In other words, all police officers of the different forces have the same training, databases, control agencies, etc., but have different leadership. Therefore we call these '*territorial divided police systems*'.

			Hierarchy	
			Integrated	**Autonomous**
Competences	**Functional**	Generic		
		Specialized		
	Geographical	National		
		Limited		

Figure 2.1 Essential characteristics of police systems

	One Force	**Different Forces**
One type of Police	Unified Police System	Territorial Divided Police System
Different types of Police		Historical Diverse Police System

Figure 2.2 Typology of police systems, according to the number of forces and types of police

In certain police systems, we observe only one police force. Mostly this kind of police system is the result of reform and therefore we call these '*unified police systems*'. Often the system is identical to the force and called the 'National Police' or 'Federal Police'.

From a conceptual point of view it is impossible that one force includes different types of police.

2.5 (De)centralised, (de-)concentrated?

Concentration refers to the geographical centre where police capacity is operating from. *De-concentration* is the opposite, and expresses the geographical distribution of capacity in different places on a specific territory. In other words, concentration/de-concentration is linked to the territorial allocation and distribution of capacity, and consequently varies according to the number of police stations on a territory.

To the contrary, a *centralised* force is a force where steering power is assembled within one central top level. *Decentralisation* refers to the delegation of power to underlying levels, within one force. In other words, centralisation/decentralisation has to do with hierarchical lines. Decentralisation can be of geographical nature, but can also be of functional nature. In other words, a centrally steered force can be de-concentrated, and a decentralised force can be concentrated.

3 Historical diverse police systems

This chapter will now discuss those police systems in Europe that are to a large extent influenced by French tradition. More precisely, this section deals with those countries that still have a military gendarmerie within their police system. A gendarmerie is a military force charged with police duties among civilian populations. In essence this comes down to the following countries: France (Gendarmerie Nationale), Italy (Carabinieri)[5], Portugal (Guarda Nacional Republicana) and Spain (Guardia Civil).[6]

The chapter does not include Austria, which also reformed its police system in 2005, with the result that the Bundesgendarmerie disappeared from the actual police framework. The same evolution can be observed in Luxembourg. In the Netherlands, there still exists a Koninklijke Marechaussee (Royal Marechaussee of the Netherlands), which is a gendarmerie force. Because this country experienced a recent dramatic police reform, this force will be discussed in section five. Greece had a gendarmerie in the past, but this was incorporated within the Greek Police Force in 1984. Because we focus on Europe, the chapter does not include other gendarmerie forces outside the European Union (EU).

3.1 The French police system

France has two national police forces, more precisely the National Police and the Gendarmerie. The National Police is the larger of the two forces. This force is responsible for policing the larger towns and cities. The Gendarmerie is responsible for the rest of the country. In addition to these two large and hierarchical forces, there are also around 5,600 more or less small municipal forces, employed, paid for and managed by the municipalities themselves (Malochet, 2008; Horton, 1995).

It was the French Revolution that changed the French police system dramatically. Emperor Napoleon Bonaparte knew the value of a strong military presence within France, while he was abroad expanding the empire. He extended the role of the Gendarmerie, and meanwhile he reinforced the role of the Ministry of Police, famously headed by Fouché, with mainly a political surveillance mandate.[7]

Police reform initiated by Napoleon Bonaparte was extended by Louis Napoleon III during his reign in the middle of the 19th century. Napoleon III came in power at a time when France was experiencing internal unrest and many citizens supported the establishment of a socialist republic. Napoleon III used the police to oppress the socialist movement. The French police were viewed as a limb of the government in a police state (Jones & Johnstone, 2011). At the same time, the Anglophile Napoleon III introduced in Paris a uniformed police in 1854, inspired by the English 'bobby', with the 'sergents de ville' (who will become 'gardiens de la paix' in 1880) strongly anchored in neighbourhoods (Deluermoz, 2012).

To understand the functioning of the National Police and the Gendarmerie, it is important to make a basic distinction between administrative and judicial competences (Monjardet, 1996).[8] Administrative competences include the maintenance of public order, the gathering of political intelligence, traffic control and other administrative tasks. Judicial competences are dealing with investigation of crime. The responsibility for administrative competences is concentrated in the Ministry of the Interior. The judicial competences are exercised by the Ministry of Justice.[9] Apart from these ministries, the Ministry of Defence was also jointly responsible for the Gendarmerie (Berlière, 1996) until 2009, and the full integration of the Gendarmerie into the Ministry of the Interior (Berlière & Levy, 2011).

The Gendarmerie today is a military force, with a strongly centralised hierarchy, a powerful head and subsequent de-concentrated territorial layers of command. The Gendarmerie is divided into the 'Gendarmerie Départementale' and the 'Gendarmerie Mobile' (Stead, 1983). From a functional point of view, the Gendarmerie specialises in the maintenance of public order, but is also engaged in criminal investigation and traffic policing.[10] In other words, the Gendarmerie should be able to perform all the policing services, judicial as well as administrative functions. The force is in other words functionally integrated. It is mostly active in smaller rural municipalities (mostly fewer than 20,000 inhabitants), while the force has competence on the whole national territory (Dieu, 2002).

Before 1941, the Gendarmerie was counterbalanced by autonomous municipal police forces, active in municipalities with more than 10,000 inhabitants, except for a dozen cities where the police forces were nationalised. In 1941, during the Vichy regime, these municipal police forces were brought together in the centralised 'Police Nationale', with important deconcentrated presence all over the country. The National Police operates under the control of the director-general of the Police Nationale. He gives instructions to the National Police. The immediate staff of the director-general includes a colonel of the Gendarmerie as liaison officer (Stead, 1983). With regard to the operational aspects, nine directorates coordinate the operational work of the National Police. The most important operational directorates are the Central Directorate of Judicial Police and the Central Directorate of Public Security. The National Police also has some directorates that can essentially be considered as intelligence agencies.

In consequence, from 1941 onwards France had two national police forces, both with broad integrated functional competences, but autonomous leadership. A certain geographical division of labour between both forces can be observed.

Since 1800 Paris has had its unique 'Préfecture de Police de Paris', integrated into the National Police (Mouhanna & Easton, 2014). This préfecture is concerned with the special needs of the metropolis, which is the seat of national government, the focal centre of administration, the site of numerous embassies and consulates, and a magnet throughout the whole year for tourists, students, artists, business people ... The Préfecture de Police functions rather autonomously with its own administrative and operational branches. The political-administrative context of Paris generated a police 'préfet', who can be considered as the almighty in the field of security in the capital (Renaudie, 2008).

From 1966 onwards, we observe the renaissance of new *municipal police forces* in the bigger cities of France (Le Goff, 2009; Malochet, 2008). These municipal forces function autonomously from the two national forces. Municipal police agents number some 20,000, in other words 7% of the global capacity of the French public police. The municipal forces function within the boundaries of the municipality (Vogel, 1993). Local police forces are considered to have a solid financial base, because they rely more on municipal resources. Some mayors are reluctant to have their own police force because of the greater responsibility and a certain philosophy of 'the Nation'.

The latest edition of the *European Sourcebook of Crime and Criminal Justice Statistics* (Aebi et al., 2014) does not mention a ratio of police officers per 100,000 inhabitants in 2011 in France. Only the previous edition (Aebi et al.,

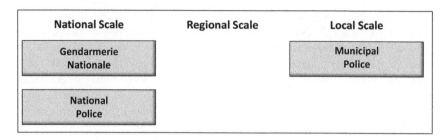

Figure 2.3 The French police system

2011) mentions a ratio of 345 police officers (excluding civilians) per 100,000 inhabitants in 2006 in France. That year, the ratio varied between the minimum of 154 (in Finland) and the maximum of 693 (in Ukraine). The mean of this ratio for all the participating countries in this work was 371 in 2006. In short, France has a police capacity that is situated under this mean ratio, but the fact that these numbers are not included in the latest (fifth) edition of the *European Sourcebook* should be a warning concerning the reliability of these figures. Eurostat mentions a global number of 203,982 police officers in France in 2012.[11]

In France we are dealing with a particular historically determined police system, with a strong central and national emphasis, hardly balanced by the relatively new local police forces (Mouhanna, 2013). All types of police forces function autonomously from each other.[12] The French system stands out as the most developed example of centralisation and the State's wish to control its citizens.

3.2 The Italian police system

Italy has a great variety of police forces. There are currently five different national police forces in Italy.[13] There is a wide area of overlap between these police forces, while there are also some areas of exclusive competence.

In the 19th century, the model of inspiration was the centralist French state, although there were also some Prussian influences. Two national forces are the most prominent, more precisely the 'Polizia di Stato' (State Police) and the 'Carabinieri' (a gendarmerie force). Small villages will normally only have Carabinieri on their territory, but both national forces are present in larger cities, which causes real competition to solve crimes involving substantial public interest or publicity (Collin, 1985).

Since the late 1790s, beginning with Napoleon Bonaparte's military conquest until 1814, most of Italy was under French domination. After the Napoleonic conquest of Italy, the king of Piedmont created a version of the French gendarmerie and reorganised pre-existing local police forces into the corps of the Carabinieri (Collin, 1985). From 1815, when the French hegemony ended, to 1848, Italy was strongly marked by disunity and fragmentation. It was in 1861 that the unification of Italy was politically completed. Italy adopted the French system of centralised administration to cope with social unrest and political instability (Canosa, 1976).

In this highly divisive atmosphere arose the need for a strong and centralised government, which called consequently for a centralised and strong police force. The Carabinieri had to act as a cohesive instrument of the political power to hold the country together (Collin, 1985). Its mission includes the protection of public order within the state, more precisely in the countryside. After having changed a few times since its inception, the force is under the dual responsibility of the Ministry of the Interior (when it concerns public order and security tasks) and the Ministry of Defence (when it concerns military tasks). It is one of the components of the armed forces, which in Italy are the Army, the Navy, the Air Force and the Carabinieri (Collin, 1999).

The origins of the Polizia di Stato go back to 1848, when the Guardia Nazionale (the national guard) was created, which was also based on the French model and created to counterbalance the Carabinieri. After its creation, this corps was transformed in 1852 into the 'Corpo delle Guardie di Pubblica Sicurezza' (Corps of the Public Security Guards). In accordance with the French police system, the officers of the Pubblica Sicurezza were placed under the authority of the Ministry of the Interior in 1890, but in 1919 this force was integrated into the armed forces (Dunnage, 1997). In 1925 Mussolini renamed the Pubblica Sicurezza the 'Corpo degli Agenti di Pubblica Sicurezza'. The name Polizia di Stato was only introduced with the reform bill of 1981 (Roodenburg, 2004; Den Boer, 1993). This reform focused to a large extent on the abolition of authoritarianism and the application of civil servant rules and norms to police officers. Consequently the reform brought the demilitarisation of the national police and syndicalisation, which are fundamental reference points for the democratic evolution of the Italian police (Lopez-Pintor & Morlina, 2003; Nolte, 2003).

Besides the Carabinieri and the National Police, there are three other state police forces. First of all the Guardia di Finanza (Finance Guard), which assists the Ministry of Finance in enforcing tax, excise customs and tariff legislation (Umberto, 2010). Second, the Corpo Forestale dello Stato (National Forest Corps), which is a law enforcement agency for the Ministry of Agriculture and Forests, controlling Italian national parks and forests. Lastly, the prison guards of the Polizia Penitenziaria (Correctional Police Corps) are also considered as policemen and are subordinated to the Ministry of Justice (Palidda, 1992).

Besides this massive presence of state police agencies, each community still has its own local police (polizia municipale), who direct traffic and issue parking fines in the cities. These have historically been troubled by inefficiency and corruption and have been marginal in law enforcement (Roach & Thomaneck, 1985).

The Italian police system makes a functional distinction between the 'polizia sicurezza' (security police) or administrative policing, and the 'polizia giudiziaria' (judicial police) or judicial policing, in line with the French system. The function of the security police is to maintain public order and to prevent crimes. The function of the judicial police, on the other hand, is repression of crime. This functional distinction runs through all of Italy's police forces. In that sense all forces are functionally integrated to a certain extent, while within the forces there exist specialised entities that are consequently not integrated (Perrodet, 2002; Bruggeman, 2014).

The municipal police can exercise all the competences of 'polizia di sicurezza', 'polizia giudiziaria' and 'polizia amministrativa', therefore this is a force with a general competence. However, 'polizia amministrativa' is its core competence and the exercise of the other functions depends on the prefect's decision at the local level, or on the prosecutor. We can state that the municipal police plays auxiliary functions in security police, occasionally it is called to play the role of judicial police, and mostly exercises administrative police functions: traffic, control of licences and of all municipal regulations of urban life, but also crime prevention at the local level, community policing, incivilities and urban disorder, etc. One important difference of municipal police is that its competence is limited to the borders of the municipality.

After the 1990s, the municipal police was strengthened and radically innovated, above all in some regions (northern and central Italy). Regions have an exclusive competence – since 2001 – in coordination, organisation and professional training of the municipal police. Its reputation has changed quite a lot in the last 20 years. Before, it was much more marginal and considered a low-level kind of police, but in the last 20 years its role in local governance of crime has been pivotal. In the Italian chapters of this volume, Rossella Selmini and Marco Calaresu describe some of these dynamics, which are part of the redistribution of responsibility in crime control and of the pluralisation of policing in Italy. There are about 60,000 municipal police officers at the national level, which means that it is the third police force after the Carabinieri (it has about the same number as the Guardia di Finanza, which, however, does not have a general competence) and is probably the largest municipal force, compared to France and Spain. Conflicts and overlaps with Carabinieri and Polizia di Stato are common.

The forces are coordinated on two levels: national and provincial. At the national level, one finds the National Committee for Public Order and Security, which seeks to promote mutual coordination and consultation between the police forces. At the provincial level, there is the Provincial Committee for Public Order and Security, which functions as an auxiliary organ for consultation (Barbagli & Sartori, 2004).

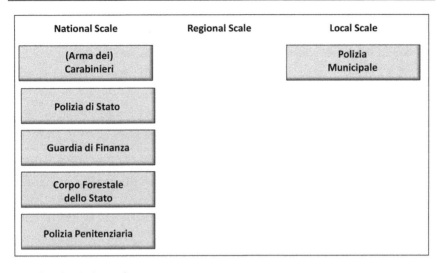

Figure 2.4 The Italian police system

The fifth edition of the *European Sourcebook* (Aebi et al., 2014) mentions a ratio of 535 police officers (excluding civilians) per 100,000 inhabitants in 2011 in Italy. The mean of this ratio for all the participating countries in this work was 386 in 2011. In short, Italy has a police capacity that is situated far above this mean ratio. Eurostat mentions a global number of 276,750 police officers in Italy in 2012.[14]

3.3 The Portuguese police system

The Second Republic was the corporatist authoritarian regime installed in Portugal in 1933. This was greatly inspired by conservative and authoritarian ideologies, and developed by António de Oliveira Salazar, ruler of Portugal from 1932 to 1968, when he was replaced by Marcelo Caetano. The Second Republic was strongly opposed to communism, socialism, liberalism and anti-colonialism. Fiercely criticised by most of the international community after World War II and decolonisation, the regime and its secret police repressed elementary civil liberties and political freedoms in order to remain in power, and to avoid communist influence and the dissolution of its empire. It was one of the longest-surviving right-wing dictatorships in Europe, outliving the fascist regimes in Germany and Italy by three decades. Only on 25 April 1974 did the Carnation Revolution in Lisbon, a military coup organised by left-wing Portuguese military officers, overthrow the Second Republic and end 48 years of dictatorship in Portugal. The dictatorial regime (1926–74) marked profoundly the development of the country at all levels, in particular those of security and the organisation of the police.

For that reason the Polícia de Segurança Pública (PSP, or Public Security Police) and the Guarda Nacional Republicana (GNR, or National Guard of the Republic) were considered as advocates of dictatorship during a long period (Agra et al., 2001).

Portugal today is a unitary state (Rodrigues, 1998). All the security forces and services are national and their cooperation is coordinated centrally by the secretary of internal security. According to Portuguese Constitutional Law the organisation of the security forces must be unique for the whole national territory. As a consequence, internal Portuguese security is based on different forces and agencies organised on a national level: the PSP, the GNR, the Polícia Judiciária (PJ, or Criminal Police) and the Serviço de Estrangeiros e Fronteiras (the Immigration and Borders Service). All these forces function according to a clear hierarchical and vertical structure (Sousa, 2003).

The responsibility for internal security is shared by two departments: the Ministry of Justice and the Ministry of the Interior. The PSP and the GNR are under the authority of the Ministry of the Interior. The Ministry of Justice is responsible for the PJ. The Serviço de Estrangeiros e Fronteiras is organised in a vertical way under the Ministry of the Interior.

The GNR is the direct descendant of the Royal Police Guard (Guarda Real da Polícia), created in 1801 in Lisbon. It took as a model the French Gendarmerie. A similar Royal Police Guard was created for Porto. In 1834 the king disbanded the Royal Police Guard in Lisbon and Porto, creating the Municipal Guards of Lisbon and Porto. In 1868 both of the Guards were put under a unified General Command, installed in barracks in Lisbon, which is still today the headquarters of the GNR (Durão et al., 2005). After the revolution of 1910, which substituted the constitutional monarchy with the republic, the new regime changed the name of the Municipal Guard to the Republican Guard (Guarda Republicana). In 1911, the name changed to National Republican Guard. In 1993 the National Republican Guard absorbed the independent Fiscal Guard (Guarda Fiscal) which became the Fiscal Brigade of the GNR.

Today the force has different local layers. The GNR has competence over the whole Portuguese territory, but is primarily present in rural areas. The GNR is competent in the domain of maintenance of public order (especially traffic security), the maintenance of the security of citizens and property, prevention of crime, the repression of fiscal infractions, collaboration with judicial authorities, police and military missions (assistance to national defence).

The PSP, civil in nature today, was in former days a paramilitary force. The mission of the PSP is to defend republican democracy, safeguarding internal security and the rights of citizens. The PSP is mostly present in larger urban areas. Due to their high visibility, the PSP is recognised by the public as the 'police' in Portugal. The PSP today contains two metropolitan commands (Lisbon and Porto), 18 districts at national level and two separate regional districts (Açores and Madeira). Furthermore, the PSP has three specialised units: an anti-confrontation unit (for football hooliganism and protests), a group for special operations (anti-terrorism and ultra-violent missions), and a protection force. The PSP is responsible for prevention of crime, the identification and arrest of criminals, and the maintenance of public order. Its mission is to a large extent identical to that of the GNR. Three functions are the exclusive domain of the PSP: the control of production, trade, use and transportation of firearms and explosives; the protection of special units; and the security of civil airports. There is no hierarchical relationship between the GNR and the PSP, but the division of labour is organised on a geographical basis.

The Polícia Judiciária is another autonomous police force. Once a criminal case starts, this force has to be notified. It is the task of the PJ to gather elements of proof. This force is strongly specialised in technical and scientific matters (Cluny, 1995).

The Serviço de Estrangeiros e Fronteiras is the last Portuguese force with police competences. It is tasked with executing Portuguese policy concerning immigration and asylum.

In 1997, the municipal police was created in Portugal. The municipal police is an administrative police operating under the direction of the mayor. The functions of municipal police are in the domains of municipal regulations and the implementation of decisions of municipal authorities, public space and local urban transport surveillance, intervention in community policing programmes, protection of buildings and municipal public facilities, and the regulation and supervision of road and pedestrian traffic.

The *European Sourcebook* (Aebi et al., 2010) mentions a ratio of 443 police officers (excluding civilians) per 100,000 inhabitants in 2011 in Portugal. The mean of this ratio for all the participating countries in this work was 386 in 2011. In short, Portugal has a police capacity that is situated above this mean ratio. Eurostat mentions a global number of 46,083 police officers in Portugal in 2012.[15]

3.4 The Spanish police system

Under Franco a tripartite system of police existed in Spain: the Civil Guard (Guardia Civil), the Armed Police (Policía Armada) and the Municipal Police (Policía Municipal). During the Franco era (1939–75), the police was reinforced and regarded as a reactionary element, associated with internal surveillance and political repression. Coercion, physical force and general violence were employed. At the end of the 19th century, the Civil Guard conducted a campaign against criminal and anarchist elements. The Municipal Police could be best described as a local autonomous traffic enforcement force, while the Civil Guard and the Armed Police were national military

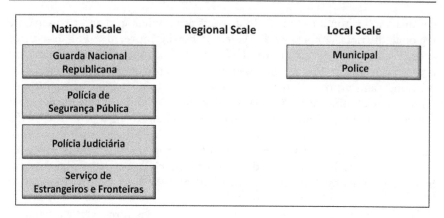

Figure 2.5 The Portuguese police system

police organisations designed to maintain control of the Spanish population and safeguard national public security (Becker & Thomas, 1973).

The Spanish Constitution of 1978 marks clearly the 'politically negotiated' end of almost four decades of dictatorship in Spain. From a constitutional point of view, Spain may be characterised from that point on as a 'regional state', in order to differentiate it from centralised and federal structures, although the Spanish system tends to operate more like a federation than a centralised state. Spain developed from a highly centralised system in which there were only two levels of government (central and local), to a tripartite system, with central, regional and local governments (Carrillo Cordero, 2003). The structures, powers and responsibilities of sub-national governments have experienced a radical transformation in the last 20 years (Recasens, 1999).

The state, the central government (Madrid), of Napoleonic tradition, has a national civilian police force (Cuerpo Nacional de Policía), the National Police, and a Civil Guard (Guardia Civil), the Spanish gendarmerie, based on the model of light infantry used by Napoleon in his European campaigns, a force of high mobility and able to patrol and pacify large areas of the countryside. On a national scale these two state forces represent the majority (two thirds) of police officers in Spain. Both forces function throughout the whole Spanish national territory. The National Police is mainly responsible for policing urban areas, whilst rural policing is generally the responsibility of the Civil Guard (Valriberas Sanz, 1999). The fact that the Guard largely operated in mostly rural and isolated parts of the country increased the risk of police violations of individual civil rights through lack of supervision and accountability. These national forces have integrated competences. The Civil Guard depends on the Ministry of the Interior (security of cities and services related to the law) and the Ministry of Defence.

The second level of independent governmental power is that of the 'autonomous communities' (comunidades autónomas), with elected governments and parliaments, for example Catalonia and the Basque Country. Catalonia has its own regional police force, the Mossos d'Esquadra, while the Basque Country has the Ertzainza. These regional forces also have integrated competences. Regional forces have a strong presence within the important metropolises in their region (e.g. Barcelona) (Domínguez-Berrueta de Juan et al., 1997).

The third level is that of the municipalities, with elected mayors (during the dictatorship they were assigned arbitrarily by central government) (Recasens & Ponsaers, 2014). The redefined and democratised municipalities gained a large degree of self-governance. The mayors became the authorities of their own local police forces. These 'Guardia Urbana' have principally functions in public security and urban traffic (Rabot, 2004).

This tripartite model, without any organic or functional hierarchy, had to base itself on reinforced coordination, which was difficult because of the bad regulations in the law of 1986 (Sanders & Young, 2002). For the autonomous communities, they were granted their own police forces, a Junta de Seguridad, to coordinate with those of the state on their territory. A Junta Local de Seguridad was also introduced for the coordination of the local police forces (where they exist) and those of the state and/or the autonomous police forces.

The *European Sourcebook of Crime and Criminal Justice Statistics* (Aebi et al., 2010) mentions a ratio of 536 police officers (excluding civilians) per 100,000 inhabitants in 2011 in Spain. With the mean of this ratio for all the participating countries in this work at 386 in 2011, Spain has a police capacity situated largely above this mean. Eurostat mentions a global number of 249,907 police officers in Spain in 2012.[16]

3.5 Lineages of the French police system

The police systems discussed in this part deal with different police forces and different types of police forces. We observed police systems that represent a long historical heritage, without dramatic recent reforms. At the centre of these systems are important national forces. They are the explicit expression of strong central national government. We observe in each country a paramilitary (in fact variations on the ancient Napoleonic gendarmerie) *and* a civil national force, for example in France the Gendarmerie Nationale versus the Police Nationale; in Italy the Carabinieri versus the Polizia di Stato, in Portugal the Polícia de Segurança Pública versus the Guardia Nacional Republicana; and in Spain the Guardia Civil versus the Policía Nacional.

Some division of labour exists between both types of forces. The paramilitary gendarmeries are mobile forces, functioning in rural areas, while the civil national police forces are mostly located on a de-concentrated basis in

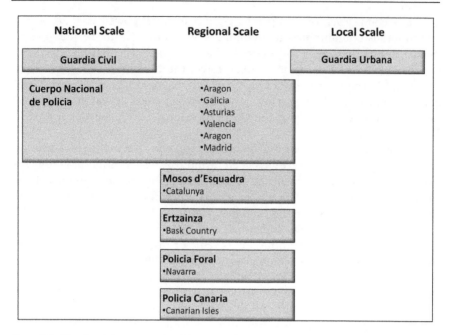

Figure 2.6 The Spanish constitutional layers and their police forces

urban areas. Both national forces function as communicating vessels, in relation to a geographical logic.

Spain (1939–75) and Portugal (1926–74) have been subject of dictatorships, which profoundly marked their development at all levels. To a certain extent these police systems had the function to protect the state and the regime against their own citizens. The political transition during the end of dictatorship hindered the development of a real criminal and security policy in a democratic logic, until the mid 1990s.

When it comes to Italy, after fascism (1922–45) and World War II, we observed the development of a democratic regime, influenced by the Cold War. The Catholic democracy, supported by the United States, systematically blocked with all its strength the access to political power for leftist movements, directed by the Communist Party. That situation facilitated certain political practices which were not always in line with the state of law and reinforced certain state apparatuses, which developed as 'isolated forces' within the society during the process of democratisation.

In short, Italy, Portugal and Spain had problems in developing a real democratic regime. Furthermore, they had a Napoleonic politico-administrative culture in common, with a central state and a bureaucratic administration that was distant from the citizen. This was translated into central state forces, double structures, some civil, some paramilitary.

Spain is to a certain extent atypical, while the central national Spanish state was confronted with important tendencies towards political regional autonomy. It is in these regions that specific regional police forces exist. This is the case with the Mossos d'Esquadra in Catalonia and with the Ertzainza in the Basque Country. They are the expression of the political will to replace national police presence with regional police forces and in that sense of the tendency towards regional political autonomy.

In these systems the national forces are counterbalanced by municipal local police forces. Bigger metropolises have specific forces (e.g. in France the Préfecture de police de Paris,[17] in Spain's Barcelona and Madrid, in Italy's Rome, and in Portugal's Lisbon and Porto), even after the nationalisation of municipal forces (e.g. France). Local steering by mayors is the expression of political local democracy.

In most of the systems a functional integration of administrative and criminal competences can be observed within the forces mentioned, but there are exceptions, for example in Italy the Guardia di Finanza, and in Portugal the Polícia Judiciária, which are autonomous national forces that are *not* functionally integrated and have an important degree of functional specialisation.

Dominantly we observe autonomous leadership of the different forces; only now and then does there exist partial hierarchical integration between different forces.

These diverse police systems, inspired by the French system, are to a large extent complex, expressing the historical development of the countries and integrating the political reality of dominantly central national democracies, taking to a smaller extent other levels of decision-making power (regional and local) into account.

4 Territorial divided police systems

Under this heading we discuss a number of European police systems that are territorially decentralised and de-concentrated. We discuss the United Kingdom (UK) and three federal states (Germany, Switzerland and Belgium).

The UK comprises four countries: England, Wales, Northern Ireland and Scotland. The UK is a constitutional monarchy with a parliamentary system. It has a two-tier model of public administration consisting of national and local governments. This institutional context is complicated by the devolution of responsibility for policing and criminal justice to the Scottish Parliament and Northern Ireland Assembly. Currently there is a lively debate on the possibility and desirability of devolving policing and criminal justice to the Welsh government, but at the moment these remain the responsibility of the English and Welsh Home Office and Ministry of Justice. This means that there is only one jurisdiction, with the consequence that the police system is the same for both countries. In this section of the chapter we limit our view to England and Wales. In Northern Ireland and Scotland we observe the dominance of real national police services, which differ strongly from the situation in England and Wales.

Apart from the UK, there is the independent Republic of Ireland, which has the national Garda Síochána (the Guardian of the Peace). This system can also not be considered as constituted out of territorial forces, as is the case in England and Wales.

Apart from the situation in England and Wales, of course, there also exist in Europe federal states. A federal state can be defined as a state with one central government and a number of regions. These regions have their own competences, which cannot be limited by the central power, their own parliament and their own government. This power equilibrium is always anchored within the constitution of a country. There are not that many federal states in Europe: Belgium, Austria, Switzerland and of course Germany. It seems evident that the federal character of a state has a certain impact on the police system of a country and federal states eventually prefer a territorial divided police system. This is the reason why a number of these systems are considered in this section. In Germany, indeed, we find a strongly decentralised system.[18] In Switzerland we find a real cantonal police at the level of each section of the federal state. Consequently, we will consider also the system of this country. The police system of the federal state of Belgium is probably the most decentralised and de-concentrated system in Europe, with a strong emphasis on the local (zonal) police, complemented by a federal police.

4.1 The police system in England and Wales

In England and Wales there are 48 counties. A county is an administrative, geographical and political boundary, which is larger than a municipality. Counties are areas used for the purposes of administrative, geographical and political demarcation. The counties may consist of a single district or be divided into several districts and have a county council. Six of the counties are metropolitan counties. The current arrangement is the result of incremental reform. Many of the counties were established in the Middle Ages somewhere between the 7th and 11th centuries. In 1974 the existing local government structure of administrative counties and county boroughs in England and Wales outside Greater London was abolished. A new set of counties was created, six of which were metropolitan. The historic county boundaries were retained wherever it was practicable.

There are 41 county forces, which form the local police forces in England and Wales, together with the Metropolitan Police and the City of London Police (Edwards & Prins, 2014). These 43 police forces are often referred to as the 'Home Office' forces, executing the 'territorial' policing of England and Wales (Mawby & Wright, 2003). They are spread all over England and

Wales, and work independently of each other. Each works under the guidelines of the Home Office. In London there are two 'constabularies'. The City of London Police is responsible for policing in the City of London, which is a separate entity from the rest of Greater London; its responsibilities include policing the major financial markets and protecting the London Stock Exchange. The Metropolitan Police Service is responsible for policing the rest of Greater London (Cohen, 1981 [1979]).

The Home Office sets guidelines which the forces have to obey, but each force has its authority which is responsible for financing the local police force. Since there are 43 local forces, there are 43 local authorities which are also working independently from each other. The counties vary in size, but every county is commanded by one chief constable. The chiefs report their activities to the Home Office and the local police authority. The police counties are financed partly by the central government and partly by local taxation. The ultimate responsibility for the police forces lies with the home secretary (Brodeur, 1995).

The structure as we know it today dates from 1829, established by the Metropolitan Police Act, and was devised by Sir Robert Peel, who was home secretary at the time (Mawby, 2003). The London Metropolitan Police, established in 1829 by him, was a centrally controlled, uniformed service, aiming at monitoring street life, and preventing crime rather than fighting it (Rodgers & Gravelle, 2012). The main shortcoming of this system was the lack of local control of the police force (Emsley, 2003). The principle underlying the structure of the early police was that the working classes would police themselves. By employing constables from the working classes, Peel hoped to ensure that the relationship between the police and the public remained close (Wall, 1998). Peel imagined a police force in which 'there was to be no caste system as in the Navy or Army'. The Metropolitan Police was to be professional and homogenous (Critchley, 1978: 52).

Along with the Metropolitan Police, other structures arose from the concerns about crime. Between 1836 and 1839, a number of police reformers suggested the implementation of one single centralised organisation. At the same time, the central government accepted that the supervision of the police institutes – except the Metropolitan Police in London – was to be a responsibility of the local governments. In 1839 a law made it possible for counties to set up their own police forces if necessary. The central government also placed its police forces under the supervision of chief constables, who were appointed by the Home Office. These centralised forces, however, were transferred to local control three years later (Emsley, 2003). The 19th century and the first half of the 20th century held the cradle for the implementation and refinement of the policing system and, by 1930, the once amateurish and chaotic system was replaced by a stable police system (Newburn, 2003).

Following a series of public scandals involving chief constables, the Royal Commission on the Police was set up in 1960. It was the first time that the principles, organisation and constitutional position of the police had been examined publicly. The main report was published in 1962 and sought to secure a system of control over the police that achieved maximum efficiency and the best use of manpower, adequate means of bringing the police to account, and proper arrangements for dealing with complaints. The Commission favoured the retention of a system of local forces but with increased central coordination. The Commission proposed to increase the size of forces and reduce the overall number of forces to allow for a more efficient administration at local level (Wall, 1998). The Royal Commission's report underpinned the Police Act 1964, which determined the responsibility for public policing to a tripartite structure of police authorities, chief constables and the Home Office.

The accountability of the police was steered by three main systems/ institutions. First of all we had the Home Office, which determines the key national policing objectives in the annual National Policing Plan, which was brought to Parliament. The key tasks of the Home Office were establishing performance targets and approving the appointment of chief constables. Second, there was the local police authority which was responsible for maintaining an effective and efficient force. This authority also determined local policing priorities, which had to be consistent with the National Police Plan. On the third level there was the chief constable, who was responsible for direction and control of the force, especially for operational matters. He or she was also responsible for achieving local and national policing objectives. The chief constable was also the manager of the local police plan in cooperation with the local police authority (Hope, 1996).

The concern with improving 'police-community liaison' was intensified following the major riots in Brixton, South London, in April 1981 which became the subject of an official inquiry led by Lord Scarman. The Scarman Report (1981) is a major reference point in the recent history of British policing, not least for its critique of militaristic policing strategies, including the aggressive 'stop and search' of young males from low-income neighbourhoods and often from ethnic minority communities on 'suspicion' of offending behaviour (Benyon, 1984; Benyon & Solomos, 1987).

The recent Police Reform and Social Responsibility Act 2011 represented a major shift in this structure, moving responsibility for public policing from police authorities to elected police and crime commissioners (PCCs), that is, from the tripartite structure introduced in 1964 to a new quadripartite structure (chief constables, Home Office, PCCs, Police and Crime Panels) (Edwards & Prins, 2014).

Next to the local police forces, which are restricted in their powers to certain areas, England and Wales also have five non-territorial police forces, which work on the whole territory. The British Transport Police, founded in 1826, is the national police force responsible for the railways. The Civil

Nuclear Constabulary is a specialised and armed service whose job it is to protect civil nuclear sites and nuclear waste and material. The Ministry of Defence Police is a civil police force that is part of the Ministry of Defence (Aydin, 1997). All the members of this service have full constabulary powers. They operate on Ministry sites, and in units throughout the UK, as their services are required. The Ministry of Defence Police is the only real national police force in the UK. The British Transport Police, the Civil Nuclear Constabulary and the Ministry of Defence Police are also referred to as the 'non-Home Office' police services. They hold a specific responsibility and execute their jurisdiction throughout the UK (Mawby & Wright, 2003). The Port of Dover Police supervises the world's busiest passenger port. Finally, the National Crime Squad works at the heart of fighting serious and organised crime. All operations of this service are dedicated to dismantling and disturbing criminal organisations. Specifically, this means fighting drugs trafficking, illegal arms dealing, money laundering, contract killing, kidnapping and extortion.

The *European Sourcebook of Crime and Criminal Justice Statistics* (Aebi et al., 2010) mentions a ratio of 248 police officers (excluding civilians) per 100,000 inhabitants in 2011 in England and Wales. The mean of this ratio for all the participating countries was 386 in 2011, meaning that England and Wales have a police capacity well below the mean ratio. Eurostat mentions a global number of 132,198 police officers in England and Wales in 2012.[19]

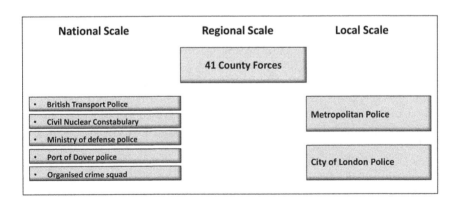

Figure 2.7 The police system in England and Wales
Note: The Metropolitan Police for Greater London is in fact a regional, not a local police force. There is major tension between the Greater London-wide priorities and the agenda of MOPAC (the Mayor's Office for Policing and Crime) and the policing priorities advanced by the 32 boroughs that constitute local government in Greater London (Edwards & Prins, 2014).

4.2 The police system in federal Germany

The German nation-state originated in 1867 with the installation of the North German Federation. In 1870/71 some southern states joined the federation. The actual name, the German Federal Republic, has been used since 1949. The 16 German 'Länder' (states) are the dominant policy level for security issues (Aden, 2004; Aden et al., 2004; Busch et al., 1985). This is the consequence of the situation in Germany when occupied by the Allied Forces after World War II. The Allied Forces took care to prevent Germany from again becoming a centralised authoritarian state as it had been between 1933 and 1945. Therefore, the 16 Bundesländer, or Länder, today enjoy a high level of autonomy in the organisation and steering of their security agencies. The Länder are also the driving force for establishing new security strategies, i.e. local crime prevention initiatives involving different state actors and non-governmental organisations (Aden, 2002; Aden et al., 2004; Busch et al., 1985). Due to the path dependencies established after World War II, Germany has a semi-decentralised police system with 16 autonomous police forces (Landespolizei) at the level of each Bundesland. The Landespolizei is the backbone of the federal police system (Aden, 2002; Aden et al., 2004; Busch et al., 1985). The police functions under the responsibility of the minister of the interior of each Landesministerium. It is at that level that political responsibility is anchored.

In 1990 the German reunification was realised, bringing together the old German Federal Republic (West Germany) and the German Democratic Republic (East Germany). In that year the six East German federal states entered the new Federal Republic. The 16 different Landespolizei forces have incorporated the former municipal police forces.[20] Each force has its own specific structure. Over time they became more similar, due to the influence of the police legislation that became more directive after 1970. Each Landespolizei force has fully integrated competences. They include the so-called 'Schutzpolizei' (protection) and the 'Kriminalpolizei' (criminal police), including all competences in the domain of traffic. The uniformed Schutzpolizei undertakes to a large extent administrative functions. The criminal police contains the SEKs (Spezialeinsatzkommandos) or special units, and MEKs (mobile commandos).[21] Each federal Land has its own police academy. At the level of each federal Land there is a 'Landeskriminalamt' (LKA) (Groß et al., 2008). LKAs belong to the Landespolizei.[22]

The federal state has two police forces: the 'Bundespolizei' (Federal Police) and the 'Bundeskriminalamt' (Federal Criminal Police Office). A number of other state and federal agencies are also involved in security issues, for example the federal customs administrations. The Federal Police is the successor of the former Federal Border Police (Bundesgrenzschutz), renamed in 2005 due to the diminishing role of border controls in the Schengen Area. By 1992, the former Federal Railway Police had already been integrated into

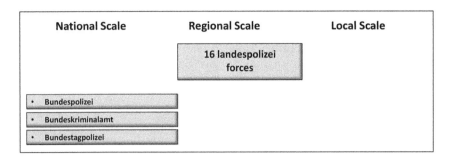

Figure 2.8 The police system in the German Federal Republic

the Federal Border Police. The Bundeskriminalamt has its headquarters at Wiesbaden (Hesse), but also maintains a satellite office in Berlin, where it is involved in the protection of government institutions and coordination with other security agencies, such as for anti-terrorism intelligence. The federal Parliament has its own small police force (Bundestagspolizei). The authority is limited to the Parliament buildings. A limited number of other federal services are also involved in security issues, such as the federal custom service. The riot police function is based on an agreement between the state and the Länder, in which military principles, training, structure and equipment are settled (Aden & De Pauw, 2014).

For the 82 million inhabitants in the German Federal Republic there are, apart from the 31,000 members of the Bundespolizei and 5,600 members of the Bundeskriminalamt, 221,000 police officers working in the 16 Landespolizei forces. These figures demonstrate the preponderance of the federal Länder to the detriment of the central state. The *European Sourcebook* (Aebi et al., 2014) mentions a ratio of 321 police officers (civilians not included) per 100,000 inhabitants in 2011 in Germany. The country scores largely under the mean average of 386. Eurostat mentions a global number of 243,982 police officers in Germany in 2012.[23]

4.3 The police system in Switzerland

Switzerland numbers about 8 millions of inhabitants. From an administrative point of view, the country is a federal republic, composed of 26 cantons (regions). Switzerland does not have an official capital city, but Bern is considered as the central metropolis in practice. Whilst Switzerland is not a member state of the EU, it nonetheless participates in the European single market and is strongly dependent on this market. The Swiss police does not exist in fact. We should rather speak of different Swiss police services as a consequence of the federal structure of the country. Switzerland has 26 codes of criminal procedure and 26 cantonal police services. Each cantonal police is subdivided into different services, more precisely into criminal services (Kriminalpolizei) and the gendarmerie (Sicherheitspolizei). According to the needs of each canton, specific services are added to this basic model, for example the police of an airport. Sometimes the traffic police is a separate service within a cantonal force; sometimes it is part of the gendarmerie.[24]

The 28 cantonal forces and additional municipal forces are the backbone of the Swiss police system. They function under the supervision of the federal authorities. The leading officers report to the cantonal and municipal police department. The coexistence and cohabitation between the cantonal and municipal forces bring specific problems concerning the division of competences and budget. This is the reason why a reflection process is ongoing concerning the integration of the municipal forces within the cantonal police (Rohrbach, 2003).[25]

Collaboration between the cantonal forces is fixed by different inter-cantonal agreements. The common efforts of the 'Conférence des Commandants des Polices Cantonales de Suisse' (CCPCS) and the 'Conférence des Directrices et des Directeurs de Police des Villes Suisses' (CDPVS) are directed towards the unification of the practices in different domains, which leads to relatively good collaboration in the combat against traditional crime (Mohler, 1997). The Swiss federal system does not lead only to inconveniences. There are also advantages to the system. Switzerland has a police system that is considered to be close to the population and is also proximate to the local authorities. Another important advantage is the flexibility to adapt to changing crime phenomena, a flexibility that is rarely observed in a centralised structure (Tschudi, 2003).

The federal government has no federal enforcement force. The enforcement and coordination of national laws are ensured by a college of cantonal police commanders. The police training is provided by cantonal academies and in the inter-cantonal Polizeischule Hitzkirch, a common initiative of 12 cantonal forces, started in 2007.

There exists a limited kind of federal police (Bellanger, 1998). The Fedpol is dependent of the federal Ministry of Justice and Police and coordinates the different police activities, especially international operations and those that demand cantonal support in the framework of criminal investigations under federal jurisdiction (e.g. phenomena such as organised crime, money laundering and terrorism).

The Ministry of Finance is responsible for the Swiss border police. A limited military police service functions within the Department of Defence. Furthermore a federal railway police is operational as a joint venture with Securitas AG, Securitrans. In case of catastrophe or large-scale rioting, the civil police services can call upon the Army, which functions in these cases under the responsibility and the command of the cantonal authority.

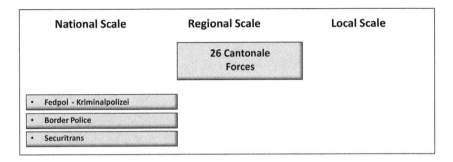

Figure 2.9 The police system in Switzerland

The *European Sourcebook* (Aebi et al., 2010) mentions a ratio of 212 police officers (civilians not included) per 100,000 inhabitants in 2006 in Switzerland. The figures for Switzerland are not included in the latest (fifth) edition of this work (Aebi et al., 2014). The average of this ratio for all participating countries was 371 in 2006, so Switzerland scores significantly below this average. Eurostat mentions a global number of 17,630 police officers in Switzerland in 2012.[26]

4.4 The police system in Belgium

The origin of the Belgian municipal police goes back to 1795 when the French occupiers set up the municipalities, thereby giving short shrift to the existing land divisions that went back to the Ancien Régime. All the municipalities became independent in 1800 and continued to exist after the independence of the country in 1830. At that time there were 2,776 municipalities, some very small. On 1 January 1977, a large-scale municipal merger was carried out, resulting initially in a total of 589 municipalities (Van Outrive et al., 1991). The Flemish Region has today 308 municipalities, the Brussels-Capital Region 19, and the Walloon Region 262. In principle, each of these municipalities had its own municipal police force prior to the reform of 1998.

The Gendarmerie was a legacy from the period when France occupied Belgium (1794–1815) and should also be seen as a Napoleonic heritage (Van Outrive et al., 1992). At the moment of independence in 1830, the Constitution stated that '*the structure and authority of the Gendarmerie will be regulated by law*'. Only in 1957 was a law on the Gendarmerie passed. Demilitarisation of the police force came much later, in 1992.

While both the above-mentioned police forces were created prior to Belgian independence, this was not the case with the criminal police at the public prosecutor's office (GPP). From 1870 onwards the magistracy started to complain about the limited impact the municipal police and the

Gendarmerie had on the level of crime. The discussion regarding the creation of a criminal police dragged on for a long time and it was only in 1919, shortly after the end of World War I, that a 'judicial police at the public prosecutor's office' was set up (Van Outrive et al., 1991).

Contrary to other European countries, it is striking that no clear, geographical or functional division of tasks between the above-mentioned police forces was ever set up. This resulted in creating an atmosphere of competition between the three forces. The notorious child abductor and murderer Marc Dutroux was arrested on 13 August 1996. It became clear that the police had lost a lot of valuable time during the investigation. The Dutroux case seriously affected public opinion and great pressure was put upon the politicians. Dutroux's escape from the court building at Neufchâteau for a short period proved to be the straw that broke the camel's back (Ponsaers & De Kimpe, 2001).

The so-called 'Octopus Agreement', dated 23 May 1998, gave rise to the fundamental reform act towards an 'Integrated Police Force on Two Levels' (WGP) of 7 December 1998 (Ponsaers, 2002). Since the introduction of the act, Belgium has had two types of police: a local police force (absorbing the municipal police and the local branches of the Gendarmerie) and a federal police force (absorbing the criminal police and the supra-local branches of the Gendarmerie). The local and federal police together make up the *integrated police*. Approximately 47,000 men and women are employed by the police. Approximately 39,000 are operational police officers. Within the framework of this reformed system, there are 'functional links between the two police levels' that are provided for by law. With respect to financing, the federal police are integrally financed nationally, while the local police are largely financed from the local municipal budgets (Cachet et al., 2008).

This reform was the first fundamental police reform in the history of the Belgian police (Bruggeman et al., 2010). The police organisation actually started at the federal police on 1 January 2001, with the local police starting one year later. At both levels – federal and local – the forces have substantial autonomy, although that does not take away the fact that they together must ensure '*integrated community policing*'. It is noticeable that the WGP has *not* given further specification to the allocation of tasks between the federal and local police forces, apart from the general statement that the local police is responsible for local and simple matters, while the federal police has to handle supra-local and complex cases. The act (WGP) lays down the functional connections between the two levels. Responsibilities for operational, integrated community policing lies at the feet of the ministers of home affairs and justice.

The system comprises 195 very diverse local zones. According to many, some of them are too small. Small police zones have difficulty in achieving the desired uniform quality and breadth of community policing. Although there is currently little interest in making zone mergers obligatory,

European police systems and metropolitan realities   49

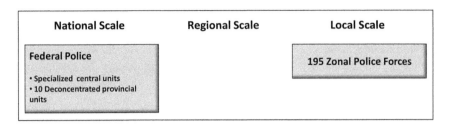

Figure 2.10 The police system in Belgium

which could affect the complex and sometimes vulnerable relationships between the local and federal police forces, scale corrections at the local police are possible for those zones that strive on a voluntary basis for upscaling. After ten years of reform, the federal police was considered to function too bureaucratically and was reorganised, simplified and rationalised, bringing the 27 de-concentrated units down to 12, at the scale of the provinces.

The *European Sourcebook* (Aebi et al., 2014) mentions a ratio of 340 police officers (civilians not included) per 100,000 inhabitants in 2011 in Belgium. The average of this ratio for all participating countries was 386 in 2011. Consequently, Belgium scores under this average. Eurostat mentions a global number of 46,784 police officers in Belgium in 2012.[27]

4.5 Legacies of feudalism and federalism

The police systems discussed under territorial divided police systems contain different police forces, but are at the same time constituted out of one type of police. In other words, here we observe a multitude of police leadership, but the kind is police in uniform. Here we are dealing with systems that are leaning on the division of the national territory in geographical entities, and in each of these territories is another force functioning with an autonomous police leadership. Each time, nevertheless, the kind of territorial force is the same. In other words, we are dealing here with police systems that are organised on a territorial basis. In some cases this dominant system is completed with some national or federal forces and/or municipal forces. The backbone of each of these systems in England and Wales, Germany, Switzerland or Belgium is respectively 'county forces', 'Landespolizei forces', 'cantonal forces' and 'zonal forces'. The dominant format is that of one type of police, with a plurality of forces.

It is striking that the division of labour in these police systems is to a large extent not functional of nature, but territorial. In short, we are dealing with functional integrated forces, which are engaged in all the aspects of police functions (administrative and criminal), but their action radius is limited to the territory (the county, the federal state, the canton, the zone) in which they are active. Every force does 'everything' in 'its' territory. It is striking that these different forces in these police systems are not hierarchically integrated. Each force has its own independent leadership and functions quite autonomously, notwithstanding that in each case we observe attempts to harmonise the functioning of the system.

Sometimes this harmonisation is stimulated by the national government (e.g. the Home Office in England and Wales). It is significant that the county forces are called 'Home Office forces', even while we keep in mind that the territorial division of England and Wales into counties is largely a legacy of feudalism. The tendency to increase national steering in England and Wales is explicitly present, without an explicit will to absorb the county forces within one national police. This observation contradicts the situation in Northern Ireland and Scotland, countries that are part of the UK but have single national police services. It is probable that these evolutions in Northern Ireland and Scotland are related to their propensity to more political autonomy and independence within the UK. In this sense we can assume that the police system of a country can be determined to a large extent by the tendency towards the formation of a new nation-state and expresses the inclination to autonomy. The reverse should also be considered: the degree of central steering of the police system will determine the possibilities for political independence.

The tendency towards unification of the police system in federal states, as for example the German Federal Republic, Switzerland or Belgium, is explicitly smaller. It is the federal structure that brings without any doubt the recognition of more autonomy for each region and less central impact. This is less the case in Belgium than in the German Federal Republic and Switzerland, where the territorial division of the police system does not follow the division in the federal regions and only a local (zonal) police is active besides the federal police (Devroe & Ponsaers, 2013). From this point of view Belgium is not unique. Also in the federal state of Austria there exists a central/federal police system, where the police is operational in the different regions, apart from the striking presence of municipal forces. In short, it is not by necessity the case that a federal state has a territorial divided police system, but it is also not a counter-indication for this reality (Ponsaers et al., 2014). From this point of view we look back to the Spanish police system, discussed earlier. Here too we recognised a 'federalising tendency' in certain regions, which led to the dominant presence of independent regional forces in these regions (such as Catalonia and the Basque Country). Again we see that the political reality of the structure of the state is reflected within the police system.

In the police systems we discussed under this section, we can observe that the territorial forces have national or federal services as counter-weights. These are to a large extent oriented towards the support of the territorial services. It is also remarkable that these territorial police systems do not contain paramilitary forces, which was still the case when we discussed the historical French tradition. It is also striking that these territorial systems have robust forces in important metropolises, which have an important weight within the global police system.

Each of the systems discussed is relatively complex, with a lot of particularities and specificities. They are to a large extent the expression of the state structure in which they function. Each of the countries has its own political history. It would go too far to sustain that we are dealing with weak democracies. Germany, for example, remains the leading reference within the European reality.

5 Unified police systems

In this section we discuss a number of European police systems that are constituted by one national police force. In other words, we are no longer dealing with one *kind* of police with different forces, but one police *force*, a unified police, operating under one unique leadership. This type of police we find in a number of European countries.[28] In Denmark we encounter a real unified police system. This system is also to a large extent territorially oriented, but can be considered a real national police.

Apart from the Scandinavian reality, we find a number of European countries that have today one National Police as a consequence of recent dramatic reforms. That is the case in the Netherlands, Northern Ireland, and in Scotland. This is the reason why we examine these countries in this section.

5.1 The police system of Denmark

Denmark has the most remarkable unified national police organisation in Europe, divided into 12 non-autonomous districts. The Danish police is a state police. Everyone who is working in the force is employed by the state and it is the state that pays all costs related to the system. In contradiction to most European countries, it is the Ministry of Justice that has the highest administrative power over the police. As well as investigation, prosecution and the maintenance of public order are part of this supervision.

This situation has been periodically discussed within Parliament. Opponents criticised the fact that justice and police are part of the same ministry, endangering the division of the executive and judicial powers. Until today the political parties have been unable to resolve this matter within Parliament (Henricson, 2004). In doing so, Denmark has in fact incorporated public prosecution into the national police, which could be called exceptional in the European context. The Danish public prosecution is not a steering instance and even from an organisational point of view is part of the police, while the prosecution of serious crime is an exception to this principle. The minister of justice is responsible for the complete chain of police-security-justice.

The Danish national police is constituted out of one central staff and 12 non-autonomous districts. Two less important districts are added to this structure. Until 2007 there existed 54 districts. Each of the actual 12+2 districts is guided by a local police leader. All districts have almost equal capacity, except for the capital city of Copenhagen. There is one national police chief. The Danish police commander functions under the authority of the minister of justice as an administrative directorate. He has operational command over the national force and important control competences. He is also responsible for the allocation of the personnel in the different districts and controls their efficient use of their means and statistical information. He does not interfere in the practical composition of the operative command in the districts. When parts of the organisation at the disposal of the commander are rendering support to a specific district, they function under the responsibility of the district commander. In other words, we can speak of hierarchical steering, based on performance agreements (Jochoms et al., 2013).

The 12 local districts within the national police are subdivided into a judicial service, a criminal service, a uniformed service and an internal service. All services have to report to the district commander, who executes the highest control. The organisational structure is to a high degree adapted to the education the personnel received. The local police is slowly evolving into a more flexible structure, without too formal a framework. Recently the difference between uniformed service and investigation was abolished. The police districts are to a certain degree decentralised, while the Ministry of Justice delegates more and more competences to the police leaders of the districts in the cities (Fyfe et al., 2013).

Apart from the organisation in districts, there exist a few services that function on a national level, more precisely: a) the Rigspolitiet, a national force that is specialised in accounting and budgeting, buildings and data control; b) the Politiets Efterretningstjeneste, or national intelligence service; and c) the Politiets Aktionsstryrke, or special force of the Danish police.

Until 1911 the police forces were paid by the municipalities, working under the hierarchical authority of the local police chiefs, assigned by the king. The municipal forces were, during the transition period until 1938, brought under the direction of the central state. The rationale behind this change was an increase in efficiency through unified management, better coordination between different police districts, and ultimately by the introduction of unified guidelines concerning the recruitment and training of police officers.

Meanwhile, Danish mayors no longer have authority over the police. They can only influence informal consultation concerning security in the region. In spite of the fact that the police is woven into several societal

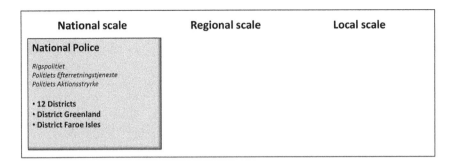

Figure 2.11 The police system in Denmark

consultations, there is no longer a formal authority relationship between the local government and the police. That is certainly the case in smaller municipalities. Since 2007 there has been a kind of district council, including the police director and the mayors of the district. The district director is formally responsible for the functioning of the district council and is also the chair of this council. Mutual consultation is foreseen. The police is supposed to draw up a local collaboration plan each year, which is consolidated within the district council. Because of the number and the intensity of public order problems in larger cities, these mayors have more impact on police policy (Henricson, 2004; Haagsma et al., 2012).

The *European Sourcebook* (Aebi et al., 2014) mentions a ratio of 196 police officers (civilians not included) per 100,000 inhabitants in 2011 in Denmark. The average of this ratio for all participating countries was 386 during that year. Denmark scores remarkably below this average. It is probable that this is related to the low population density in Denmark. Denmark has hardly any metropolises and is to a large extent a green rural area (Haagsma et al., 2012). Eurostat mentions a global number of 10,758 police officers in Denmark in 2012.[29]

5.2 The police system of the Netherlands

The Netherlands had a long evolution towards a national police. In 1945, immediately after World War II, the Netherlands experienced chaos. A lot of houses were bombarded and the police was very weak (Fijnaut, 2007). In the Dutch municipalities of 25,000 inhabitants or more, the so-called municipal police was present. The mayor of the municipality was 'head of the police' and responsible for the local police. The municipal council could demand that the mayor give more attention to the police. The mayor was responsible for public order and the prosecutor was responsible for criminal aspects. The administrative leadership of the municipal police was in the hands of the minister of the interior.

In 1945 the government decided that the municipal police should stay in the larger cities, while the Rijkspolitie (the police of the kingdom) was installed. This new force became active in smaller cities and municipalities. The administrative supervision for this new force was in the hands of the minister of justice. A new police system was introduced, composed of the municipal police and the Rijkspolitie. Apart from those forces there was the Royal Marechaussee, already installed in 1814, which was a centrally steered police force with a military structure, in fact a gendarmerie.

In April 1993, the Dutch police was reorganised. The Rijkspolitie was abandoned. The work in the municipalities without municipal police was given to the new *regional police* and other tasks were transferred to the National Police Service Force (KLPD). At that time, the Dutch police system resembled strongly that of England and Wales, with 25 autonomous regional forces which were territorially oriented, each with its own police leadership, complemented by a few central national services (KLPD). The police chief had the daily command over his regional force. The regional triangular consultation between the mayor of the largest municipality of the region, the prosecutor and the police chief of the regional force determined the security policy within the region. Besides this, each municipality had the right to its own triangular consultation with its own mayor (Ponsaers et al., 2012). Each region contained a number of districts, and each had a district chief. Each district was composed of a number of local entities. The number of police officers was determined by the number of inhabitants of the region and the frequency of crime there. On the occasion of the reform all tasks concerning civil aviation were transferred to the Royal Marechaussee. In 1998 this Marechaussee became an independent part of the Army. Since that time the force is no longer considered part of the police system.

Despite the reform of 1993, the system continued to generate criticism (Prins et al., 2012). In the end, the government decided in January 2013 to reform the system anew. This ultimate reform concluded the discussion on the organisation of the police. All parts of the police system were included in one force, the Dutch National Police. Since then the police has functioned under the authority of the new Ministry of Security and Justice. The 25 regional forces and the KLPD were restructured into ten sub-national entities (plus one for the Dutch Antilles), a national unit, a police service centre and the police academy. The regional entities of the national police are the backbone of the new police system (Vlek & Van Reenen, 2012).

The territories of the sub-national entities are equal to the new geographical limitations of the judicial system. A sub-national entity is composed of districts, (support) services and staff. Each district is composed of basic teams, an investigation unit and a so-called 'flexible team'.[30] In case of crisis the police collaborates with the fire brigade and medical ambulance services within the so-called security region. The mayor and the public prosecutor have the supervision of the local commitment of the police. These

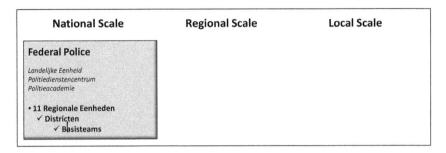

Figure 2.12 The police system in the Netherlands

two parties make agreements in the local triangular consultation with the police. Within this consultation the priorities are determined, based on the integral security plan of the municipality and national priorities (Fijnaut, 2012).

The *National Unit* is to a large extent the descendant of the former KLPD. It is composed of a staff, a national operational centre, a national investigative unit, a national information service, a national service for operational collaboration, a service for infrastructure, a service for surveillance and protection, a special force, and a national management team for planning and capacity management. Apart from that, the national police has a national concern service, the service centre for the police. In this centre an important part of support is covered. The management of the national police is focused on human resources, facility management, finances, provision of information and communication. The police academy, the training centre of the police, is provisionally not a formal part of the national police, but over time it seems to be being absorbed by the organisation (Fyfe et al., 2013).

The *European Sourcebook* (Aebi et al., 2014) mentions a ratio of 230 police officers (civilians not included) per 100,000 inhabitants in 2011 (thus before the actual reform) in the Netherlands. The average of this ratio for all participating countries was 386 during that year. The Netherlands scores significantly below this average. Eurostat mentions a global number of 39,735 police officers in the Netherlands in 2012.[31]

5.3 The police system of Northern Ireland

Today Northern Ireland has a national police force, the Police Service of Northern Ireland (PSNI). It is the successor of the former Royal Ulster Constabulary (RUC), which, in turn, was the successor of the Royal Irish Constabulary (RIC) in Northern Ireland.

Policing in Ireland started in the mid-18th century, in the form of the Dublin Metropolitan Police (Ellison & Smyth, 2000). It was established under British rule, and was seen by the Irish people as an extension of that nation-state (Punch & Bisschop, 2009). During the 19th century the British government became increasingly convinced that a militarised police force would be the only way to maintain their dominance in Ireland. The result was the creation of the Peace Preservation Force, a 'compromise between a fully-fledged centralised police force and the extensive use of the military in a policing role' (Ellison & Smyth, 2000: 12). Over time this force became increasingly centralised and when the RIC was installed in 1836, the military nature of the force was clear, despite objections to a 'continental' (French) style of policing. The overall result that was the RIC was a symbol of the British rule for the Irish people, and consequentially, the force was detested by them.

From the late 19th century on, the majority of people living in Ireland wanted the British government to grant some form of self-rule to the island. The nationalists (known as republicans, mainly Catholics) sought to gain Home Rule, which would give Ireland autonomy in internal affairs, without breaking up the UK. However, a significant minority (known as the unionists or separatists, republicans, mainly Protestants) was opposed to this idea, because it implied maintaining the connection with Britain and 'betrayed' the so-called pan-Irish political union (of *Northern* and *Southern* Ireland). The last group retained control of a fraction of the Ulster Volunteer Force (UVF), a loyalist paramilitary group in Northern Ireland (Lundy & McGovern, 2001).

During the general election of 1918, the traditional Irish Parliamentary Party lost almost all of its seats to the unionists of Sinn Féin. Guerrilla warfare raged across Ireland, leading to the Anglo–Irish War. The authorities created the (mainly ex-UVF) Ulster Special Constabulary to aid the RIC and introduced emergency powers to put down the Irish Republican Army (IRA). Many died in political violence. In 1920 the British government partitioned the island into *Northern* Ireland and *Southern* Ireland. From 1922 on Northern Ireland stopped being part of the UK and became part of the newly created Irish Free State. A new dominion for the whole island of Ireland was established, but Northern Ireland immediately exercised its right to opt out of the new dominion. This way Northern Ireland became a new autonomous region (Kempa, 2007).

The first years after the transition were marked by bitter violence, particularly in Belfast. The IRA was determined to oppose the partition. The police force of Northern Ireland became the RUC (Mulcahy, 2006). This resulted in a high number of ex-RIC officers being integrated into the newly formed RUC (Ellison & Smyth, 2000). An undercurrent of RIC ideals remained in the RUC. Northern Catholics did not join the new force in great numbers. Despite symbolic changes, the RUC remained a centralised paramilitary force under direct political influence.

'The Troubles' was a period of ethno-political conflict in Northern Ireland, conventionally dating from the late 1960s and considered to have ended with the Belfast 'Good Friday' Agreement of 1998. The RUC played a key role during 'the Troubles' (Stamer, 2007). An important milestone in the worsening relationship between the British Army and Irish nationalists was the Falls Curfew of July 1970, when British troopers imposed a curfew on west Belfast. The appearance in 1970 of the Provisional IRA, a campaign of violence by loyalist paramilitary groups and the killing of unarmed civilians in Derry by the Parachute Regiment on 30 January 1972, called 'Bloody Sunday', brought Northern Ireland to the brink of civil war. In March 1972, the British government pushed through emergency legislation that prorogued the Northern Ireland Parliament and introduced direct rule from London. A year later the British government dissolved the Parliament of Northern Ireland and its government (Jarman, 2004).

By the 1990s, the tension between the IRA and British security forces convinced a majority inside the republican movement that greater progress might be achieved through negotiation rather than violence at this stage (Lamb, 2008). Increased government focus on the problems of Northern Ireland led in 1998 to the Belfast Agreement, signed by eight parties (Engel & Burruss, 2004). To adhere to the agreement, the Independent Commission on Policing (ICP) was set up to make proposals on the changes needed within the RUC. The resulting *Patten Report* (Patten Report of the Independent Commission on Policing for Northern Ireland, 1999) detailed many institutional changes required to recreate the police system in line with the Belfast Agreement. This report shows a more community-oriented approach to policing. However, the report notes that realistically, implementation of all of the proposals will only be possible in conditions of political stability and with an end to paramilitary violence (O'Rawe, 2007).

Ultimately, the RUC was replaced by the Police Service of Northern Ireland on 4 November 2001, in essence a national police force. Although the majority of PSNI officers were still from the Protestant community, this dominance is not as pronounced as it was in the RUC because of affirmative action policies. The PSNI has one chief constable, who is assisted by a deputy chief constable and the senior management team. He is appointed by the Northern Ireland Policing Board, subject to the approval of the minister of justice for Northern Ireland. Each district is headed by a chief superintendent. Districts are divided into areas, commanded by a chief inspector and they in turn are divided into sectors, commanded by inspectors. In 2001 the old police divisions and sub-divisions were replaced with 29 District Command Units (DCUs), roughly according to the local council areas. In 2007 these 29 districts were replaced again by eight districts in anticipation of the local restructuring of the public administration. In other words, we are dealing with a decentralised yet united police force (Punch & Bisschop, 2009), with the Northern Ireland area divided into four urban and four rural police districts. These districts are run by a chief superintendent and operate with a degree of autonomy with specific district policies, priorities and initiatives for community safety. The PSNI aims to be a proactive,

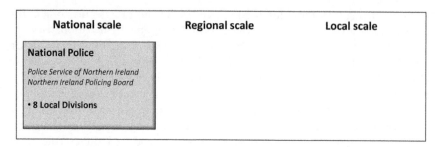

Figure 2.13 The police system in Northern Ireland

community-oriented police force based on professionalism and working with the community to create a safer Northern Ireland.

To support the PSNI in becoming a more transparent, accountable and legitimate organisation, the police system incorporates the Policing Board (PB) to ensure an effective, efficient, impartial, representative and accountable police service which will secure the confidence of the whole community. This is supplemented by the police ombudsman, who provides a complaints system considered to be impartial, independent and effective (O'Rawe & Moore, 2000).

The *European Sourcebook* (Aebi et al., 2014) mentions a ratio of 139 police officers (civilians not included) per 100,000 inhabitants in 2011 in Northern Ireland, significantly below the average for all participating countries of 386. Eurostat mentions a global number of 13,400 police officers in Northern Ireland in 2012.[32]

5.4 The police system of Scotland

Scotland is part of the sovereign state of the United Kingdom, together with England, Northern Ireland and Wales. During the 1990s three of them (Scotland,[33] Wales[34] and Northern Ireland[35]) voted in favour of a limited form of autonomy. There is a rather strong political tendency in Scotland advocating for independence. A national referendum was planned in September 2014 concerning this issue, which resulted in a vote against full independence. Although the Scottish Parliament does not dispose of sovereign state power, it is engaged actively in competences such as taxes, national insurance, etc. (Donnelly & Scott, 2008).

Before the 19th century Scotland had no municipal police. During the 19th century municipal forces gradually replaced city guards, vigilantes or soldiers. The first municipal force was that of Glasgow, which appeared in 1800. Rapidly other Scottish cities followed this example. Since then it is clear that the central state has been less steering in Scotland than in England and Wales. The Scottish cities and municipalities decided to a large degree on their own police forces, without central intervention (Barrie, 2008). In 1862 the police of Glasgow had a force of about 700 officers and the police of Edinburgh one of about 300 members.

After World War II a number of important changes were introduced in the Scottish municipal forces, such as the installation of a common police academy. The Police (Scotland) Act of 1967 created a legal framework for the organisation of a territorial police in Scotland, as in England and Wales. In 1975 the local administration was created. As a consequence of this reorganisation, the number of local forces was reduced to eight for the whole Scottish territory. Amongst other changes, the police of Glasgow was integrated in the Strathclyde Police. The structure of the eight forces was continued after the reorganisation of the local administration in 1996, indicating territorial divided forces (Fyfe et al., 2013).[36]

In 2012 the Police and Fire Reform Act was realised after intensive consultation.[37] It was this act that installed the national police service of Scotland (Seirbheis Phoilis na h-Alba). The new Scottish national police was implemented on 1 April 2013. It is the successor of the former system of territorial divided forces, with the forces absorbed into a unified police force, functioning on the whole Scottish territory. The Scottish national police has 14 local divisions (Fyfe et al., 2013). A number of central services were also created, for example the Scottish Police Services Authority (a public administration of the Scottish government, responsible for certain central services) and the Scottish Police Authority (to which the Scottish police has to render accountability) and the Scottish Crime and Drug Enforcement Agency (Scott, 2008). The national force has broad 'crime scene' investigative possibilities and laboratory facilities. The force is strongly engaged in crime prevention.

The *European Sourcebook* (Aebi et al., 2010) mentions a ratio of 329 police officers (civilians not included) per 100,000 inhabitants in 2011 in Scotland. The average of this ratio for all participating countries was 386 during that year. In short, Scotland scores below this average. Eurostat mentions a global number of 17,496 police officers in Scotland in 2012.[38]

5.5 Reform and unification in Europe

In a number of European nation-states we find police systems that have integrated all components of the former police system into one national police. System and force become identical this way. Logically, we can no longer speak of one 'type' of police. Mostly observers qualify this situation as national police forces or unified police. These systems are characterised by the fact that we deal with one leadership, which is responsible for the whole force and structure. This kind of system brings hierarchical integration within the different components of the organisation.

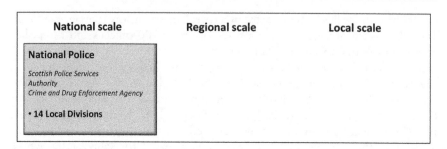

Figure 2.14 The police system in Scotland

This situation has as a consequence that the national police structure is financed by the national authorities. The financing by lower policy levels is much more modest, or non-existent. The role of local authorities, or mayors, is minimal.

It is striking that these systems are functionally integrated by necessity. There is only one force, and it is that force which has to perform '*all*' police tasks, judicial as well as administrative in nature. It is also remarkable that most of these systems are internally structured according to a territorial division and not according to functional specialisations. They are territorially divided and oriented forces, with an umbrella organisation. In most cases we can observe structures encompassing large geographical entities, which are again subdivided into smaller territories. In most Scandinavian countries this is still the reality, as in Sweden, Norway or Finland.

Besides this reality, there are a number of specific central services, which are impacting in a less important way on the global system. The territorial police work stays the backbone of these systems, which means that each of the districts, divisions, regional entities, etc. has territorial competence on the whole national territory.

A number of the national systems that we discussed are recent creations, but not all. This is the case in the Netherlands and in Scotland, to a lesser extent in Denmark and Northern Ireland. Notwithstanding this observation, all unified systems are the result of reform, constructed out of the old bricks of former systems. We observe that these unified systems no longer have military components. Gendarmerie-like elements are no longer part of these national systems.[39]

In specific cases this national formation of one force is complemented by an increasing tendency towards independence and the formation of a nation, as in Northern Ireland and Scotland. In this context we refer to the situation in Catalonia (Spain). However, this is not always the case, as in Denmark and the Netherlands, where reform was induced by considerations concerning efficiency.

Real municipal forces are barely still a part of these national systems, but this does not prevent the national organisation from guaranteeing solid local entities in metropolitan areas. It is striking that in such countries the policy functions concerning police and justice are also united, as is the case in Denmark, but also in the Netherlands. In Northern Ireland and Scotland, we did not observe this evolution.

6 Conclusion

We can distinguish three types of police systems in Europe: a) historical diverse police systems, b) territorial divided police systems, and c) unified police systems. The functioning of these different structures varies dramatically.

6.1 The cost

When we observe the police capacity per 100,000 inhabitants in the countries under study (Figure 2.15), we conclude that this ratio fluctuates dramatically, with a spike to the top for Spain, and Denmark as the outlier at the bottom.

When we calculate the average police capacity according to the type of police systems we distinguished (Figure 2.16), we observe clearly that the historical diverse police systems consume much more police capacity than both other police systems.

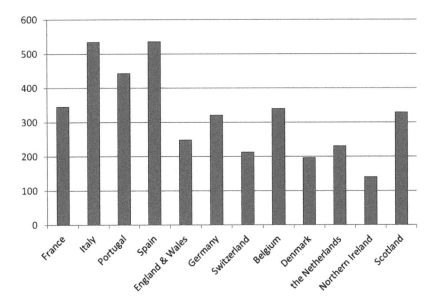

Figure 2.15 Police capacity per 100,000 inhabitants in the countries under study, 2011 (Aebi et al., 2014)[40]

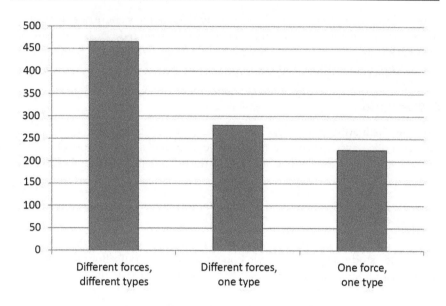

Figure 2.16 Police capacity per 100,000 inhabitants according to the typology

Between territorially divided police systems and unified systems the observed differences are much smaller. This is rather astonishing, while the creation of a national police and the subsequent dramatic reform is mostly sustained by the argument that a unified police is much more cost effective. Observing this marginal difference more carefully reveals that in fact both kinds of police systems are constructed in the same way: we are dealing with territorially divided systems also when we are dealing with unified national systems.

Reform towards a national police leads nevertheless to nationalisation of costs. Military parts of the system disappear mostly, with these parts sometimes becoming part of the Army. In any case, it seems that demilitarisation is a pre-condition for dramatic reform. It is also striking that national police systems have a great need for strong local entities in metropolises.

In specific cases we observe the construction of national police systems as an instrumental means for political ends. Examples are the Spanish police system and the national police forces of Northern Ireland and Scotland. In contradiction to what we expected, federal states do not by necessity have a territorial divided police system. This is nevertheless the case in the Federal Republic of Germany. Apart from structural differences between the different countries, we can observe that community policing became the dominant police philosophy in Europe. Structure seems more likely to differ than culture.

6.2 Different metropolitan realities

While the weight of metropolitan areas in Europe has clearly become more important, this reality is not really systematically reflected in the different national police systems. In the historical diverse police systems we observe a continuity in the importance of the centrality of nation-states. In unified police systems we encounter the consolidation of national interests, without a strong emphasis on metropolitan policing. It is in territorial divided police systems that we can observe the capacity to include the metropolitan reality better and more flexibly within the system.

Often nation-states anticipate the metropolitan rise by creating regulations that leave large room for manoeuvre at the discretion of metropolitan authorities. The local elective representation of metropolitan inhabitants by political leaders becomes a central question in local governance and translates into growing participation and/or resistance by the civil society in decision making. Government becomes, more than ever, governance by consent (Devroe, 2013).

Nevertheless, the political governing model of European metropolises is not identical throughout Europe (Devroe et al., 2014). Some can be identified as *city-states*. Berlin, for example, combines different functions: it is simultaneously the capital of the country, one of the 16 autonomous German Länder and, as the most important metropolis of Germany, also one of the three city-states of the country. The mayor of Berlin is thus at the same time prime minister of the state (Land) and mayor of the city-state (Aden, 2014). Certainly, there are other governance models in Europe than the city-state.

Some metropolises are in fact *capital cities of regions, with a large degree of autonomy*, for example, the city of Barcelona[41] (Recasens & Ponsaers, 2014). Barcelona is the capital city of the Catalonian autonomous region. The political dominance of the regional government in Catalonia, based in Barcelona and striving for regional independence, is striking compared to that of the Spanish central government in Madrid, but also compared to the position of the mayors in Catalonia.

A third model of governing is that of the *metropolis under the national authority*. In these metropolises the nation-state and its government still largely dominates the local reality. A typical historical example is Rome, being submitted to the power of the Italian central state[42] (Bruggeman, 2014). Only to a small extent and very slowly is more political power delegated today to Italian regions, provinces and municipalities in Italy. Paris also matches this configuration to a large extent.

6.3 Internal pluralisation of policing

European metropolises and their local governance challenge the traditional concept of national police systems in various ways (Ponsaers et al., 2014).

This is largely obtained by *pluralising the police function* (Jones & Newburn, 2006a). This pluralisation is to a large extent an *internal* process, barely influencing the shape of national police systems. In varying ways we can observe different police forces functioning on the territory of each metropolis. Sometimes there is a dominance of national services (e.g. in Paris), under the political responsibility of the national government; sometimes the territory is principally policed by a metropolitan police (e.g. in London), guided (and financed) by the local authority, but used also by the national government. In other metropolises we can observe a complex mixture of local, regional and national police forces, functioning according to different policy agendas on the territory of the same metropolitan area (e.g. in Brussels or Rome). In this framework we can observe a multitude of 'public safety regimes' (Edwards & Hughes, 2012).

In contradiction to the growing importance of metropolises, we observe also police reform programmes in certain European countries reducing the plurality of policing to one national force (e.g. in Amsterdam, the Netherlands). The meaning of these legal-constitutional changes in metropolitan police configurations is not yet extensively articulated in terms of shifting political power in earlier studies. Does this mean that national/federal government tries to strengthen its symbolic position to the detriment of metropolitan governance, and why?

6.4 External pluralisation of policing

Pluralisation of policing is also an *external* process. More than ever before we observe the appearance in certain metropolitan areas of new *non*-police configurations, in other words new ('light blue') uniformed surveillance agencies (e.g. public wardens, guardians, stewards …), while in other metropolises this phenomenon is marginal. It is remarkable that this evolving reality is not part of shifts in national police systems. These changes can only be studied in the framework of local monographs and especially through the comparison of different metropolises in one and the same country.

We can observe the same geographical variability when it comes down to voluntary activities of citizens in the domain of security (e.g. Neighbourhood Watch programmes). Non-commercial initiatives by citizens are banned in Berlin, and in Paris civil self-defence initiatives are not tolerated. The same variation can be observed in the rise of outsourcing of private commercial security agencies by public authorities and the dissemination of competences, soft as well as harsh (Edwards & Hughes, 2012).

Despite the observed pluralisation of the regular public police, the 'dark blue' police seems to maintain its central position in the domain of security in European metropolises. It seems that we are observing merely a process of diversification, no more than that. It does not mean that the steering of the whole configuration, or ultimately the monopoly of legal violence, is transposed to other actors in the field. It is not obvious that a real 'web of policing' is woven, a security network including all actors, resulting from this evolution (Prins et al., 2012). For example, in Barcelona no formal functional ties exist between the public and the private sector. Mostly the question of if there is real cooperation between both sectors remains unanswered. Most of the time that collaboration is limited to specific situations or spaces (e.g. in football grounds in Berlin). It is our deduction that these external forms of plural policing are to a large extent determined by push and pull factors of local decision-making power, and affected by political compromise or ideology. Only an in-depth study of the situation on the territory of specific European metropolises can shed light on this local reality.

Notes

1 The authors are grateful for the very useful information and suggestions from Adam Edwards, Rossella Selmini, Jacques de Maillard, Christian Mouhanna and other authors in this volume.
2 On the occasion of the panel on the Policing European Metropolises Project, during the 14th Annual conference of the European Society of Criminology in September 2014 in Prague.
3 Notwithstanding the shrinking political weight of European nation-states, Europe does not have an operational police force, despite the existence of Europol.
4 Italy, for example, has different police forces. Some are functioning at national level (Polizia di Stato, Carabinieri, Guardia di Finanza, etc.), while others are present at (supra-)local level (Polizia Provinciale, Polizia Municipale, etc.). All these different components together are considered to constitute the national Italian police system.
5 This chapter makes abstraction of the gendarmerie of San Marino, an enclaved microstate surrounded by Italy, and of the Corps of Gendarmerie of Vatican City.
6 In the French-speaking cantons of Switzerland the 'gendarmeries' are in fact the uniformed civil police and therefore are not considered in this chapter.
7 The first creation of a national police force was carried out by King Louis XIV, who created the first national police of Paris to maintain public order. Napoleon created the first judiciary force, but he is well known for his spies (police officers without uniforms).
8 Monjardet make the difference between three functions: administrative, judicial, but also security (answering to the citizens' demands) to stress the fact that in France the Police Nationale does not fulfil the last function.
9 However, the minister of justice has no power over the judicial police force, which is under the command of the minister of the interior. This is a tremendous problem for the magistrates.
10 Some observers stress the fact that the gendarmerie used to be a real community policing force. Mouhanna (2011) stresses that Anglo-Saxon authors often mistake military force (nature) and military way of acting (function) in respect to the French gendarmerie.
11 See http://appsso.eurostat.ec.europa.eu/nui/show.do?dataset=crim_plce&lang=en and http://ec.europa.eu/eurostat/statistics-explained/index.php/File:Police_officers, _2002%E2%80%9312_YB14.png
12 We should note that there are various attempts at coordination: the Gendarmerie Nationale is now part of the Ministry of the Interior, there are conventions

between municipal and national police forces. The préfet, at the level of the department, is in charge of coordination (and there are weekly meetings between Gendarmerie Nationale, Police Nationale, prosecutor and préfet). There are also ways (rather informal) in which the mayors can influence the national police.

13 There are actually six, if we include the Provincial Police, a local police in charge of environmental control at the province level, under the general coordination of the regional governments. However, since provinces were abolished and transformed during 2014 in the Metropolitan District, this police force will be – probably – absorbed by the municipal police.

14 See http://appsso.eurostat.ec.europa.eu/nui/show.do?dataset=crim_plce&lang=en and http://ec.europa.eu/eurostat/statistics-explained/index.php/File:Police_officers, _2002%E2%80%9312_YB14.png

15 See http://appsso.eurostat.ec.europa.eu/nui/show.do?dataset=crim_plce&lang=en and http://ec.europa.eu/eurostat/statistics-explained/index.php/File:Police_officers, _2002%E2%80%9312_YB14.png

16 See http://appsso.eurostat.ec.europa.eu/nui/show.do?dataset=crim_plce&lang=en and http://ec.europa.eu/eurostat/statistics-explained/index.php/File:Police_officers, _2002%E2%80%9312_YB14.png

17 It should be stressed that the prefecture of police is not a municipal police; there is no real municipal police force in Paris. For further reading, see de Maillard, 2015.

18 In Austria the police is the responsibility of the federal Ministry of the Interior, in Vienna. The system was reformed in 2005, which led to the consolidation of the federal police (Bundespolizei), the federal criminal police (Bundeskriminalamt) and the Bundesgendarmerie in nine federal command structures at the level of the federal state. Apart from that, Austria has 21 municipal forces. We will not consider this system further in this chapter.

19 See http://appsso.eurostat.ec.europa.eu/nui/show.do?dataset=crim_plce&lang=en and http://ec.europa.eu/eurostat/statistics-explained/index.php/File:Police_officers, _2002%E2%80%9312_YB14.png

20 It was in München in 1975 that the last municipal police was abolished in the federal state of Bayern.

21 The SEKs are to a large extent the consequence of the confrontation of the police with left terrorism in Germany during the 1970s.

22 Brandenburg and Saarland are exceptions. Here the LKAs are independently organised.

23 See http://appsso.eurostat.ec.europa.eu/nui/show.do?dataset=crim_plce&lang=en and http://ec.europa.eu/eurostat/statistics-explained/index.php/File:Police_officers, _2002%E2%80%9312_YB14.png

24 Mostly municipal forces are added to the cantonal forces. Cities such as Zurich, Bern and Lausanne have their own criminal police within their municipal police force, apart from the municipal gendarmerie. In Geneva, the municipal police has competences that are limited to the recording of infringements.

25 In French cantons like Fribourg, Neuchâtel or Vaud reform projects were elaborated. In the German-speaking canton Bern a fusion at cantonal level was realised in 2007. The urban cantons like Genève were less touched by these organisational and management problems because essential police tasks like public order, public security and judicial police were mostly covered by the cantonal police (Sigrist, 2009).

26 See http://appsso.eurostat.ec.europa.eu/nui/show.do?dataset=crim_plce&lang=en and http://ec.europa.eu/eurostat/statistics-explained/index.php/File:Police_officers, _2002%E2%80%9312_YB14.png

27 See http://appsso.eurostat.ec.europa.eu/nui/show.do?dataset=crim_plce&lang=en and http://ec.europa.eu/eurostat/statistics-explained/index.php/File:Police_officers,_2002%E2%80%9312_YB14.png
28 It is striking that a number of Scandinavian countries have such a police system. The Swedish system is rather similar to the system in England and Wales, but has (in contradiction to the British system) an umbrella organisation for the 21 county forces and the Swedish National Police Council (Rikspolisstyrelsen), the so-called 'Swedish Police Service'. The system in Norway resembles the Swedish. Also this system is inspired by that of England and Wales. This system also has an umbrella organisation, the Norwegian Police Service (Politiog lensmannsetaten), containing the central National Police Direction, seven special services and 27 police districts. Finland has one single police organisation, which functions under the authority of the Ministry of the Interior and the supervision of the National Police Council. There are 11 police departments within the police organisation. We leave these systems aside. The organisational structure is to a large extent territorially oriented and does not reflect the integration of different components in one single integrated organisation. We are dealing with the composition of different territorially oriented organisations under one policy umbrella. In this sense, the dominance of a unified police in Scandinavia is a myth.
29 See http://appsso.eurostat.ec.europa.eu/nui/show.do?dataset=crim_plce&lang=en and http://ec.europa.eu/eurostat/statistics-explained/index.php/File:Police_officers,_2002%E2%80%9312_YB14.png
30 The tasks of basic teams are: first point of contact, delivering first aid and non-urgent reports steered by the central dispatch, investigation of frequent crime and enforcement (of juvenile violence, events, hotel and catering industry, mental health care, traffic, surveillance of foreigners, environmental and executive tasks). Basic teams have investigative capacity for tackling frequent delinquency. The investigative unit of a district is responsible for high-impact crime. It delivers support to the basic teams (Bruggeman & Ponsaers, 2011).
31 See http://appsso.eurostat.ec.europa.eu/nui/show.do?dataset=crim_plce&lang=en and http://ec.europa.eu/eurostat/statistics-explained/index.php/File:Police_officers,_2002%E2%80%9312_YB14.png
32 See http://appsso.eurostat.ec.europa.eu/nui/show.do?dataset=crim_plce&lang=en and http://ec.europa.eu/eurostat/statistics-explained/index.php/File:Police_officers,_2002%E2%80%9312_YB14.png
33 The creation of the Scottish Parliament through the Scotland Act 1998 was a consequence of a referendum of all registered domiciles in Scotland in 1997.
34 The creation of the National Assembly for Wales was a consequence of a referendum vote by all registered domiciles in Wales in 1997.
35 The creation of the Northern Ireland Assembly in 1998 was a consequence of the Belfast Agreement (colloquially known as the Good Friday Agreement), and was negotiated by elected representatives of the main political parties in Ulster.
36 Besides these forces there existed others, such as the British Transport Police, the Ministry of Defence Police, the UK Atomic Energy Authority Police and the National Criminal Intelligence Service (NCIS), but these forces fell under the responsibility of the UK rather than that of the Scottish government.
37 Consult: www.scotland.gov.uk/Publications/2011/09/15110325/0
38 See http://appsso.eurostat.ec.europa.eu/nui/show.do?dataset=crim_plce&lang=en and http://ec.europa.eu/eurostat/statistics-explained/index.php/File:Police_officers,_2002%E2%80%9312_YB14.png
39 In the Netherlands there is still the Royal Marechaussee, which is rather a part of the army than of the police.

40 The recent edition of the *European Sourcebook* (fifth edition) did not include the figures for France and Switzerland. We refer to the fourth edition of the *European Sourcebook* for these countries.
41 The Spanish Constitution of 1978 distinguishes three autonomous levels of political power: the central government, the so-called 'autonomous communities', and municipalities with elected mayors.
42 As originally Italy was a patchwork of small kingdoms and dwarf states, between 1825 and 1870 (later empowered by Mussolini), the political choice was made to form a strong central state.

Bibliography

Aden, H. (2002) 'Preventing crime, mobilizing new actors and tendencies towards a repressive roll-back: German security and crime prevention policies in the 1990s', in P. Hebberecht, D. Duprez (eds), *The Security and Prevention Policies in Europe*, Brussels: VUB Brussels University Press, 133–116.

Aden, H., De Pauw, E. (2014) 'Policing Berlin. From separation by the "iron curtain" to the new German capital and a globalised city', in P. Ponsaers, A. Edwards, A. Verhage, A. Recasens i Brunet (eds), *European Journal of Policing Studies*, Special Issue Policing European Metropolises, Antwerpen/Apeldoorn: Maklu, 2(1): 13–29.

Aden, H., Domingo, B., Maguer, A., Stephens, M. (2004) 'Policing and internal security', in H. Compston (ed.), *Handbook of Public Policy in Europe: Britain, France and Germany*, Basingstoke: Palgrave-Macmillan, 39–48.

Aebi, M.F. et al. (2010) *European Sourcebook of Crime and Criminal Justice Statistics* (fourth edition), The Hague: Boom Juridische Uitgevers.

Aebi, M.F. et al. (2014) *European Sourcebook of Crime and Criminal Justice Statistics* (fifth edition), European Institute for Crime Prevention and Control, affiliated with the United Nations (HEUNI), Helsinki: Hakapaino Oy.

Agra, C., Quintas, J., Fonseca, E. (2001) 'De la sécurité démocratique à la démocratie de sécurité: le cas Portugais', *Déviance et Société*, 25(4): 499–513.

Aydin, A.H. (1997) *Police Organisation and Legitimacy: Case Studies of England, Wales and Turkey*, Aldershot: Avebury.

Barbagli, M., Sartori, L. (2004) 'Law enforcement activities in Italy', *Journal of Modern Italian Studies*, 9(2).

Barber, B. (2013) *If Mayors Ruled the World: Dysfunctional Nations, Rising Cities*, New Haven, CT: Yale University Press.

Barrie, D.G. (2008) *Police in the Age of Improvement: Police Development and the Civic Tradition in Scotland, 1775–1865*, Cullompton: Willan Publishing.

Bayley, D.H., Shearing, C.D. (1996) 'The future of policing', *Law and Society Review*, 30(3): 585–606.

Bayley, D.H., Shearing, C.D. (2001) *The New Structure of Policing: Description, Conceptualization, and Research Agenda*, Washington, DC: National Institute of Justice.

Becker, H., Thomas, Ch. (eds) (1973) *Police Systems of Europe: A Survey of Selected Police Organisations*, Springfield, IL: East Lawrence Avenue.

Bellanger, F. (1998) 'Administration et police en Suisse', *Annuaire Européen d'Administration Publique*, 21: 25–240.

Benyon, J. (ed.) (1984) *Scarman and After*, Oxford: Pergamon Press.

Benyon, J., Solomos, J. (eds) (1987) *The Roots of Urban Unrest*, Oxford: Pergamon Press.
Berlière, J.M. (1996) *Le monde des polices en France*, Bruxelles: Editions complexe.
Berlière, J.M., Levy, R. (2011) *Histoire des polices en France*, Paris: Nouveau Monde editions.
Brodeur, J.P. (1995) *Comparisons in Policing: An International Perspective*, Avebury: Ashgate Publishing Limited.
Bruggeman, W. (2014) 'Policing Rome', in E. Devroe, P. Ponsaers, W. Bruggeman, E. De Pauw, M. Easton (eds), *Orde van de Dag*, n°68, *Policing in Europese Metropolen*, Mechelen: Kluwer, 27–36.
Bruggeman, W., Easton, M., Devroe, E., Ponsaers, P. (2010) 'Conclusie: Kijken naar de toekomst van de politie', in W. Bruggeman, E. Devroe, M. Easton (eds), *Evaluatie van 10 jaar politiehervorming*, Panopticon Libri n°4, Antwerpen-Apeldoorn: Maklu, 281–285.
Bruggeman, W., Ponsaers, P. (2011) 'Nederlandse politiehervorming, gezien vanuit een Belgisch perspectief', in *Tijdschrift voor de Politie*, Jg. 73, nr. 10, Amsterdam: Reed Business, 23–26.
Busch, H., Funk, A., Kauß, U., Narr, W.D., Werkentin, F. (1985) *Die Polizei in der Bundesrepublik*, Frankfurt/Main and New York: Campus.
Cachet, L., De Kimpe, S., Ponsaers, P., Ringeling, A. (eds) (2008) *Governance of Security in the Netherlands and Belgium*, Den Haag: Boom Juridische Uitgevers, Reeks Het groene gras, 356.
Canosa, R. (1976) *La polizia in Italia dal 1945 ad oggi*, Bologna: Il Mulino.
Carrillo Cordero, F. (2003) 'El Modelo policial español y la descoordinación policial', in E. Linde Paniagua, J. Pérez Vaquero (eds), *La coordinación de las policies*, Madrid: Editorial Colex.
Cluny, A.F. (1995) 'O relacionamento da Polícia Judiciária com o Ministério Público e o poder judicial em Portugal', *Revista do Ministério Público*, 64: 67–77.
Cohen, P. (1981 [1979]). 'Policing the working class city', in M. Fitzgerald et al. (eds), *Crime and Society*, London: Routledge & Kegan Paul.
Collin, R.O. (1985) 'The blunt instrument: Italy and the police', in J. Roach, J. Thomanick (eds), *Police & Public Order in Europe*, Worcester: Bullings & Sons Ltd.
Collin, R. (1999) 'Italy: a tale of two police forces', *History Today*, 49, 27–33.
Crawford, A., Lister, S., Blackburn, S., Burnett, J. (2005) *Plural Policing: The Mixed Economy of Visible Patrols in England and Wales*, Bristol: The Policy Press.
Critchley, T.A. (1978) *A History of the Police in England and Wales*, London: Constable.
Deluermoz, Q. (2012) *Policiers dans la ville, La Construction d'un ordre public à Paris (1854–1914)*, Paris: Publication de la Sorbonne, 408.
de Maillard, J. (2015) 'Des acteurs en quête de légitimité dans la production de l'ordre public urbain. L'exemple des inspecteurs de sécurité de la Ville de Paris', *Déviance et Société* 2015/3, 39.
Den Boer, M. (1993) *The Italian Police and European Police Cooperation*, Edinburgh: University of Edinburgh.
Devroe, E. (2013) 'Local political leadership and the governance of urban security in Belgium and the Netherlands', *European Journal of Criminology*, 10(3): 314–325.
Devroe, E., Ponsaers, P. (2013) 'Reforming the Belgian police system between central and local', in N.R. Fyfe, J. Terpstra, P. Tops (eds), *Centralizing Forces? Comparative*

Perspectives on Contemporary Police Reform in Northern and Western Europe, The Hague: Boom Legal Publishers/Eleven, 77–98.

Devroe, E., Ponsaers, P., Bruggeman, W., De Pauw, E., Easton, M. (eds) (2014) 'Policing in Europese Metropolen', *Orde van de Dag*, 68, Mechelen: Kluwer, 92.

Dieu, F. (2002) *La Gendarmerie, secrets d'un corps*, Toulouse: Editions complexe.

Domínguez-Berrueta de Juan, M., Fernando Pablo, M., Fernández de Gatta Sánchez, D. (1997) 'Reforma policial y constitución: algunas claves para su interpretación', in *Constitución, policía y fuerzas armadas*, Madrid: Marcial Pons.

Donnelly, D., Scott, K. (2008) 'Policing in Scotland', in T. Newburn (ed.), *Handbook of Policing* (second edition), Cullompton: Willan Publishing, 182–203.

Dunnage, J. (1997) *The Italian Police and the Rise of Fascism*, Westport: Praeger.

Durão, S., Gonçalves, C.G., Índias Cordeiro, G. (2005) 'Vadios, mendigos, mitras: práticas classificatórias de la Polícia en Lisboa', *Revista da Faculdade de Ciências Politicas e Sociologia da Universidade Complutense de Madrid*, 42(3): 121–138.

Edwards, A., Hughes, G. (2012) 'Public safety regimes: Negotiated orders and political analysis in criminology', *Criminology and Criminal Justice*, 12(4): 433–458.

Edwards, A., Hughes, G., Lord, N. (2013) 'Urban security in Europe: Translating a concept in public criminology', *European Journal of Criminology*, 10(3): 260–283.

Edwards, A., Prins, R. (2014) 'Policing and crime in contemporary London. A developmental agenda?', in P. Ponsaers, A. Edwards, A. Verhage, A. Recasens i Brunet (eds), *European Journal of Policing Studies*, Special Issue Policing European Metropolises, Antwerpen/Apeldoorn: Maklu, 2(1): 61–93.

Ellison, G., Smyth, J. (2000) *The Crowned Harp: Policing Northern Ireland*, London: Pluto.

Emsley, C. (2003) 'The birth and development of the police', in T. Newburn (ed.), *Handbook of Policing*, Cullompton: Willan Publishing Ltd, 66–83.

Engel, S., Burruss, G. (2004) 'Human rights in the new training curriculum of the police service of Northern Ireland', *International Journal of Policing Strategies and Management*, 27(4): 498–511.

Fijnaut, C. (2007) *De geschiedenis van de Nederlandse Politie*, Den Haag: Boom Uitgevers.

Fijnaut, C. (2012) *Het nationale politiekorps – achtergronden, controverses en toekomstplannen*, Amsterdam: Uitgeverij Bert Bakker.

Fyfe, N., Terpstra, J., Tops, P. (eds) (2013) *Centralizing Forces? Comparative Perspectives on Contemporary Police Reform in Northern and Western Europe*, The Hague: Eleven Publishers.

Groß, H., Frevel, B., Dams, C. (2008) 'Die Polizei(en) in Deutschland', in H. Groß (ed.), *Handbuch der Polizeien Deutschlands*, Wiesbaden: VS Verlag für Sozialwissenschaften, 11–44.

Haagsma, J., Smits, I., Waarsing, H. (2012) *Blauw, hier en daar*, Apeldoorn: Reed Business.

Henricson, Ib. (2004) *Politiret*, 3 udgave, Jurist- og okonomforbundets Forlag.

Hope, T. (1996) 'Communities, crime and inequality in England and Wales', in T. Bennett (ed.), *Preventing Crime and Disorder: Targeting Strategies and Responsibilities*, Cambridge: Institute of Criminology.

Horton, C. (1995) *Policing Policy in France*, London: Policy Studies Institute Publishing.

Jarman, N. (2004) 'From war to peace? Changing patterns of violence in Northern Ireland, 1990–2003', *Terrorism and Political Violence*, 16(3).

Jochoms, M., Cachet, L., van Sluis, A., Sey, A., Ringeling, A. (2013) *Contested Police Systems, Changes in the Police Systems in Belgium, Denmark, England & Wales, Germany and the Netherlands*, Reeks Het Groene Gras, The Hague: Eleven International Publishers.

Jones, M., Johnstone, P. (2011) *History of Criminal Justice*, Waltham MA: Anderson Publishing.

Jones, T., Newburn, T. (eds) (2006a) *Plural Policing: A Comparative Perspective*, London: Routledge.

Jones, T., Newburn, T. (2006b) 'Understanding plural policing', in T. Jones and T. Newburn (eds), *Plural Policing: A Comparative Perspective*, London: Routledge, 1–11.

Kempa, M. (2007) 'Tracing diffusions of policing governance models from the British Isles and back again: Some reflections for democratic reform in troubled times', *Police Practise and Research*, 8(2).

Lamb, M. (2008) 'A culture of human rights: Transforming policing in Northern Ireland', *Policing*, 2(3).

Le Goff, T. (2009) *Les polices municipales en Ile de France*, Paris: IAU Ile de France.

Loader, I. (2000) 'Plural policing and democratic governance', *Social and Legal Studies*, 9 (3): 323–345.

Loader, I., Walker, N. (2001) 'Policing as a public good. Reconstituting the connections between policing and the state', *Theoretical Criminology*, 5(1): 9–35.

Lopez-Pintor, R., Morlina, L. (2003) *Italy and Spain, Civilian Control of the Military and the Police*, Stanford: Stanford Institute for International Studies.

Lundy, P., McGovern, M. (2001) 'Politics of memory in post-conflict Northern Ireland', *Peace Review*, 13(1).

Malochet, V. (2008) *Les policiers municipaux*, Paris: PUF.

Manning, P.K. (1997) *Police Work, The Social Organization of Policing* (second edition), Long Grove, IL: Waveland Press Inc.

Mawby, R. (2003) 'Models of policing', in T. Newburn (ed.), *The Handbook of Policing*, Cullompton: Willan Publishing, 15–40.

Mawby, R., Wright, A. (2003) 'The police organisation', in T. Newburn (ed.), *The Handbook of Policing*, Cullompton: Willan Publishing, 169–195.

Mohler, M.H.F. (1997) 'Les expériences de la Suisse en matière de coopération policière tant entre les cantons qu'entre les autorités fédérales et cantonales', in R. Bieber, A.-C. Lyon, J. Monar (eds), *Justice et affaires intérieures – l'Union européenne et la Suisse*, Berne: Stämpfli, 126–131.

Monjardet, D. (1996) *Ce que fait la police, sociologie de la force publique*, Paris: La Découverte.

Mouhanna, Ch. (2011) 'Rural policing in France: The end of genuine community policing', in R.I. Mawby, R. Yarwood, *Rural Policing and Policing the Rural. A Constable Countryside?* Farnham: Ashgate, 45–57.

Mouhanna, Ch. (2013) 'Reforms in France: Irreversibly spiralling into (more) centralization', in N. Fyfe, J. Terpstra, P. Tops (eds), *Centralizing Forces? Comparative Perspectives on Contemporary Police Reform in Northern and Western Europe*, The Hague: Eleven Publishers, 23–39.

Mouhanna, Ch., Easton, M. (2014) 'Policing Paris. "Out of" or "still in" Napoleonic time', in P. Ponsaers, A. Edwards, A. Verhage, A. Recasens i Brunet (eds),

European Journal of Policing Studies, Special Issue Policing European Metropolises, Antwerpen/Apeldoorn: Maklu, 2(1): 94–109.

Mulcahy, A. (2006) *Policing Northern Ireland: Conflict, Legitimacy and Reform*, Cullompton: Willan.

Newburn, T. (2003) 'Policing since 1945', in T. Newburn (ed.), *Handbook of Policing*, Cullompton: Willan Publishing Ltd, 84–105.

Nolte, G. (2003) *European Military Law Systems*, Berlin: De Gruyter Rechtswissenschaften Verlag.

O'Rawe, M. (2007) 'Human rights, transitional societies and police training: Legitimating strategies and delegitimating legacies', *St. Johns Journal of Legal Commentary*, 22.

O'Rawe, M., Moore, L. (2000) 'Accountability and police complaints in Northern Ireland: Leaving the past behind?', in A. Goldsmith, C. Lewis (eds), *Civilian Oversight of Policing: Governance, Democracy and Human Rights*, Oxford: Hart Publishing.

Palidda, S. (1992) 'Les forces de sécurité en Italie', in J.M. Erbes et al. (eds), *Polices d'Europe*, Paris: L'Harmattan, 235–266.

Patten Report of the Independent Commission on Policing for Northern Ireland (1999) 124.

Perrodet, A. (2002) 'The Italian system', in *European Criminal Procedures*, Cambridge: Cambridge University Press, 348–351.

Ponsaers, P. (2001) 'Reading about "community (oriented) policing" and police models', *Policing: An International Journal of Police Strategies & Management*, 24(4): 470–496.

Ponsaers, P. (2002) 'On evaluating "community (oriented) policing" through other police models', in T. Van den Broeck, Ch. Eliaerts (eds), *Evaluating Community Policing*, Brussels: Politeia, 51–76.

Ponsaers, P., Bruggeman, W., Bisschop, L., De Kimpe, S. (eds) (2012) 'Bestellen en Schalen', in *Themanummer Bestellen en Schalen, Orde van de Dag*, 57, Mechelen: Kluwer, 6–11.

Ponsaers, P., De Kimpe, S. (2001) *Consensusmania – Over de achtergronden van de politiehervorming*, Leuven/Leusden: ACCO, 283.

Ponsaers, P., Edwards, A., Verhage, A., Recasens i Brunet, A. (eds) (2014) *European Journal of Policing Studies*, Special Issue Policing European Metropolises, Antwerpen/Apeldoorn: Maklu, 2(1).

Ponsaers, P., Tange, C., Van Outrive, L. (eds) (2009) *Regards sur la police – Insights on Police, un quart de siècle de recherche sur la police en Europe et dans le monde anglo-saxon – Quarter of a Century of Research on Police in Europe and the Anglo-Saxon World*, Ecole des Sciences Criminologiques Léon Cornil, Bruylant, Bruxelles/Brussels, 607.

Prins, R.S., Cachet, A., Ponsaers, P., Hughes, G. (2012) 'Fragmentation and interconnection in public safety governance in the Netherlands, Belgium and England', in M. Fenger, V. Bekkers (eds), *Beyond Fragmentation and Interconnectivity*, Amsterdam: IOS Press.

Punch, M., Bisschop, L. (2009) 'United Kingdom: Legacy of the founders of the research on police', in P. Ponsaers, C. Tange, L. van Outrive (eds), *Insights on Police: Quarter of a Century of Research on Police in Europe and the Anglo-Saxon World*, Bruxelles/Brussels: Bruylant.

Rabot, A. (2004) 'The implementation and evaluation of community policing in Spain: Results and future prospects', *European Journal of Crime, Criminal Law and Criminal Justice*, Martinus Nijhof Publishers, 12(3): 213–231.
Recasens, A. (1999) 'Police', *European Journal of Crime, Criminal Law and Criminal Justice*, Martinus Nijhof Publishers, 7(3): 397–411.
Recasens, A., Ponsaers, P. (2014) 'Policing Barcelona', in P. Ponsaers, A. Edwards, A. Verhage, A. Recasens i Brunet (eds), *European Journal of Policing Studies*, Special Issue Policing European Metropolises, Antwerpen/Apeldoorn: Maklu, 2(1): 110–128.
Renaudie, O. (2008) *La Préfecture de Police*, Paris: LGDJ.
Roach, J., Thomaneck, J. (1985) *Police and Public Order in Europe*, Kent: Croom Helm Ltd.
Rodgers, C., Gravelle, J. (2012) 'UK policing and change: Reflections of policing worldwide', *Review of European Studies*, 4(1).
Rodrigues, J.N.C. (1998) 'Para um novo conceito de Polícia', *Revista Portuguesa de Ciência Criminal*, 8(3): 389–408.
Rohrbach, E. (2003) 'Das Projekt "Polizei Thun". Über die Zusammenlegung der Stadt- und Kantonspolizei Thun', *Kriminalistik*, 5: 385–388.
Roodenburg, H. (2004) 'Social control in Europe, history of crime and criminal justice series', in *Social Control in Fascist Italy, the Role of the Police*, Norman: Ohio State University.
Sanders, A., Young, R. (2002) 'From suspect to trial', in M. Maguire, R. Morgan, R. Reiner (eds), *The Oxford Handbook of Criminology*, Oxford: Oxford University Press.
Scott, A.J. (ed.) (2001) *Global City-Regions: Trends, Theory, Policy*, Oxford: Oxford University Press.
Scott, K. (2008) 'The Scottish crime and drug enforcement agency: From common police service to "MacFBI"', *The Police Journal*, 46–56.
Sigrist, A. (2009) 'Suisse: une recherché disparate pour un monde policier éclaté', P. Ponsaers, C. Tange, L. Van Outrive (eds), *Regards sur la police – Insights on Police, Un quart de siècle de recherche sur la police en Europe et dans le monde anglo-saxon – Quarter of a Century of Research on Police in Europe and the Anglo-Saxon World*, Ecole des Sciences Criminologiques Léon Cornil, Bruxelles/Brussels: Bruylant.
Sousa, A.F. (2003) 'Polícia administrativa: autoridades, órgãos e competências', *Revista de Estudos Jurídico-Políticos*, 9: 63–111.
Stamer, Q. (2007) 'Monitoring the police service in Northern Ireland in complying with the Human Rights Act 1998', *Policing*, 1(1).
Stead, P.J. (1983) *The Police of France*, London: Macmillan.
Terpstra, J., Stokkom, B. van, Spreeuwers, R. (2013) *Who Patrols the Streets? An International Comparative Study of Plural Policing*, Den Haag: Eleven International Publishing.
Tschudi, H.M. (2003) 'Lokale und regionale Verantwortung: Der Schweizer Föderalismus als Vor- oder Nachteil für die Sicherheit in den Städten', in Konferenz Der Städtischen Polizeidirektorinnen Une Polizeidirektoren Kspd Und Dem Polizeidepartement Der Stadt Zürich (Ed.), *Urbane Sicherheit im 21. Jahrhundert. Referate und Podiumdiskussion der Tagung vom 12. September 2003*, Zürich, Basel: Genf, Schulthess, 25–40.

Umberto, S. (2010) 'The Guardia di Finanza and the prevention of and fight against organized crime', *Rivista di Criminologia, Vittimologia e Sicurezza*, 4(1), Società Italiana di Vittimologia.

Valriberas Sanz, A. (1999) *Cuerpo nacional de policía y sistema policial español*, Madrid: Ediciones jurídicas y sociales, 229–287.

Van Outrive, L., Cartuyvels, Y., Ponsaers, P. (1991) *Les polices en Belgique, Histoire socio-politique du système policier de 1794 à nos jours*, Bruxelles: Vie Ouvrière, 336.

Van Outrive, L., Cartuyvels, Y., Ponsaers, P. (1992) *Sire, ik ben ongerust. Geschiedenis van de Belgische politie, 1794–1991*, Leuven: Kritak.

Vlek, F., Van Reenen, P. (eds) (2012) *Voer voor Kwartiermakers, Wetenschappelijke kennis voor de inrichting van de Nationale Politie*, Politie & Wetenschap Overzichtsstudies, Amsterdam: Reed Business.

Vogel, M. (1993) *Les polices des villes entre local et national: l'administration des polices urbaines sous la IIIe République, thèse de sciences politiques*. Grenoble: IEP.

Wall, D.S. (1998) *The Chief Constables of England and Wales: The Socio-Legal History of a Criminal Justice Elite*, Dartmouth: Ashgate.

Part II

Convergence

The dominance of national states in agenda setting

Chapter 3

France

Governing metropolises: The false pretences of metropolisation

Jacques de Maillard and Christian Mouhanna

In France, the centralisation of public security started being challenged by policy-makers toward the late 1970s, but changes really commenced in the 1980s, following in particular the 1983 Bonnemaison report (Bonnemaison, 1983). The main dynamics of the process can be described as follows: the rallying of local and regional governments around security issues; the design and release of contractual tools enabling the State and local governments to handle security and prevention matters collaboratively; the rise of private security forces; the interlacing of prevention and repression issues (Le Goff, 2008).

More generally, a 'movement of de-monopolisation of the legitimate use of force' (Roché, 2004: 65; de Maillard, 2005) can be said to be occurring, both in terms of security-producing policy-making – split between the municipal, national and European levels – and in terms of operational implementation, carried out by a variety of local organisations, public transport operators, corporations, etc.

This new configuration has three major characteristics: a) The number of players increases, such that security ceases to be a State monopoly. Many actors are then mobilised, from local governments to security companies through semi-public organisations, associations or even individuals. b) Negotiation becomes paramount, as evidenced by a proliferation of such legal instruments as framework agreements, partnership protocols, agreements on objectives, etc. c) In the aftermath of the Bonnemaison report, cross-sectoral approaches have flourished, as more and more socio-urban issues are being tackled from multiple angles. Proactive prevention and repressive action are no longer perceived as mutually exclusive but rather as complementary, or even confused (Ferret & Mouhanna, 2005).

The present chapter intends to explore these dynamics by questioning the underlying logic of how municipalities mobilise their resources and the nature of their exchanges with local representatives of central government agencies. The *metropolisation* of policies is then questioned. By metropolisation, we mean not only the consequences of the creation of these new inter-municipal local government entities known as 'metropolises', but also a process whereby public authorities – including the Police and Gendarmerie, as well as local and regional governments – tackle the challenge of producing forms of action that take into account economic, demographic and (as far as we are concerned here) criminal flows whose logics cannot be contained within classical municipal boundaries.

Given the heterogeneity of local situations – both in terms of security patterns and responses, and in terms of how municipal police forces are organised[1] – it was felt that a clear description of the French situation would best be achieved by working on four metropolises, differing in size and historical background: Paris, Lyon, Toulouse and Strasbourg. We show how the very construction of these metropolises illustrates both the limits of local governance in the field of security and the manoeuvring of central authorities to maintain their dominant position in this area.

I The emergence of local regimes of security

Ever since 1941, mayors had been relegated outside the field of security. In 1982, the Bonnemaison policy gave them an opportunity to reinvest it, mainly – at first – as managers of social crime prevention schemes known as 'municipal delinquency prevention councils'.[2] However, they gradually started hiring officers tasked with public space surveillance and social regulation missions – such as municipal police, whose numbers have increased threefold in three decades, but also local mediators, whose job consisted in reinvesting public spaces, thereby preventing them from being confiscated, and most importantly in defusing potential conflicts regarding their use. Simultaneously, closed-circuit television (CCTV) became increasingly popular in French cities, regardless of their size, to protect public spaces. More generally, urban spaces were equipped and redesigned using technologies and measures pertaining to situational prevention. This does not mean that the social treatment of crime through educational measures and youth activities was entirely dismissed by municipalities. However, it has been progressively marginalised for the last 20 years,[3] being considered relatively inefficient and not visible enough to meet the expectations of populations who are confronted on a daily basis by disorder and vandalism (broken windows, soiled mailboxes, idle youths occupying stairwells and entrance lobbies …). Similarly, social workers were relegated to the background by new professionals such as 'risk management engineers' and 'municipal security experts', who act as the link between territories (the security demands of the population), techniques (partners) and politicians. This municipal expertise, backed by technical and human resources, ultimately enabled mayors to weigh in on the production of security and question the actions of central government agencies.

However, this broad depiction of the approach of public security and prevention by municipalities needs to be refined on the basis of local case studies. While such developments as the creation – or reinforcement – of municipal police forces, the management of contract-based arrangements or the use of CCTV tend to be shared, individual municipal policies are rather idiosyncratic.[4] In this respect, we find local public safety regimes (Edwards & Hughes, 2012) to be an interesting concept. In the remainder of the chapter, limits to the decentralisation of metropolitan policing are explored through reference to four case studies: Paris, Lyon, Strasbourg and Toulouse. These four cases are particularly relevant for our analysis for political and institutional reasons: Paris has been governed by a left-wing coalition since 2001 and has the institutional and political specificities of a capital; Lyon has been headed by a socialist mayor since 2001 with a constant involvement on public security issues; Toulouse and Strasbourg have been marked by political changes over the last 15 years and raise the question of policy continuity despite political changes.

1.1 Paris and the unabating grip of the state

Paris is no doubt the place where the State's grip is the strongest and most enduring. While over the years various mayoral candidates have wielded the threat of creating a municipal police force, the city of Paris still does not boast one to this day (Mouhanna & Easton, 2014). Still, it is not entirely devoid of resources as far as prevention and public safety are concerned, with about 650 security inspectors (inspecteurs de sécurité) – not exactly a plethora, though, for a major city with a population of more than 2 million – whose policing competences are limited in scope by the health and sanitary regulations of the city of Paris. Their job is to enforce these regulations, especially local business policing measures, and to protect municipal property, including the parks and gardens (de Maillard et al., 2015). Faced with specific insecurity issues and tensions in some areas, the city council also created night correspondents (correspondants de nuit) in the early 2000s. About 150 such officers are tasked with keeping a night watch and offering mediation services. Finally, the city of Paris, in close partnership with the Prefecture of police, has developed an extensive CCTV network of more than 1,000 cameras covering public spaces. In January 2015, the city council signed a contract with the Prefecture of police, the Parquet de Paris (i.e. the public prosecutor), and the Rectorat (Ministry of Education). The 'Contrat parisien de prévention et sécurité' (Parisian contract of prevention and security) follows up on a previous contract dating back to 2009 and sets three priorities for 2015–20: a) preventing juvenile delinquency through civility education and by combating truancy, recidivism, radicalisation, addiction …; b) protecting vulnerable persons, preventing woman and family abuse, offering victim support; and c) improving public peace, i.e. combating street prostitution and drugs, securitising communal spaces.

Of all these issues, a couple have grown to become major concerns: the occupation of shared spaces, by street peddlers or idle youths in stairwells and entrance lobbies for instance; and the protection of tourists in the heart of Paris (de Maillard & Zagrodzki, 2015). Although the city has gradually developed prevention and security resources, its position remains one of relative weakness. Contrary to what happened in London, the management of the Paris police force never shifted towards the municipality and remains in the hands of a state-appointed prefect of police.[5] At the political level, demands for the creation of a municipal police force in Paris were never satisfied, and the Socialist municipality in power since 2001 has remained extremely prudent on this topic, considering that claiming this competence would be too politically risky by making them appear too repressive and too selfish. In Paris, the mainstream political reading is that public policing is the responsibility of national forces, referring to a view of equality at a national scale between citizens. Many demonstrations that take place in Paris are directed against the central government and not the city authorities. Interestingly, this position did not vary over the 2001–14 period (the two terms of B. Delanoé, the Socialist mayor), even though the Socialist mayor and his team vocally and consistently opposed (right-wing) national security policies (Mouhanna, 2010). Terrorist threats have only contributed to reinforcing this centralising trend in Paris, since all special weapons and tactics (SWAT) teams and terrorism-intelligence units belong to the National Police or Gendarmerie forces.

1.2 Lyon: asserting strategic municipal power

Lyon offers an utterly different picture. The city started developing a CCTV network as early as the 1990s, rather early compared to other large French cities. The efforts of the then centre-right mayor were pursued by his Socialist successor, elected in 2001: in 2014, Lyon was covered by 414 cameras. The 2001 municipal elections proved highly charged, with security being the major campaign theme and very few differences in the candidates' respective positions after a series of spectacular burglaries had put the protection of central district businesses in the spotlight.

The city of Lyon boasts a significant municipal police force comprising 325 officers (6.8 per 10,000 inhabitants) equipped with rubber-ball riot guns, and a professionalised technical staff including specialised security officials and a situational prevention engineer, all under the umbrella of a general security division (Délégation générale à la sécurité), headed by a commissaire (police superintendent) on secondment from the National Police. Situational prevention has been taken very seriously, leading to the creation of a Situational Prevention Commission[6] whose purpose is to identify ways to avoid anything that might facilitate insecurity in urban spaces (dimly lit areas, corridors, isolated corners, etc.), as evidenced by CCTV deployment. No sooner was the mayor elected in 2001 than he made a point to state his determination to fight crime: 'I will bring tangible, direct, and concerted responses to these criminal acts that threaten to tear apart the social fabric in our districts' (quoted in Freyermuth, 2013: 107). He subsequently recruited in his cabinet the former chief of staff of the local National Police directorate,[7] and took a series of legislative measures against prostitution under the combined pressure of the residents and the prefect, which triggered some turmoil in the mayor's own camp.[8] The mayor of Lyon's rhetoric has traditionally focused on the necessity of maintaining a balance between prevention and security, assigning a high value to public peace for the residents while insisting that victims need protection, as shown by this programme for the 2014 municipal elections: 'reconciling resolution and justice so that everyone in the city, regardless of their district, can safely live and travel, work or have a good time' (AEF Sécurité, 2014). Lyon could be said to represent a developmental regime in which a conventional focus on assertive criminal justice and law enforcement has been augmented by situational methods of risk management and, as such, an exemplar of how the social crime prevention envisaged by Bonnemaison has now been eclipsed.

1.3 Strasbourg: a partnership-based municipal policy

The city of Strasbourg's policy has been relatively prudent, rather less enforcement-oriented than Lyon, in these matters. In the late 1990s, in a context of recurring urban unrest (especially on New Year's Eve), the Socialist mayor created a public peace department (service de tranquillité publique) by putting together various disparate units, including the municipal police force. The focus on security was reinforced after the victory of the conservatives at the 2001 mayoral election. A former commissaire was recruited to head the public peace department, along with other former officers from the Ministry of the Interior, as chief of the municipal police and coordinator of the local security contract (contrat local de sécurité), respectively. His enduring presence lent significant stability to municipal security policies in Strasbourg, in spite of a political changeover in 2008. This is particularly noticeable as far as CCTV is concerned, since the left-wing municipality never challenged the investments made in this area: about 330 cameras cover the territory of the Eurométropole – as the local intercommunal entity is known – most of them in the historic centre. In 2012, the municipal police force comprised 157 officers (3.6 per 10,000 residents). Campaigning for re-election in 2014, the incumbent (and finally re-elected) mayor insisted on 'the determined action aiming to prevent petty crime, remind citizens of the rules that make it possible to live together, and support victims' (AEF Sécurité, 2014). Partnerships between the State and local governments are a defining feature of the Strasbourg area: a local security contract was signed in 2003, renewed and extended in 2009 (becoming an 'intercommunal prevention and security contract') and is being reviewed on a regular basis ever since 2011. This contract defines three priorities: a) a series of actions targeting young people who are exposed to crime (civic education, respect in shared spaces, mediation at school, prevention of recidivism); b) preventing family and woman abuse, supporting victims; and c) improving public peace (relying on CCTV, mediation and specialised prevention teams). Strasbourg could be considered an example of a 'progressive' regime whose agenda combines social reform (civic education, support for vulnerable populations) with risk management (pervasive CCTV surveillance). Moreover, as will be shown below, Strasbourg is characterised by a strong supra-communal dimension.

1.4 Toulouse: towards more stringent repressive policies?

Security policies in Toulouse have a history of varying with political changeovers. The 1990s and 2000s were marked by a relative stability, with a limited municipal police force (175 officers, i.e. four per 10,000 residents), mainly tasked with preventive missions, and a restrained use of CCTV: 16 cameras. A public peace office (office de la tranquillité) had been created and acted mainly as a mediator in cases of neighbourhood disturbances. The shift to a right-wing majority in 2014, however, seems to have triggered some changes, even though it is still too early to assess them accurately. During his campaign, the future mayor had insisted that his intention was to 'develop a resolutely pragmatic policy. Pragmatic indeed, since we certainly do not plan to fight the dogmatic methods of the current municipality – which considers the security of Toulouse residents to be the sole responsibility of the State – with a dogmatic approach of our own' (AEF Sécurité, 2014). The mayor then recruited a former police officer in his cabinet, appointed a clearly repressive deputy mayor in charge of security, significantly increased staffing levels in the municipal police force (with a target of 300 officers by 2017), and funded more CCTV surveillance (with a target of 300 cameras by 2017). While preexisting schemes were continued, they became more repressive: the public peace office remains but was rebranded as 'Allo Toulouse' – suggesting a reactive operational hotline – and no longer includes a mediation team; municipal decrees against public consumption of alcohol have been reinforced. Decrees have been promulgated to fight prostitution in specific districts; a special unit comprising municipal police, mediators and social workers has been put together to address the presence of fringe elements in the public space; and a council for the rights and duties of families has been created to tackle deviant acts by minors. Even though the current dynamics cannot yet be fully assessed, the Toulouse context and outlook thus clearly appear repressive, based on the cooperation of national and municipal police forces, the allocation of new resources to the municipal police and the reinforcement of CCTV surveillance.

1.5 Balancing between local assertiveness and state control

As mentioned above, action regimes vary: some cities favour an aggressive approach from municipal police forces (Lyon, or even Toulouse since 2014), while others, such as Strasbourg, proceed more cautiously. Then there is Paris, which does not even have a municipal police force. Other differentiating parameters include reliance on regulatory devices such as anti-prostitution decrees, the mayor's political discourse, and the more or less extensive use of CCTV. To quote the two most contrasting cases, the historical influence of the Prefecture of police and the absence of any municipal police force generate sharply asymmetrical exchanges in favour of the National Police in Paris, while in Lyon, the reinforced resources of the municipal police and the expertise built over time by the municipality have paved the way for more balanced relations.

Common features do appear, however. All of these cities have developed cooperative security governance approaches. The increasing reliance on contract-based relations and similar forms of partnership, such as task forces, means that more and more local spaces for negotiation end up being institutionalised. This is epitomised by such agreements as the 'coordination agreements' (conventions de coordination) signed between the national and municipal police forces, which define their respective hours and areas of responsibility, thus helping to determine whether a given action should be conducted jointly or separately.

Mayors – especially mayors of major cities, who enjoy better connections to the Ministry of the Interior – may weigh in on the national agenda setting and/or obtain increased staffing resources. One key aspect of this is the fact that one representative may be elected to several positions (cumul des mandats). As a result, in many large and major cities, the mayor is also a member of Parliament or a senator, a configuration that can be leveraged advantageously (primarily in a fight for resources) at the national level.

This cooperative approach of governance, however, needs to be twice nuanced. First, a look at the respective levels of staffing makes it clear that central public security forces vastly outnumber their counterparts (see Table 3.1).

Numbers speak for themselves: municipal police account for a mere 7.1% of all police staff in the whole country. Even looking at actual public security forces only, more than 78,000 National Police officers belong to the central

Table 3.1 Compared staffing levels of security forces

National Police	National Gendarmerie	Municipal Police
144,858*	100,049**	19,325***

Source: Ministry of the Interior.

* Real staffing as of 31 December 2011. ** Real staffing as of 31 December 2012. *** Staffing as of 31 December 2011.

security division and thus directly contribute to enforcement, and the numbers are similar in the Gendarmerie: the central State still boasts a large predominance here. To be sure, local and regional governments do fund some resources – facilities and equipment – that alleviate the budgets of the National Police and Gendarmerie, and negotiations are regularly conducted between the prefect, the commissaire and the mayor, all of which contributes to attenuating these discrepancies. Still, municipalities and the National Police are bonded by interdependencies that remain asymmetric, and local governments have limited influence on State police at the local level. Elected officials may complain about the lack of personnel and/or raise police awareness on some specific crimes or trends, but they have no say in the objectives or means of action of the National Police. This sets the State apart among players in the field, since it is both in a position to design the regulatory framework of the negotiation and at the head of (by far) the largest public security force.

Which introduces our second caveat: exchanges between the national and municipal police forces are rather asymmetrical too. Coordination agreements between them usually entrust repressive missions to the former, and consider that primary interventions should usually be conducted by the municipal police, with the central force providing support and following up on the judicial level. Municipal police have extremely limited legal powers compared to their National Police colleagues: being only adjunct judicial police officers (agents de police judiciaire adjoints), as opposed to judicial police officers, they are not allowed to make arrests and conduct investigations. Even though CCTV networks are operated by municipalities, footage is directly transmitted to the National Police and no report of any kind is due in return. In Toulouse, the new mayoral team's decision to resume night interventions was welcomed by the National Police, who see this as a way of complementing their own interventions at a time of increasingly scarce resources ... and as an opportunity to remotely control interventions by municipal police. One interesting hypothesis here is that the role of the State is becoming partially differentiated. On the one hand, as far as the management of public security staffing goes, its position is one of almost absolute monopoly, which enables it to maintain extended resources and keep by far the upper hand in the management of public security. On the other hand, regarding broader forms of control and prevention, the State is but another player in localised negotiation processes. Ever since the early 2000s, the State's strategies have been characterised by constant to-ing and fro-ing between contradictory national and local policies. At the national level, policing policies have consistently been result oriented and strongly influenced by performance indicators, which has induced a recentralisation process with little encouragement for local partnerships, while locally the State has fostered the development of concerted local prevention and security strategies.

2 Metropolisation as a discontinuous process hurting co-production

Another key aspect of the ambiguous relationships between national and municipal authorities in the 'co-production' of security policies is 'metropolisation'. This is a broader process of reform in French public administration in a search for more effective and efficient metropolises to adapt to globalisation. In the historical context of the French nation-state, however, metropolisation encounters two fundamental features that explain how difficult it is to develop coherent and stable local security regimes.

2.1 The adverse effect of dispersed competences on security policies

The first feature is communal fragmentation. As of 1 January 2016, the French territory was subdivided into more than 35,800 communes, each with its own municipal council and mayor, who in turn is endowed with specific prerogatives in matters of security. While these communes vary hugely in terms of their area and population, 31,500 of them have fewer than 2,000 residents (INSEE, 2010). These modest demographics are compounded by commensurately modest financial resources that make it impossible for them to recruit salaried officers. Even the larger metropolises considered in this chapter are somewhat fragmented. The Toulouse metropolis, for example, is composed of 37 communes,[9] Lyon 59,[10] and Strasbourg 28.[11]

Pursuing a trend that started as early as the 1990s, and given a general reluctance by communes to merge, successive central governments have sought to encourage synergies around such public policies as transportation, waste and water management, economic action and urban planning. To make them able to compete with other European cities, the largest conurbations have been given the status of metropolis (Maptam Act, 24 January 2014, and Notre Act, 7 August 2015). These entities are managed by an assembly of delegates from the communes, which designates a president, but no specific election is organised to confer this assembly a democratic legitimacy of its own.

The above-mentioned metropolises were created on 1 January 2015 by aggregating communes in conurbations with more than 400,000 residents.[12] For these communes, the move involved delegating the following competences: economic, social and cultural development; public transportation; housing; sewage treatment and water management; fire fighting; environment and waste management. Theoretically, the design and implementation of crime prevention schemes is also supposed to be managed at the metropolitan level. However, this does only have a limited impact on policing per se, at least as far as protection and repression are concerned. Mayors tend to cling to their prerogatives in the field of security, reluctant as they are to share them. For one thing, elected officials are the ones who will be held accountable by the electorate if and when a feeling of insecurity arises. Furthermore, the authority conferred by protecting their fellow citizens is considered by mayors as a key element of their legitimacy and continuing appeal to the electorate.

The second defining feature of the French political and administrative system is its stacked – and non hierarchical – nature. While the commune is the smallest form of government, it is by no means the only one and sits at the bottom of an imposing pile. Not only are communes integrated into intercommunal management bodies such as metropolises, but they also form part of a 'département' (hereafter referred to as 'department'; adj. 'departmental'), which in turn belongs to a 'region', both of which have their own elected officials, whose agenda, however, often has little in common with the day-to-day preoccupations of mayors. This vertical fragmentation does affect how security and prevention matters are dealt with. Social work and welfare, specialised prevention, or the management of juvenile delinquency and child abuse, for instance, are typically managed at the department level. Yet municipal police forces and local security regulations fall within the realm of mayoral power, hence the difficulty of 'marrying' municipal security policies and social or prevention actions initiated by the department. In fact, this involves investing rather heavily in a partnership, a somewhat complicated affair when stakeholders tend not to agree, because of political or ideological opposition, or bureaucratic competition. As a result, some communes have developed their own mediation system to overcome what they consider to be a deficient approach from their departmental counterparts.

This double movement of fragmentation – horizontal as well as vertical – has several consequences. To begin with, consistent management becomes challenging: splitting competencies between the various authorities hardly contributes to the proper design of inclusive security policies embracing all fields of public action – housing, prevention, repression, social action, employment, etc. Next, elected officials of the various echelons waste significant time arguing with their counterparts. Mayors can be tempted to 'outsource' their problems, expelling difficult families or exporting potentially disorderly activities to neighbouring communes. Third, in times of budget restrictions, local governments take exception to funding certain types of actions, preferring to let other stakeholders deal with the problem. The lack of financial commitment to crime prevention from many departments is glaringly obvious.[13] Finally, geographical compartmentalisation hurts the development of capital-intensive services that can only be achieved by pooling resources. Intercommunal police forces are extremely rare.[14] At the scale of a metropolis, each police force in each commune – assuming there is one – has its own organisation, its own city-backed budget, its own equipment – weapons, vehicles, radios, all subject to variations – and its own employment doctrine, with no reference whatsoever to its neighbours.[15] In one and the same conurbation, one commune may very well choose to have an armed, repressive municipal police force when one of its immediate neighbours focuses exclusively on public peace and mediation, and yet another on traffic and parking issues – depending on the vision of the respective mayors. That is not to say that no attempts at pooling resources have been made. For one thing, as far as prevention is concerned, metropolises currently tend to assume a number of responsibilities hitherto devoted to departments. In addition, discussion arenas have been created to foster a dialogue among elected officials and encourage them to think outside the municipal box and at the intercommunal scale. For instance, local security and crime prevention councils (Conseils locaux de sécurité et de prévention de la délinquance – CLSPDs) acting at the communal level were created as early as the 1980s. They are composed of elected officials, salaried members of the municipal services, municipal as well as National Police and/or Gendarmerie officers, representatives of the public prosecutor (Procureur de la République), and representatives of various organisations acting in the field of security and prevention. These councils have now been duplicated at the scale of the metropolis and dubbed intercommunal security and crime prevention councils (Conseils intercommunaux de sécurité et de prévention de la délinquance – CISPDs). Cooperation in the field of prevention and security comes in rather different flavours from one metropolis to another. While the Strasbourg CISPD seems to be based on genuine cooperation, things are different in Toulouse where local CLSPDs are still calling the shots and the CISPD remains an empty shell. In Lyon and Toulouse, despite the initiatives of the mayor of the central city in both cases – see above – cooperation with the other communes in the metropolis is very limited.

The contrast between a city like Strasbourg and the others is also apparent in the field of CCTV surveillance. In France, installing and managing CCTV networks is a communal prerogative. In the Strasbourg metropolis, video surveillance is managed by an intercommunal entity, whereas in Lyon or Toulouse it remains municipal, which creates a geographically discontinuous coverage of public areas. This is another case of municipal priorities taking precedence over the broader picture of the conurbation, even though elected officials unanimously insist that crime has become increasingly mobile and communal boundaries have been blurred by urban development, to the point of becoming obsolete. To a certain extent, communes remain trapped in an obsidional or siege-like mentality: the discourse of some mayors clearly suggests that crime comes from the other communes, and that protection is needed against the outside world.

The current limits of communal investment in intercommunal security can be apprehended through a series of striking examples that show how permanent reluctance can be. Lyon offers a good illustration, insofar as this commune enjoys a very specific legal status whereby traffic policing regulations are now in the hands of the president of the metropolis – of which most local elected representatives had argued in favour when the text was drafted. In practice, though, the opposite is true: the management of traffic policing has remained a prerogative of mayors.[16] In order to reconcile actual practice with the letter of the law, it has been jointly agreed that the communes will draft and vote for traffic regulations, which will then be merely rubber-stamped by the metropolis. This backwards step was then rationalised along the lines of traffic problems being too local by nature to be treated at the metropolis level. This case provides a good insight into the difficulties that may arise when trying to define a security policy at a level – that of the metropolis – which may seem somewhat removed from highly localised issues.

Paris offers an even more complex case. The Greater Paris metropolis was born on 1 January 2016 and covers 130 communes, four departments and 6.98 million residents. The aforementioned fragmentation process is again quite perceptible. While the city of Paris still does not have its own municipal police force and only enjoys extremely limited policing prerogatives given the ubiquitous presence of the Prefecture of police, neighbouring communes have long developed significant municipal forces, not to mention major CCTV networks. The wealthiest among them have managed to mobilise the necessary financial resources, leaving the poorest suburbs to 'do what they can' with little or no municipal police.

Like the other metropolises, the Greater Paris city-region has created an entity to coordinate prevention operations at its level, since this competence is a prerogative of municipalities. A metropolitan council of security and crime prevention has been established by law; it must be consulted for advice and before the prefect of police and prefect of the Ile de France region, approve the crime prevention plan of the metropolis. Short-term benefits are not guaranteed, however, given the ridiculously low level of funding of the metropolis of Paris as compared to the budgets of individual communes.

Moreover, the council's security coordination plans are less ambitious than was initially projected. Each commune maintains its monopoly in the field, with municipal police forces whose composition and operational activities depend, as anywhere else, on the mayor and local finances. Similarly, CCTV networks are not interconnected and no plan seems to be emerging on this aspect. At a time when the continuity of the urban fabric and daily travels of the residents – crisscrossing the entire conurbation for both work and entertainment purposes – traverse municipal boundaries and in a context where criminals are also thought to have become increasingly mobile, municipalities keep reasoning at the traditional scale in the field of security (Le Goff & Malochet, 2015).

In the Paris area, just as in the other metropolises, a clear discrepancy exists between policies implemented in mutualised sectors – such as transportation and urban planning – and security policies that apparently fail to inspire a similar degree of collaboration. Common policies can only be achieved if policy-makers think outside the local box and in terms of the 'metropolis'. However, mayors and their teams can only be elected by defending a municipal agenda, especially as far as security is concerned. In addition, territorial division is often based on socio-economic breakdowns that tend to set apart, on the one hand, wealthy communes supporting business parks, well-off residents and the will to 'defend oneself' against criminals from the outside, and on the other, more modest communes with a high proportion of social housing and limited tax resources. Administrative boundaries are thus compounded by invisible but real boundaries that segregate populations who, while they do share the same spaces on a daily basis at work, do not in fact live together. Obviously, these geographic and social rifts also appear within the communes themselves, with sometimes sharply contrasting neighbourhoods in one and the same city. However, demographic changes within the metropolis, combined with a rise in real estate prices in upmarket neighbourhoods and the gregarious tendencies of the richest categories of the population, have contributed to the increasing homogeneity of many of these communes, which in turn makes it difficult for mayors to garner support for 'pooling' policies. This segmentation process is illustrated most vividly by the resistance by several affluent communes to compulsory social housing projects, which they consistently refuse to implement in spite of the penalties incurred. As a consequence, communal fragmentation remains the norm.

If a supra-communal vision of security issues can be said to be in the making at all, it certainly proceeds more from national agencies – i.e. the National Police – than from local elected officials and their municipal police units. Territorial breakdown and the specific nature of security as a central theme in municipal politics stand in the way of any truly ambitious metropolitan policy in the field – contrary to what pundits predicted a decade ago when they envisioned the rise of powerful local police forces.

2.2 Persistently ubiquitous national forces

While local governments, due to their fragmented and 'localised' nature, are having a hard time outgrowing their boundaries to implement meaningful security policies at the supra-communal scale of the metropolis, the opposite is true for national policing agencies, which are engaged in a reorganisation process aiming to leave behind their traditional divisions and broaden their scope. Ever since the early 2000s, the Ministry of the Interior has been engaged in cost-cutting, merging and concentration processes. The initial step was to take advantage of new information and communication technologies to merge departmental command centres, first in the Gendarmerie, then in the National Police.[17] Next, these technical advances were leveraged to implement general HR management tools that reach far beyond the metropolis itself. While each commissariat (police station) or Gendarmerie brigade used to enjoy a modicum of autonomy – with National Police officers permanently appointed to a given district – staff management is now performed at a higher echelon. Although this does not mean that local PN (Police Nationale) or GN (Gendarmerie Nationale) chiefs have lost all visibility and authority over their troops, it certainly makes it a lot more challenging for them to carry out any local policy. Police calls are received and patrols dispatched above them. Police officers appointed to the police station of a given city are often used to respond to calls from other communes, which makes it trickier to negotiate arrangements directly with local elected officials and to meet their demands. 'Quieter' communes will eventually complain of having their own supply of National Police 'consumed' by unruly neighbours, and become increasingly adamant that a 'proprietary' municipal police force is needed.

Both organisations have thus redesigned their operations based on a supra-communal vision of demands and forces. In practice, the departmental director of public security for the National Police, and the group commander (commandant de groupement) for the Gendarmerie each manage a departmental command centre which takes incoming calls, dispatches police patrols and intervention units, and analyses crime patterns, delivering statistics that serve as a basis for discussion with communes.

This supra-communal – and even supra-metropolitan – movement of concentration has intensified ever since the end of community policing in France, which had seen many smaller police stations opened in urban areas and stable groups of policemen appointed to the corresponding districts on a full-time basis. This policy was terminated in 2003, forcing ground police officers to relinquish any territorially specific strategy.

For the moment, however, this concentration process is hindered by the fact that two (often competing) forces with fairly distinct cultures – civilian vs. military – still coexist. While the Gendarmerie has theoretically left the Ministry of Defence to join the ranks of the Ministry of the Interior since 2009, a proper merger of the GN into civilian policing has not yet been initiated, as is the case in other European countries. At the metropolitan scale, this duality is also a factor. While the Greater Paris metropolis is entirely contained within the police area, which covers the entire conurbation under a single umbrella, the other metropolises in our sample are split, some communes being under police jurisdiction and others governed by the Gendarmerie. For more than a decade these jurisdictions have been gradually redesigned to adjust the PN/GN breakdown to changing demographics and the geographical expansion of urban areas. Still, in spite of these adjustments – which, it must be said, have been pretty limited, for the sake of preserving everyone's habits, including the officers, elected officials, and residents – the breakdown remains, even though it hardly fits today's urban realities. Only four out of 37 communes in the Toulouse metropolis, for instance, fall under police jurisdiction, i.e. 528,700 residents out of 725,000. In Lyon, the proportion is 18 out of 59, i.e. 1.08 million residents out of 1.28.

While the largest communes have been able to develop competences in terms of crime analysis and prevention, where the management of CCTV networks is one of their prerogatives, the balance of power remains similar, even when they boast significant municipal police forces. Mayors have little or no say in how PN and GN staff are deployed in their jurisdiction; they have to 'make do' with the agenda of the national forces which, more often than not, are the only ones with a global perspective on security in the metropolis, when each municipality is focusing on its own territory. At the metropolitan scale, often for want of a proper perspective on the broader picture, the metropolis is unable to set the agenda – contrary to the PN. At the communal level, municipal police forces, in spite of their best efforts, will always be dependent, constrained as they are by their limited judiciary – and non-existent investigative – prerogatives.

It does not follow that local elected representatives are totally absent from the security game. Metropolises are led by powerful officials with strong national political connections – key figures and inescapable partners. While they may not yet have properly addressed the field of security, inter-communal policies are gradually appearing in other related fields: education, urban planning, transportation, social action and inclusion, even health care. Ultimately, each of these sectoral policies has to do not only with prevention, but also with security proper. Failing to integrate the security dimension in these policies is likely to generate tensions with the central State in the medium or even short term. Given the budget restrictions the State is subject to – not unlike local governments – it may not be in a position to assume this central role for much longer in an increasingly complex game.

3 Conclusion

The way local security is governed in France has undergone dramatic changes over the last 35 years. Local authorities (especially municipalities) have reinforced the capacities of action by developing specific expertise and hiring staff (especially municipal police). Local partnerships have been set up, where prevention and security actions are debated and implemented. Most of the time these new local regimes are 'hybrid', as they combine social prevention and situational prevention measures, as well as repressive tactics. Our four case studies demonstrate that there may exist variations between localities depending upon the political resources of the mayor, presence of the National Police forces and political orientations of the municipality.

However, these local regimes remain fragile. Central authorities are reluctant to pass security policy-making prerogatives down to local governments. When community policing – the last attempt at a policy combining prevention and repression – was abandoned, National Police forces were told to focus exclusively on the latter and communes where asked to take care of the former. This allocation of tasks raises a few questions, pertaining in principle to its relevance and in practice to its operational implementation. Is it at all possible for any security force to focus essentially on its repressive function while delegating prevention to others entirely? Local governments do not appear excessively keen on being confined to a restricted field and consistently attempt to infiltrate what is supposed to be the State's sphere – even though they possess neither the legal competences nor the resources to do so. As far as they are concerned, state agencies at the local level are also saddled with a rather unstable position and need to engage in a constant dialogue with local elected representatives. The resulting permanent negotiation process implies considerable, time-consuming and costly to-ing and fro-ing of local interactions involving not only mayors and commissaires or Gendarmerie officers, but also local and national elected representatives.

The political and administrative fragmentation of the French territory has contributed to maintaining the predominant position of state agencies in the practical, day-to-day elaboration of local security policies. Elected representatives may not conduct major repressive operations without the active support of the National Police. The need to focus specifically on their commune has historically prevented mayors from developing a global perspective on metropolitan security policies. The PN and the GN were all the more ready to do so, when they were simultaneously relieved of any involvement in matters of proximity, henceforth reasoning exclusively in terms of the metropolis or the department. In spite of major territorial administrative reforms – which mostly ratified an existing metropolisation process, already experienced by residents used to travelling to their workplace, school, favourite place of entertainment, etc. – and in spite of the many supra-communal policies generated in various areas of public action by said metropolisation, mayors cannot seem to accept the idea of sharing their (limited but real) prerogatives in the field of security – yet. The resulting void was filled by a strong comeback of national security agencies at this particular scale. Sub-national variations in metropolitan policing agendas exist but, even so, these are not crucial in explaining metropolitan policing in France which continues to be driven by national government and its police forces which dwarf municipal police services in size and expenditure. This leads us to a partial bifurcation: on policing issues, the state monopoly is only moderately attuned, although on prevention issues the state is only one actor amongst others in a process of local negotiation.

Terrorist attacks and threats recently generated concerns that contributed to further reinforcing the idea that the central State ought to be in charge of security policy-making. The dominant position of national forces has been reinforced by the globalisation of threats, the designation of national and international networks as generating these threats, and the mobility of aggressors. The result is a paradoxical situation whereby the metropolitan scale appears too small considering such threats, yet too big for implementing prevention methods that require extremely localised interventions: mayors have – or should have – sufficient knowledge of their residents to help identify those who may be considered a threat.

However, budget constraints and the constant vilifying that has plagued successive national governments in the field of security suggest medium- and long-term trends that may shift the course of events away from this Napoleonic security management model. Because metropolises are gaining momentum, because they are led by elected representatives who are going to need a brand of legitimacy best built by using security as a seduction device for wooing voters, because said elected representatives will be in a position to negotiate their involvement in security policy-making with central governments, the balance may shift. Still, national security agencies remain powerful, united against outside influences, and recognised as possessing real expertise in the field, which should be enough to weigh on the other side and preserve their dominance.

Notes

1. Cayrel & Diederichs, 2010.
2. 'Conseils intercommunaux de sécurité et de prévention de la délinquance', which became 'Conseils locaux de sécurité et de prévention de la délinquance' (local security and delinquency prevention councils) in 2002.
3. The 2000s reinforced this trend (especially through the adoption of the 2007 crime prevention law, while N. Sarkozy was minister of the interior, which favours more repressive devices at the local level), but they do not represent a turning point, because just after the Bonnemaison report, some voices rose up against this 'overly permissive' policy.
4. Regarding CCTV, for instance, a 2011 study of the 60 largest French cities by OWNI showed that 100% of right- and centre-right-controlled cities were equipped, against 60% of left-wing-controlled cities, with one camera per 1,858 inhabitants vs. one per 4,961 inhabitants, respectively.
5. In France, the prefect is the local representative of the State.
6. Commission de prévention situationnelle.
7. Chef d'état major de la direction départementale de la police nationale.
8. www.rue89lyon.fr/2011/11/10/chasse-prostituees-7-arretes/
9. The 725,000 residents of the Toulouse metropolis live in 37 communes, including the city of Toulouse and its 453,000 residents, eight other towns with more than 10,000 residents, the smallest commune harbouring only 245 residents.
10. The Lyon metropolis is home to 1.281 million residents spread over 59 communes whose populations vary from 1,000 to 500,700 for Lyon itself. In spite of its extended range of competences, the metropolis has no security commission.
11. The Strasbourg metropolis has 473,000 residents, 274,400 of whom live in the central city.
12. Ten on 1 January 2015; 12 on 1 January 2016.
13. www.lagazettedescommunes.com/170679/action-sociale-contraints-a-la-depense-les-departements-reagissent/
14. Rapport d'information de MM. François Pillet et René Vandierendonck, fait au nom de la commission des lois n°782 (2011–12) – 26 septembre 2012.

15 Cayrel & Diederichs, 2010.
16 www.lagazettedescommunes.com/316241/la-metropole-de-lyon-contourne-la-loi-m aptam-en-matiere-de-police-de-circulation/
17 We are referring here to the departmental presence of national policing agencies, as opposed to any services reporting to the department government.

Bibliography

AEF Sécurité (2014) 'Dossier: élections municipales', www.aef.info.
Bonnemaison, G. (1983) 'Rapport de la Commission des maires pour la sécurité "Face à la délinquance: prévention, répression, solidarité"', ed. La documentation Française, Paris.
Cayrel, L., Diederichs, O. (2010) *Le rôle et le positionnement des polices municipales*, Paris: Inspection générale de l'Administration.
de Maillard, J. (2005) 'The governance of safety in France. Is there anybody in charge?', *Theoretical Criminology*, 9(3): 325–343.
de Maillard, J., Zagrodzki, M. (2015) 'Plural policing in Paris. Variations and pitfalls of cooperation between national and municipal police forces', *Policing & Society*, 1–14, doi:10.1080/10439463.2015.1046454
de Maillard, J., Zagrodzki, M., Benazeth, V., Zavlaski, V. (2015) 'Les inspecteurs de sécurité de la Ville de Paris, des acteurs en quête de légitimité dans la production locale de l'ordre', *Déviance et société*, 39(3): 295–319.
Edwards, A., Hughes, G. (2012) 'Public safety regimes: Negotiated orders and political analysis in criminology', *Criminology and Criminal Justice*, 10(3): 260–283.
Ferret, J., Mouhanna, C. (eds) (2005) *Peurs sur les villes*, Paris: PUF.
Freyermuth, A. (2013) 'L'offre municipale de sécurité: un effet émergent des luttes électorales', *Revue internationale de politique comparée*, 20(1): 89–116.
INSEE (2010) www.insee.fr/fr/themes/document.asp?ref_id=ip1217.
Le Goff, T. (2008) *Les maires, nouveaux patrons de la sécurité?* Rennes: Presses Universitaires de Rennes.
Le Goff, T.Malochet, V. (2015) 'Le grand Paris de la sécurité', *Note rapide de l'Institut d'aménagement et d'urbanisme – Ile de France*, 702.
Mouhanna, C. (2010) 'Security in Paris: How political and administrative organisational complexities eclipse real issues', in M. Cools et al., *Police, Policing, Policy and the City in Europe*, The Hague: Eleven International Publishing.
Mouhanna, C., Easton, M. (2014) 'Policing Paris. "Out of" or "still in" Napoleonic time?', *European Journal of Policing Studies*, 2(1): 94–109.
Roché, S. (2004) 'Vers la démonopolisation des fonctions régaliennes: contractualisation, territorialisation et européanisation de la sécurité intérieure', *Revue Française de Science Politique*, 54(1): 43–70.

Chapter 4

Portugal

Urban security governance in Portugal: Key elements and challenges

Carla Cardoso and Josefina Castro

1 Introduction

The framework of the present analysis is based on the academic debates evidenced by criminological and security governance literature concerning the major transformations in urban security and policing in advanced democratic countries in the last decades. Security governance is increasingly recognised as a multiple and diffuse concept encompassing a 'constellation of institutions, whether formal or informal, governmental or private, commercial or voluntary, that provide for social control and conflict resolution, and that attempt to promote peace in the face of threats (either realized or anticipated) that arise from collective life' (Dupont et al., 2003: 332). In fact, as highlighted by several scholars, these dichotomies are still associated with a traditional view and therefore are inadequate to capture a reality that is especially hybrid.

Plural policing or the shift from 'police to policing' (Bayley & Shearing, 2001, 2008; Loader, 2000) is pointed out as one of the elements of this new governance and is conceived as the fragmentation and diversification of policing provision in different agencies and agents, the correlated end of the monopoly by the state and public police, and the transfer of functions and responsibilities from the public to the private and voluntary sectors. Policing is now being widely provided by institutions other than the state, more visibly by private companies on a commercial basis, and by communities on a volunteer basis (Bayley & Shearing, 2001, 2008).

These developments have been regarded as elements of a broader process in the reconfiguration of contemporary governance, namely the nature and powers of the nation-state from a hierarchic bureaucracy toward a greater use of markets and quasi-markets, especially in the provision of public services. Despite divergences concerning the meaning of these transformations, their explanatory factors and their consequences, one of the central points of the debate, which differentiated the approaches that have theorised the governance of security within criminology, namely governmentality, governance and regime analysis, refers to the role and the state's position in this 'new' configuration. The 'hollowing-out of the state' (Rhodes, 1994; Jessop, 2004) or the diffusion of responsibilities within and outside the state and its relationship with processes such as globalisation, internationalisation, and the shift from welfare to neo-liberal rationality, are central aspects shared by these different analytical perspectives (e.g. Johnston & Shearing, 2003; O'Malley, 2005; Rose et al., 2006).

Although the theoretical debate has been often marked by the conflation between ontological, epistemological and normative levels of analysis, even within the same line of theoretical approach, one of the questions that divides the perspectives, as highlighted by Edwards and Hughes (2012: 434), is the focus of analysis, emphasising the political rationalities that underlie the state powers or 'emphasizing the processes of diffusion of political power through networks and programs of governance'.

A central question, pointed out by Jones and Newburn (2008) and Crawford (1999), is whether the transformations represent a truly qualitative break with the past, something that is assumed by the governance scholars. Another question is the interpretation of what the new role of the state is (or should be) in 'network governance' or 'nodal governance' and their implications. In these terms a distinction can be observed between those that search for a 'neutral' view of the role of the sovereign nation-state, conceiving it as only one node of a broader and diverse network (Shearing & Wood, 2003; Johnston & Shearing, 2003), highlighting the opportunities for citizen participation and social cohesion that are opened by the new actors of governance and its arrangements, and those that continue to interpret the changes in terms of its relations with authoritarian state interventions or that focus the analysis on the mechanisms of the 'regulatory state', stressing, at least in symbolic and legitimacy terms, the singular position of the state.

While recognising the presence of central aspects of the pluralisation of security and policing in Portuguese urban contexts, namely the exponential growth of private security since the 1980s, the appeal to the participation and responsibility of individual citizens in security and crime prevention, the pluralisation of policing functions and the way they are modelled by consumerism, the central state remains the dominant actor in the provision, regulation and distribution of security in urban contexts.

The present chapter will focus on the sphere of urban security, community safety and policing in Portugal, and in particular in the metropolitan areas of Lisbon and Porto. It will not focus on supranational governance in spite of being aware of its relevance for the understanding of the internal security field. The main questions that guide our analysis are: What are the main axes of the current configuration of plural policing in Portugal? How does it relate to major trends in urban security governance and to the broader changes in the role of the state? The first part presents an overview of the developments of security in Portugal and key elements of the Portuguese context of contemporary urban security governance. Second, we will analyse the current configuration in terms of three major vectors: a) public/private; b) central/local; c) law enforcement and criminal justice/prevention.

2 Urban security overview

2.1 From 1974 until the mid-1990s

After a period of almost 50 years of dictatorship (1926–74), the conceptualisation and development of crime and security policies were inseparable from the reorganisation of the public administration and judicial systems. The *Carnation Revolution* was initially a military coup in Lisbon on 25 April 1974, organised by the Armed Forces Movement, composed of military officers who opposed the regime. This movement led to the fall of the authoritarian 'Estado Novo' in Portugal and ended war in the colonies. Political power was taken over by a military junta during a two-year transitional period known as PREC (Processo Revolucionário em Curso, or Ongoing Revolutionary Process), characterised by social turmoil and power disputes between left- and right-wing political forces. The two national police forces, the Polícia de Segurança Pública (PSP) and the Guarda Nacional Republicana (GNR), were considered as advocates of dictatorship and were no longer authorised by the new political power to maintain public order or to control demonstrations. This task was assigned to the military 'revolutionary' forces (Pinto, 2010; Cerezales, 2008). In the context of political instability and economic crisis, the primary concern of the provisional governments was to ensure conditions for economic reconstruction and political legitimacy through the stabilisation of the democratic regime. It was therefore necessary to implement reforms by restructuring services in order to adapt them to the principles enshrined in the democratic Constitution of 1976 and to the social and political transformations demanded by Portuguese society.

As noted by several authors, unlike Spain, Portugal underwent a transition without negotiations or pacts between the dictatorial elite and opposition forces, having as a consequence a severe crisis of the state (Fishman, 2010; Pinto, 2010). The situation was aggravated by the simultaneous processes of transition to democracy and decolonisation. The decolonisation process required the integration into Portuguese society of half a million Portuguese people from the African colonies. In turn, this unprecedented movement provided the society with qualified human resources which gave a relevant contribution to the construction of a democratic state. Until the formation of the first constitutional government in May 1976, the revolutionary period was characterised by strong social and political tensions.

In terms of urban security, the maintenance of public order and crime prevention was a key element in achieving a balance between, first, the promotion of tolerance and respect for civil rights and liberties and, second, the need to control social disorder which were perceived as threats to the post-dictatorial state and the construction of a democratic order.

The adaptation of police forces to democratic principles required a rupture with the dual legacy of the past – the dictatorship and the post-revolutionary period. The movement of purges affected the political elites, the members of the dictatorial political and military elite, the civil service and the private sector. Being the police one of the pillars of the previous regimes, associated with political and social repression they did no escape from these measures. After the abolition of the political police, the reorganisation of the security forces started with the abolition of the 'riot police'.[1] These measures, however, were not enough to modify the public image of the security forces and rehabilitate them.

As a consequence, the legitimisation of the post-revolutionary police was a slow process. During the 1980s, and following several incidents and complaints about the abuse of police powers, a report produced by the ombudsman recommended reforms to the recruitment and training of police officers, including a greater emphasis on human rights, and the creation of legal mechanisms to render the police more accountable for the use of their powers. As a consequence, policing was increasingly conceived in terms of enforcing the rule of law and protecting civil rights and freedoms. The principal measures, regarding the police, were addressed towards strengthening human and material resources as well as their professional qualifications. Since the 1980s several schemes have been introduced to raise police educational and training standards and provide higher education for police officers, namely the creation of the Higher Institute for Police Sciences and Internal Security.[2] Altogether, those measures aimed to change the public image of the police, and to promote a closer cooperation between these state agents and the citizens. This purpose was considered to be fundamental in order to overcome a perceived lack of trust in police inherited from the previous political regime and is maintained until present in the policy discourse.

During this period, concerning policing, crime prevention was primarily treated as a matter of deterrence, addressed through more or less policing and greater or lesser police visibility, often not involving any substantial change in the conception of the functions and traditional ways of conducting police work. Security policies were essentially directed towards two types of problems: a) a hybrid configuration between petty crimes and disorder which were seen as major threats and offences against the democratic state (from popular protests to terrorism); and b) since the late 1970s, the trafficking and use of drugs. In fact, the 'drug' phenomenon dominated the political and social agenda during the 1980s and 1990s due to its power to bring together social and security problems and because of its territorial visibility (associated with certain problematic neighbourhoods in Lisbon and Porto). Thus, the drug problem became the subject of a mobilisation of national and local policies that clearly exceeded the maintenance of order and repression of the phenomenon *per se*. Indeed, it constituted a precursor of the most visible changes in the handling of crime and security that occurred from the first half of the 1990s.

During the 1980s, the polarisation of the crime and insecurity debate around the drug problem was evident, in particular the association between drug abuse, trafficking and petty crime and societal insecurities in both political and media discourse. The increasing public concern had a strong impact on the functions of the judicial system and revealed the rigid organisation of control mechanisms around security forces and the penal system. It was in this context that in 1987 'Projecto Vida'[3] was established by the Presidency of the Council of Ministers. This project introduced an integrated and multi-modal approach to the drug problem, comprising the repression of drug trafficking alongside strategies for prevention, treatment and the reintegration of drug users. These strategies entailed the progressive extension of a network of treatment facilities, measures and programmes aimed at rehabilitating drug addicts and reducing their stigma and social rejection. The emphasis on cooperation between public and private agencies and between central and local authorities made this programme a prototype for innovations in crime prevention that emerged in the mid-1990s.

2.2 From mid-1990s to mid-2000s

The 1990s were marked by a political stability and confidence in socioeconomic prosperity that had been enhanced by the accession of Portugal to the European Economic Community in 1986. During this period there was also greater investment in social protection measures and programmes that aimed to increase well-being, prevent social exclusion, and reduce poverty and inequality.

At the same time this period was characterised by a greater emphasis on crime and security issues in the media, political discourse and public opinion. Argument about urban security during this period has revolved around several trends: a) the increasing levels of crime in the context of a weakening of formal and informal controls generated by the transition from dictatorship to democracy; b) the opening up of Portuguese society and related changes in urban lifestyles; c) the increasing concern of public opinion and the mass media with the perceived relationship between insecurity and immigration, social exclusion and deprived neighbourhoods, particularly in the country's two main urban conurbations of Lisbon and Porto; and d) the association between these problems and the increase in crime and insecurity in urban areas. From that moment on, these issues were given unprecedented media coverage and attention in political debates. Although the drug problems remained present in this configuration, their importance receded in the face of other phenomena, in particular juvenile delinquency, violence and organised crime.

It was actually in the 1995 election campaign that the accent of the political discourse gave emphasis to social policies around crime and insecurity.

The construction of the welfare state itself was understood to be an element of crime prevention, given the explicit recognition within political discourse that the social causation of crime lies beyond the narrow action of the criminal justice system and should be tackled through general social policies addressed towards the improvement of life conditions and directed, in particular, towards the most vulnerable groups.

During this period the major developments in urban security emphasised:

- The assumption that the 'criminal issue' was complex and multidimensional, and therefore required an integration of crime prevention policies and strategies. This idea expresses the decentralisation and expansion of the concept of crime, which was, traditionally, locked within the boundaries of the formal control system and particularly within the core police and criminal justice system.
- The proliferation of measures and programmes that combine mixed preventive strategies, social and situational, often directed at different objectives (e.g. prevention of crime and victimisation, prevention of exclusion and marginalisation, fear of crime reduction, promotion of confidence in the police and institutions, social cohesion, promotion of informal social control), and also to different targets (offenders and potential offenders, victims and potential victims, social groups, and specific contexts such as vulnerable or at-risk territories).
- The growing relevance of preventive approaches with particular emphasis on the local territory and context.
- The emergence of a culture of partnership which was inseparable from the appeal to 'the community' and co-responsibility, in alliance with the progressive recognition of the state's incapacity to handle these problems unilaterally.

Altogether these elements go hand in hand with the increased adoption of a managerial approach, namely a client-oriented approach, the adoption of efficiency and efficacy indicators within police forces and the growth of the practices of contracting out. Finally, in those developments it is possible to detect the influence and transfer of policies implemented by other countries and European Union (EU) institutions to Portugal.

As we will describe later, urban security is still largely a 'top-down', national state-led agenda, both in its definition and implementation (the central state remains undoubtedly a cornerstone in the definition and implementation of policies and security strategies).

2.3 From 2000s to present

Although the elements described in the previous period are still present, two major key aspects that emerged in the last decade characterise the current configuration: the reform of the Internal Security System (culminating in the Internal Security Law in 2008[4]) and the adoption of austerity policies (from 2010 onwards).

The internal security reform

During this period security governance has focused largely on whether or not to adopt a new organisational model, including merging police bodies and/or changing the territorial allocation of resources and functions. The principal arguments for the reform were to promote the rationalisation of resources and the efficiency of the system by improving the coordination between security forces and services at national and local levels and by better clarifying the respective areas of responsibility. This reform was preceded by two studies commissioned by the government[5] in 2006, which argued for a system of internal security that overcomes problems of integration, coordination and information sharing, both at national and international levels. Internally, the main shortcomings detected are: the multiplicity of different and non-articulated powers and the lack of coordination between the various levels of administration; the lack of a coordinating body for crime prevention as well as the need for a national crime prevention strategy; and finally, the lack of a systematic system for evaluating policy responses. However, despite this rhetoric of 'multi-level governance', the proposals are focused on different models of the internal reorganisation of the national police forces and thus remain emphatically state centred.

The elements that support the need to reform are: the perceived transnational security threats, specifically organised crime and terrorism; at the national level, the increase in criminality observed until 2008; and the reform of central state administration to reduce expenditure.

Under the 'auspices' of austerity

After the 'euphoria' of the period between 1985 and 1998, there has been growing concern about Portugal's relative lack of economic development, scientific, technological and organizational capacity. Portugal belongs to the group of Southern European countries that have suffered most from the impact of the economic and financial crisis and related problems of sovereign debt, and has been subject, along with Greece and Ireland, to an Adjustment Programme. The high debt, both private and public, combined with a chronic trade deficit and mediocre gross domestic product (GDP) growth since 2000 accentuated the clear impacts on social and economic vulnerability even before the bailout from the 'Troika' constituted by the European Commission, the European Central Bank and the International Monetary Fund in April 2011. In fact, Portugal became the first country, in

2000, to be subjected to the EU's Excessive Deficit Procedure under the Stability and Growth Pact.

During this period unemployment rates have increased (2001 4.0%; 2006 7.6%; 2011 12.7%; 2012 15.5%; 2013 16.2%; 2014 13.9%; 2015 12.5%),[6] as has household debt, with the middle class being the most affected. 'The gap between rich and poor was already wide before the crisis and has remained broadly unchanged since. In 2008, Portugal had the sixth-most unequal income distribution and was the most unequal European country' (OECD, 2013: 48).

In terms of the impact of the crisis and the austerity policies on security, it can be said that defying predictions made by politicians, media and opinion makers, and against the arguments used by police forces in order to claim more resources, increases in public disorder and crime have not been observed. More objectively, recorded crime shows a downward trend in recent years at the national level, and also in the metropolitan areas of Lisbon and Porto. The number of police effective during this period remained stable (see Figure 4.1). Moreover, unlike the situation in Greece (Xenakis & Cheliotis, 2013), the urban centres of Lisbon and Porto have been revitalised as a consequence of increasing tourism and related commercial activity. The mass protests against government austerity measures in Lisbon and Porto were in general peaceful, and the police forces kept a low profile.

The crisis has not been accompanied by a politicisation of security and crime issues. On the contrary, public security and crime have become secondary concerns, both in public opinion and in political discourse, to other economic and social concerns, primarily unemployment and poverty. In fact, crime control was kept out of political debate by a broad consensus between the major political parties. It is also important to note that in Portugal there has not been the 'punitive turn' in criminal justice perceived in other Western countries. Despite the decline of social welfare policies during this period, there has not been a discernible emphasis on 'get tough' policies. Apparently, welfarism still remains a relevant element in the legitimacy of criminal policies and in the role of the state in exercising its coercive force.

The major priorities in urban security, as they are presented by the national authorities,[7] are similar to those before the crisis: the repression and prevention of violent and organised crime, terrorism, sex crimes, drug trafficking, domestic violence, and crimes against the most vulnerable citizens. White-collar crime, cybercrime and human trafficking are also included in the priorities. Nevertheless, the more prevalent crimes in large urban areas are petty theft, such as pickpocketing, smash-and-grab, residential and business burglaries, and drug offences. In terms of policing, the national implementation and development of 'proximity policing' programmes oriented to the protection of the most vulnerable citizens (e.g. women, children and the elderly) and to specific contexts (e.g. schools, commercial areas and activities) are also presented as main priorities.

3 Analysing contemporary urban security governance in Portugal

Aiming to describe the continuities and discontinuities between public discourses, decisions actually taken, action and its results, we will analyse the current Portuguese context in three vectors that, in our view, are essential in this comparative exercise on plural policing and urban security governance: a) public/private; b) central/local; c) law enforcement and criminal justice/prevention.

3.1 Public/Private

Urban security in Portugal is highly dependent on national government through the direction of the Ministry of Internal Administration (MAI). At local level, the security is mainly assured by two national police bodies: the PSP (Public Security Police), a civil police; and the GNR (similar to the French Gendarmerie), a military force. These police forces are responsible for the internal security and the protection of citizens' rights under the jurisdiction of the MAI. In addition, there are other national security forces with more specialised functions: the judiciary police (Polícia Judiciária, or PJ, a criminal investigation police), particularly focused on violent and organised crime under the jurisdiction of the Ministry of Justice; and the immigration and borders service (Serviço de Estrangeiros e Fronteiras, or SEF) under the jurisdiction of the MAI. The internal security system also includes the Intelligence Services, the Maritime Police and the Aeronautic Authority. All the security forces and services are national and their cooperation is coordinated centrally by the secretary of internal security. According to Portuguese Constitutional Law (article 272) the organisation of the security forces must be unique for the whole national territory.

The PSP and the GNR are the forces mainly in charge of criminal prevention and the maintenance of public order. Together they represent about 85% of the expenditure and staff of the MAI. The main criteria for the distribution of functions between them are territorial, the PSP being responsible for policing urban areas, whilst rural policing is generally the responsibility of the GNR. In many municipalities the two forces coexist, being responsible for distinct areas. These forces also share criminal investigation competences with the judiciary police.

The metropolitan commands of the PSP in Lisbon and Porto depend directly on the National Directorate and are structured in police divisions responsible for the municipalities. Each command also includes specialised divisions (Transportation Security, Airport Security, Traffic Regulation, and

Criminal Investigation). There are also special units whose functions are not territorially defined as they intervene across the country in situations of a serious threat to security or in special complex cases (Corps of Intervention, Group of Special Operations, Personal Security and Inactivation of Explosives).

This structural differentiation is mainly focused on what can be considered the core issues of internal security, and it is accompanied by a relatively recent differentiation that is most noticeable in functional terms: the emphasis on prevention and proximity, on subjective security and the related appeal for the participation of citizens in local security strategies (e.g. RASI;[8] Castro et al., 2012; Agra et al., 2002).

Concerning the provision of policing by private actors, the most relevant development is the growth of commercial private security. From the late 1980s there has been an expansion of the private security sector. Even in a country with a low crime rate, as is the case in Portugal, private security has expanded (Rodrigues, 2011). According to the last *Annual Report on the Private Security Sector in Portugal*,[9] developed by the Private Security Council (a consultation body of the MAI) in 2013, 36,113 active private security guards were registered (345 guards per 100,000 inhabitants; the police numbers were 436 per 100,000 inhabitants). Figure 4.1 illustrates the trend of private security guards and public police officers in the last decade.

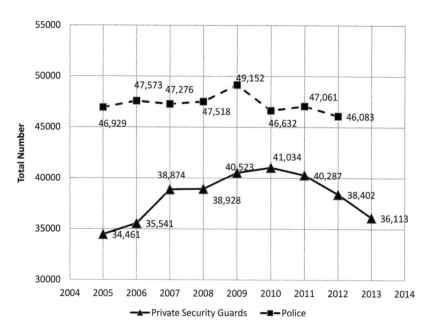

Figure 4.1 Total number of police officers and private security guards in Portugal in the last decade
(Sources: Eurostat and *Annual Report on the Private Security Sector in Portugal*)

According to Law No. 34/2013, of 16 May 2013, private security activity is defined as the provision of services to third parties by private entities and the organisation, by any entities and for their own benefit, of self-protection services. The training of private security personnel is also considered a private security activity.

The private sector is officially understood as subsidiary and complementary to the security services and its relevance is recognised both in the protection of people and property and in the prevention and deterrence of illicit activities. Private security services have a duty to provide public authorities with all the assistance requested from them. In case of intervention by the public police or security services in places where private security companies operate, these companies are obliged to put their human and material resources under the command of those forces. In addition, they have special duties, such as immediately reporting to the judicial or police authority the practice of any crime of which they become aware.

In urban semi-public and private spaces, private security is the main actor. The activity of private security comprises the services of monitoring movable and immovable assets and the control of entrance, personal protection, monitoring alarms and video surveillance, carriage, custody, treatment and distribution of valuable goods, the inspection of luggage and passengers at ports and airports, and inspections of tickets on public transport.

The state has been particularly active in the regulation of this sector (e.g. DL94/2002, 12 April; DL 35/2004, 21 February; DL 38/2008, 8 August; DL 34/2013, 13 May). The national police (PSP), through the Department of Private Security, is responsible for the licensing and supervision of private security activities and for the training and supervision of private security personnel. At a national level, the Board of Private Security includes representatives of businesses and workers in the sector and also certain public entities responsible for areas where private security is especially relevant, such as the financial sector and sports. At a local level, there are departments of the PSP that are responsible for promoting cooperation between public and private security, particularly at certain mass events such as sporting events and concerts. The illicit use of private security is considered a crime.

The legal regulation of the sector not only allows the use of private security, but in certain situations it is mandatory the adoption of private security systems and measures. For instance, the state requires the adoption of private security systems in: bars and clubs that have spaces for dance and are licensed to sell alcohol; credit institutions and financial companies; big commercial units; petrol stations; and sport events. In some circumstances, and with special permission from the PSP, the private guards can stop and search – namely in sport events, airports and ports – but only in entrances, whilst in the interior of these venues stop and search is only permitted by the public police.

The state is one of the main customers of private security, since most public buildings (such as public schools and universities, municipalities, hospitals, etc.) have private security. In turn, the private sector can hire the services of police officers, namely for policing private spaces (e.g. supermarkets) and also specific events organised both by private and public entities. These kind of services are authorised by police authorities.

In sum, the state has a prominent role in the private security sector by: a) regulating and supervising the sector; b) being a key consumer of private security; c) cooperating in the policing of particular contexts and events; and d) competing for the same services (providing services to private entities).

Concerning private policing under non-commercial auspices, there is a growing mobilisation of agencies and other private actors around security and criminal prevention. This mobilisation is, however, usually motivated by the action of public authorities, particularly the police. We can mention as more relevant:

- The involvement of retailers in 'proximity policing' programmes (see section 3.3, below) in urban centres of Lisbon and Porto.
- The involvement of associations and private entities in community prevention programmes and local social networks even if they do not have crime prevention as a primary objective, but are aimed at the reduction of social exclusion and the promotion of social welfare.
- The financing of closed-circuit television (CCTV) implementation, particularly in public spaces, such as nightlife areas of Lisbon and Porto by retailer associations. However, in Portugal the implementation of CCTV in public areas is rare and needs special permission from the Portuguese Data Protection Authority.

Initiatives such as Neighbourhood Watch or other citizen-driven crime prevention measures are not observed and are not tolerated by the Portuguese authorities.

3.2 Central/Local

Portugal, with a population of 10.5 million, has a complex administrative structure. At the first level, the country is divided into two autonomous regions (the Azores and Madeira archipelagos) and continental Portugal. These two autonomous regions have political and administrative statutes and self-government bodies. Although in the 1990s public debate about regionalisation intensified, culminating in 1998 with a referendum in order to implement statutory and political regions with some degree of autonomy, there was a low turnout, with 52.4% of the electorate abstaining, and 63.5% of those who did vote rejecting the proposal for regionalisation.

The 18 'districts' are the territorial administrative subdivisions of mainland Portugal. It was the area of jurisdiction of a civil governor, who acted as the local delegate of the central government. However, in 2011, a decree extinguished the civil governments, transferring most of their functions to other bodies. At the second level, the 308 municipalities are the more consistent and stable division of the country. These are constituted by deliberative and executive bodies elected by residents. The municipalities are subdivided into civil parishes,[10] the smallest units and their presidents also democratically elected by residents. In addition, Law No.11/2003 (13 May 2003) allows the municipalities to organise themselves into inter-municipal communities and metropolitan areas.

The creation of the metropolitan areas of Lisbon and Porto was a response to the increasing need to coordinate supra-municipal and inter-municipal investments and activities in areas such as public transport, sanitation, environmental resources, civil protection and territorial planning. These metropolitan governments have a deliberative, an executive and a consultative board. The deliberative board is constituted by all the mayors, the executive board is elected by the municipal assemblies from a list of candidates, and the consultative board is constituted by representatives of relevant institutions, entities and organisations in the metropolitan region (Law No. 75/2003). In Portugal, there are two metropolitan areas, Porto and Lisbon, which together account for about one third of the entire Portuguese population and attract considerable migration from interior regions of the country and immigration from outside the country. The Metropolitan Area of Porto (AMP) is constituted by 17 municipalities with a population of approximately of 1.6 million (population density: 861 inhabitants per square kilometre (km^2)). The municipality of Porto has 237,591 residents (population density: 5,736 inhabitants/km^2). The Metropolitan Area of Lisbon (AML) is constituted by 18 municipalities of Greater Lisbon and the Setubal Peninsula with a population of approximately 2.8 million (population density: 966 inhabitants/km^2). The municipality of Lisbon has 547,631 residents (population density: 6,532 inhabitants/km^2).

Although security is one of the areas included in the legal framework of metropolitan areas, in fact neither AMP nor AML have a specific agenda on this issue. To reiterate, the governance of security in Portugal is highly centralised, being dependent of central government through the jurisdiction of the MAI. However, since the late 1990s there have been signs of decentralisation as indicated by the creation of municipal police and local security councils.

The municipal police are administrative organisations operating under the direction of the mayor. According to the Law No. 19/2004 (20 May), the functions of the municipal police are: a) monitoring compliance with municipal regulations; b) effective implementation of the decisions of municipal authorities; c) the surveillance of public space, including the surrounding areas of schools, in coordination with the security forces; d) surveillance of local urban transport, in coordination with the security forces; e) intervention in community policing programmes in schools or with specific groups of citizens; f) protection of buildings and municipal public facilities; and g) regulation and supervision of road and pedestrian traffic.

In the same period, the Municipal Safety Councils in all municipalities across the country (Law No. 33/1998 of 18 July) were created. The objectives of the boards, with consultative purposes, are: a) to contribute to a deeper understanding of the safety situation at a local level; b) to formulate proposals for solving marginalisation and safety problems and to participate in prevention activities; c) to promote discussion about measures against crime and social exclusion; d) to evaluate requests directly related to safety issues and social inclusion; e) to monitor and support actions directed, in particular, at drug prevention and other social problems.

In spite of their responsibility for the maintenance of public order and the protection of local communities, in cooperation with national forces, the primary focus of municipal policing is on the regulation of urban traffic. This is also observed in Lisbon and Porto, where, differently from other urban areas, the municipal police is constituted by police officers from the PSP but under the direction of the mayor. Public awareness of the local safety councils is negligible.

As contrasted with other European countries, there is little appetite amongst municipal authorities in Portugal for increasing their role in the governance of security. There is little evidence that municipal authorities are using their administrative competences and regulatory powers to create new controls on anti-social behaviour and disorder. In general, the role of the mayor is to make visible to the central government the security problems at a local level. In short, local security is regarded as a matter entrusted to the police and to the central state, and not subject to negotiation between local and central government, in contrast with other areas such as education, public transportation and social housing.

This does not mean that crime is not a concern of local government. On the one hand, crime prevention and repression are in general assigned exclusively to the national police and this is evident in the discourses of the local authorities and municipal police who are careful to demarcate their more limited interventions in urban security. On the other hand, the intervention by municipalities in crime prevention is understood as indirect, through the pursuit of social policies and improvements in the quality of life. These local policies are mainly directed at what are perceived to be the 'social causes of crime' and related problems (e.g. inequality, prostitution, drug abuse). Moreover, there is a consensus that local policies should prioritise reductions in the fear of crime. Currently, reducing the fear of crime amongst residents and tourists, especially in Lisbon and Porto, is clearly a central concern in local authorities' discourse. This is justified by the perception that fear of crime is excessively high compared to registered crime. Indeed, the current consensus is that problems of crime are effectively under control and that the metropolitan areas of Lisbon and Porto are perceived as 'safe'. This approach of using social policies and interventions to reduce the fear of crime is referred to by local authorities as 'security in the broad sense'.

In this context, between the late 1990s and the first decade of the 2000s, in the metropolitan areas of Lisbon and Porto, the municipalities developed, in conjunction with the central government, initiatives for 'security in the broad sense'. Thus, in 1996, the 'Porto City Contract', an initiative of the central government (Ministries of Interior, Justice, Education and Health) and the Porto municipality with the participation of private agencies, was implemented. The main objective was to develop an integrated programme promoting urban safety with a multi-agency approach to problems of drug addiction, prostitution and victims of domestic violence. At the core of this programme was the Permanent Safety Observatory, coordinated by the University of Porto.

In 2008, the MAI promoted the creation of Local Safety Contracts with municipalities. These contracts integrated different strategies, actors and agencies, namely the national and municipal police, public services and private agencies at a local level. The municipalities and the civil governors were responsible for diagnosis, programme conception, coordination and evaluation. Despite the often-vague formulation of objectives and activities, these contracts combined different strategies: situational prevention, proximity policing, renewal of the built environment, social interventions and strategies intended to enhance mechanisms of informal social control. Despite contingencies in the development of the 34 local contracts, in general, the agencies and activities that were included under the umbrella of the programmes were already present before the contracts, and so this programme was mainly a way to aggregate and better coordinate already existing resources. Less than three years later, in 2011, the extinguishing of the competences of the civil governors motivated by the austerity measures, led to a rapid and 'silent death' of the programme without much resistance from the local authorities or other institutions involved. Recently, the programme of socialist government (2015–2019) announced a "new generation" of the local security contracts.

In sum, from the local authority's perspective, security is not defined as an autonomous field of action, being instead formulated in terms of welfare and social policies. Lisbon takes an exceptional position, while it formulates an explicit policy agenda for the area of security, having a department within the municipality itself with responsibilities in this area, and claiming to have a proactive role and active participation in problem solving in security matters. This position is accomplished by a strategy led by the municipal police, which is singular in the Portuguese context: the development of community policing programmes. The delimitation of this intervention area is mainly made according to their distinction over the proximity policing implemented by the national police which coexists without problems in the same areas.

3.3 Law enforcement and criminal justice/prevention

From what we have been saying, despite the security pluralisation, 'everything still happens within the state framework' (Ferret, 2004: 62) in the management of urban security. In the absence of a real local driven policy agenda for urban security, the focus of analysis should move from the tensions between state and non-state agents, at local and national levels, which are emphasised by governance analysis, and should instead focus on an analysis of the national security agenda. As some authors have pointed out (Johnston, 2006; Crawford, 2006; Ferret, 2004), more attention should be given to the uncertainties and contingencies that influence the state action and the competing objectives of governing agents and the various police organisations.

Since the mid-2000s it is possible to identify two key tendencies in the formulation of security policies. First, an emphasis on sharing responsibility between central government, local administration and civil society, together with the promotion of social cohesion and prioritising the needs and expectations of citizens. The aim was to adapt the police work to local contexts whilst maintaining its national character, the 'proximity policing' programme being its most successful outcome. Second, the need to reform the Internal Security System, notably by improving coordination mechanisms and a rationalisation of resources. The realisation of this agenda culminated in what we call the 'security-criminal justice' complex.[11]

Proximity policing

The proximity policing programme brings together and organises at a national level all proximity policing programmes that began in the 1990s as pilot projects implemented by the national police (GNR and PSP), into two independent teams, the EPAV (teams of proximity and support to the victim) and EPES (teams of the 'Safe School Programme'). The central aim of this programme is the improvement of the relationship between police and citizens, bringing them into a closer 'proximity'. The two dimensions of this integrated programme – EPAV and EPES – have their origins in two previous programmes, 'INOVAR' and the 'Safe School Programme', respectively.

The 'Safe School Programme' is a community policing programme implemented at national level in 1992 by the MAI and the Ministry of Education. Implementation was the responsibility of the police and it was regulated by these ministries. The general aim is to promote 'a culture of safety in schools', thereby contributing to the affirmation of the school community as a privileged space of youth integration and socialisation. The specific objectives of this programme include: the identification of risky behaviours and disorder in schools and surrounding areas; the participation in activities aimed at preventing risky behaviours and promoting self-protection; to inform and assist school authorities in the identification of at-risk youth and their referral to the relevant authorities; to support victims of crime and their referral to the relevant authorities; and data collection and analysis about criminality, violence and victimisation in the school community. In order to achieve these goals, the development of systematic cooperation and permanent exchange of information between the police and the educational community is required. At the same time, the programme contributes to the reinforcement of the liaison between schools and other community resources.

Domestic violence, which has been the object of increased public concern, has motivated different kinds of programmes and measures aiming to promote cooperation between public services and private agencies. In 1999, the government created the 'INOVAR' project[12] under the direction of the MAI. The main objective was to improve the relationship between the national police (PSP and GNR) and the community within a 'proximity' policing philosophy. The measures included the renewal of police stations with better services for victim assistance (namely, the creation of a special office for victim attendance; specific training for police agents; a database with information about community resources for assisting victims). In the implementation of these activities a relevant role was given to the police as a key player in the fostering of institutional networks with private organisations (e.g. non-governmental organisations), and public services (e.g. hospitals, social security) at the local level, stressing the idea of 'policing with and for the community' (Tyley, 2008: 376). Currently, these objectives are integrated into the 'proximity policing' programme and the national police have adopted an assessment tool in order to define the level of risk in each case of domestic violence, therefore aiming to define preventive measures and, in collaboration with the penal justice system, to support prosecution.

Analysing the developments of the proximity policing programmes, implemented at local level by national police forces, it is observed that their main targets are different actors, contexts and sectors of activity. In addition to police patrols, these programmes provide information to citizens and potential victims on how to reduce victimisation opportunities and adopt protection measures. The concept of 'proximity' translates the logic of the implemented programmes better than the concept of 'community': a police-centred and a top-down conception of the production of social order. In fact, the aim is to reduce the distance between the state and citizens considered more vulnerable and at greater risk of victimisation according to their characteristics (age, gender, etc.) or the activity sector in which they operate (schools, trade, tourism). Thus it is a 'de-territorialised' model of prevention in the sense that it does not require any reference to a specific community. Ultimately, if there is a community, it is the 'national community'. In this sense, the concept of proximity should not be confused with the idea of devolving responsibility for the production of security to local communities themselves. In spite of the policy discourses claiming the establishment of a partnership between police and citizens in the co-production of security, the police have a dominant role in the definition of problems and in the strategies to address them.

The victim-oriented logic of these programmes gives to the police action a status of 'public service' (prudential advice and support for citizens' self-protection), and demarcates it from the traditional functions of law enforcement or reactive responses centred on identifying and blaming particular offenders without hampering the accomplishment of surveillance, gathering of information and problem-oriented functions. Moreover, the proximity programme provides another means of legitimising the police beyond their capacity to reduce crime. This proximity can also be extended by the use of social networks (e.g. Facebook, Twitter) for closer communication with citizens. This more abstract conception of proximity allows these programmes to circumvent successfully what would be their obvious territorial deployment: the disadvantaged and problematic neighbourhoods, locales where it would be much harder for the police to maintain the commitment to this new model of 'public policing', avoiding the slipping into aggressive order maintenance or zero tolerance and maintaining a more comfortable distance from crime-oriented policing. Moreover, this strategy is in line with the understanding of security by municipal authorities and local agencies, focused on the improvement of quality of life, reduction of fear of crime, and social policies. In other words, the adopted model of proximity allows the overcoming of the 'tension between targeting the poor and risky, and the commitment to a "social" form of universalism' (Stenson, 2008: 9).

Thus, although we cannot posit that proximity programmes contribute to increased community cohesion or 'bonding capital', they are undoubtedly a pacifying element in the citizen-state relationship, a fact that is not irrelevant at a time when the ideal of the welfare state has been challenged. Of course, the maintenance of the integrated programme of proximity policing puts difficulties in the management of resources at a time when they are more limited. Hitherto, however, no movement to reduce or reallocate responsibility for proximity policing, for example to municipal police forces, can be observed.

The rationale behind the 'proximity policing', as has just been characterised, can be contrasted with the community policing programme implemented by the Lisbon municipal police in certain areas and constitutes a unique case at national level. This model of community policing, which commenced in 2008 as an alternative model of policing, aims to establish a closer relationship between the municipal police and the community. In general, the experiences already implemented aimed to reduce fear of crime, by intervening in the underlying factors, including physical disorders, interventions in the public space or in social disorders, such as conflicts between neighbours.

There are essentially two differentiating elements put forward in relation to the proximity policing implemented by national police: a) the bottom-up character – that is, the objectives are established by community representatives and not by the municipal police; and b) the eminently preventive nature. Concerning the former aspect, the core element of this model and different from the proximity policing model is that community policing works 'with' the community and the proximity model works 'for' the community. Thus, it is noted that the role of the community in the programme design and implementation and, consequently, the situated character of each programme, which objectives, actions and functioning, are conceived upon the needs and local resources through diagnosis and monitoring. The 'community' is understood and treated as both actor in and target of intervention. The strategy is to select urban areas where locally based initiatives were already implemented and in which it is possible to constitute a 'security working group' charged to conduct a diagnosis and an action plan. The management team of municipal police play a key role in boosting these groups, although, as stated, the aim is to create conditions for it to work autonomously, regardless of their presence. The 'community' is defined and covers local institutions and organisations, both public and private, and citizens residing or engaged in other activities (e.g. commercial) in the project area.

Regarding the second point, the programme is seen as having a crime prevention function, by addressing the physical and social conditions that could promote criminal activities. Besides participation by the management team, municipal police officers participate by referring problems they detect to the authorities which have the powers to respond.

The 'security-criminal justice' complex

The developments in mid-2000 that culminated in the publication of the Internal Security Law in 2008 epitomise internal tensions in the state governance of security, particularly in the way security is linked to criminal justice policies.

The Internal Security Law, as mentioned above, was justified by the Socialist government based on the perceived inadequacy of the internal security system in place since the 1980s (Internal Security Law No. 20/87 of 12 June 1987). It was argued that this inadequacy arose as 'the result of an outdated internal and international conjuncture' (Resolution of the Council of Ministers 45/2007 of 19 March 2007), both in terms of the nature of the present threats and by coordination deficits, particularly between the various police forces and security services. Thus, the reform aims to bridge the deficits of coordination in the fields of prevention, public order, criminal investigation and information systems, and increase cooperation at national and international levels. As stated in the same resolution of the Council of Ministers, the cornerstone of this reform is the 'creation of an integrated internal security system, headed by a secretary-general, with similar status to the secretary of state and directly dependent on the prime minister'.

It was precisely this secretary-general who aroused the greatest criticisms of the new Internal Security Law. These criticisms, made by political forces and by justice sectors, namely the judiciary, centred on the excessive centralisation of powers. Effectively, the new law grants the secretary-general coordination, management, control and operational competences over the police forces and security services, namely the PJ, GNR, PSP and SEF. The problems arising in relation to such powers include the competences that these entities have, as criminal police bodies, in the field of criminal investigation. Indeed, the Law of the Organisation of Criminal Investigation,[13] published under the same reform, gives to the secretary-general the following functions: a) the distribution of powers between the criminal police bodies in order to avoid conflicts; b) to ensure the sharing of resources and support services according to the needs of the criminal police body; and c) to ensure the functioning and access to the integrated criminal information by all criminal police forces, according to their needs and competences. This solution of the concentration in a single person, who depends directly on the prime minister, of competences related to the security forces and services even when they act in criminal investigations, and in that case, under the functional dependence of the public prosecutor, which is intended to be autonomous, deserved a heated debate. The Supreme Judicial Council even pointed out that it constituted a 'veritable invasion of criminal investigation by the executive power'. This apparent conflation between justice and security, or at least the establishment of a continuum, with overlapping areas between each sphere, is also reflected in the creation, during the same period, of the first Framework Law of Criminal Policy[14] in 2006. This law defines the objectives, priorities and guidelines for crime prevention, criminal investigation, prosecution, execution of sentences and security measures.

The significance of this for our analysis is how this legal and institutional complex articulates, for the first time in the Portuguese context, what is denominated by Valverde (2008) as scales, jurisdictions and temporalities that could enhance the coexistence of conflicting legal orders.

4 Conclusion

In general, we can observe elements that are conceptualised by several scholars as shifts in the governance of security, namely the expansion of private security services and technologies as well as some measures that intended to decentralise security governance (e.g. municipal police, local security contracts). However, the governance of urban security in Portugal is largely dependent on central state and national police forces and its diversification is primarily internal to these police forces. In that sense, 'urban security' is still under the scope of 'public security' or 'national security', in which the national police forces are truly the only entities that have a planned approach to security problems at the local level. In spite of that, this situation does not seem to cause any tension between local and central authorities, to the extent that local authorities do not complain or seek greater control over the security agenda. Instead, tensions and competitiveness are observed mainly in the distribution of competences and powers between the different police forces.

Plural policing is recognised not so much in the decentralisation of security from sovereign state to the private sector or local authorities, but mainly within the national police. It is accompanied by an erosion of the traditional identity of public police based on law enforcement and 'crime fighting'. Criminal justice, risk management and social justice represent the goals and agendas of the internal pluralisation of public security. However, the Portuguese experience questions whether there is a local governance of security as such, at least in the manner that has been described in the international literature on urban security governance, whether in terms of network governance analysis (Shearing & Wood, 2003; Johnston & Shearing, 2003) or regime analysis (Edwards & Hughes, 2012; Edwards & Prins, 2014), since in Portugal local networks are centrally directed. As Rhodes (2007: 1256) argues, '[l]ocal networks cease to be local networks when they are centrally manipulated or directed'. In effect, when networks are centrally managed, horizontal relationships are transformed into vertical relationships. In sum, the state maintains a prominent role by triggering and financing action, by 'steering and rowing', even under the impact of austerity-driven spending cuts and rhetoric about the virtues of 'less state'.

Another element that is quite distinctive in the Portuguese experience in comparison to conceptions of governance in the international literature, is the fact that the national police seem to have survived, relatively unscathed, the crisis of the state and its institutions following the financial crisis of 2008. Several factors may help to understand this 'state of grace' enjoyed by the police in a context of social, political and economic crisis:

- The historical process of adaptation to democratic legitimacy and the process of rehabilitation of the public image of security forces, which were felt by the population as core elements in the maintenance of the longest dictatorship in Western Europe.
- The above changes were, mainly from the 1990s, accompanied by investment in training and recruitment, contributing to the image of

greater professionalism, competence, along with greater openness and proactivity in the relationship with civil society.
- The growing media coverage of the police 'achievements' in combating crime and their diversifying functions, especially those that refer to the logic of proximity, prevention and service delivery. Also this image of competence and professionalism has not been contradicted by any rise in crime in recent decades.
- Finally, there has been a consensus amongst national governments led by different political parties over the need to depoliticise policing and ensure the national police remain above party politics. This national consensus and the apparent "de-politicization" contribute to enhance the positive reputation of the national police regardless of the political "colour" of municipal authorities.

Being a project that aims to foster comparative analysis, we are aware that the differences found in the Portuguese experience might be interpreted in terms of the characteristic traits of a transition process that naturally is becoming blurred as the country approaches European standards. Such an interpretation implies an inevitability that devalues the socio-political and socio-cultural embedded realities, which constitute the basis of an historical and comparative analysis, and assumes a homogeneity, which is far from existing in the 'European model'.

A deeper understanding of the Portuguese configuration would require, as suggested by Ferret (2004) about policing in continental Europe, a social, historical and political dimension of analysis that goes beyond the scope of this chapter.

The understanding of the current landscape of the provision and regulation of security and policing in Portugal and, more broadly, the nature and processes of governance, requires at least the acknowledgement that current convergences and divergences emerge from a framework that is not characterised by a consistent tradition of local and regional government, a well-developed welfare state and an advanced economy.

Concerning the dominance of the central state, the reasons are multiple and deeply rooted in the Portuguese history. The administrative tradition has been characterised by increasing centralisation since the early 19th century. The revolution of 1974 and the democratic Constitution did not substantially change the highly centralised nature of society and the state in political, social, economic and administrative terms (Barreto, 1984). The integration into the EU has played an undeniable role in the current configuration of governance, facilitating and even imposing the participation of sub-state levels through the delivery of resources (Silva & Syrett, 2006). In spite of these dynamics, however, the central government departments maintain a pre-eminent role in government directly or through their services at the local level.

It is undeniable that in the last 15 years elements have been accentuated in the programmes and actions of the governments that invoke the theses of a 'hollowing state' that emerged alongside other elements associated with the neo-liberal rationality, such as privatisation, public-private partnerships, contracting out and new public management.

The state and public administration reforms have been justified based on the criticism of bureaucratic state, the need to maximise the efficiency, effectiveness and accountability of public institutions, as well as the emphasis on individuals' responsibility as a means to compensate the limits of the sovereign state. At the same time, we observe over the years the expansion of the 'regulatory state'. Nevertheless, until the current crisis and the Troika's structural adjustment programme, the reform of the state was invariably justified in terms of the 'modernisation of the country' in order to align it with European standards of development and well-being. In fact, the compatibility between these arguments and the construction of the welfare state was never significantly contested. On the contrary, welfarism and the reform of the state were regarded as elements of the same social and economic project: the development of the country toward a more egalitarian, participative and inclusive democracy (Rodrigues & Reis, 2012; Fishman, 2010).

The crisis and the austerity of recent years have further developed this longstanding debate about the centralisation of government in Portugal, accentuating the economic component of the argument, given the vulnerability of politics and sovereignty, caught between the external impositions of international bodies and the pressures of the markets. The 'emaciating of the state', the exaltation of private initiatives and the significant cuts in public expenditure are justified as 'necessary evils', in order to prevent the collapse of government and to save the welfare state, in particular the most emblematic sectors, such as social security and the national health system. The vulnerability of the Portuguese economy was never a good basis for neo-liberal reforms. In addition, the national economy has always been heavily dependent on central government, which was formed not as a mere regulatory state but as a catalyst and facilitator of private or public-private initiatives that European funds have made possible. As Barreto (1984: 196) writes, in Portugal 'almost everything grows in the shadow of the state, under its inspiration and guidance'. The stagnation of the economy from the beginning of this century and the growing indebtedness of companies, families and the state, made more than ever visible this secular dependency between political, economic and financial power.

In sum, the 'hollowing out of the state' has always been conceived as a product of the necessary reconciliation between the expectations of the Portuguese for a more social state and the conditions and contingencies of the economic basis for this state. In these terms the ideal of the welfare state, in spite of the challenges, remains a support for the legitimacy of state action and remains a relevant capital that no political force dares to dismiss.

Notes

1 Companhia Móvel da PSP.
2 Instituto Superior de Ciências Policiais e Segurança Interna.
3 Integrated into the National Plan to Combat Drugs (Resolution of the Council of Ministers n. 23/87, 21 April).
4 Lei de Segurança Interna de 2008 – Law n.° 53/2008, 29 August 2008.
5 'The Study for the Rationalisation of Structures of GNR and PSP' ('Estudo de Racionalização das Estruturas da GNR e PSP', Accenture, 2006); and 'The Study for the Reform of the Organisational Model of the Internal Security System' ('Estudo para a reforma do modelo de organização do sistema de segurança interna', Instituto Português de Relações Internacionais da Universidade Nova de Lisboa, 2006).
6 Pordata, www.pordata.pt.
7 Law n.°17/2006, 26 May 2006 (Lei-Quadro de Política Criminal); Law n.°38/2009, 23 May 2009; Law n.°72/2015, 20 July 2015 (Leis de Política Criminal).
8 *Relatório Anual de Segurança Interna* – RASI (Portugal Annual Report on Internal Security), Sistema de Segurança Interna-Gabinete do Secretário Geral, 2014, available online: www.portugal.gov.pt/media/6877606/20150331-rasi-2014.pdf
9 Relatório Anual de Segurança Privada, 2014.
10 In Portuguese, 'Freguesias'.
11 With this term we refer to an integrated internal security system, which is extremely centralised and which represents a hybrid fusion of the notions of criminal justice (including all the guarantees for fair trial) on one hand, and security (including vague references to threats and suspicions) on the other.
12 Resolução de Conselho de Ministros n°6/99 (Resolution of the Council of Ministries).
13 Law n.° 49/2008, 27 August 2008.
14 Lei-Quadro de Política Criminal (Law n.° 17/2006, 23 May 2006).

Bibliography

Agra, C., Quintas, J., Fonseca, E. (2002) 'From democratic security to a securitarian democracy: The Portuguese example', in P. Hebberecht, D. Duprez (eds), *The Prevention and Security Policies in Europe*, Brussels: VUBPress.

Barreto, A. (1984) 'Estado Central e Descentralização: antecedentes e evolução, 1974–1984', *Análise Social*, XX: 191–218.

Bayley, D.H., Shearing, C.D. (2001) 'The new structure of policing. Description, conceptualization, and research agenda', *National Institute of Justice. Research Report* (NCJ 187083).

Bayley, D.H., Shearing, C. (2008) 'The future of policing', in T. Newburn (ed.), *Policing Key Readings*, Cullompton: Willan Publishing, 715–732.

Castro, J., Cardoso, C.S., Agra, C. (2012) '(Social) crime prevention in Portugal', in P. Hebberecht, E. Baillergeau (eds), *Social Crime Prevention in Late Modern Europe. A Comparative Perspective*. Criminologische Studies, Brussels: VUBPress.

Cerezales, D. (2008) *Estado, Regímen y Orden Público en el Portugal contemporâneo*. PhD thesis, Universidad Complutense de Madrid.

Crawford, A. (1999). *The Local Governance of Crime: Appeals to Community and Partnerships*, Oxford: Oxford University Press.

Crawford, A. (2006) 'Networked governance and the post-regulatory state?: Steering, rowing and anchoring the provision of policing and security', *Theoretical Criminology*, 10, 449–479.
Dupont, B., Grabosky, P., Shearing, C. (2003) 'The governance of security in weak and failing states', *Criminal Justice*, 3: 331–349.
Edwards, A., Hughes, G. (2012) 'Public safety regimes: Negotiated orders and political analysis in criminology', *Criminology and Criminal Justice*, 12/4: 433–458.
Edwards, A., Prins, R. (2014) 'Policing and crime in contemporary London: A developmental agenda?' *European Journal of Policing Studies*, 2/1: 61–93.
Ferret, J. (2004) 'The state, policing and "old continental Europe": Managing the local/national tension', *Policing & Society*, 14, 49–65.
Fishman, R.M. (2010) 'Rethinking the Iberian transformations: How democratization scenarios shaped labor market outcomes', *Studies in Comparative International Development*, 45, 281–310.
Jessop, B. (2004) 'Hollowing out the nation state and multi-level governance', in P. Kennett (ed.), *A Handbook of Comparative Social Policy*, Cheltenham: Edward Elgar, 11–25.
Johnston, L. (2006) 'Transnational security governance', in J. Wood, B. Dupont (eds), *Democracy, Society and the Governance of Security*, New York: Cambridge University Press.
Johnston, L., Shearing, C. (2003) *Governing Security*, London: Routledge
Jones, T., Newburn, T. (2008) 'The transformation of policing? Understanding current trends in policing systems', in T. Newburn (ed.), *Policing. Key Readings*, Cullompton: Willan Publishing, 733–749.
Loader, I. (2000) 'Plural policing and democratic governance', *Social & Legal Studies*, 9, 323–345.
OECD (2013) *Portugal: Reforming the State to Promote Growth*, Better Policies, Paris: OECD Publishing.
O'Malley, P. (2005) 'Policing, politics and postmodernity', in T. Newburn (ed.), *Policing. Key Readings*, Cullompton: Willan Publishing.
Pinto, A.C. (2010) 'Coping with the double legacy of authoritarianism and revolution in Portuguese democracy', *South European Society and Politics*, 15, 395–412.
Rhodes, R.A.W. (1994) 'The hollowing out of the state: The changing nature of the public service in Britain', *The Political Quarterly*, 65, 138–151.
Rhodes, R.A.W. (2007) 'Understanding governance: Ten years on', *Organization Studies*, 28, 1243–1264.
Rodrigues, J., Reis, J. (2012) 'The asymmetries of European integration and the crisis of capitalism in Portugal', *Competition and Change*, 16: 188–205.
Rodrigues, N. (2011) *A Segurança Privada em Portugal – Sistema e Tendências*, Almedina.
Rose, N., O'Malley, P., Valverde, M. (2006) 'Governmentality', *Annual Review of Law and Social Science*, 2: 83–104.
Shearing, C., Wood, J. (2003) 'Nodal governance, democracy, and the new "denizens"', *Journal of Law and Society*, 30(3): 400–419.
Silva, C.N., Syrett, S. (2006) 'Governing Lisbon: Evolving forms of city governance', *International Journal of Urban and Regional Research*, 30(1): 98–119.
Stenson, K. (2008) 'Governing the local: Sovereignty, social governance and community safety', *Social Work and Society*, 6: 1–14.

Tyley, N. (2008) 'Modern approaches to policing: Community, problem-oriented and intelligence led', in T. Newburn (ed.), *Handbook of Policing* (second edn), Cullompton: Willan Publishing, 373–345.

Valverde, M. (2008) 'Analysing the governance of security: Jurisdiction and scale', *Behemoth. A Journal on Civilization*, 1: 3–15.

Xenakis, S., Cheliotis, L.K. (2013) 'Spaces of contestation: Challenges, actors and expertise in the management of urban security in Greece', *European Journal of Criminology*, 10: 297–313.

Chapter 5

Finland

Policing regimes in transition in the Nordic countries: Some critical notes from the Nordic reality

Sirpa Virta and Jari Taponen

The Nordic way of policing is usually described as democratic, uncontroversial and civilian in outlook and style. A prevailing image is that policing reflects the egalitarian values of Nordic people and societies. From a political point of view, Nordic metropolises can be characterised as 'metropolis under the national authority' where the state is the main actor responsible for policing and security. Local elected politicians and local political decision-making bodies have no role in defining policing, police tasks or the allocation of resources for policing. Nordic police cooperation reflects the close geographical and social connections between Nordic countries. This cooperation takes multiple forms and it is based mainly on institutionalised practices and on formal agreements between the Nordic countries' police organisations.

This chapter discusses the context-dependent elements of policing in metropolises, including the increasing influence of the European Union (EU) in shaping policing in the Nordic countries, the role of local politics and politicians in centralised police systems, and the significance of 'structural trust' and trust towards the police. Policing in the Nordic countries is facing increasingly complex threats and problems so it is legitimate to ask whether the situation will be the same in the future. There are also significant differences between the Nordic countries in many security- and policing-related developments. It is argued that policing regimes in the Nordic countries are changing due to both internal and external pressures. Policing regimes in Nordic metropolises can be characterised as multi-level governance in an increasingly complex political environment. In order to develop a theoretical understanding of these policing regimes in transition, some fine-tuning of concepts is suggested. To illustrate this transition and to exemplify metropolitan policing in the Nordic context, the chapter considers current developments in the policing of Helsinki, the capital of Finland.

I Introduction

There is a common understanding that there is something unique and exceptional in the Nordic countries and therefore also in the policing of these countries. The Scandinavian, or Nordic, model has been characterised by many criminologists as consensual, social democratic and welfare oriented, non-punitive and inclusive (Crawford, 2009; Esping-Andersen, 1990; Lappi-Seppälä, 2011). The liberal values, which include freedom of expression, equality, privacy, transparency and the rule of law, form the heart of Nordic social life. However, the current and rapidly changing policy environment in the Nordic countries, in Europe and globally is challenging these basic values in practice. The increasing complexity of the political and security environment, the EU effect and the emerging arrangements for cooperation in societal security will have significant consequences for metropolitan policing in the Nordic countries. These developments lead us to question if there is still a stable policing regime seen in the Nordic countries, as it used to be, and what the future policing regime in Nordic metropolises will be. How significant are contextual elements in each country? So far, it has been argued that in order to understand the Nordic police one has to know something about the broader governmental model of Nordic welfare, which is characterised by a strong state, generous and universal welfare systems, and high economic productivity. Today, the model has been under considerable pressure and its weakened position has influenced the police too (Hoigård, 2011: 265).

Denmark, Norway, Iceland, Sweden and Finland are by definition Scandinavian countries, or Nordic countries.[1] The term Nordic country is preferred in this chapter, because the location in Northern Europe is a common denominator of all these countries. Finland has not always been called a Scandinavian country, and there is the special term of 'Fenno-Scandia' for the Scandinavian countries including Finland. Finland is in many ways different to the other Nordic countries. Perhaps the most important factor is the language difference. Finnish is not part of the Nordic linguistic family, because its common roots are with the Estonian and Hungarian languages. The Norwegians, the Swedes and the Danes can more or less easily understand each other, but Finnish is from a totally different linguistic family. This has been recognised in Nordic police studies as a difficulty, especially in comparative research (Hoigård, 2011: 265). Furthermore, although Swedish is the second official language in Finland, it is used mainly only by people who have it as their mother tongue.

The general security landscape of the individual Nordic countries is also very different. Finland has the longest EU border, with Russia. The contemporary international political situation in Ukraine and Russia effects both the external and internal security politics in Finland more than in other Nordic countries. Denmark, on the other hand, is located in continental Europe. It is easy to drive by car to Denmark from other parts of Europe, and from Copenhagen to Malmö, but usually one has to take a ferry or fly to the other Nordic countries. Finland, Sweden and Norway have large Arctic areas in the North. Policing the North is becoming increasingly common business for the police, border guards, emergency services and customs of these countries. For instance, the police of Finland and Sweden have agreed on common cross-border patrolling and search and rescue operations. Norway is not part of the EU, and Finland and Sweden are not in the North Atlantic Treaty Organization (NATO). There are many institutional, area-based and cultural differences which are more or less relevant in the context of policing and especially in policing Nordic metropolises.

2 Societal security and the changing security environment

Recently, due to the rapidly changing international security environment and common threats like terrorism, pandemics and climate change, Nordic cooperation on issues of civil security has been enhanced. The emerging concept of *societal security* covers civil, non-military, security cooperation between the five Nordic countries. Since 2009, the so called Haga process (Haga I Declaration, Nordic Ministerial Meeting on Civil Protection and Emergency Preparedness in Stockholm, 27.04.2009) has produced the new concept of societal, or comprehensive, national security, which co-exists with military-led planning for wartime. This new concept emphasises the protection of society as a whole, with its own complex mechanisms, values and culture – rather than reducing security to the maintenance of physical boundaries or the protection of individuals considered in isolation from one another (Bailes & Sandö, 2014).

The Haga process goes hand in hand with the development of policing strategies in the Nordic countries. The organisations and planning processes are still separate but in some cities and areas in Finland, for instance, strategic planning and operational planning is increasingly coordinated across police, emergency and disaster management services and in concert with the contingency planning and preparedness of the military. This increasing cooperation can be witnessed in the development of joint safety and security plans. Resilience has emerged as the common rationale for public safety regimes in these joint plans and under the auspices of the new concept of societal security. Preparedness has become an important aspect of policing in big cities, but it is still too early to evaluate whether it has superseded more traditional social security and crime prevention agendas. Preparedness is focused on general safety and security matters (evacuation plans, impact analyses, anticipatory negotiations, etc.) and what should be done in the event of major incidents such as terrorist attacks. This development suggests that hard security measures (often from the perspective of traditional national security) will begin to shape local policing agendas within Nordic countries as well as the character of police cooperation between them.

In this chapter, the characteristics of Nordic police systems and policing are discussed, as well as the pressures and challenges they face from domestic, European and global environments. The meaning and role of the state, and the common understanding of the state, are traditionally very different in the Nordic countries compared with many other European countries. Consequently, the political role of the municipalities, cities or metropolises in defining policing strategies or resources is also very different in the Nordic countries when compared with many other European countries. Trust and confidence towards the police will be discussed too. The chapter will address the hypothesis and criteria of the Policing European Metropolises Project, from the Nordic perspective, acknowledging the value of the comparative approach adopted in this project whilst suggesting some adaptation of the concept of metropolitan policing to accommodate the Nordic experience.

The Policing European Metropolises Project, comparing policing regimes within and between EU member states, is an interdisciplinary research project. Police and policing studies' theoretical and methodological approaches usually come from many disciplines, mostly from criminology, but also from political science, international relations, public administration, governance and management studies and sociology. In order to understand the significance of contextual elements, organisational processes, institutional arrangements, policies and strategies, politics and emerging threats, an interdisciplinary approach is needed. Recently, in criminology and other fields of inquiry, complexity theory and the idea of complex adaptive systems have become popular in explaining the rapidly changing environment of organisations and regimes as well as their capacities to adapt to this environment. Questions asked by John Grieve (2014: 141), 'Is policing a simple or complex task?' and 'Can complexity theory help us answer that question?', will guide the analysis. From an international perspective, the Nordic welfare model still creates better societies than the others, but when the Nordic police and policing environment of the 2010s and 1990s are compared, the differences are striking (Hoigård, 2011: 266).

Old and new elements of policing exist side by side in the Nordic countries, but it has been argued that something new has happened in the Nordic police during the last 10–20 years. Neo-liberal ideology has reached Nordic countries and the Scandinavian welfare state model is under pressure. It is exposed to increasing privatisation and outsourcing of public services and to increasing social inequalities. One significant element in politics has been the rise of right-wing populist parties that are represented in the national parliaments. There are differences between the right-wing populist parties in Nordic countries, but there are similarities concerning stricter immigration policy and a harsher criminal justice policy. They have weakened the political culture of consent in Scandinavia and introduced a culture more attuned to conflict. In this political culture organised crime, cross-border crime and terrorism are perceived as the new threats, along with immigration, which is identified as a major challenge for policing (Hoigård, 2011: 332–333).

The Nordic Council of Ministers and Pohjola-Norden[2] have adopted the concept of societal security (comprehensive security) in the Haga I

Declaration (2009) and in several subsequent policy documents concerning the development of Nordic cooperation in matters of civil security. The main addition to the traditional approach is the cooperation between civil authorities, in particular the police, and the military and defence authorities (Nordiska Samarbetet i Samhällssäkerhet, 2014). Increasingly there are joint rescue and emergency exercises and the police have begun to take preparedness more seriously. Improving the processes of preparedness, in cooperation with other authorities, is one of the new priorities for the police in Finland (the Ministry of the Interior Action Plan, 2016).

The *whole systems approach* to security promoted by the Haga process requires new conceptual and theoretical tools informed by a multi-disciplinary approach to research. In these terms, theories of networked governance provide a means of addressing the complexity arising out of the Haga process. It is possible to identify three forms of complexity: cognitive complexity (and wicked problems), strategic complexity and institutional complexity. Complexity theory has become popular in political science, criminology and governance studies recently, having originally emerged in the natural sciences. Given its in-depth approach to complexities and complex systems, it addresses complexity in a new way and provides a new, interesting and promising perspective on the complexities involved in governance networks (Koppenjan & Klijn, 2014: 157). The whole systems approach is based on Niklas Luhmann's theory of social systems (Luhmann, 1995), and it is suggested that his systems theoretical approach provides a useful addition to understanding the causalities and interdependencies in societal security and in the context of policing metropolises in general, as well as in the specific context of Nordic policing development (Virta & Branders, 2016).

3 Policing the Nordic countries

The number of inhabitants in Sweden is approximately 9.4 million, in Denmark 5.5 million, in Finland 5.4 million, in Norway 4.9 million and in Iceland 0.3 million. In Finland there are only 1.37 policemen per 1,000 inhabitants, while in Norway the number is 1.69, in Denmark 1.96, in Iceland 2.06 and in Sweden 2.13 (National Police Board, 2014). Existing research suggests people in the Nordic countries trust the police. In international comparisons of popular trust in police, the four top countries standing out from the others are all Nordic (Kääriäinen, 2007: 419). Nordic police cooperation reflects not only a close geographical and social connection between the countries but also a similar history, producing these high levels of trust (Kleiven, 2012: 70).

All Nordic countries have unified, state-organised police forces under the political supervision of a separate government minister (in Finland it is the minister of the interior, in the other countries it is the minister of justice).

With the exception of the security agencies, professional and administrative responsibility is delegated to a separate bureau with a chief executive employed for a definite term. The chief reports to the responsible minister. Each country is divided into police districts with a considerable degree of independence in budget responsibility, personnel policies and resource priorities (Hoigård, 2011: 268).

The degree of internal and external pluralisation of the police function is low in all Nordic countries. Although the Nordic police have a larger proportion of generalists compared with many other countries, specialisation is increasing. Comparing the range of tasks for the police in the Nordic countries, Hoigård shows that there are some variations among them concerning police functions (see Table 5.1).

Depending on the definition of metropolis (size, number of inhabitants, status), there are not many cities in the Nordic countries that one can call a metropolis. Copenhagen and Stockholm are metropolises, but also Oslo, Reykjavik and Helsinki could be defined as metropolises due to their status as capitals. Tampere is the centre of a large area of 45 cities and municipalities, and hosts the Police Headquarters of a big police department in central Finland. From a political point of view, the Nordic metropolises can be characterised as 'metropolises under national authority' where the national state dominates local decision making. Locally elected politicians and decision-making bodies have no role in defining policing, police tasks or the allocation of resources for policing.

Table 5.1 Range of tasks for the police in the Nordic countries

	Norway	Sweden	Denmark	Finland
Security service	X		X	X
Safety building, public order	X	X	X	X
Crime fighting (prevention, investigation)	X	X	X	X
Integrated prosecution duties	X		X	
Civil law-related tasks	X			
Passport-related tasks	X	X		X
Administrative duties	X	X	X	X
Immigration-related tasks	X			
Border control	X	X	X	
Rescue services, other crisis handling	X			

Source: Hoigård, 2011: 281.

Denmark, Finland, Iceland, Norway and Sweden have always cooperated closely. Nordic police cooperation includes formal and informal arrangements and, for instance, a system in which officers are stationed in countries other than their place of origin to work on subjects of strategic interest. These officers operate with domestic police authority regardless of their nationality. The system was originally implemented to combat drug offences, but since 1996 it has covered all forms of transnational crime (Hoigård, 2011: 272). In the northern parts of Finland, Sweden and Norway new models of cross-border cooperation have emerged involving joint patrols with border guards and customs officers, rescue and emergency service personnel. This innovation is based on national legislation in each country, bilateral and multilateral agreements, and institutionalised practices.

The Nordic Passport Union was established in 1954 – a border-free zone where all citizens could pass without a passport. It was an early version of the contemporary Schengen Agreement and the idea of free movement across borders. The first agreement of Nordic police cooperation was signed in 1972, and its revised version in 2003. The current formal framework is the Agreement on Nordic Police Cooperation 2012. In addition to these, there are other arrangements concerning, for instance, wider regional cooperation, like the establishment of the Baltic Sea Task Force including Russia (1998) (Kleiven, 2012: 63–68). In most cases the police cooperation takes place at the purely operational level, ranging from coordinated traffic control, public order policing and contracting out services, to cooperation in criminal case investigations and the development of new tools for the police. The Nordic Police Cooperation Agreement (2012) and agreements between the national police commissioners also fall under the Schengen regulations by which the Nordic countries are bound (National Police Directorate, 2010: 24).

4 The essence of the state

According to Cecilie Hoigård, no comprehensive scientific attempts have been made to describe police development in recent decades in the various Nordic countries. However, in her article 'Policing the North' (2011) there is a comparative approach which gives an excellent picture about many similarities and ideals of the police that have their roots in the ideology of the welfare state. The essence and role of the state in Nordic countries is an important contextual element in the analysis of their metropolitan policing regimes. There is a strong legalistic state tradition that seeks to guarantee a stable democratic political system, social welfare, justice and equality. The essence of the state is seen as a common will, as a positive rather than negative or repressive presence in citizens' lives. This tradition has significant consequences for the analysis of Nordic policing regimes because it is contrary to the general view and approach to the state in critical studies of policing where it is generally assumed that sovereign state power is a dangerous presence in social and political life (an evil), or at best a presence whose force is only to be prevailed upon at moments of last resort (a necessary evil). In either case, the state is postulated as a standing threat to the liberty and security of citizens. Much less is it assumed that the state can play a positive role in producing the forms of trust and solidarity between strangers that are essential ingredients of secure democratic societies (Loader & Walker, 2007: 25).

In the welfare state model, public authorities have the responsibility to ensure that all citizens have access to basic economic, social, educational and cultural goods and services. The state remains an important supplier of these public goods and retains a major interventionist role in society. Police philosophy in the Nordic countries is built on these ideals and can be summarised in the following terms (Hoigård, 2011: 274–275):

- *Integration*. The principle of integration is that the police are locally anchored. Reciprocal dependency forms the basis for a good society, where informal thick ties are more important than formal thin ties, and informal social control is more efficient than formal control. Informal control works both ways and is the best way to avoid abuses of police power. Personal contact creates confidence. Personal proximity provides deeper understanding about the best ways to prevent and combat criminality.
- *Civilian features*. Nordic police philosophy, which emphasises a civilian, not a military, face is closely connected to the tasks of the police.
- *Decentralisation*. The police cannot be locally anchored without being decentralised. Access to good police services should not depend on where one lives.
- *Generalism*. The police ought to be capable of carrying out a variety of different tasks. The individual police officers must have all-round competence. A generalist police also provides better interaction with people, which contributes to public confidence.
- *Statewide unification*. The strong position of the state in the Nordic welfare model implies that all police activity be state-organised in a unified police organisation. All police duties and jurisdictions are gathered together within one organisation.

It is not a surprise, then, that in the Nordic countries community policing is not a specialism, but rather it is the logic of policing in general. Therefore, attempts to import into the Nordic countries in 1990–2010 an Anglo-American model of community policing as a police specialism failed to some extent (Virta, 2002; Peterson, 2010). However, the ideals of civil, decentralised, generalist police are not predominant and eternal principles. According to Hoigård (2011), they can be viewed as located on the end of the continuum: a decentralised police versus a centralised police; a locally anchored police versus an internationally anchored police, and so on. The recent police reforms in the Nordic countries have been seen not as a break with old ideals but as a necessary development and concretisation of these ideals: the development of society necessitates an adjustment of police work and how it is organised in the context of internationalisation, a more threatening crime scene, demographic changes in which immigration is problematised, international police cooperation and a new managerialism in the age of austerity (Hoigård, 2011: 276). In this respect, comparative research about the adaptation of different policing systems to apparently common, global challenges, has the potential to inform arguments about better governing complexity.

5 Policing Helsinki, the capital of Finland

In Finland the state is responsible for security and policing. The Ministry of the Interior and the National Police Board (NPB) are the main actors defining strategies and action plans for the police and policing. The strategies are implemented in local police departments, through the national police performance management system. As noted above, this model of governing can be described as the metropolis under national authority. In the remainder of the chapter, policing strategies in Helsinki are considered as an example of metropolitan policing in Nordic countries.

In Finland, cities and municipalities are independent (municipal self-governance is in the Constitution). As a state authority, the Helsinki Police Department (HPD) is steered, maintained and controlled by the Ministry of the Interior and by the National Police Board. Security and policing strategies of the EU, and the government's security strategies are taken into account in national policing strategies. In addition to the formal structure of policing policy making and since 2000, networking and partnership practices, voluntary cooperation and government-driven local security planning have been institutionalised as a key component of local security governance. In Finland, there are no strong political interests or political competition in defining policing strategies and their outcomes either at the national level, in Parliament, or at the local level in city councils (there are no elected mayors in Finland). The degree of internal and external pluralisation of policing is low. The volume of private security business is growing, but its role and mandate are narrow, and it is steered and controlled by the Ministry of the Interior and the police. However, due to the rapidly changing security and policing landscape (for instance, flows of asylum seekers) and political changes, common to all Nordic countries, it is legitimate to ask whether policing in Finland will remain as *a*political as it is now.

Finland is a large and sparsely populated country. About 5.4 million Finns live in a geographically large country, but most of them on the southern coast and in big cities. The number of police officers is 7,389 (in 2014). There are 1.37 policemen per 1,000 inhabitants. The number of policemen per

1,000 inhabitants has remained relatively low in Finland compared with the other Nordic countries (Haraholma & Houtsonen, 2013: 65). The police are considered reliable, and in 2015, 90% of Finns expressed trust in the police (HS, survey 03.12.2015). Finland continues to be a safe country in general terms. Another significant contextual element is the long and strong legalistic state ('Rechtstaat') tradition that has guaranteed a stable democratic political system, social welfare, justice and equality. This legalistic tradition of governance has not weakened, although welfare society and social security systems have become more contested politically, while the social democratic approach is losing its leading role in thinking (Virta, 2013a: 353). Old and new elements of policing exist side by side in the Nordic countries, but as noted above, it has been argued that policing is changing in response to the breakdown of the Scandinavian welfare state model (Hoigård, 2011: 332–333).

There is only one police organisation which performs all police tasks, and it is internally structured according to territorial divisions and not according to functional specialisms. The provision of police powers are laid down in the Police Act, for which the Ministry of the Interior is responsible. It includes general provisions and principles concerning police work. Policing in Finland has meant historically the core tasks of the police, specifically law enforcement. Strategic thinking, strategies and strategic management have been more or less imported from abroad, such as in 1990–95 with the New Public Management reform ideas, and by policy transfer of Anglo-American policing innovations like community policing (Virta, 2002, 2013b). Since 2001 the strategy processes of the Ministry of the Interior (including the police) have been linked with the performance management processes of the state public administration. Today, the strategies are implemented through performance contracts between the National Police Board and the local police departments (Juntunen, 2015).

Finland has had a centralised state police organisation since the first year of state independence in 1917. After the years of war in 1939–44, the development of the police and policing has been stable, there have been no special political interests involved in the development, and the organisational changes have been rational, incremental and rare. The main drivers for change and development have been in line with the reforms of the public sector in general (for instance, the New Public Management and related reforms like management by results). The recent police reforms in 2009–15 have been implemented in three phases. The reforms have followed a similar trajectory to that in Denmark (Holmberg & Balvig, 2013) in terms of a process of administrative restructuring that has reduced the number of police districts from 90 down to 24 and further down to 11. These processes of geographical restructuring have created larger territorial policing units at regional and local levels. However, the context of the changes in Finland has been different from that in Denmark, because they have largely been driven by a need to address a declining police budget and are underpinned by a commitment to the principles of New Public Management with a focus on increasing efficiency and improving the quality of service for the public (Haraholma & Houtsonen, 2013).

Helsinki, as the capital of Finland, has a police department with a unique position among the other police departments in the country, in that geographically the area or territory of the metropolis forms the area or district of the HPD. Local policing has been increasingly enmeshed in networks and partnerships despite the fact that there is a centralised national police system in Finland. The formation of networks and partnerships has been the main objective of the experiment in community policing since 1999. This more systematic, strategic approach to local policing meant that local safety planning was to be formulated and implemented with local authorities. In 2001, 203 cities and municipalities (less than half of all cities and municipalities) had some kind of safety plan. In many cases, small municipalities had made regional plans together (Virta, 2002: 195–196). In the Finnish concept of local safety planning, local is a geographical concept rather than communitarian. The first wave of local safety plans (1999–2003) witnessed a significant expansion in the formation of local security partnerships. This expansion was especially significant in cities where the safety planning process was integrated into the more established annual welfare strategy (Virta, 2013a: 345).

One significant factor is that local safety planning is voluntary and needs responsible leaders and leadership in order to be successful. National strategies, like the Strategic Police Plan 2015 and the Internal Security Programme 2012, are persuasive by nature and include recommendations, and therefore the local police and local authorities can ignore them if they have other priorities or competing interests. The annual performance contract between the NPB and a particular local police department may or may not include local safety planning and performance targets for cooperation with the local authorities and other actors. The situation varies a lot in different parts of the country. Because there is no legislation concerning local safety planning and the status of the plan, it has been recommended by the Ministry of the Interior that the plans should be ratified at city councils in every fourth year.[3] In some cities, like in Helsinki, the Safety and Security Plan of the City of Helsinki (2016) is part of the city's strategy portfolio, but in cities that are located in the area of large police departments (like, for instance, in Tampere, which is one of 45 cities and municipalities in the area of the Central Finland Police Department), the situation is very different.

The EU programmes such as the Tampere Programme for Freedom, Security and Justice 1999, The Hague Programme 2004 and the Stockholm Programme 2009, as well as the EU Internal Security Strategy 2010, have been very influential in the development of Finland's security governance and strategies. In the same way, the EU-level policing strategies of counter-terrorism, organised crime and prevention have been influential in the development of policing strategies in Finland. The Ministry of the Interior was responsible for the preparation and implementation of the Internal Security Programmes of 2004, 2008 and 2012. In these programmes a very broad definition of safety and security was adopted, involving measures for social crime prevention and specific measures such as the prevention of violent extremism and radicalisation (Virta, 2013a).

Global, European and domestic developments in reaction to emerging security threats have changed the way of thinking about security governance. Preparedness, civic protection, resilience and contingency planning have been reconciled with prevention and other internal security policies. The concept of comprehensive security (also called societal security) has emerged, first in the context of Nordic cooperation in the field of civil security, and it has been used in security strategies as an umbrella concept, covering all securities (from emergency and rescue services, organised crime, cross-border crime, crime prevention to immigration services, customs and border guards). This is a new phenomenon, but it is seen both in government strategies (for instance, in the Security Strategy for Society, prepared by the Ministry of Defence, Government Resolution 16.12.2010) and some new local safety plans (The Safety and Security Plan of the City of Helsinki, 2016).

The strategies of the government and the ministries set general agendas for security governance, but it is up to the Ministry of the Interior and the NPB whether and how much they are to be taken into account in their policing strategies and action plans, and performance targets and contracts between them and the local police departments. However, the policing strategies are usually in line with the main national strategies and their general objectives (Juntunen, 2015).

5.1 From police strategies to performance contracts

The police have had a more strategic orientation in management since 1999, linked with the introduction of performance management systems. This has meant that the strategy of the police takes account of the government's performance targets (and economic realities like budget cuts) as well as the strategy of the Ministry of the Interior. The NPB plans, manages, develops and oversees police and policing across the country, as well as the performance of local police departments in accordance with the performance targets. It also plays a major role in communicating the needs and priorities of the police to political decision makers (in the Parliament), and the reverse. There are several specific strategies concerning, for instance, counter-terrorism, organised crime and crime prevention. They are prepared by the police, and they follow the objectives and means of the respective EU strategies.

The funding and its allocation for the local police departments in Finland is in the hands of the NPB. The current Strategic Police Plan (2015)[4] has four strategic goals: ensuring safety and security, preventing crime, efficient provision of services, and maintaining trust and influencing the development of society. The goals are very general by nature, but the plan includes the actions too, so it could be called an action plan. At the end of the plan, there are the main indicators (five to eight indicators per each strategic goal). The indicators are also general by nature (volumes of actions, etc.). The plan describes what the police is doing, and how the organisation is led and managed, but it is difficult to find measurable objectives and clear priorities for societal outcomes. The performance contracts between the NPB and the local police departments are based on funding allocated to them by the state budget, and they reflect the national strategic goals and priorities. If the local departments do not reach the goals and priorities, there are no financial or other consequences.[5]

5.2 Local safety planning and local policy agenda setting

There has been a long tradition of the community policing style since the 1960s in Finland. Anglo-American community policing has been implemented since 1996, and it has been argued that local security networks and local safety planning can be seen as an outcome of community policing policy and of more general crime prevention policies of the government and the Crime Prevention Council of the Ministry of Justice. From the beginning, since 1999, the formation of partnerships for local safety planning processes were in most cases a police initiative. It was seen as one of the main measures of a community policing strategy[6] and its implementation. Local coalitions included representatives from governmental agencies, municipalities, voluntary organisations, churches and private businesses. The main aim was to set policy objectives and make a local (or regional) safety plan or 'security strategy', 'policing plan', 'crime prevention plan' – the nomenclature depended on the specific focus defined in local policy-making processes (Virta, 2002: 197).

Local safety planning was institutionalised by the first Internal Security Programme in 2004, but there is no legislation on it. The processes, practices and the roles of the local safety plans in guiding policing policies vary a lot throughout the country. Current local safety plans are implementing the Internal Security Programmes (2008 and 2012), whereas the first wave of the plans (from 1999) implemented the community policing strategy of the police. The focus in earlier plans was on crime prevention. The Internal Security Programmes, which are in line with European internal security and home affairs and justice strategies, have guided local safety plans since 2004. The contents of the current local safety plans vary, but the main focus is on prevention of social exclusion. There are also new goals such as a reduction of tensions between groups of people and the protection of critical infrastructure (Virta, 2013a: 350).

5.3 Helsinki – the capital of Finland

Helsinki is the capital of Finland and the only metropolis in the country. There are 620,700 inhabitants (in 2015) in Helsinki, but 1.1 million inhabitants in the metropolitan area that includes the cities of Espoo, Vantaa and Kauniainen. Helsinki is located near Tallinn, the capital of Estonia. It takes only one to two hours by ferry from Helsinki to Tallinn, but there is also a preliminary agreement (HS 05.01.2016) between the two cities about planning to build a tunnel under the sea in the near future (the tunnel would mean 30 minutes by train from city to city). The closest metropolis is St Petersburg in Russia. There is the main large airport of Finland in Helsinki, and five large ship terminals, the implication of this being lots of tourists and other international traffic and businesses. Helsinki is also the most multi-cultural city in Finland. The biggest minorities of people from other countries are Russians, Estonians and Somalis (43% of all people of foreign origin in Helsinki) (www.stat.fi, www.hel.fi). Therefore, the policing environment and circumstances are quite different in Helsinki from in Tampere and central Finland.

Political decision making at the metropolitan level is concentrated in the elected city council and municipality. In Helsinki, security is one of the nine 'core values' of the city. Security is seen as an important element for growing tourism, business competitiveness and inward investment. The perspective is more social security and welfare oriented than crime prevention oriented. The strategy is very clear in defining policing (crime prevention, public order) as the task of the police (The Strategy of the City of Helsinki 2013–2016). The political leaders or the members of the city council have no formal power over police strategies or operational matters in Helsinki; the municipality cannot engage the police in their policy. However, based on a long tradition of practical cooperation, there are a lot of municipal authorities involved in the police-led local safety planning processes, street-level cooperation projects and various crime prevention initiatives. The local safety planning process, then, produces the framework for this practical cooperation (The Safety and Security Plan of the City of Helsinki 2016).

5.4 The police and policing in Helsinki

The Helsinki Police Department, established in 1826, is one of the 11 local police departments in Finland. Due to the status of Helsinki as the capital, and because one fifth of the Finnish population live in the city and the metropolitan area around it, the HPD is the biggest police department. There are about 1,300 policemen (2.06 policemen per 1,000 inhabitants) in Helsinki, which is more than in the other parts of the country.

The number of crimes reported to the police in Helsinki has been reduced since 2010, as in Finland in general, but it remains still higher than in the other parts of the country. Due to the location of Helsinki, there are specific types of crimes not appearing in other parts of the country, for example so called 'hit-and-run' robberies, when criminals come usually by ferry from the Baltic countries and leave the country right after the robbery.[7] The police in Helsinki work together with the Customs and Border Guard in order to prevent and fight international organised crime, human trafficking and other serious crime. There is a special model of institutionalised cooperation between these three authorities in Finland (so called PTR-cooperation: Police, Customs and Border Guard cooperation).

There is also a lot of operational and street-level cooperation with private security companies, voluntary associations and municipal authorities.[8] The HPD started the community policing reform in 2007. The implementation of the national Community Policing Strategy (2007) was an important starting point, and the HPD Strategy for 2008–12 had a special initiative of developing a new and innovative community policing model for the whole department and the city of Helsinki. The other significant initiative was launched in 2008, that of 'virtual community policing' and the first community policing officers in social media. Social media and mobile technology have become an important part of policing in giving advice and informing citizens, but also inviting them to report. The whole process of implementation of the national Community Policing Strategy has resulted in a systematic, holistic and strategic approach to local policing (and thus not as a police specialism) in Helsinki, as well as in Finland in general.

International police cooperation between European and other metropolises is part of operational policing in Helsinki, but there are no objectives or statements for it in the policing plans and performance contracts. The police are involved in various European task forces (Police Chiefs' Task Force, Capital Cities' police leaders group, etc.), and other policing and security networks. In addition to informal cooperation and information exchanges, there are cooperation agreements and institutionalised cooperation practices between the HPD and the police organisations of Tallinn, Stockholm and St Petersburg.

5.5 The politics of policing and the main policing strategies

Annual performance contracts between the NPB and the HPD are based on the national strategies of the police (Strategic Police Plan 2015, and specific strategies like the Strategy for Preventive Policing 2014) and of the Ministry of the Interior (Internal Security Programme 2012, the forthcoming Internal Security Strategy 2016). The performance contract 2016 includes general objectives of the police and the detailed objectives of the HPD, and as an appendix the Action Plan of the HPD. The general objectives include the promotion of security, more effective crime prevention (through, for instance, intelligence-led policing practices and social media), quality of services, and more productivity. The requirements of the government to save money (due to budget cuts) are taken into account (The Performance Contract between the HPD and the NPB, 2016).

The special objectives of the HPD prioritise the development and improvement of its own competences, for criminal investigation, immigration and asylum, strategy for fighting cybercrime, multi-agency and multi-professional teamwork, rather than societal outcomes. There are, for instance, no specific objectives for crime reduction. Also the Action Plan includes mostly descriptions of the measures to be implemented, improvement of internal processes and development initiatives. So the desired outcome of policing as a whole is seen to be an accomplishment of more effective internal processes (The Performance Contract 2016 and its Action Plan – appendix).

The Safety and Security Plan of the City of Helsinki (2016) is the framework for the policing partnerships, multi-agency cooperation and multi-professional teams. It is seen as an important element for building and sustaining everyday security and welfare. Local safety planning processes have been institutionalised in Helsinki with the first Security Strategy of Helsinki (2001), followed by the Everyday Safety strategy in 2006, and the Safety and Security Plan of Helsinki 2011–2014. The planning process is chaired by the Steering Group, which has members from the top administrative level of the city of Helsinki, Rescue and Emergency Services and the HPD (police chief). The practical processes for cooperation amongst these agencies have been divided into three levels: the strategic level (reconciled with the other welfare strategies of the city of Helsinki), action plans and different security-related initiatives of the city as a whole, and particular plans and initiatives in different areas of Helsinki (in the suburbs, shopping mall areas, etc.) (The Safety and Security Plan of the City of Helsinki, 2016).

The Safety and Security Plan of the City of Helsinki (2016) is a coordination document rather than a genuine strategy with definite objectives, but it clearly describes how the city and the police are working together. It includes all cooperation initiatives, working methods (multi-professional teams of different authorities for preventing youth crime, etc.) and priorities. There is a systemic approach in the strategy – for example, it identifies the interdependencies between alcohol consumption, public order disturbances and criminal activities. The general priorities in 2016 are:

- Welfare in general (main means: prevention of social exclusion, social work and prevention of alcohol and drugs problems)
- Traffic safety, road policing
- Welfare of children and young people (youth work, child care)
- Criminality (prevention of violence, burglary, robbery)

- Visible surveillance, crime prevention
- Integration of immigrants

(The Safety and Security Plan of the City of Helsinki, 2016)

In addition, there are 13 different projects and cooperation models listed (most of them youth work, social work or other special projects, in which the police have a minor role). These projects are accountable to their particular funding bodies, as projects are financed by a variety of sources, but they are seen as part of the implementation of the Safety and Security Plan of the City of Helsinki. The outcome of the strategy, however, is not evaluated as a whole. In an interview[9] conducted in September 2015, Police Chief of Helsinki Lasse Aapio argued that there is no local political steering of safety and security planning in Helsinki, certainly no particular ideological interest amongst local politicians in policing issues. The cooperation works well and happens between the police, the city authorities and the voluntary sector, as a part of public administration processes, according to the principles of good governance.

Policing in Helsinki has been adaptive and flexible in responding to current security challenges and changes, as cooperation between the HPD and the city authorities, other state authorities (Customs, Border Guard), international partners (the police of Tallinn, Riga, Vilnius, St Petersburg and Stockholm) and the voluntary sector has been further enhanced. The police and the city authorities, with other partners, have produced the Safety and Security Plan of the City of Helsinki (2016), which provides a framework for security governance. This development could readjust the relationship between local and national authorities in the future.

The degree of internal and external pluralisation of policing is low. The new non-police configurations (community support officers, 'light blue' agencies) do not exist, nor do significant voluntary activities of citizens (neighbourhood wardens). The volume of private security businesses is growing, but their role and mandate are still small in public policing and security governance, and controlled by the state authorities (the Ministry of the Interior and the police).

It remains to be seen whether current challenges, such as the flow of asylum seekers (approximately 35,000 in 2015), the rise of the extreme right in party politics and in street demonstrations, and economic pressures for cutting public sector budgets will change the big picture of metropolitan policing in Finland in the near future. Immigration and the integration of migrants are included in the safety and security strategies for Helsinki, which is the city where most immigrants to Finland live, and prevention of violent extremism has become a part of the policing strategy, stimulated in particular by the influence of broader EU strategies on counter-terrorism. Due to the rapidly changing security and policing landscape and political changes, common to all Nordic countries, it is important to ask if policing in Finland will remain as *a*political in the future.

6 Policing in transition in the Nordic countries

The ideals of Nordic policing have been under considerable pressure during the past decade. The most eye-opening event was the attacks on 22 July 2011, launched by Anders Breivik on government offices in Oslo and, subsequently, against the Workers Youth League summer camp on Utoya Island. It is argued that this transformed policing not just in Norway but in all Nordic countries (Hoigård, 2011: 288). As a consequence, the state has remained as a central actor and national security has become more important in the field of policing, especially in Nordic metropolises. State and police organisations have become more dependent on common European policies and strategies of immigration control, counter-terrorism, security and policing. In the field of cyber-terrorism and cyber-criminality the interdependencies are even stronger. The Nordic countries are no longer seen as 'sanctuaries', either in the eyes of citizens or in the eyes of refugees and immigrants. A common perception is that the promise of Nordic welfare societies has been lost as more extreme political movements and voices gain support. There has been a turn in policing towards pacification and public order tasks, even war-like police operations, as seen in the Husby Riots in Stockholm in May 2013 (Hörnqvist, 2014).

The EU is an important institution for international police cooperation in the Nordic countries. The Norwegian police have cooperation agreements with the EU and Europol (the European Police Office), even though the country is not an EU member state. All Nordic countries have been part of the Schengen Agreement since 2001, even though neither Iceland nor Norway is a member state of the EU (Hoigård, 2011: 272). Policy analyses of the impact of the main EU security and policing strategies in several member states show how they are shaping national and local policing (Virta, 2011). The strategies, like the whole policy domain of the EU's 'Area of Freedom, Security and Justice', are based on common EU-wide threat assessments. Perhaps the most important consequence, in the context of the Policing European Metropolises Project, has been the reconciliation of local policing/ community policing strategies, tactics and practices with national security, notably counter-terrorism strategies, tactics and practices, in the Nordic countries' policing regimes. This development has brought the state and the police into neighbourhoods in new ways. The consequent attempt to reconcile community policing with intelligence-led policing for national security and counter-terrorism purposes may not, however, respect the philosophical elements and objectives of community policing, notably trust in communities and the protection of human rights (Virta, 2011: 201).

Another important trend in this current 'transformative moment in policing' is the centralisation of police organisations (Terpstra & Fyfe, 2013: 1). There have been police reforms in many European countries recently, and in all the Nordic countries police reforms have brought about drastic reductions in the number of police districts: for instance, in Finland from 90 to 11, in Norway from 57 to 24, and in Sweden from 118 to 21, with further reductions to come (Holmberg & Baldvig, 2013: 55). The centralisation of police organisation in Finland has been fast (three reforms, one after another, in 2009–14), and whilst it is too early to evaluate the impact of these reforms, it seems the centralisation of management and administrative tasks along with the reduction of top management staff and the number of police departments' headquarters, all undertaken as part of the government's austerity drive to reduce public expenditure, has not resulted in major changes in the big cities but has mainly had an impact in rural areas (Haraholma & Houtsonen, 2013). Despite this organisational centralisation, there is a common strategic view that local policing in the Nordic countries should not be weakened and that metropolitan policing in particular is in need of more political attention and resources. However, one cannot avoid the impression that police organisations and their leaders, as well as politicians, are very confused about the future of policing and the core tasks of the police, given this increasingly complex policing policy environment (see for instance, Virta, 2008; Wennström, 2013).

In all Nordic countries, there is a clear and increasing focus on citizens' perceptions of safety and police responsibility for this. The importance of partnerships with other organisations on a local level is strongly emphasised and also the private security industry is growing (Hoigård, 2011: 333). Partnerships and safety and security networks are mentioned as primary goals, rather than tools or means to an end, in many policing and security strategies in Finland. This has led to various kinds of partnerships and networks of the state and municipal authorities, voluntary sector and associations. Urban security governance is a complex field of multilevel and multiagency cooperation, where traditional crime prevention and community safety seem to be taken over by preparedness, contingency planning, protection and resilience (Virta, 2013: 343). Increasing interdependencies and cooperation have not led, however, to joint governance or shifts in the tasks and duties of the authorities.

Networks and partnerships should be studied and evaluated further, in order to assess their outcomes and whether they have changed the policing regime. Pluralisation has not meant (at least in Finland) shifts in tasks, duties, responsibilities and resources; on the contrary, it seems that the police is concentrating more and more on the 'core tasks' of crime fighting and public order. The role of the state in general is strengthening, due to the political situation (in Ukraine and Russia) and new security threats (Islamic State fighters), but this trend has also been visible in the Nordic countries recently because of developments in internal security, in particular the increase in riots, extreme politics and hate crime, etc.

There is a common concern in the Nordic countries that trust towards the police, and the state and government in general, cannot be sustained in this new environment. According to a comparative study, Nordic countries have had the highest levels of trust towards the police (amongst 16 European countries). It is argued that this is due to the perceived integrity of public administration, with negligible problems of corruption, and the earlier investment in welfare services. There is also a special phenomenon called 'generalised trust' which is characteristic of the Nordic countries. It refers to the notion that citizens' basic attitude towards other people is trusting and that people are willing to cooperate with each other (Kääriäinen, 2007: 412, 420). These specific and generalised forms of trust are significant factors in police legitimacy, and the future and success of policing in Nordic metropolises is dependent on their sustainability. However, there is alarming evidence that the situation may be changing: explanations for the Stockholm riots, according to interviews with residents of the Husby neighbourhood in which they occurred, include references to systematic police harassment, neo-liberal restructuring of the welfare state, a lack of political participation and a deep disappointment that welfare society promises had not been kept by government (Hörnqvist, 2014: 5). The measured trust of the Finns towards the police is still high (90%) according to the latest survey (HS 03.12.2015), but it seems that it describes 'generalized trust' or 'structural trust', and is not dependent on environmental factors. It does not seem to correlate with the citizens' perceptions of insecurity, which have increased (HS 17.01.2016).

7 Conclusions

The comparative approach to research adopted in the Policing European Metropolises Project is rightly located within a focus on the governance of multilevel (European, state, regional and local) and inter-organisational (partnerships, networks) relationships (see Chapter 1 of this volume). These are context-dependent elements and more significant in some metropolises than in others. The influence and role of the EU are important in shaping local policing in the Nordic countries. The essence and role of the state are different in the Nordic countries than in many other European countries. The state is the main actor, and also by citizens, the state and the police are seen as the main and most preferable provider of security and safety. Local politicians and city and municipal authorities have almost no role in defining policing, police tasks and resources.

Systems theory and complexity theory offer additional perspectives to policing regimes. As argued, policing in Nordic metropolises is complex and this complexity is growing due to politics and developments within the EU, other international security developments, domestic political and economic developments, political violence, criminality. Social cohesion, trust and the welfare society are threatened. Policing and security networks will need to evolve into complex adaptive systems in order to safeguard comprehensive security. A complex adaptive system is defined as a collection of individual agents with the freedom to act in ways that are not always totally predictable, and whose actions are interconnected so that the action of one part changes the context for other agents. Complex adaptive systems are modular in nature and are made up of subsystems. The basis of complexity theory is that it is the behaviour of the overall system rather than the individual components of the system that needs to be the focus of inquiry (Pycroft, 2014: 22–25). Policing systems, including regimes in European metropolises, and their interaction with each other, need to be analysed as complex systems. Much can be learnt through a deeper understanding of interdependencies and complexities of police systems.

Notes

1 In comparative analysis the group of the Nordic countries may vary; the analysis often does not include Iceland and/or Finland (for instance, Crawford, 2009). In Hoigård's (2011) article Iceland is included in general analysis, but not in detailed comparative tables.
2 The Nordic Council of Ministers and Pohjola-Norden form the official network for the development of Nordic cooperation between the five Nordic countries (www.norden.org).
3 The period of municipal and city council elections.
4 The National Police Board has published the Strategic Police Plan (2015), which is the main strategy of the police. The performance contracts between the NPB and the local police departments are based on this strategy.
5 This is the weakness of the current performance management system.
6 There was no written strategy document about community policing in Finland in 1999 (nor before), but there was 'the development paper' of the Police Department of the Ministry of the Interior, which outlined the principles and general goals of local safety planning (Linjauksia lähipoliisimallista, 1999, Ministry of the Interior).
7 The police (especially the Serious and Organised Crime Unit of the HPD) works together with the police of Estonia, Latvia and Lithuania in these cases (interview with Detective Chief Inspector Jukka Larkio, HPD, 18 November 2015).
8 The police decide the strategic and operational partners case by case, and municipal authorities and other actors make their own decisions (whether to take part or not). The principles of good governance and good practices are important drivers for cooperation in practice, not political interests, steering or impulses.
9 The interview with Police Chief Lasse Aapio was conducted on 1 September 2015, in his office at the HPD Headquarters.

Bibliography

Bailes, A., Sandö, C. (2014) *Nordic Cooperation on Civil Security: The Haga Process 2009–2014*, Institute of International Affairs, University of Iceland.
Brunsson, N. (2009) *Reform as Routine. Organizational Change and Stability in the Modern World*, Oxford: Oxford University Press.
Crawford, A. (2009) *Crime Prevention Policies in Comparative Perspective*, Cullompton: Willan Publishing.

de Lint, W., Virta, S., Deukmedjian, J. (2007) 'Simulating control: A shift in policing', *American Behavioural Scientist*, 50(12): 1631–1647.

Esping-Andersen, G. (1990) *The Three Worlds of Welfare Capitalism*, Cambridge: Polity Press.

Grieve, J. (2014) 'The Stephen Lawrence inquiry: A case study in policing and complexity', in A. Pycroft, C. Bartollas (eds), *Applying Complexity Theory. Whole Systems Approaches to Criminal Justice and Social Work*, Bristol: Policy Press, 141–158.

Haraholma, K., Houtsonen, J. (2013) 'Restructuring the Finnish police administration', in N. Fyfe, J. Terpstra, P. Tops (eds), *Centralizing Forces? Comparative Perspectives on Contemporary Police Reform in Northern and Western Europe*, The Hague: Eleven, 59–76.

Hoigård, C. (2011) 'Policing the North', *Crime and Justice*, 40(1): 265–348.

Holmberg, L., Baldvig, F. (2013) 'Centralization in disguise – The Danish police reform 2007–2010', in N. Fyfe, J. Terpstra, P. Tops (eds), *Centralizing Forces? Comparative Perspectives on Contemporary Police Reform in Northern and Western Europe*, The Hague: Eleven, 41–58.

Hörnqvist, M. (2014) 'The fluid legitimacy of the Husby riots', *Criminology in Europe. Newsletter of the European Society of Criminology*, 13(1): 4–7.

Juntunen, A. (2015) *Linking Strategy and Performance Management. Case: Ministry of the Interior. Acta Universitatis Tamperensis 2097*, Tampere: Tampere University Press.

Kääriäinen, J. (2007) 'Trust in the police in 16 European countries. A multilevel analysis', *European Journal of Criminology*, 4(4): 409–435.

Kleiven, M.E. (2012) 'Nordic police cooperation', in S. Hufnagel, C. Harfield, S. Bronitt (eds), *Cross-Border Law Enforcement*, Taylor & Francis, 63–75.

Koppenjan, J., Klijn, E.-H. (2014) 'What can governance network theory learn from complexity theory?' in R. Keast, M. Mandell, R. Agranoff (eds), *Network Theory in the Public Sector. Building New Theoretical Frameworks*, New York: Routledge, 157–173.

Lappi-Seppälä, T. (2011) 'Explaining imprisonment in Europe', *European Journal of Criminology*, 8(4): 303–328.

Loader, I., Walker, N. (2007) *Civilizing Security*, Cambridge: Cambridge University Press.

Luhmann, N. (1995) *Social Systems*, Stanford, CA: Stanford University Press.

National Police Board (2014) *Statistics*, Finland.

National Police Directorate (2010) *The Police in Norway*.

Peterson, A. (2010) 'From Great Britain to Sweden – The import of reassurance policing. Local police offices in metropolitan Stockholm', *Journal of Scandinavian Studies in Criminology and Crime Prevention*, 11, 25–45.

Pycroft, A. (2014) 'Complexity theory: An overview', in A. Pycroft, C. Bartollas (eds), *Applying Complexity Theory. Whole Systems Approaches to Criminal Justice and Social Work*, Bristol: Policy Press, 15–38.

Terpstra, J., Fyfe, N.R. (2013) 'Introduction: A transformative moment in policing', in N. Fyfe, J. Terpstra, P. Tops (eds), *Centralizing Forces? Comparative Perspectives on Contemporary Police Reform in Northern and Western Europe*, The Hague: Eleven, 1–22.

Virta, S. (2002) 'Local security management: Policing through networks', *Policing: An International Journal of Police Strategies and Management*, 25(1): 190–200.

Virta, S. (2008) *Policing Meets New Challenges. Preventing Radicalization and Recruitment*, Tampere: University of Tampere, CEPOL and Police College publication. www.cepol.europa.eu/E-Library.

Virta, S. (2011) 'Re/building the European Union: Governing through counter-terrorism', in V. Bajc, W. de Lint (eds), *Security and Everyday Life*, New York: Routledge Advances in Criminology, 185–211.

Virta, S. (2013a). 'Governing urban security in Finland: Towards the "European model"', *European Journal of Criminology*, 10(3): 341–353.

Virta, S. (2013b). 'Finland', in M. Nalla, G. Newman (eds), *Community Policing in Indigenous Communities*, Boca Raton, FL: CRC Press, Taylor & Francis Group, 247–255.

Virta, S., Branders, M. (2016) 'Legitimate security? Understanding the contingencies of security and deliberation', *British Journal of Criminology*. doi:10.1093/bjc/azw024

Wennström, B. (2013) 'Police reform in Sweden: How to make a perfect cup of espresso', in N. Fyfe, J. Terpstra, P. Tops (eds), *Centralizing Forces? Comparative Perspectives on Contemporary Police Reform in Northern and Western Europe*, The Hague: Eleven, 157–172.

Other references

Helsingin kaupungin strategiaohjelma 2013–2016 (The Strategy of the City of Helsinki). www.hel.fi

Helsingin kaupungin turvallisuussuunnitelma 2016 (The Safety and Security Plan of the City of Helsinki).

HS 03.12.2015; 05.01.2016; 17.01.2016 (*Helsingin sanomat*, the biggest newspaper in Finland).

Internal Security Programme 2004, 2008 and 2010. Ministry of the Interior, Finland.

Linjauksia lähipoliisimallista. Helsinki: Ministry of the Interior Publications, 1999.

Nordiska Samarbetet i Samhällssäkerhet. Oslo: Pohjola-Norden Publications, 2014.

Security Strategy for Society. Government Resolution 16.12.2010.

Strategic Police Plan. The Police of Finland. 2015. www.poliisi.fi

The *Action Plan* of the Ministry of the Interior (incl. the police) of Finland, 20.01.2016.

The performance contract between the HPD and the NPB, 2016 (not public).

Tilastokeskus (the centre for statistics), 2015. www.stat.fi

Chapter 6

Slovenia

Metropolitan policing in post-socialist countries: The case of Slovenia

Maja Modic, Branko Lobnikar, Bernarda Tominc, Andrej Sotlar and Gorazd Meško

Since the fall of the Berlin Wall, policing in Central and Eastern Europe has gone through profound changes, as has the development of formal social control institutions in cities in these countries. First, the *pluralisation* of social control institutions, which encompasses different state police organisations (e.g. state police, gendarmerie, custom services, etc.), local community police organisations (e.g. municipal police or city wardens), and private security institutions, has influenced the transfer of responsibility for security provision from the state to local communities, and even to private entrepreneurs and individuals. Second, the *participation of civil society* in the preparation and implementation of security strategies and in fostering *accountability mechanisms* for police institutions has become a crucial aspect of effective security policy at the national and the local levels. As a consequence, the *public-private model of policing* has developed as a reaction against too narrow and too traditional a concept of policing in Central and Eastern Europe after World War II. The concept of plural policing in Eastern and Central Europe can be characterised in terms of the blurring of distinctions between state versus local, and public versus private actors, such that the state loses its predominant position, especially in those local (urban) areas, where security problems are most acutely experienced and reported. In this conception security problems are tackled by various policing stakeholders seeking local solutions to local problems. In Eastern and Central Europe this is taking place through processes of localisation, specifically through the decentralisation of national police forces on the one hand, and the development of city/local police organisations, subordinated to mayors or local authorities, on the other. The purpose of this chapter is to discuss these trends and particularities in post-socialist policing and to illustrate them through reference to developments in the Central European state of Slovenia.

I Introduction

In discussing changes in the structures and processes of policing in the context of the transition of police organisations in Central and Eastern Europe and specifically in Slovenia, a typical post-socialist society, we will first consider the general characteristics, trends and changes in policing. We then shift the focus of discussion from the state (national) to the local level, since the transformational processes in policing have not taken place simultaneously and independently but have often, especially in the 'new democracies', proceeded from reforms at the level of the state to the regions and then to local communities.

It is difficult to find a common definition of post-socialist countries from the area of Central and Eastern Europe; however, in the broader historical sense, it can be defined by the areas formerly covered by the German Empire or the Weimar Republic and the Habsburg monarchy and its successors, the Austrian and Austro-Hungarian Empire (Johnson, 1996). Over the last century, this geographic area has witnessed the rise and fall of nations, the succession of political regimes, as well as democracy in action and the worst manifestations of totalitarianism (Meško et al., 2014).

As noted by Caparini and Marenin (2005) police reform in post-conflict settings has received much attention recently from both academics and practitioners, while comparative studies of transformations of policing systems in countries are less common – an exception to the rule is a handbook on policing in Central and Eastern Europe (CEE) (Meško et al., 2013a). This work suggests that, at present, there is a diversity of states in this post-Soviet region, ranging from the nearly consolidated democracies of Central and Eastern Europe to various authoritarian regimes (Caparini & Marenin, 2005). Authors note that some common experiences in the structure and functioning of socialist policing continue to influence the development of post-socialist police organisations and criminal justice systems in CEE countries. Policing in the former communist systems of Central and Eastern Europe were based on the model developed in the Soviet Union and subsequently exported to client regimes. While Western European democracies underwent a process of liberalisation in their criminal justice and penal policies after World War II, including the abolition of the death penalty and the development of alternatives to imprisonment, the criminal justice systems of Central and Eastern European countries did not experience the same type of transition. Compared to the West, official crime rates in Central and Eastern European countries were very low. Since state socialist ideology held that crime was by definition a capitalist phenomenon that was supposed to disappear with the achievement of communism, a lower 'recorded' crime rate confirmed the superiority of the communist system over the capitalist system (Caparini & Marenin, 2005). With the commencement of the post-socialist transition in the 1990s, Central and Eastern European states faced a triple challenge: overcoming the communist legacy in their criminal justice systems; reforming the police to reflect principles of democratic policing, including international standards in human rights; and contending with the actuality of crime and public fear of crime. Post-communist states faced the task of building criminal justice systems that were more democratic and transparent (Caparini & Marenin, 2005). The political turbulence accompanying this post-Soviet transition had a direct impact on policing, including the development of formal social control institutions in cities, specifically processes of pluralisation, the increased participation of civil society and measures to improve the accountability of various policing stakeholders. In turn, these can be clarified and exemplified through reference to policing in the two principal cities of Slovenia, the capital Ljubljana and the second biggest city, Maribor.

2 Changes in the concept of policing in Central and Eastern Europe: localisation, privatisation and Europeanisation

Political democratisation is a precondition and 'driving force' of various reforms to policing, from decentralisation to pluralisation and privatisation in former European socialist countries, including the Eastern part of Germany post-reunification. Attitudes toward democratic changes significantly influence the legitimacy of police organisations. Therefore, it is not surprising that in many post-socialist countries police officers who participated in campaigns against democratic reforms were fired and replaced by newly socialised officers or they simply lost their ranks during the post-Soviet transition. In Poland, such processes were related mostly to members of the special militia forces (Paun, 2007), but also to other police officers. For example, Haberfeld (1997) reports that as many as half of the Polish police officers lost their jobs during the transition. After German reunification, police officers in the former German Democratic Republic were prevented from joining the united German police if there was evidence of their participation in the suppression of democratic protests or of their involvement with the secret political police, the Stasi (Jobard, 2004). Jenks (2004) also discusses the sacking of police officers in the Czech Republic. In Slovenia, this process of lustration was never officially implemented in the public police whilst employees of the former secret police were 'retired' (Meško & Klemenčič, 2007). The public police (*Milica*) played an important role in the process of Slovenian independence, which related to democratisation itself, and this is one reason why the majority of police officers kept their jobs (Meško et al., 2014). Since the 1990s, Central and Eastern European countries have followed the implementation of new policing models imported from Western liberal democracies, and premised on the protection of human rights, transparency, demilitarisation, decentralisation, community policing principles and plural policing.

Pluralisation as a worldwide trend, commencing in the West, has also become a reality in Central and Eastern European policing. Public (national) police organisations are losing their exclusive role in policing as once typical police activities are being transferred to 'new police forces' – other private, state and/or local organisations, which in some cases have not been primarily established to perform police tasks (Jones & Newburn, 2006). Closely connected to the idea of plural policing is the idea of a private-public model of policing. According to Ponsaers (2001), who identified and described various policing models, the public-private model of policing emerged as a reaction against both too narrow and too traditional a conception of policing. The public-private model is based on the observation that private and public police have gradually developed in conjunction with each other (Ponsaers, 2001). The principal concepts of this police model are fragmentation, bifurcation, redistribution of policing functions, disintegration, interaction between police, consumerism, privatisation, the more encompassing concepts of (in)security, civilian oversight and accountability (Ponsaers, 2001: 487). In the following sections the main characteristics of policing in some Central and Eastern European countries are presented.

2.1 Localisation of policing in Central and Eastern Europe

Lobnikar, Sotlar and Modic (2015) note the increasing trend of city/local police or traffic wardens established by and subordinated to mayors or local authorities, as a part of the decentralisation of police and security functions. These police organisations are located between the state police and private policing entities on the emerging continuum of plural police actors, and provide public security in local environments such as metropolises.

In Austria local police forces exist in some of the municipalities (37 out of 2,354). These are municipal police services, subordinated to the mayor, and are in charge of policing matters within their own jurisdiction. Municipal police agencies cannot be established in a municipality with a Federal Police authority; consequently, they exist mainly in small and medium-sized municipalities. However, the larger municipalities with Federal Police authorities have another possibility for local security provision – they can set up local guards, which are tasked with maintaining public order, night patrolling and traffic enforcement. In some cases, these guards are employed full-time within a municipal administration but in most cases they are employed by private security firms contracted by the municipal authorities (Wenda, 2014). Since the 1990s, this kind of outsourcing has also become a reality for the Federal Police, with the privatisation of security checks at airports and other facilities including the justice courts, embassies, car registration procedures and the regulation of traffic in road construction areas (Edelbacher & Norden, 2013).

In the Czech Republic municipalities have had the power to establish municipal police services since 1991, working in cooperation with the national police force to provide additional security in enforcing municipal regulations and dealing with minor offences and incivilities (Foltin et al., 2013).

Since 2009 municipal administrations in Serbia have had the power to establish municipal police services performing similar functions (Kešetović, 2013).

In Hungary, the national police hold the executive powers in security provision, but contemporary challenges, such as large-scale events, and a lack of staff and technical support, provide new opportunities for private security and civil initiatives. The most evident example of the latter is the Hungarian Civil Guard, a civil organisation of unarmed yet uniformed citizens, performing certain police tasks, mostly protecting neighbourhoods and patrolling in marked civil cars (Leyrer, 2013).

In Slovenia public policing organisations include the national police, municipal warden services, the financial administration, established in 2014 by merging the Customs Administration and the Tax Administration, and the judicial police. Private organisations include commercial security and private detective services. Cooperation between all the members of the plural policing family, especially between the police and private security officers as the most numerous organisations, remains the main challenge in the field of plural policing in Slovenia (Nalla et al., 2009; Sotlar & Meško, 2009). In Slovenia, police and municipal wardens perform the majority of security tasks. Here we need to emphasise a substantial difference. As Sotlar and Dvojmoč (2015) point out, certain differences arise with regard to the status of the municipal wardens/guards, compared with other policing actors, in particular the state police. When comparing salaries, it can be found that the starting salary of a municipal warden ranks two wage grades lower than the salary of a police officer with the same qualifications. In January 2013, the gross earnings of an entry-level municipal warden were around €892 and those of a police officer some €965 per month (Ministrstvo za notranje zadeve, 2013).

2.2 Privatisation of policing in Central and Eastern Europe

As noted, all post-socialist countries from CEE encountered significant challenges in transforming their policing structures. After the fall of the Berlin Wall, the CEE countries registered sharp increases in crime and public fear of crime along with the perception that the state police were unable to adequately assure personal safety and the protection of property. These factors also contributed to the widespread emergence of private policing and security firms (Caparini & Marenin, 2005). Consequently privatisation is having a profound impact on policing and the provision of security, throughout the area of Central and Eastern Europe. Bayley and Shearing (2001) have argued that this broad trend heralds a fundamental transformation in the governance of security, involving the separation of those who authorise policing from those who actually perform policing. In other words, state or local governments no longer exclusively carry out policing (Caparini & Marenin, 2005).

This process of privatisation is more evident in some countries than in the others. A quick look into the ratio between (public) police officers and private security officers gives us some insight into this trend. For example, private security officers in the Czech Republic and Serbia outnumber police officers, while the number of private security officers in Poland and Hungary is as much as twice and three times (respectively) higher than the number of police officers (COESS, 2011). In post-conflict societies (Croatia, Serbia, Bosnia and Herzegovina, Former Yugoslav Republic of Macedonia) private security organisations are an important factor, as they ensure security and also offer employment opportunities for demobilised soldiers and police officers (Sotlar, 2009).

Despite increasing research into the pluralisation and privatisation of policing, less attention has been devoted to how 'new' policing bodies can be held accountable in the public interest. Lessons from the considerable research into the trust and legitimacy of the (public) police (McConville & Shepherd, 1992; Sunshine & Tyler, 2003; Tyler, 2011), which clearly demonstrates that the police depend on adequate public support in order to function successfully, suggest that issues of trust and legitimacy in plural policing are likely to become an increasing focus of concern (Lobnikar et al., 2015).

2.3 Europeanisation

The other major trend in the post-socialist transition is the Europeanisation of policing in Central and Eastern Europe, culminating in the accession of CEE states to the European Union (EU) in 2004 and 2007. This has expedited the shift toward civil, non-military features of policing and acted as a pressure for greater convergence in policing amongst CEE countries. Europeanisation is most evident in the close cooperation between national police organisations and in adhering to increasingly uniform police standards and procedures. Europeanisation is also facilitated by the impact of EU policing organisations such as Europol (European Police Office), Frontex (European Agency for the Management of Operational Co-operation at the External Borders of the Member States of the European Union), CEPOL (European Police College), AEPC (Association of European Police Colleges), and MEPA (Mitteleuropäische Polizeiakademie) (Meško & Furman, 2014; Meško et al., 2014).

These three major trends, of pluralisation, localisation and Europeanisation, clarify the different pressures driving metropolitan policing in post-socialist societies. It is primarily in metropolitan policing that these different tendencies have to be accommodated, in particular the simultaneous commitment of effort and resources to more intense international cooperation, to local, community-oriented policing, and to the governance of an increasing plurality of public and private actors (Meško et al., 2014). Understanding how these different tendencies are accommodated in specific localities helps to differentiate and explain processes of convergence and diversity in metropolitan policing across CEE countries. In the remainder of the chapter, this accommodation is illustrated through reference to metropolitan policing in the particular context of Slovenia, a strategically significant Central European state located at the intersection of the Balkans and Western Europe.

3 The impact of transformations in Central and Eastern Europe on local policing: the case of Slovenia

3.1 Slovenian policing

Slovenia is a Central European country covering 20,237 square kilometres (km^2), and bordering Italy to the west, Austria to the north, Hungary to the east and Croatia to the south. After World War II, Slovenia joined the Socialist Federal Republic of Yugoslavia where it remained until 25 June 1991 when it gained independence following the results of a plebiscite on sovereignty and independence. In the next two decades, Slovenia became a member of major global, political, security and economic organisations including the United Nations (UN), EU, North Atlantic Treaty Organization (NATO), Council of Europe (COE), Organization for Security and Co-operation in Europe (OSCE), and Organisation for Economic Co-operation and Development (OECD) (Statistical Office of the Republic of Slovenia, 2011; Government of the Republic of Slovenia, 2012).

The beginnings of the Slovenian police date back to the period of the Austro-Hungarian Empire, when the Gendarmerie Corps was founded in 1849. After World War I and the disintegration of the Austro-Hungarian Empire, Slovenia, along with its existing gendarmerie, became part of the newly established Kingdom of Serbs, Croats and Slovenians. Between 1945 and 1991, the Slovenian police formed part of the Yugoslav police force called the 'Milica' (militia).

After Slovenia gained independence in 1991, the old practices of social control were abandoned, the militia was transformed into the police, and reforms designed to bring the Slovenian police closer to Western policing ideals were introduced. The Slovenian police service employed 8,808 personnel: 5,911 uniformed police officers, 1,720 non-uniformed police officers, and 1,177 remaining police personnel (without police powers), or one police officer for every 267 inhabitants (Ministry of the Interior & Police, 2014). Slovenia belongs to the group of countries with 400–499 police officers per 100,000 inhabitants.

According to the Police Organisation and Work Act (Zakon o organiziranosti in delu v policiji, 2013), the Slovenian police service is a body within the Ministry of the Interior and performs its tasks on three levels – national (General Police Directorate), regional (eight police directorates), and local (police stations) – with its headquarters located in Ljubljana. Police stations are headed by commanders and classified according to the tasks they perform: police stations, traffic police stations, border police stations, maritime police stations, airport police stations, mounted police stations, service dog handler stations, and police stations for compensatory measures (Ministry of the Interior, Police, 2015g). The area of each police station is divided into police districts, which comprise the jurisdiction of one or more municipalities, or only a part of the municipality. Police districts are intended to implement the social role of the police and are headed by community policing officers who are responsible for preventive tasks within local communities and for implementing the social role of the police (Kolenc, 2003; Ministry of the Interior, Police, 2015g).

In Slovenia, according to the research conducted by Meško, Sotlar, Lobnikar, Jere and Tominc (2012), citizens are mostly concerned about traffic safety, natural and other disasters, and their quality of life, particularly their economic opportunities. In the prevention of crime and disasters the police are an integral and permanent actor. The police serve as an initiator, as a partner and as a supporter in more than 100 preventive activities that have taken place or are still ongoing. In their efforts to improve community policing, community policing officers cooperate mostly with local communities, educational institutions and social services. The police are also part of preventive activities initiated by other public administrative agencies including the ministry responsible for transport and the ministry responsible for social affairs, and by local administrations at the behest of mayors, local security councils, by schools and non-governmental organisations (NGOs).

3.2 Policing in Slovenian local communities

State policing in Slovenia is centralised with one national, state-funded police force, operating at national, regional and local levels. The local authorities have no power to conduct any oversight in the operation of the state police or to influence the appointment of their local-level commanders. Generally, local authorities have a negligible influence on the work of the police (Meško et al., 2013b). However, the Local Self-Government Act (Zakon o lokalni samoupravi, 2007) provides municipal mayors with the power to establish formal police-local community partnerships for dealing with problems in their cities or municipalities. Police officers, municipal wardens, representatives of schools, social services, private security companies, associations, non-governmental agencies and private security companies are members of these local safety councils. These consultative bodies are considered a part of the strategy of community policing and were introduced to enable an organised way of setting priorities for crime prevention and safety at the local level (Meško & Lobnikar, 2005; Meško et al., 2006; Ministry of the Interior, Police, 2013a). Therefore, by cooperating with the police within local safety councils, local authorities can influence police work to some extent, particularly in the analysis of the local security situation, the development of safety strategies and the organisation of round tables and public forums (Kolenc, 2003). As a prelude to discussing the conduct of these councils in the two main cities of Slovenia, it is helpful to understand the context of policing in Ljubljana and Maribor.

The capital city of Slovenia, Ljubljana, is populated by 286,307[1] inhabitants (SI-STAT, 2015) and covers an area of 274.99 square kilometres (City of Ljubljana, 2014). Ljubljana Police Directorate recorded 45,912[2] criminal offences in 2013, of which more than two thirds are recorded in the capital city Ljubljana (Ministry of the Interior, Police, 2014a). In Ljubljana[3] five police stations along with the traffic police station, mounted police station and service dog handler station are responsible for the safety of the city and its residents. In these units there are 197 police officers per 100,000 inhabitants (Ministry of the Interior, Police, 2015a) covering the area of 274.99 km^2, which is divided into 49 police districts, these being the basic geographic areas where community policing officers perform their duties (Ministry of the Interior, Police, 2015e). Local safety councils are organised at the level of the city (Ljubljana Council for citizens' safety and the Municipal Council for road safety) and at the level of residential quarters (19 safety councils) (Ministry of the Interior, Police, 2015c; Municipality of Ljubljana, 2015).

Maribor is the second largest Slovenian city and a sort of informal centre of the eastern part of the country. It is a university town and the seat of the Municipality of Maribor, which extends over 147.5 km^2. In November 2012, there were just under 108,000 inhabitants, which means that the density of people was 730 inhabitants per km^2 (Municipality of Maribor, 2013). On a daily basis approximately 29,000 workers commute to Maribor from the surrounding communities and suburban settlements (TRAMOB – izdelava načrta trajnostne mobilnosti v mestu in okolici, 2013). Additionally, 24,350 students commute to Maribor on a daily basis (Gabrovec & Bole, 2009). In Maribor[4] the police tasks are performed by police officers working in two police stations, the traffic police station and the mounted police and service dog handler station (Ministry of the Interior, Police, 2015b). These units cover an area of 147.5 km^2 (Municipality of Maribor, 2013) and employ 203 police officers per 100,000 inhabitants. Their territory is divided into 18 police districts (Ministry of the Interior, Police, 2015f). There is one city safety council (Municipality of Maribor safety council) and 18 safety councils organised on the level of residential quarters (Municipality of Maribor, 2015; Ministry of the Interior, Police, 2015d).

Residents of the municipality elect the mayor through direct elections. The mayor represents and acts on behalf of the municipality. The mayor also represents the municipal committee and convenes and chairs the sessions of the municipal council, but does not have the right to vote. The mayor proposes the municipal budget and the final account of the budget, as well as decrees and other acts within the competence of the municipal council, and is responsible for the implementation of decisions passed by the municipal council (Zakon o lokalni samoupravi, 2007).

In order to satisfy the needs of inhabitants in accordance with the Local Self-government Act (Zakon o lokalni samoupravi, 2007), a municipality performs the following duties and functions of relevance for the safety and quality of life of its citizens:

- regulate, manage and provide a framework for local public services within its jurisdiction;
- promote the services of social welfare for pre-school institutions, for the basic welfare of children and the family, and for socially threatened, disabled and elderly people;
- provide for protection of the air, soil and water sources, for protection against noise and for collection and disposal of waste, and to perform other activities related to protection of the environment;
- regulate and maintain water supply and power supply facilities;
- construct, maintain and regulate local public roads, public ways, recreational and other public areas;
- regulate traffic in the municipality and perform tasks of municipal public order;
- exercise the supervision of local events;
- organise municipal services and local police, and ensure order in the municipality;
- provide for fire safety and organise rescue services;
- determine offences and fines for offences violating municipal regulations and inspect and supervise the implementation of municipal regulations and other acts.

In Table 6.1 the numbers of reported crimes in the period 2010–14 in Ljubljana, Maribor and the whole country are presented. One can see that the majority of crimes (more than 40% of all crimes) reported in Slovenia, are committed either in Ljubljana or in Maribor.

A municipal warden service has been established in both cities. The main legal basis for their operation is an Act on Local Police[5] (Zakon o občinskem redarstvu, 2006), which defines the control of misdemeanours as the primary function of the municipal warden service including the power to issue fines to offenders. However, they are obliged to notify the police when they find an offence for which the perpetrator is prosecuted. They cooperate with the police in other ways as well, mostly in preventive activities and in mixed patrols (Sotlar & Dvojmoč, 2015; Zakon o občinskem redarstvu, 2006).

According to Article 30 of the Act on Local Police (Zakon o občinskem redarstvu, 2006), jurisdiction over the work of municipal wardens is held by the Ministry of the Interior; moreover, other ministries hold jurisdiction in

Table 6.1 Number of reported crimes in the period 2010–14 in Ljubljana and Maribor compared to Slovenia

Number of reported crimes	2010		2011		2012		2013		2014	
Ljubljana	30,775	34.39%	32,336	36.45%	31,450	34.40%	32,096	34.21%	30,408	34.76%
Maribor	6,129	6.85%	6,052	6.82%	6,403	7.00%	6,268	6.68%	5,907	6.75%
Slovenia – all	89,489	100%	88,722	100%	91,430	100%	93,833	100%	84,474	100%

Source: Ministry of the Interior, Police, 2011a, 2011b, 2012a, 2012b, 2013b, 2014a, 2014b, 2015a, 2015b.

accordance with their respective working areas. The specific tasks of municipal wardens can be defined in more detail by executive acts or municipal decrees. Each municipality is obliged to prepare and enact a municipal safety plan, which defines the role of the municipal warden service in accordance with specific municipal needs and requirements. The Act on Local Police defines their following tasks as: ensuring safe and unobstructed road traffic in residential areas; ensuring road and environmental safety; providing safety on public paths, recreational and other public spaces; protecting public assets, natural and cultural heritage; maintaining public order and peace; managing the prosecution process in line with legislation; and keeping records regarding formal measures.

The Ljubljana municipal warden service is primarily tasked with all the general tasks the law defines. Their tasks are also defined in the *Strategy of community-oriented work of Ljubljana municipal wardens* (City Council of the Municipality of Ljubljana, 2011), adopted by the City Council in 2011. In this strategy it is noted that despite a primarily repressive role, the warden service also performs preventative tasks. Ensuring children's safety in traffic, managing traffic during special events, presentations of their work and cooperation with schools (offering lectures on traffic safety) are some of the activities the authors of the *Strategy* mention along with the intention to implement more preventive activities in the future. Another area defined by the *Strategy* is building a partnership with other local- and national-level bodies and residents. Within this idea, they especially emphasise cooperation with the Ljubljana Police Directorate, focusing on everyday cooperation with community policing officers. In 2014, the municipal warden service employed 53 people who carried out 101,032 various measures within the scope of their work. According to their annual report, the most frequent measures relate to email communications with residents, which enables a quicker response to public questions (Ljubljana municipal warden service, 2015).

The Maribor municipal warden service performs all general tasks provided by the law. It functions as an inter-municipal warden service, jointly established by 18 municipalities with Maribor municipality being the focus of its activities and measures. According to the annual report for 2014 (Maribor municipal warden service, 2015), it is evident that the majority of measures relate to policing traffic, including the protection of the most vulnerable groups in traffic – children, pedestrians and disabled persons. In 2014 Maribor municipal warden service employed 18 people who addressed 27,176 misdemeanours (Maribor municipal warden service, 2015).

When it comes to private commercial security agencies in Slovenia, one cannot differentiate between the national level and the level of metrópolises. There are eight forms of private security in Slovenia and all are represented in Ljubljana and Maribor. Private security firms may apply for one or more licences for the following forms of private security: the protection of people and property; protection of persons; transportation and protection of currency and other valuables; security at public gatherings; security at events in catering establishments; the operation of security control centres; design of technical security systems; and implementation of technical security systems. In 2015, there were 149 registered private security firms, of which only a few of the biggest possessed all eight licences (Ministry of the Interior, 2015). Private security firms employ around 6,400 security guards. The biggest private security in Slovenia is Sintal d.d. from Ljubljana, followed by Varnost Maribor d.d. from Maribor. It is estimated that between 2,500 and 2,700 private security guards operate in the area of Ljubljana,[6] and around 1,200 in Maribor.[7] Also, according to the same estimation, up to 55% of all private security business in Slovenia is carried out in Ljubljana, while the share in Maribor represents around 20%.

Activities of private security firms are mainly regulated by the Private Security Act (Zakon o zasebnem varovanju, 2011), but also the Public Gathering Act (Zakon o javnih zbiranjih, 2011). Metropolises usually contract private security firms for the protection of their institutions (e.g. City Hall, administrative bodies of the city, companies and institutes owned by the city such as schools, nurseries, cultural buildings, etc.) and public events. More important clients for private security firms are numerous economic entities, such as shopping malls and supermarkets. One can assume that this has at least an indirect impact on security in both cities. The functions and obligations of private security firms must be within legislation that regulates private security and is specified in a contract. Private security personnel can use only entitlements/measures defined by the Private Security Act. Security officers are obliged by the same law to immediately notify the nearest police station, or file charges with the public prosecutor's office, when they discover a criminal offence is being planned, is in the process of being executed or, subsequently, that an offence has been committed, for which an offender is prosecuted. Private security firms are mainly supervised by the Inspectorate for Interior Affairs and the Police (both are bodies within the Ministry of the Interior). To a certain extent, they are also supervised by other inspectorates and by the clients who hire their services. There are several contacts between private security officers and local police officers cooperating on operational matters. Private security firms inform local police units about the criminal offences that come to their attention and hand over the offenders they apprehend to the police. There is also close cooperation between private security and police in the organisation of public, especially sporting, events and securing public spaces in which they also cooperate with the municipal warden services. It is expected that the above-mentioned forms of cooperation will be further strengthened as a consequence of the Protocol on Mutual Cooperation between the Chamber for the Development of Slovenian Private Security and the General Police Directorate (Protokol o medsebojnem sodelovanju med Zbornico za razvoj slovenskega zasebnega varovanja in Generalno policijsko upravo, 2013). Generally speaking, private security firms are mostly hired in order to perform primary and secondary (situational) crime prevention (Meško, 2002), and are responsive to the needs and demands of their clients rather than to citizens or society as a whole.

4 The challenges of local policing in Slovenia

This analysis of policing in post-socialist countries suggests that there are some common trends. However, we agree with Ponsaers, Edwards, Recasens i Brunet and Verhage (2014) that policing is context-specific and needs to be understood in terms of the effect of particular historical circumstances and political choices.

As regards the legislative difference between policing in Ljubljana and Maribor, the fact is that in Slovenia the area of providing security is under state patronage. The same legislative regulation for all institutions of plural policing is a major driver of convergence in policing policy agendas in both cities. From the criminal justice point of view according to the Criminal Procedure Act (Zakon o kazenskem postopku, 2014), all security stakeholders (including NGOs and citizens) can report a crime or make a complaint to the public prosecutor, but it is also possible to make the complaint to the police or the courts. The police and courts are obliged to accept the complaint and report it to the public prosecutor. The same also goes for misdemeanours. Therefore the first conclusion is that few differences can be discerned in the powers and duties of policing in these cities given that the regulation of policing is very centralised in Slovenia. The second conclusion is that the majority of security tasks are performed by the national police and municipal wardens who are subject to this centralised state direction.

However, new forms of security provision have emerged throughout the region and private security companies have become major suppliers of services previously provided by the state. As it was noted, in Bulgaria, another post-socialist country, and in Austria, an older democracy, local governments are empowering private security companies to perform policing tasks for city authorities. This proliferation of private security companies and their ambiguous links with public police organisations requires further study, particularly in relation to any implications for the governance of security and how this might vary between localities.

All analysed policing institutions possess powers, which in certain ways and to various extents exceed the powers of civilian residents. Therefore, oversight and control of these institutions is essential for the protection of legality and ensuring the legitimacy of their conduct. In Slovenia, civilian oversight of complaints of ill treatment by the police was introduced by the Police Act 1998 (Zakon o policiji, 1998) and reinforced by legislation in 2013. Following the ruling of the European Court of Human Rights in the cases of *Rehbock v. Slovenia* (in 2000) and *Matko v. Slovenia* (in 2006), a Department for the Prosecution of Officials was established in the Office of the State Prosecutor General in 2007. Civilian oversight of policing was further enhanced through the complaints procedures outlined in the Organisation and Work of the Police Act (Zakon o organiziranosti in delu v policiji, 2013). The Ministry of the Interior is responsible for the overall monitoring and supervision of the resolution of complaints, and the police are responsible for considering complaints in reconciliation procedures and for certain other tasks in the complaint procedure (Lobnikar et al., 2014). The control over municipal warden services is more or less in the hands of state ministries rather than municipal authorities. The Local Police Act (Zakon o občinskem redarstvu, 2006) does not allow municipalities to have full autonomy with regard to the functioning of municipal warden services. Article 30 thus specifies the jurisdiction of the Ministry of the Interior to implement the Act while other ministries have jurisdiction in accordance with their working areas.

The limited formal authority that municipalities have to set local policing agendas is also emphasised in the regulation of the warden services employed by these municipalities. Thus, the Ministry of the Interior is responsible for supervising the legality of the work of municipal authorities, municipal administrations and municipal warden services (Sotlar & Dvojmoč, 2015). Although mayors have responsibility for resolving any complaints about warden services, the appointment of heads of municipal warden services is not bound to the mandate of the mayor. Rather, this is an official appointment for five years such that heads of warden services remain in position, even if senior policy makers in City Hall, including the mayor, are replaced. However, notwithstanding these constitutional-legal relationships, it would be naive to underestimate the informal role and political power of mayors in shaping policing in their municipalities. The position of the mayor in any city is especially controversial if they find themselves involved in criminal proceedings. Such proceedings clarify the conflictual relationship between the state police investigating a mayor who is, in turn, responsible for the operational performance of municipal warden services. The intensive cooperation between the police and warden services is jeopardised in these circumstances where it is highly unlikely to find the much-needed synergy between the two institutions (Sotlar & Dvojmoč, 2015). In turn, the control of private security agencies is defined in the Private Security Act (Zakon o zasebnem varovanju, 2011). If one feels their rights or freedoms have been violated by the actions of a security guard, they can file a complaint with the licensee who was the security guard's employer at the time of the act. The licensee's duty is to consider the complaint and, within 30 days, notify the complainant whether the complaint is well founded. In case the security guard's action has elements of a criminal offence or misdemeanour, the licensee is obliged to notify the police (Zakon o zasebnem varovanju, 2011).

One of the main challenges both in Maribor and Ljubljana arises from the notion of the function of the local police. Mayors do not have a direct impact on the functioning of the state police; however, they are able to influence the operational work of municipal warden services and, in some instances, can use this influence for their own instrumental advantage, for example in maintaining order in the local environment through imposing penalties, without seeking public consent. Such an approach can lead to public mistrust toward the work of the municipal warden service. An instance of this in the municipality of Maribor was the serious revolt of the population against the warden service after speed cameras were installed on the streets of their city[8] (Mekina, 2012). By contrast, however, the municipal authority in Ljubljana has adopted a less instrumental use of the wardens, seeking the consent of local residents by introducing the concept of a community-oriented warden service (City Council of the Municipality of Ljubljana, 2011). Even so, the lack of respectability and acceptance of municipal wardens amongst the public is common for both cities, at least in comparison with public attitudes toward the state police. It is this politicised role of the wardens, along with the increasingly significant but under-regulated role of the private security sector in policing cities, which emphasises the growing significance of metropolitan policing within the post-socialist countries of CEE.

Notes

1 Data as of 2014 (SI-STAT, 2015).
2 This represents approximately 47% of the country's recorded crimes (93,833 in 2013) (Ministry of the Interior, Police, 2014b).
3 Altogether 22 police units operate within Ljubljana police directorate, but we focus only on those units that operate within the area of the municipality of Ljubljana. These units employ 550 police officers (Ministry of the Interior, Police, 2015h).
4 Altogether 17 police units operate within Maribor police directorate, but we focus only on those units that operate within the area of the municipality of Maribor. These units employ 219 police officers (Ministry of the Interior, Police, 2015b).
5 This is an official translation into English, but it is misleading, as in Slovenia there is no policing body that could be referred to as the local police. The literal translation for the title of this act is simply 'Act on municipal warden service'.
6 This would give a ratio of between 871 and 940 private security officers per 100,000 inhabitants.
7 This would give a ratio of 1,111 private security officers per 100,000 inhabitants.
8 In December 2012 thousands of demonstrators went out onto the streets and protested against the mayor at that time. The main reason was his idea to install fixed speed cameras, which recorded 70,000 offences in just a few days. The concession for operating the speed cameras was given to a private company, which was supposed to receive approximately 93% of all fines and in return would renew the city's traffic-light system. Most of the 30 cameras were set on fire by the demonstrators (Mekina, 2012). Later on, the newly elected mayor suspended the decision to introduce speed limit cameras in the city of Maribor.

Bibliography

Bayley, D.H., Shearing, C.D. (2001) *The New Structure of Policing: Description, Conceptualization and Research Agenda*, Washington, DC: National Institute of Justice.

Caparini, M., Marenin, O. (2005) 'Crime, insecurity and police reform in post-socialist CEE', *The Journal of Power Institutions in Post-Soviet Societies* [online], 2. Retrieved from http://pipss.revues.org/330.

City Council of the Municipality of Ljubljana [Mestni svet Mestne občine Ljubljana] (2011) *Strategija v skupnost usmerjenega dela mestnega redarstva Mestne občine Ljubljana* [Strategy of community-oriented work of Ljubljana municipal wardens].

City of Ljubljana (2014) *Statistical Yearbook Ljubljana 2013*. Retrieved from www.ljubljana.si/file/1541944/statistical-yearbook-2013eng.pdf.

COESS (2011) *Private Security Services in Europe: Facts & Figures 2011*. Retrieved from www.coess.eu/_Uploads/dbsAttachedFiles/Private_Security_Services_in_Europe-CoESS_Facts_and_Figures_2011%281%29.pdf.

Edelbacher, M., Norden, G. (2013) 'Policing in Austria: Development over the past twenty years, present state and future challenges', in G. Meško, C.B. Fields, B. Lobnikar, A. Sotlar (eds), *Handbook on Policing in Central and Eastern Europe*, New York: Springer, 15–31.

Foltin, P., Rohál, A., Šikolová, M. (2013) 'Policing in the Czech Republic: Evolution and trends', in G. Meško, C.B. Fields, B. Lobnikar, A. Sotlar (eds), *Handbook on Policing in Central and Eastern Europe*, New York: Springer, 57–81.

Gabrovec, M., Bole, D. (2009) *Dnevna mobilnost v Sloveniji* [Daily mobility in Slovenia], Ljubljana: Geografski inštitut Antona Melika ZRC SAZU. Retrieved from http://giam.zrc-sazu.si/sites/default/files/9789612541187.pdf.

Government of the Republic of Slovenia (2012) *About Slovenia*. Government Communication Office. Retrieved from www.vlada.si/en/about_slovenia/.

Haberfeld, M.R. (1997) 'Poland: "The police are not the public and the public are not the police": Transformation from militia to police', *Policing: An International Journal of Police Strategies & Management*, 20(4): 641–654.

Jenks, D. (2004) 'The Czech police: Adopting democratic principles', in M. Caparini, O. Marenin (eds), *Transforming Police in Central and Eastern Europe*, Münster: LIT Verlag, 115–127.

Jobard, F. (2004) 'The lady vanishes: The silent disappearance of the GDR police after 1989', in M. Caparini, O. Marenin (eds), *Transforming Police in Central and Eastern Europe*, Münster: LIT Verlag, 49–68.

Johnson, L.R. (1996) *Central Europe: Enemies, Neighbors, Friends*, New York: Oxford University Press.

Jones, T., Newburn, T. (2006) *Plural Policing*, London: Routledge

Kešetović, M.Ž. (2013) 'Serbian police: Troubled transition from police force to police service', in G. Meško, C.B. Fields, B. Lobnikar, A. Sotlar (eds), *Handbook on Policing in Central and Eastern Europe*, New York: Springer, 217–239.

Kolenc, T. (2003) *The Slovene Police*, Ljubljana: Ministry of the Interior of the Republic Slovenia, Police, General Police Directorate.

Leyrer, R. (2013) 'Finding the right path of policing in Hungary', in G. Meško, C.B. Fields, B. Lobnikar, A. Sotlar (eds), *Handbook on Policing in Central and Eastern Europe*, New York: Springer, 115–129.

Ljubljana municipal warden service (2015) *Poročilo o delu mestnega redarstva Mestne občine Ljubljana v letu 2014* [Annual report on the work of the Ljubljana municipal warden service 2014], Ljubljana: The Municipality of Ljubljana. Retrieved from www.ljubljana.si/file/1618172/letno-poroilo-2014.pdf.

Lobnikar, B., Sotlar, A., Modic, M. (2015) 'Do we trust them? Public opinion on police work in plural policing environments in Central and Eastern Europe', in G. Meško, J. Tankebe (eds), *Trust and Legitimacy in Criminal Justice: European Perspectives*, Cham: Springer, 189–203.

Lobnikar, B., Šumi, R., Meško, G. (2014) 'Police integrity surveys and implementation of findings within the Slovenian police', in J.L. Hovens (ed.), *Building Police Integrity: A Post-conflict Perspective*, The Hague: Royal Netherlands Marechaussee, 249–271.

Maribor municipal warden service [Medobčinski inšpektorat in redarstvo Maribor] (2015) *Poročilo o delu Medobčinskega inšpektorata in redarstva Maribor za leto 2014* [Annual report on the work of Maribor municipal warden service 2014]. Retrieved from www.lex-localis.info/files/1876602f-4f89-40f1-aaad-2e5bb98e25c5/63571449309 2051579_7.tocka.pdf.

McConville, M., Shepherd, D. (1992) *Watching Police, Watching Communities*, London: Routledge.

Mekina, B. (2012) 'The placid people's revolt', Voxeurop.eu, 14 December. Retrieved from www.voxeurop.eu/en/content/article/3163301-placid-people-s-revolt.

Meško, G. (2002) *Osnove preprečevanja kriminalitete* [Basics of crime prevention], Ljubljana: Visoka policijsko-varnostna šola.

Meško, G., Fields, C.B., Lobnikar, B., Sotlar, A. (2013a). *Handbook on Policing in Central and Eastern Europe*, New York: Springer.

Meško, G., Furman, R. (2014) 'Police and prosecutorial cooperation in responding to transnational crime', in P. Reichel, J. Albanese (eds), *Handbook of Transnational Crime and Justice*, Los Angeles, CA: Sage, 323–352.

Meško, G., Klemenčič, G. (2007) 'Rebuilding legitimacy and police professionalism in an emerging democracy: The Slovenian experience', in T.R. Tyler (ed.), *Legitimacy and Criminal Justice*, New York: Russell Sage Foundation, 84–115.

Meško, G., Lobnikar, B. (2005) 'Policijsko delo v skupnosti: razumevanje uvoženih idej, njihova kontekstualizacija in implementacija', in V.G. Meško, M. Pagon, B. Dobovšek (eds), *Izzivi sodobnega varstvoslovja*, Ljubljana: Fakulteta za policijsko-varnostne vede, 89–109.

Meško, G., Lobnikar, B., Jere, M., Sotlar, A. (2013b). 'Recent developments of policing in Slovenia', in G. Meško, C.B. Fields, B. Lobnikar, A. Sotlar (eds), *Handbook on Policing in Central and Eastern Europe*, New York: Springer, 263–286.

Meško, G., Nalla, M., Sotlar, A. (2006) 'Cooperation on police private security officers in crime prevention in Slovenia', in V.E. Marks, A. Meyer, R. Linssen (eds), *Quality in Crime Prevention*, Norderstedt: Books on Demand, 133–143.

Meško, G., Sotlar, A., Lobnikar, B. (2014) 'Policing in Central and Eastern Europe: Past, present and future prospects', in M.D. Reisig, R.J. Kane (eds), *The Oxford Handbook of Police and Policing*, Oxford: Oxford University Press, 606–623.

Meško, G., Sotlar, A., Lobnikar, B., Jere, M., Tominc, B. (2012) *Občutek ogroženosti in vloga policije pri zagotavljanju varnosti na lokalni ravni* [Feelings of insecurity and the role of police in local safety provision], CRP(V5-1038 A): poročilo ciljnega raziskovalnega projekta. Ljubljana: Fakulteta za varnostne vede.

Ministry of the Interior [Ministrstvo za notranje zadeve] (2013) *Vrednost plačnih razredov* [The value of the wage classes]. Retrieved from www.mnz.gov.si/fileadmin/m nz.gov.si/pageuploads/SOJ/2013/130718_preglednica_vrednost_placnih_razredov.pdf.

Ministry of the Interior (2015) *Seznam imetnikov licenc na dan 5.3.2015* [The list of licence holders as of 5 March 2015]. Retrieved from www.mnz.gov.si/si/mnz_za_va s/zasebno_varovanje_detektivi/zasebno_varovanje/evidence_vloge_in_obrazci/.

Ministry of the Interior, Police [Ministrstvo za notranje zadeve, Policija] (2011a). *Poročilo o delu Policijske uprave Ljubljana za leto 2010* [Report on the work of the Police Directorate of Ljubljana for 2010]. Retrieved from http://policija.si/images/ stories/PULJ/PDF/Statistika/LetnoPorocilo2010.pdf.

Ministry of the Interior, Police [Ministrstvo za notranje zadeve, Policija] (2011b). *Poročilo o delu Policijske uprave Maribor za leto 2010* [Report on the work of the Police Directorate of Maribor for the year 2010]. Retrieved from http://policija.si/ images/stories/PUMB/PDF/statistika/LetnoPorocilo2010.pdf.

Ministry of the Interior, Police [Ministrstvo za notranje zadeve, Policija] (2012a). *Poročilo o delu Policijske uprave Ljubljana za leto 2011* [Report on the work of the Police Directorate of Ljubljana for the year 2011]. Retrieved from http://policija.si/ images/stories/PULJ/PDF/Statistika/LetnoPorocilo2011.pdf.

Ministry of the Interior, Police [Ministrstvo za notranje zadeve, Policija] (2012b). *Poročilo o delu Policijske uprave Maribor za leto 2011* [Report on the work of the Police Directorate of Maribor for the year 2011]. Retrieved from http://policija.si/ images/stories/PUMB/PDF/statistika/LetnoPorocilo2011.pdf.

Ministry of the Interior, Police [Ministrstvo za notranje zadeve, Policija] (2013a). *Policijsko delo v skupnosti* [Community policing], Ljubljana: Ministrstvo za notranje zadeve, Policija.

Ministry of the Interior, Police [Ministrstvo za notranje zadeve, Policija] (2013b). *Poročilo o delu Policijske uprave Ljubljana za leto 2012* [Report on the work of the Police Directorate of Ljubljana for the year 2012]. Retrieved from http://policija.si/ images/stories/PULJ/PDF/Statistika/PULJ_Letno_porocilo_2012.pdf.

Ministry of the Interior, Police [Ministrstvo za notranje zadeve, Policija] (2014) *About the Police.* Retrieved from www.policija.si/eng/index.php/aboutthepolice.

Ministry of the Interior, Police [Ministrstvo za notranje zadeve, Policija] (2014a). *Poročilo o delu Policijske uprave Ljubljana za leto 2013* [Report on the work of the Police Directorate of Ljubljana for the year 2013]. Retrieved from http://policija.si/ images/stories/PULJ/PDF/Statistika/PULJ_letnoporocilo2013.pdf.

Ministry of the Interior, Police [Ministrstvo za notranje zadeve, Policija] (2014b). *Poročilo o delu policije za 2013* [Annual report on the work of the police 2013], Ljubljana: Ministrstvo za notranje zadeve, Policija. Retrieved from www.policija.si/ images/stories/Statistika/LetnaPorocila/PDF/LetnoPorocilo2013.pdf.

Ministry of the Interior, Police [Ministrstvo za notranje zadeve, Policija] (2014c). *About the Police.* Retrieved from www.policija.si/eng/index.php/aboutthepolice (accessed January 10, 2016).

Ministry of the Interior, Police [Ministrstvo za notranje zadeve, Policija] (2015a). *Poročilo o delu Policijske uprave Ljubljana za leto 2014* [Report on the work of the Police Directorate of Ljubljana for the year 2014]. Retrieved from www.policija.si/ images/stories/PULJ/PDF/Statistika/PULJ_LetnoPorocilo2014.pdf.

Ministry of the Interior, Police [Ministrstvo za notranje zadeve, Policija] (2015b). *Poročilo o delu Policijske uprave Maribor za leto 2014* [Report on the work of the

Police Directorate of Maribor for the year 2014]. Retrieved from www.policija.si/index.php/policijske-uprave/pu-maribor/statistika.

Ministry of the Interior, Police [Ministrstvo za notranje zadeve, Policija] (2015c). *Posvetovalna telesa. Policijska uprava Ljubljana* [Consultative bodies. Ljubljana Police Directorate]. Retrieved from http://policija.si/index.php/policijske-uprave/pu-ljubljana/posvetovalna-telesa.

Ministry of the Interior, Police [Ministrstvo za notranje zadeve, Policija] (2015d). *Posvetovalna telesa. Policijska uprava Maribor* [Consultative bodies. Maribor Police Directorate]. Retrieved from http://policija.si/index.php/policijske-uprave/pu-maribor/pu-maribor.

Ministry of the Interior, Police [Ministrstvo za notranje zadeve, Policija] (2015e). *Vodje policijskih okolišev. Policijska uprava Ljubljana* [Community policing officers. Ljubljana Police Directorate]. Retrieved from http://policija.si/index.php/policijske-uprave/pu-ljubljana/vodje-policijskih-okoliev.

Ministry of the Interior, Police [Ministrstvo za notranje zadeve, Policija] (2015f). *Vodje policijskih okolišev. Policijska uprava Maribor* [Community policing officers. Maribor Police Directorate]. Retrieved from http://policija.si/index.php/policijske-uprave/pu-maribor/vodje-policijskih-okoliev.

Ministry of the Interior, Police [Ministrstvo za notranje zadeve, Policija] (2015g). *About Police Stations*. Retrieved from www.policija.si/eng/index.php/aboutthepolice/organization/69.

Ministry of the Interior, Police [Ministrstvo za notranje zadeve, Policija] (2015h). *Police Stations*. Retrieved from www.policija.si/eng/index.php/policestations#PP_LJ.

Municipality of Ljubljana (2015) *The City Council of the City of Ljubljana*. Retrieved from www.ljubljana.si/en/municipality/city-council/.

Municipality of Maribor [Občina Maribor] (2013) *Mestna občina Maribor v številkah 2012* [Municipality of Maribor in numbers 2012]. Retrieved from www.maribor.si/dokument.aspx?id=19541.

Municipality of Maribor [Občina Maribor] (2015) *Varnostni sosvet* [Safety council]. Retrieved from www.maribor.si/podrocje.aspx?id=164.

Nalla, M., Johnson, J.D., Meško, G. (2009) 'Are police and security personnel warming up to each other? A comparison of officers' attitudes in developed, emerging, and transitional economies', *Policing: An International Journal of Police Strategies & Management*, 32(3): 508–525.

Paun, C. (2007) *Democratization and Police Reform*, Berlin: Freie Univerzizät Berlin.

Ponsaers, P. (2001) 'Reading about "community (oriented) policing" and police models', *Policing: An International Journal of Police Strategies & Management*, 24(4): 470–497.

Ponsaers, P., Edwards, A., Recasens i Brunet, A., Verhage, A. (2014) 'Policing European metropolises', *European Journal of Policing Studies*, 2(1): 345–354.

Protokol o medsebojnem sodelovanju med Zbornico za razvoj slovenskega zasebnega varovanja in Generalno policijsko upravo [Protocol on Mutual Cooperation between the Chamber for Development of Slovenian Private Security and the General Police Directorate] (2013) Retrieved from www.zrszv.si/images/PROTOKOL-ZRSZV-POLICIJA.pdf.

SI-STAT (2015) *SI-Stat Data Portal*. Retrieved from http://pxweb.stat.si/pxweb/dialog/statfile1.asp.

Sotlar, A. (2009) 'Post-conflict private policing: Experiences from several former Yugoslav countries', *Policing: An International Journal of Police Strategies and Management*, 32(3): 489–507.

Sotlar, A., Dvojmoč, M. (2015) 'Municipal warden services in the pluralised policing environment in Slovenia', *Revija za kriminalistiko in kriminologijo*, 66(4): 330–341.

Sotlar, A., Meško, G. (2009) 'The relationship between the public and private security sectors in Slovenia: From coexistence towards partnership?' *Varstvoslovje*, 11(2): 269–285.

Statistical Office of the Republic of Slovenia (2011) *Statistical Portrait of Slovenia in the EU 2011*. Ljubljana: Statistical Office of the Republic of Slovenia. Retrieved from www.stat.si/eng/pub.asp.

Sunshine, J., Tyler, T. (2003) 'The role of procedural justice and legitimacy in shaping public support for policing', *Law and Society Review*, 37(3): 513–547.

TRAMOB – *izdelava načrta trajnostne mobilnosti v mestu in okolici* [TRAMOB – planning of sustainable mobility in the city and its surroundings]. (2013). Maribor: Mestna občina Maribor. Retrieved from www.maribor.si/dokument.aspx?id=21254.

Tyler, T. (2011) 'Trust and legitimacy: Policing in the USA and Europe', *European Journal of Criminology*, 8(4): 254–266.

Wenda, G. (2014) 'Municipal police in Austria: History, status quo, and future', *SIAK – Journal for Police Science and Practice*, 4: 74–86. Retrieved from http://dx.doi.org/10.7396/IE_2014_G.

Zakon o javnih zbiranjih [Public Gathering Act] (2011) *Uradni list Republike Slovenije* (64/11).

Zakon o kazenskem postopku [Criminal Procedure Act] (2014) *Uradni list Republike Slovenije* (87/14).

Zakon o lokalni samoupravi [Local Self-government Act] (2007) *Uradni list Republike Slovenije* (94/07).

Zakon o občinskem redarstvu [Act on Local Police] (2006) *Uradni list Republike Slovenije* (106/06).

Zakon o organiziranosti in delu v policiji [Act on Police Organization] (2013) *Uradni list Republike Slovenije* (15/13).

Zakon o policiji [Police Act] (1998) *Uradni list Republike Slovenije* (49/98).

Zakon o zasebnem varovanju [Private Security Act] (2011) *Uradni list Republike Slovenije* (17/11).

Part III

Divergence

Active city-regions pursuing their own policing agendas

Chapter 7.1

Italy

Urban policing in Italy: Some reflections from a comparative perspective

Rossella Selmini

1 Introduction

On 19 February 2015, hundreds of hooligans, supporters of the Rotterdam football team Feyenord, invaded the historic centre of Rome, engaged in vandalism and riots with the police, and damaged the 15th-century 'Fontana della Barcaccia' by Bernini, in Piazza di Spagna.

These events gave rise to a fight between the mayor of Rome, the prefect and the 'questore'.[1] The mayor complained publicly about the inefficiency of the state police control and their inability to protect public goods, such as old historical monuments, the right of 'tourists and unarmed citizens' to walk safely in the city, and the rights of local shop owners, who suffered from both vandalism and economic losses, since they had to shut down for many hours to avoid further damages.

The prefect and the questore replied sharply, reaffirming the correctness of their choices, reporting that they deployed 1,600 policemen in the city who prevented even more serious events, including degeneration of the vandalism into riots which would have risked injuries and deaths.

In Italy, public security and public order ('sicurezza e ordine pubblico') are constitutionally competences of the national state. However, as I explain in detail below, since the beginning of the 1990s, following a common European trend, cities and regions, responsible for a new field of local public policy defined as 'local urban security', have tried to play a role in this arena.[2] For a long time, they were quite successful. Results included a new infrastructure of local crime prevention and community safety initiatives and new forms of policing urban space. These were planned at the local level, coordinated and funded in many cases by the regional governments, with no involvement of the national state. The conflict between the mayor of Rome and the representatives of the national state marked, however, the conclusion of a turning point in a process that went on for many years and symbolically represents a sort of withdrawal by local governments from the sphere of urban security and the reestablishment of traditional roles and divisions of responsibility. This is not just a return to the old (pre-1990s) times when the national government and national police were in charge of all matters of security, at every territorial level, but a new phase. The borders are still being redesigned and conflicts – different in their content from those of past years – continue to characterise Italian institutional and political life. Several lessons from this episode can provide critical and theoretical understanding of the changing shape of Italian governance of crime at the local level and of connected changes in policing of urban life.

In this chapter I explore some conceptual issues related to changing forms of urban social control and policing with a focus on Italian cities, and in a comparative perspective. I rely upon a number of different theoretical perspectives, particularly those that focus on dynamics of state sovereignty and redistribution of powers (Garland, 1996, 2001), on how governance unfolds at the local level (Crawford, 1999; Johnston & Shearing, 2003), including recent integrations of the idea of governance offered by 'regime analysis' (Edwards & Hughes, 2012), combined with theories of urban social control and pluralisation of policing (Beckett & Herbert, 2008; Crawford, 2006; Jones & Newburn, 2006). My analysis is based on a comparative perspective, aimed at singling out how ideas, concepts, practices and policies recur in different contexts and how they are adopted – or not – in different places or times. The 'adoption process' implies also an 'adaptation', i.e. that the local context reshapes those flows according to its own specific needs and interests (Newburn & Sparks, 2004). This process of adaptation is the result of many structural and cultural factors and, starting from a convergent 'global' dynamic characterised by homogenisation, gives rise to local – sometimes quite important – divergences in the development of the new forms of governance of local security policies[3] and policing.

Although undoubtedly we are witnessing a massive process of policy transfer, particularly from the United States to European countries, and a prominent 'convergence' dynamic, local peculiarities still matter, and the policy transfer process is quite a complex one. Understanding better when and on which issues local peculiarities matter will improve, I believe, our broader knowledge of the alleged process of global homogenisation of cultures and practices of control at the local level.[4] I use the concept of 'security policies' broadly, although my focus is on those strategies, practices and measures that mostly aim to reinforce urban control and policing at the local level.[5]

2 Responsibilisation strategies 'all'italiana'

In this part of the chapter I show the importance, from a theoretical point of view, of analysis of the political and institutional contexts in which these policies developed and of issues of centralisation/decentralisation. A relevant literature has analysed in general the dynamics of decentralisation of national policies and of allocation of duties that were traditionally performed by national states to other entities (local bodies, a variety of public or private agencies, citizens, organisations, and the private market), often in the framework of a crisis of power and legitimacy of the nation-states (Castells, 1997). Garland's (1996) article, 'The limits of the sovereign state', remains an important theoretical starting point for what concerns the field of crime control. Garland's work is based on the idea that crime control strategies in the United States and Britain (and probably elsewhere, as he suggests) have been characterised in recent decades by important changes in the sovereign power of the state in crime control. Since the sovereign state was no longer able to control different fields of social life, contradictory responses were developed. On the one hand, as Garland clearly stated, the sovereign state tries to redistribute responsibility for crime control to different actors in society (a variety of agencies, private citizens, profit and non-profit organisations, etc.). On the other hand – since the political costs of this redistribution might be severe – at the same time the sovereign state tries to reaffirm its monopoly on crime control. As a result, contradictory discourses, policies and practices over crime control have been proposed at different levels and at the same time. The responsibilisation strategy represented thus a way to deal with contradictions, retaining at the same time the capacity of the state to control the process, particularly thanks to partnerships and multi-agency coordination.[6]

This process occurred in Italy as well, but with importantly different trajectories in content and time. These differences are mostly a consequence of the peculiar history of the formation of the Italian unitary state and its governmental bureaucracies, of specific features of Italian institutional and constitutional arrangements, and of state relationships with civil society and the private market. The formation of the Italian state is a complex process that started in 1861 after a process of forced reunification of distinct smaller kingdoms, with different cultural and legal traditions and a remarkable disparity in economic development.[7]

These issues, together with the fascist dictatorship that Italy experienced for more than 20 years, left many marks on the development of Italian 'sovereignty'. The central government was perceived at the same time as oppressive and distant from the citizens (as a result of the forced process of reunification and of the dictatorship legacy). The attempt to build a strong central state able to rule a fragmented country has been constantly undermined by economic and structural features, political instability, backwardness of state bureaucratic apparatuses and the never-ending disparity between the northern and central areas and the south.

What occurred in Italy, for a long period, was a self-responsibilisation of cities (mostly located in the north and the centre of the country) in the matter of urban security and policing. The development of local initiatives in this field between the mid-1990s and the second half of the 2000s was promoted by the cities, supported – in a negotiated, not coercive framework – by regional governments,[8] with few subterranean conflicts with the national government which was unable to stop these developments and also apparently not much interested in trying to control them. Cities found support – resources, technical assistance and political empowerment – in regional governments, which were, like the cities, interested in expanding their fields of competence, and at the same time, were less bureaucratic and better technically equipped for regulation of crime prevention and local policing. At the beginning of the 1990s, a new law introduced the direct election of mayors by the citizens. This resulted in an increase in mayors' political and institutional legitimacy in dealing with different aspects of urban life and its increasing complexity, above all in the largest Italian cities and metropolises. In the same period regional governments become more powerful and showed a capacity for policy innovation in a variety of their competences.[9]

Urban security and policing represented a perfect field for a struggle for more autonomy, more resources and more political visibility. Planning, coordination, funding and negotiations of priorities occurred at the regional level between regional governments and mayors. The general constitutional rules on the sovereignty powers of the national state concerning 'public security and public order' remained untouched,[10] but development of urban security policies and a new form of policing at the local level was admitted, tolerated and even ignored.

Since the municipal police were mostly in charge of the implementation of these new policies, this implied that urban policing at the local level was increasingly the province not of the national but the municipal police. We could interpret this dynamic as a different, unintentional way to implement responsibilisation strategies, based on a *laissez-faire* approach. Local governments implicitly redefined the borders of the state intervention by exercising their new powers in tackling the very local, mundane, routine petty thefts, muggings, burglaries and drug dealing. These are the phenomena included in the vague category of urban disorder that feeds feelings of insecurity in citizens. National government and national police were better equipped to deal with 'serious crime' (which in Italy is almost a synonym for Mafia-type crime and corruption) and with 'internal security', i.e. the protection of the state from external attacks (terrorism and related phenomena).

This does not mean, of course, that national police stopped having responsibility for crime at the city level, but that a new scenario of urban policing emerged. The relative autonomy of regions and cities to play their roles for more than a decade also represented an attempt to develop a new set of policies. Since they had to be different from those of the traditional criminal justice system, they were also partially based, at least in the early years, on a different rationality in which enhanced crime prevention and community policing were viewed as strategies in a policy agenda more oriented toward inclusion and social justice.

3 Centralisation and the punitive turn

At the end of the first decade of 2000 this picture changed radically. The national government stepped in and increasingly reduced local governments' powers in the field, opening a new era of national activism by the Ministry of the Interior and its apparatuses. As a consequence of this new national strategy a remarkable change occurred in the infrastructure of local security policies.[11] They are now mostly ruled by a national law (Law 15/2009 'Disposizioni in materia di sicurezza pubblica') and by related decrees of the minister of the interior that impose guiding principles for local authorities in operating crime and urban disorder programmes, and, more recently, in the organisation and duties of the municipal police.

In this new framework, the national government has clearly turned toward a 'tough' approach to crime (Mosconi, 2010), mostly based on increases in control measures, on criminalisation of behaviour, including behaviours that were once considered expression of social deprivation and marginality, and on increasing severity of national laws concerning punishment for street crime and violent behaviour. There are several steps in this new dynamic.

First, a national programme for urban safety was launched in 2009, diverting funds to local crime prevention measures based mostly on closed-circuit television (CCTV) and other situational measures in urban design.[12] Second, the national government strongly enforced 'agreements' or 'protocols' (the so-called 'patti per la sicurezza') with local governments. This is a pre-existing form of partnership for implementation of local safety plans that was never very successful and which replicated the experiences of the French 'contrats de sécurité' (Le Goff, 2004) and similar mechanisms for coordination of crime prevention and policing at the local level. In the new phase, the leading role of the local prefectures in defining priorities and measures is stressed and a national model for partnership is imposed by the minister of the interior.

Finally, partially new administrative orders and municipal by-laws, regulated by national laws or ministerial decrees, replaced – as the only tolerated practice of local governance of crime – the earlier infrastructure created jointly by cities and regional governments.

Administrative orders had long been used by mayors to control some forms of disorder and incivility, but with some important restrictions in time, space and content. A decree of the minister of the interior in 2008 eliminated these restrictions, defined extensions and limits in detail, and transformed traditional mayoral practices into semi-criminal measures.[13] These orders are now aimed at routine control – and not just on the grounds of urgency – of 'behaviours' and 'situations' related to crime or disorder.

Mayors – in their new role of government officers – can issue an administrative act 'in order to prevent and to eliminate serious dangers that are a threat for public safety and for urban safety'[14] in a variety of situations.

These include urban decline, physical and social disorder, prostitution and drug dealing, begging, alcohol abuse, illegal sale of goods, illegal occupation of public spaces, offences to 'public decency', etc. If the orders – based on administrative powers at a first step – are breached, the consequence is a (minor) criminal violation, punished with a fine. The widespread use of these orders, especially in the biggest cities, remarkably reshapes urban policing at the local level, with municipal police becoming heavily involved in zero tolerance-type strategies (Ruga Riva, 2010; Selmini, 2013).

This radical shift is the result of a full implementation of a responsibilisation strategy, in Garland's sense. The state, on the one hand, re-establishes its sovereign role in crime control, including in the 'grey' area of local security policies which was for years in the control of local authorities. Mayors – although acting as 'state officers' – are politically responsible for the operation of policies towards citizens that are no longer local, but are decided and controlled by the centre. In 2011 the Italian Constitutional Court declared that administrative orders were partly unconstitutional; however, they are still widely used by mayors, and they have often been transferred (in order to circumvent the 2011 decision) into municipal police by-laws. Together with centralisation – with some degree of responsibilisation of other actors – local policies and local policing strategies have shifted towards a more punitive and exclusionary approach.

Why did the shift occur? What is going on in Italy seems to be a different step in a centralisation–decentralisation dynamic that has been quite common in many Western countries in recent decades, at different levels, but which in Italy is characterised by a higher level of institutional fragmentation and political instability (Selmini, 2005). There are no other actors who can play a significant role, differently from contexts in which local governance is characterised by a wide range of networks and centres of interest (Johnston & Shearing, 2003; Crawford, 2006).

A second, often neglected issue in the analysis of changes in contemporary crime control policies in general is the importance of increasing reductions in public expenditure that directly affected the local governments, particularly the regions. Although the reduction of public sector budgets has been a necessity for many European governments, in Italy this reduction has affected local governments on a much higher scale. Urban policing and security policies became a luxury that local governments can no longer afford, especially since this field of policy never became an established competency of local governments and was not therefore easy to defend from cutbacks.[15] The financial crisis has, among its many detrimental effects, entirely reconfigured institutional conflicts among cities, regions and the national state, with the latter regaining all the power of its sovereignty. In a country where 'pluralisation' of policing mostly means a redistribution of responsibilities among public-funded police forces, the impact on crime control is quite important.[16]

Why, however, did mayors, after years in which they struggled to gain more powers in control of crime and disorder at the urban level, enthusiastically embrace the new regime imposed in 2008? I would speculate that this turn towards centralisation of policing and security policies is a further evidence of the fragmented institutional and political Italian contexts, in which conflicts, unstable alliances and changeable partnerships are the rule (Melossi & Selmini, 2009). There are, however, other explanations. Some studies show that the administrative orders gave mayors legitimacy in intervening at the local level that previous partnerships with the regions did not provide. Even though the administrative orders did not prove to be very successful in solving the problems they were meant to address (Selmini, 2013), the mayors nonetheless believed that they had real power in their hands (Galantino & Giovannetti, 2012).

Recently, however, some mayors, especially in the biggest cities, overwhelmed by the increasing complexity of their role, made even worse by the strictures of incredibly limited resources, have been increasingly rejecting any involvement in urban policing and have demanded state intervention. The events in Rome described in the introduction provide an example of this new phase, which coexists with the contradictory above-mentioned dynamic.

4 Governance through partnership

Another important conceptual framework, albeit related to the responsibilisation strategy, are the studies of governance (Crawford, 1999; Johnston & Shearing, 2003). This refers first to a new mentality in organising social control that implies new practices of negotiation and cooperation among different actors involved in providing security. To keep the new system of social control working and to avoid excessive fragmentation and inconsistencies, new institutions and new regulations and patterns are created under the umbrella of 'partnership coordination'. Once again, a comparative analysis that considers how the partnership model unfolds in different European contexts shows interesting features.

In Italy we can observe again both peculiarities and some similarities with what is occurring in the rest of Europe. Partnership is, first of all, extremely limited, in several ways: the number and type of actors involved, the kinds of instruments used to organise negotiations and to coordinate actors, the goals of the negotiations, and the imbalance of power among the 'contractors'. The much more complex strategy of governance – with a variety of networks, agencies, actors and instruments to foster cooperation and manage conflict – seems to be embodied only in the so-called 'patti per la sicurezza', formal, semi-contractual agreements between municipalities and prefects. This strategy of contractualisation was first adopted between the end of the 1990s and the first half of the 2000s.

These 'first generation pacts', consistent with dynamics described above, were characterised by a low, ritualistic and primarily bureaucratic involvement of national government representatives, by attempts of mayors to emphasise their role in urban security, by limited goals and by even more limited contents. Some studies showed that they represented mostly the first attempt of the national state to control the activism of local governments in the field of crime control, in order to avoid a blurring of boundaries of the power constitutionally attributed to them[17] and to re-establish state sovereignty in a symbolic way (Calaresu, 2013). Many of these agreements were never implemented, as a confirmation of the 'avoiding' strategy of the state that I mentioned before.

The turning point of 2008, however, implied also a change in the regulation of partnerships through the so called 'patti per la sicurezza'. Consistent with the new role that the central government wants now to play, these 'second generation pacts' are instruments that do not negotiate, but mostly impose a list of activities and duties for the municipalities, which also must support most of the costs (Calaresu, 2013). Competition and conflict, still evident in the first period, disappeared in the second stage. Bifurcation of tasks (with local governments mostly involved in marginal and auxiliary roles, often limited to 'social prevention') instead of integration of activities, is the rule. The role of the municipal police in urban policing has been ambiguously redesigned, in both a reactive and a proactive way. The agreements' contents reproduce the political agenda of the moment, emphasising street crime and incivilities, targeting marginal populations, mentioning social intervention and crime prevention mostly as 'decorative' elements (Sozzo, personal communication, 14 November 2014). Local communities, other non-state actors and the private sector are rarely involved: an important feature, above all in a comparative perspective, that once again shows how these dynamics remain mostly inside the border of the public sector.

Local governance of crime and urban policing, through the centralising turn of 2008, represented above all by the practices of administrative orders and security agreements, is definitively centralised. Complexity is reduced, real cooperation is absent, conflicts are controlled and other actors are absent from the official picture.

5 Police, plural policing and changes in social control in the city

In this final section, I link together conceptual perspectives from the studies of the (apparent?) crisis of the sovereign state and studies on governance with contemporary and older ideas on the changing shape of formal social control. There are, of course, many theoretical overlaps between these studies. Stanley Cohen, for instance, in developing some aspects of Foucault's work, mentions a process of erosion of the state's monopoly in the control of deviance and crime that resulted in the creation of 'wider, stronger and different nets' of control (Cohen, 1985: 38). Contemporary post-social control perspectives have refined and developed these seminal ideas, developing related concepts like 'plural policing' (Jones & Newburn, 2006), investigating the role of communities and private citizens in the 'widening the net process', and showing how the post-disciplinary forms of control reinforce the expansion of the market in regulating behaviour.

I focus here on how the concepts and practices related to the idea of pluralisation of policing have been adopted and reshaped in the Italian context, from both an external and an internal perspective. I also consider changes occurring in social control in the city.

Conspicuous features of the conflictive dynamics between central and local governments are the reconfiguration of police presence and tasks in the city, and competition between national polices forces and the municipal police. As explained elsewhere in this volume (see Devroe and Ponsaers), in Italy there are two main national police forces, the 'Polizia di stato' and the 'Carabinieri', with a general competence, plus municipal police and some smaller specialised national police corps.[18] The municipal police, with 60,000 officers, have a general competence as well, but they usually perform mainly administrative functions and have limited territorial competence within the borders of the municipality. Municipal police, however, increased in numbers and power between the beginning of the 1990s and the first half of the 2000s, coinciding with the expansion of the role of cities in local governance of crime. The constitutional reform of 2001 reinforced regional powers for coordination, organisation and professional training of municipal police, who remained, however, dependent on the mayor and hired by the municipality. This police force – much stronger in Italy compared with the corresponding municipal polices in France and Spain – represented the most important actor in the development of local security plans (Bricocoli & Cristalli, 2004; Selmini, 2010). That was because of its less rigid structure, the greater flexibility of its competences, the capacity to perform both proactive and reactive roles, a deep knowledge of the local context, and the closest relationships with citizens.

Urban policing at the local level, thus, was increasingly shared by three police forces, with the municipal force gradually coming to play the most important role. The national police, in coincidence with the first signs of a centralisation process, began to compete on the grounds of 'community policing' – also as a result of the transfer of these concepts from abroad.[19] Municipal police were competing in performance of more repressive and aggressive duties without abandoning their more 'community-oriented' nature.

In such a context, pluralisation of policing, as described by the literature, is quite limited in Italy. It is mostly an internal police process involving public police forces which fight with each other in order to obtain greater visibility and resources, and is an important feature of the institutional conflict among cities, regions and central government that I described above. Attempts at coordination have occasionally been successful, under specific, contingent circumstances. However, an institutional culture of cooperation never developed because of the unwillingness of the central state either to delegate authority or to reform the police forces, and because of the great professional culture differences between the more backward and repressive national police (Palidda, 2000) and Carabinieri, and the more modernised, community-oriented and well-trained municipal police.

When internal pluralisation occurred, it involved a new public actor: the Army. After 2008, when the national government turned to an authoritarian, command-style approach in local security policy and policing, the national government launched a programme for the involvement of military agents in patrolling the streets of the 34 biggest cities.[20] The programme, emphatically defined as 'Operazione Strade sicure' (Operation Safe Street), aimed to reinforce the sovereign state presence at the urban level, using the image and strength of the Army, the most symbolically important of the state's powers.

Consistently with the general and ongoing process of centralisation of local governance, municipal police are experiencing a devaluation of their role. Their activities and roles are increasingly under the control of the national government, and not the mayors. This occurs in different ways: by means of narrower control exercised by the prefects at the local level, through the implementation of administrative orders, and finally also through the 'security contracts'. The precise rules about the extent and the quality of municipal police duties are decided not as a result of negotiation, but are imposed by the prefect. 'External' pluralisation of police activities – which in Italy is quite limited – is so far affecting only the municipal police tasks, and mostly concerns the traffic control-related activities, in order to reinforce municipal police involvement in crime and urban disorder control.

This does not mean, of course, that privatisation of some police or parapolice activities are not occurring in Italian cities. However, the phenomenon seems to be neither remarkable nor increasing.[21] Other forms of pluralisation of policing, for instance those described by Loader as 'policing below government' (Loader, 2000), do not seem to be important in the redesign of urban control. In the recent past, thanks to the stimulation of local authorities, citizen involvement in crime prevention practices at the neighbourhood level was promoted (Melossi & Selmini, 2009). In the current centralisation stage, community involvement remains a rhetorical commitment in government reports and papers that mostly plays a 'decorative role'. The definition of 'sicurezza partecipata' refers to an abstract idea of citizens who are supposed to 'participate' in the construction of everyday security at the local level, but there are no practices or programmes in place to achieve this goal.

The very low level of community involvement in crime control and prevention is demonstrated by the failure of any attempt to develop in Italy practices like the Neighbourhood Watch programmes in other countries. Several factors can explain why such programmes were never adopted in Italian cities. The main factor is that relationships between the citizen and the state are remarkably different in Italy than in Anglo-American contexts. The state is perceived by citizens as distant, and police forces' working styles have always emphasised authority and refused accountability. As a result of the complex historical process of state formation, the instability of institutions and the inefficiency of state bureaucracies, civil society has low expectations of the state and its institutions (including the police). This has severely limited its capacity for reaction and civic mobilisation[22] (La Spina, 1993: 58).

The lack of knowledge about the extent and activities performed by other actors, above all private police, provides no basis for a broader and more sophisticated understanding of the pluralisation of policing in Italy.

6 Conclusions

In this chapter I explained the development of local security policies and changes in urban policing in Italian cities using theoretical insights from studies on local governance of crime, on restructuring of state sovereignty in crime control, and on policing. These insights are important for understanding processes and dynamics that have been ongoing for several decades in European cities, and for their capacity to explain worldwide processes. Analysis of local contexts, however, shows important peculiarities which, without rejecting the broader, global framework, add new dimensions for a better understanding of those same global processes. Convergence is evident and prevalent, but divergences are important. I showed how in the Italian case, for instance, the restructuring of the sovereign state, the responsibilisation strategies, the features of the infrastructure for local governance, and the shapes of policing and control at the urban level have similarities with broader processes occurring in the Western world, but also differences in shape and time. These divergences are the result of specific local factors, including the particular process of state formation, the fragmentation of the institutional Italian framework, the conflict between centralisation and decentralisation that has characterised Italy in the last two decades, and the peculiarity of the Italian police apparatus.

With the disappearance of the infrastructure of crime prevention and control created by the alliance between regional governments and cities, we are also witnessing the disappearance of an attempt to develop an alternative and transformative agenda for crime control. This agenda was based on the empowerment of cities, mayors and local communities, on negotiation regimes instead of coercive controls, on security policies that, despite some ambiguities, were mostly characterised by a social inclusion rationality, a proactive policing strategy, and an attempt to balance crime control and rights. The new centralisation stage represents not only a delegitimation of local powers, but also a turn towards more punitive, exclusionary policies that target marginal social groups and reinforce control and punishment at the local level in different ways. The politics of 'austerity' represented a fundamental step in this turn. As Hallsworth and Lea wrote, 'the State is back, and it is beginning to look rather unpleasant' (Hallsworth & Lea, 2011: 142).

Notes

1 In Italy the prefect is the representative of the national state at the local level. There are about 100 prefects, corresponding to the territories of provinces (districts). The 'questore' is the chief of the national police forces that operate at the level of the city.
2 In other European countries the same policy field was described in different words: 'new crime prevention' (Robert, 1991) and 'community safety' in the UK (Crawford, 1999). Despite the different terms, relating to different legal and institutional traditions of various countries, the content of these policies is very similar, and it includes a variety of preventive and control measures.
3 See Newburn and Sparks (2004), and also the attempt by Edwards and Hughes (2005: 6) to conceptualise this dynamic comparison with reference to the search not for uniformity nor uniqueness, but for necessary and contingent relations, and to define 'convergence'.
4 Most of the comparative studies focus on the hypothesis of a homogenisation of criminal policies across the Western countries, and some show that the convergence process, though clear and accelerated, is still far from homogenisation of penal cultures and practices, for instance concerning punishment (Cavadino & Dignan, 2006).
5 Crime prevention programmes, which in Italy are included under the umbrella of 'security policies', are not considered in this chapter, unless they are aimed at social control, as is the case for situational crime prevention programmes, which I consider as part of broader policing strategies.
6 Garland makes it clear that this process is not simply a downloading of responsibilities and tasks, but a much more complex 'new form of governing at a distance' and 'new mode of exercising power' (Garland, 1996: 454).
7 The process of unification in the country was not smooth before or after 1860. Territorial fragmentation and large differences in the quality of life, from the economically developed and progressive regions of the north to the more rural, underdeveloped and Mafia-controlled areas of the south, are still an important feature of Italy. For a detailed account of the construction of the Italian national state, see Duggan (2008), and on the difference between the different areas, Putnam (1993).
8 At the beginning of 2000, 11 regions had enacted laws that regulated local security and community safety at the local level and coordinated the organisation of municipal police which, though directly under the authority of the mayors, were nonetheless under the broader supervision of regional governments (Braghero & Izzi, 2004). This was a result of a 2001 constitutional reform that, though in an ambiguous way, declared that the 'administrative local police' was an exclusive competence of the regions.
9 A process supported also at the European level, as demonstrated by the mantra on the importance of 'subsidiarity' and the 'Europa delle regioni' (A Europe of Regions) slogans that we can find in many European Union documents of the period.
10 The only change was the new competence of the region in 'administrative local police', which established a power of general coordination of municipal police at

the local level, leaving the same police under the direct rule of municipalities. The reason behind this ambiguity was mostly a concern about transforming municipal police into a new 'regional' force.
11 That, of course, did not happen suddenly but was the result of a longer, though covert, process that started a few years earlier.
12 See article 61, section 18, Law 6 August 2008 n. 133: 'Fondo per la realizzazione di iniziative urgenti per il potenziamento della sicurezza urbana e la tutela dell'ordine pubblico.' Once again, the label used is the one of 'urban safety' interpreted as a part of 'public safety' and therefore a competence of the national government.
13 These are quite similar – even though the legal basis is different – to the antisocial behaviour orders implemented by the New Labour government in the UK during the first decade of 2000 (Burney, 2005) and other hybrid civil laws or individual orders in US cities (Beckett & Herbert, 2009).
14 This is the first national legal definition of 'urban safety': 'A public good to protect and defend, inside local communities, through the improvement of civic rules, and with the aim to improve the quality of life in urban centres, and, finally, to strengthen social cohesion' (Ministerial Decree 5 August 2008).
15 A proposed national law aimed at creating a coordinated system of competences among regions, cities and the central state was promoted in 2003, but was never discussed by the different governments in charge after that year.
16 How politics of austerity impacted on policing still is – with few exceptions (see Millie & Bullock, 2013) – a very understudied issue, which deserves more attention in future studies on policing and security.
17 Almost all these agreements begin with a definition of safety, where it is clarified that the national government has responsibility in crime repression and public order, while local governments are responsible for the maintenance of a quiet and peaceful urban life. The concept of safety is divided into two different levels: local control and repression, for which responsibility belongs to national agencies; and local community reassurance and promotion of citizens' well-being, for which responsibility is mainly allocated to local governments.
18 This creates a situation of competition, conflicts, overlapping of duties and competences, and inefficiency that, though occasionally denounced, has never resulted in any kind of rationalisation or reform (Cornelli, 2003).
19 At the beginning of the 2000s both the national police and the Carabinieri launched their national programmes of 'community policing', defined as 'Polizia di prossimità', from the French model of 'police de proximité', and 'carabinieri di strada' (street Carabinieri). In a situation of 'market saturation', giving the widespread presence of municipal police at the neighbourhood level, both national programmes failed. For a detailed analysis of national police attempts to embrace a 'community policing' philosophy, see Bertaccini (2006) and Della Porta and Reiter (1994).
20 A phenomenon that, unexpectedly, did not gave rise to any public concern or protest, except occasional complaints by police unionists. The phenomenon of the Army patrolling the streets and performing roles in urban control is a relatively new issue that deserves more attention by scholars (see Brodeur, 2010; Graham, 2010).
21 However, in Italy, the paucity of studies and of data on private policing and broadly on the process of commodification of security does not allow much speculation on this point.
22 This is mostly true for the south of the country. In the north, characterised by a much higher level of civic participation (Putnam, 1993), citizen activism was mostly channelled, at least until the beginning of the 1990s, towards political participation.

Bibliography

Beckett, K., Herbert, S. (2008) 'Dealing with disorder: Social control in the post-industrial city', *Theoretical Criminology*, 12(1): 5–30.
Beckett, K., Herbert, S. (2009) *Banished. The New Social Control in Urban America*, New York: Oxford University Press.
Bertaccini, D. (2006) 'La "nuova riforma" della polizia italiana: i discorsi e le pratiche ufficiali di "polizia di prossimità" in Italia', in M. Pavarini (ed.), *L'amministrazione locale della paura*, Firenze: Carrocci, 65–140.
Braghero, M., Izzi, L. (2004) 'Le leggi regionali in materia di sicurezza urbana', in R. Selmini (ed.), *La sicurezza urbana*, Bologna: il Mulino.
Bricocoli, M., Cristalli, F. (2004) *Sicurezza urbana, prossimità e territorio. Culture e pratiche della polizia locale in Lombardia*, Milano: Franco Angeli.
Brodeur, J.P. (2010) *The Policing Web*, Oxford: Oxford University Press.
Burney, E. (2005) *Making People Behave. Anti-social Behaviors, Politics and Policy*, Cullompton: Willan.
Calaresu, M. (2013) *La politica di sicurezza urbana. Il caso italiano (1994–2009)*, Milano: Franco Angeli.
Castells, M. (1997) *The Power of Identity, vol. II of The Information Age: Economy, Society and Culture*, Oxford: Blackwell.
Cavadino, M., Dignan, J. (2006) 'Penal policy and political economy', *Criminology and Criminal Justice*, 6(4): 435–456.
Cohen, S. (1985) *Visions of Social Control: Crime, Punishment, and Classification*, Cambridge: Polity Press.
Cornelli, R. (2003) 'Le forze di polizia: situazione attuale e prospettive di riforma', in M. Barbagli (ed.), *Rapporto sulla criminalità in Italia*, Bologna: Il Mulino, 575–609.
Crawford, A. (1999) *The Local Governance of Crime: Appeals to Community and Partnerships*, Oxford: Clarendon Press.
Crawford, A. (2006) 'Policing and security as "club goods": The new enclosures?' in J. Wood, B. Dupont (eds), *Democracy, Society and the Governance of Security*, Cambridge: Cambridge University Press, 11–138.
Della Porta, D., Reiter, H. (1994) 'Da "polizia del governo" a "polizia dei cittadini"? Le politiche dell'ordine pubblico in Italia', *Stato e mercato*, 48: 433–465.
Duggan, C. (2007) *The Force of Destiny: A History of Italy Since 1796*, London: Penguin. Italian translation (2008) *La forza del destino. Storia d'Italia dal 1796 ad oggi*, Bari: Laterza.
Edwards, A., Hughes, G. (2005) 'Editorial', special issue of *Theoretical Criminology*, 9(3): 259–263.
Edwards, A., Hughes, G. (2012) 'Public safety regimes: Negotiated orders and political analysis in criminology', *Criminology and Criminal Justice*, 12(4): 433–458.
Galantino, M.G., Giovannetti, M. (2012) 'La stagione delle ordinanze sulla sicurezza. Il punto di vista degli attori coinvolti', *Studi sulla questione criminale*, 2, 55–82.
Garland, D. (1996) 'The limits of the sovereign state: Strategies of crime control in contemporary society', *British Journal of Criminology*, 36(4): 445–471.
Garland, D. (2001) *The Culture of Control: Crime and Social Order in Contemporary Society*, Oxford: Oxford University Press.
Graham, S. (2010) *Cities Under Siege: The New Military Urbanism*, London: Verso.

Hallsworth, S., Lea, J. (2011) 'Reconstructing Leviathan: Emerging contours of the security state', *Theoretical Criminology*, 15(2): 141–157.
Johnston, L., Shearing, C. (2003) *Governing Security. Explorations in Policing and Justice*, London: Routledge.
Jones, T., Newburn, T. (2006) 'Understanding plural policing', in T. Jones and T. Newburn (eds), *Plural Policing. A Comparative Perspective*, Abingdon: Routledge.
La Spina, A. (1993) 'Le strategie informali di autotutela del cittadino: significato, presupposti, linee di tendenza', *Quaderni di sociologia*, 37(4): 42–62.
Le Goff, T. (2004) 'Réformer la sécurité par la coproduction: action or rhétorique?' in S. Roché (ed.), *Réformer la police et la sécurité. Les nouvelles tendances en Europe et aux Etats Unis*, Paris: Odile Jacob, 82–104.
Loader, I. (2000) 'Plural policing and democratic governance', *Social and Legal Studies*, 9(3): 323–345.
Melossi, D., Selmini, R. (2009) 'Modernisation of institutions of social and penal control in Europe: The "new" crime prevention', in A. Crawford (ed.), *Crime Prevention Policies in Comparative Perspective*, Cullompton: Willan, 153–176.
Millie, A., Bullock, K. (2013) 'Policing in a time of contraction and constraint: Re-imagining the role and function of contemporary policing', *Criminology and Criminal Justice*, 13(2): 133–142.
Mosconi, G. (2010) 'La sicurezza dell'insicurezza. Retoriche e torsioni della legislazione italiana', *Studi sulla questione criminale*, V(2): 75–99.
Newburn, T., Sparks, R. (2004) 'Criminal justice and political cultures', in T. Newburn, R. Sparks (eds), *Criminal Justice and Political Cultures. National and International Dimensions of Crime Control*, Cullompton: Willan, 1–15.
Palidda, S. (2000) *Polizia post-moderna. Etnografia del nuovo controllo sociale*, Milano: Feltrinelli.
Putnam, R.D. (1993) *Making Democracy Work: Civic Traditions in Modern Italy*, Princeton, NJ: Princeton University Press.
Robert, P. (1991) 'Les chercheurs face aux politiques de prévention', in P. Robert (ed.), *Les politiques de prévention de la delinquance a l'aune de la recherche. Un bilan international*, Paris: L'Harmattan, 13–27.
Ruga Riva, C. (2010) 'Diritto penale e ordinanze sindacali. Più sanzioni per tutti, anche penali?' *Le Regioni*, 1–2: 385–396.
Selmini, R. (2005) 'Les politiques italienne de sécurité: qui govern, l'Etàt, les Regions ou les Villes?' in S. Roche (ed.), *Réformer la police et la sécurité. Les nouvelles tendances en Europe et aux Etats Unis*, Paris: Odile Jacob, 143–168.
Selmini, R. (2010) 'Cosa fa la Polizia Municipale e come cambia la sua identità', *Quaderni di Citta sicure*, 36: 85–125.
Selmini, R. (2013) 'Le ordinanze sindacali in materia di sicurezza: una storia lunga, e non solo italiana', in S. Benvenuti et al. (eds), *Sicurezza pubblica e sicurezza urbana. Il limite dei poteri di ordinanza dei sindaci stabilito dalla Corte Costituzionale*, Milano: Franco Angeli, 52–165.
Wood, J., Dupont, B. (2006) 'Introduction: Understanding the governance of security', in J. Wood, B. Dupont (eds), *Democracy, Society and the Governance of Security*, Cambridge: Cambridge University Press, 1–10.

Chapter 7.2

Italy
Policing and urban control in Rome and Milan: A view from the southern edge of Europe

Marco Calaresu and Rossella Selmini[1]

1 Introduction

In this chapter we describe and discuss the politics of policing in the two biggest Italian cities, Rome and Milan. The empirical focus of this intra-national comparison is on the formulation of policy agendas for policing, seeking to differentiate sub-national from national variation in policing, and context-dependent characteristics from any macro-tendencies (Edwards & Prins, 2014: 405–411). The two cities' agendas are analysed for seven years (2007–14), a period characterised in Italy by remarkable financial and economic pressures on public bodies (see Selmini in this volume), by increasing centralisation (Calaresu, 2013, 2016, 2017), and by an extension of punitive measures and crime controls at the urban level (Selmini in this volume). Our analysis shows that the two cities dealt with these changes differently, with Milan showing a resistance to the national tendencies described above, and Rome being characterised by an ambiguous and fragmented policy agenda, apparently more influenced – even if with some conflicts – by the national government programmes. We argue that this divergence is mostly the result of the powers available to the mayors, of their political ideology, of some features of their biography and of their political careers, and of the divergent economic and social trajectories that characterised Milan and Rome in the last decade.

In this chapter, we first discuss our research questions and methodological issues. We then briefly examine the context, i.e. the evolution of urban security policy in Italy and the socio-demographic profiles of the two cities. In the core section, we analyse the formulation of policing agendas in Rome and Milan as they emerged through the adoption of 'Security Pacts' (hereafter referred to as SPs) and 'Administrative Orders' (hereafter referred to as AOs). It is argued that SPs and AOs are the most significant documents to understand changes in policing and urban security at the local level in Italy. Finally, in our conclusions, we discuss how processes of divergence and convergence in policing policy agendas unfolded in the two Italian metropolises.

2 Research questions and methodological issues

The current academic debate over policing in European metropolises[2] suggests a number of competing theoretical propositions about the significance of sub-national variation in the politics of policing (see Devroe et al. in this volume). The different theses formulated by scholars can be divided into two main tendencies in governing processes: a tendency towards convergence and a tendency towards divergence. In the former case, sub-national variation in the governance of policing would be negligible: due to the predominance and the projection of nation-state power (Stenson, 2008; Hallsworth & Lea, 2011), and in the latter case – concerning the governing of social conflicts – divergence due to competition amongst city-regions (Sassen, 2001; Bowling & Sheptycki, 2012).

It is fair to wonder, therefore, whether in the Italian case, for the 2007–14 period, a process of divergence can be found, rather than a process of convergence in public policy 'talk' and 'decisions' about policing (Brunsson, 1989; Pollitt, 2001). The empirical focus of comparison in this work, then, is on the formulation of policing policy agendas seeking to differentiate sub-national from national variation (Edwards & Prins, 2014, Recasens i Brunet & Ponsaers, 2014). We also differentiate context-dependent qualities, such as the 'Barcelona-ness' and 'Paris-ness' of policing (Ponsaers et al., 2014), from macro-tendencies, such as policing during times of crisis and austerity (Hough, 2013; Millie & Bullock, 2013).

From a methodological point of view, this implies the use of the multiple-embedded case study, a research design that allows discussion – through intra-national comparisons of the metropolitan cities of Rome and Milan – of convergences and divergences in the two cities' policing agendas and how they should be interpreted. We acknowledge limitations inherent in this methodological choice: focusing research on police agenda setting deliberately ignores research on the implementation of policy goals and their outcomes, and potential gaps between 'talk', 'decisions' and policing 'in action'. Nevertheless, using this approach, we can address specific theoretical issues, raising relevant questions for comparative research such as: is there a predominant actor, and who is responsible for formulating the agenda and establishing a coalition of support for it? Is there competition amongst rival policing agendas? Is the role of the national state more important in defining agendas, responding to pressures from a 'transnational state system' or from local peculiarities (Bowling & Sheptycki, 2012)? Last but not least, how are centralisation and decentralisation dynamics unfolding in the Italian case (Crawford, 1999; Johnston & Shearing, 2003)?

Methodologically, the work is based on qualitative analyses of institutional and political documents, describing policy agendas in the national context and in the selected cities. Official documents are good empirical sources for the study of agenda setting, being the product of institutionalised life and, concerning our aims and scope, for the study of the formulation of policing policy agendas (Corbetta, 1999: 453). In particular, we focus on the SPs, signed in Italy between governmental agencies and local governments, and on the AOs, adopted by city mayors for security issues, which are considered here as the most important instruments for the design of policing and control at the urban level in Italy.

3 The evolution of urban security policy in Italy

Before the 1990s, Italian policy makers showed little or no interest in urban security policy, concentrating their attention instead on policies for fighting crime in general and organised crime in particular (Triventi, 2008: 90). At the beginning of the 1990s, however, Italy experienced a generalised increase in local governments' powers, as a consequence of new rules on the direct election of mayors and of a constitutional change in 2001 that gave the regions more powers including responsibility for local policing. Those reforms focused on the delegation of powers to lower levels of government, generating 'more charismatic mayors' (Giovannetti, 2009), and are consistent with a broader process – occurring in the Western world – that emphasises the responsibilisation of actors other than the national state in the fields of crime control and prevention, together with a restructuring of the sovereign state (Garland, 1996). This process is characterised by an important role played by regional governments, which provide policy statements, resources and regulatory instruments that in many other countries are national government responsibilities (Selmini, 2005), and implied a greater visibility and involvement of municipal police corps in urban control (see the chapters by Selmini, and by Devroe and Ponsaers in this volume). Even without formal competences related to public order and security, local forces gradually acquired a 'substitute' function of public order management (Pavarini, 2006). The significance of regions and cities also had an influence on the rationality of programmes that were mostly – though not only – oriented to social justice and to an idea of security balanced by freedom and the enhancement of civil rights, as contrasted with a purely punitive approach (Selmini in this volume).

From 2007, however, the national government began to assert a stronger role in urban control and crime prevention strategies, 'opening a new era of national activism by the Ministry of the Interior' (Selmini in this volume). This centralisation was made possible by national laws passed in 2008 and 2009[3] by the new right-wing government, whose principles were then re-shaped in a variety of governmental acts that reveal the new discourses and decisions about urban policing. Several governmental documents of the seven years under study (2007–14) dictate choices about national and local priorities concerning policing, crime control and prevention at the local level. Examples are the so-called 'Performance Plans and the Guidelines of the

Minister of the Interior' and the 'Agenda of the Government about Local Authorities, Security and Immigration', both released annually by the minister of the interior. These plans, with little variation, assert that urban security is a matter of 'public security' and that problems at the local level must be dealt with through cooperation between national and local governments, through a strategy defined as 'integrated security' or, alternatively, as 'shared security'. An example of this centralisation is the decision of the national government in 2008 to appoint the prefects – the heads of prefectures, i.e. the representatives of the state at the local level – as special commissioners for 'mobile populations' for the cities of Rome, Milan and Naples, where the presence of illegal settlements of (above all) Roma people is highest. Prefects – and their decisions – replaced the mayors, once the only officials responsible for this subject at the local level.[4] This priority for metropolitan policing was also reflected in the first national programme for funding local projects of urban security, which, in addition to emphasising the control of Roma people, also promoted enhanced surveillance of urban populations through the implementation of closed-circuit television (CCTV) schemes across Italian cities.[5] In short, through a variety of normative and regulatory instruments, the national government attempted to re-establish its role in defining local policing agendas, in deciding priorities and tools for intervention, and consequently weakening the previous infrastructure for urban policing which was based on the alliance between regions and municipalities.

The turn towards centralisation was accompanied by a shift towards a more punitive model of crime control that emphasises street crime, immigration and the control of mobile populations such as Roma people, and other vulnerable groups who are seen as mainly responsible for crime and as a threat to public security. This shift is demonstrated, for instance, by the decision (started in 2008) to routinely involve military agents in patrolling the streets with a primary function of policing and urban control (Ministero della Difesa, 2015), and by a national pact entitled, 'Thousands of Eyes on the City' that gives CCTV companies and private police a new role in policing and urban control (Ministero dell'Interno & ANCI, 2010). Considering these documents altogether, the national government strategies and priorities after 2007 were centralisation (although presented as 'integrated security') and a tougher approach on crime that, despite the distance in space, time and cultural context, resembles the 'zero tolerance' strategies adopted in New York City in the past.[6]

In this context, SPs and AOs have became two of the most important tools to set local agendas for policing in Italian cities (Pizzetti, 2012; Selmini, 2013; Calaresu, 2016, 2017). On 20 March 2007, a framework agreement on urban security was signed between left-wing Minister of the Interior Giuliano Amato, the National Association of Municipalities (ANCI), and the mayors of the ten metropolitan cities. The national pact was designed to initiate as many agreements (SPs) as possible between the prefectures, the municipalities, the provinces and the regions, thereby generating different institutional configuration (Calaresu & Tebaldi, 2015). According to scholars, the instrument of SPs was used by the national government to impose, rather than negotiate, a list of activities and duties on the peripheral actors, such as municipalities (Selmini, this volume; Calaresu, 2016), which are also mostly in charge of the costs of this 'new form of governing at a distance' (Garland, 1996: 454).

As for the AOs, these acts traditionally express the mayors' power to address urban problems such as safety and public hygiene. This power was enlarged and strengthened in two different ways. First, it was made clear by Law N° 125/2008 that mayors were acting as national government officers, and not as elected representatives of the community (Selmini, 2013). Second, these orders became unlimited in time, and broader in their content (Moroni & Chiodelli, 2014). In addition, with the Ministerial Decree of 5 August 2008, the government indicated the areas and situations in which mayors were entitled to issue administrative orders. In this new situation, mayors became extremely dependent on the priorities indicated by the national government and also because AOs have to be approved by the prefect. According to some scholars, these modifications transformed traditional mayoral practices into hybrid semi-criminal measures (Selmini in this volume; Di Ronco & Peršak, 2014), with municipal police[7] often involved in zero tolerance strategies (Ruga Riva, 2010). Although on 7 April 2011 the Italian Constitutional Court declared that these new kinds of AOs were partly unconstitutional concerning the unlimited time of possible enforcement, mayors have continued to use these orders (constantly reissuing them), or have transferred them into municipal police regulations, thus creating what has been defined as a 'municipal criminal law' (Ruga Riva, 2008).

Taken altogether, SPs and AOs redesigned the whole system of policing and urban control, creating a model in which the national government decides priorities, distribution of resources, and instruments, and mayors become state officers under the control of the prefect. A new alliance,[8] based on a clear asymmetry of powers, defines practical and symbolic roles of policing actors, and shifts the focus from social and community crime prevention at the local level to risk management and criminal justice. The success of this attempt to centralise metropolitan policing agendas and to delimit the discretion available to municipalities and their mayoral leaders cannot, however, be inferred from this reform of the national policing system. Given the dependence of national authorities on the resources of municipal actors to translate national priorities into action, it is necessary to compare and contrast actual metropolitan policing agendas. The remainder of the chapter compares and contrasts policing agendas in the two largest cities in Italy, Rome and Milan. The two cities have been a particular focus of national policing priorities, i.e. about mobile populations and Roma people, and therefore provide a critical test of how successful the post-2007 attempt to centralise metropolitan policing agendas has been. In the section below, we will highlight the social and economic standing of Rome and Milan relative to other Italian and European metropolises.

4 A short socio-demographic profile of Rome and Milan

Rome and Milan are among the most densely populated metropolises in southern Europe. Rome, with 2,872,659 inhabitants (ISTAT, 2014), is the biggest city in Italy and the fourth largest in the European Union (EU) (EUROSTAT, 2012). Milan is the second most populous Italian city, with 1,337,885 inhabitants (ISTAT, 2014), 13th most populous in the EU and, in recent years, the third most populous metropolitan area in Europe (OECD, 2006: 31). The territory of the province of Rome experienced a significant increase (199%) in the number of foreign residents over a decade (2001–10). The city of Milan also recorded a sizable increase in the same period (148%), with an even more dramatic increase in the provincial territory (480%) (Giovannetti & Gramigna, 2013: 45–48).

Being the capital of the Italian Republic, the city of Rome hosts the principal institutions of the country, including the Presidency of the Republic, the government (and the ministries), the Parliament, the main judicial courts and the diplomatic representatives. While Rome is the Italian political capital, Milan is the business centre, hosting the Italian Banking Association, the Italian Stock Exchange, the headquarters of some of the largest Italian publishing groups, private television and Internet companies, a large number of media and advertising agencies, and many national and international fashion and design companies.

From an economic point of view, Milan and Rome, respectively, in 2014 had gross domestic products (GDPs)[9] per capita of US$41,147 and $38,025 (Parilla et al., 2015). To better understand the importance of the two cities in an international perspective, it could be said that if the metropolitan areas of Rome and Milan were countries, they would be, respectively, the world's 67th (roughly the size of Oman) and 50th (approximately the size of Qatar) largest economies by GDP (IMF, 2015). Nonetheless, it should be noted that due to the financial crisis that started internationally in 2007, both Rome and Milan are suffering in numerous economic performance indicators. According to several indices, they have not yet recovered to pre-recession levels of employment and GDP per capita (Parilla et al., 2015: 9, 32–33). Both are among the 'main fallers'[10] within the top 100 cities ranked by projected urban economy growth rates and GDP by 2025 (PwC, 2009: 25).

A benchmarking among the ten metropolitan areas in Italy shows that the area of Rome, in 2013, was the first in the country for the number of stock companies, exceeding those of Milan (Provincia di Roma, 2014: 67). The economy of Rome is characterised by relative absence of heavy industry and manufacturing services (in which the capital is ranked in the last spot among the ten metropolitan cities), while it is ranked first for the relative presence of companies active in the fields of education, health and social services, rental, travel agencies and business support, plus other service activities (Infocamere – Movimprese, 2013). The capital area is also ranked highly for the relative presence of companies involved in the hotel and travel industries, artistic activities, and entertainment and fun (Infocamere – Movimprese, 2013), proving itself one of the most important tourist destinations in the world (Bremner, 2015). Inside the city boundaries is Vatican City, the only worldwide example of an independent state located within a city: religious tourism is an additional pole of attraction for the city (in 2016 Rome was to host the Jubilee of Mercy).

Milan was ranked in first place in 2013 for 'business vitality', and has ranked first for incidence of enterprises in the service sector, and for information and communication companies (Infocamere – Movimprese, 2013). Its role in tourism also should not be underestimated: for example, the recent EXPO 2015 (Universal Exposition) experience attracted about 20,000,000 visitors in six months (*Ansa*, 9 October 2015). This seems to confirm that tourism is an increasingly important part of the city's economy.

5 The policing agenda setting in Rome and Milan

5.1 Security pacts and administrative orders in Rome

The first 'Patto per Roma sicura' (Pact for the Safety of Rome, hereafter referred to as PSR1) was approved on 18 May 2007 (Comune di Roma, Prefettura di Roma, Provincia di Roma and Regione Lazio, 2007), within 60 days of the signing of the national pact by the minister of the interior (Ministero dell'Interno, 2007). The Pact was settled by a left-centre council (run by Walter Veltroni from 2006 to 2008), with the presence of a left-centre national government led by Romano Prodi from 2006 to 2008. The new right-centre administration run by Gianni Alemanno (2008–13) decided to sign its own pacts with the prefecture, the region and the province, respectively on 29 July 2008 (The Second Pact for the Safety of Rome, referred to as PSR2) and 21 December 2011 (The Third Pact for the Safety of Rome, referred to as PSR3) (Comune di Roma, Prefettura di Roma, Provincia di Roma and Regione Lazio, 2008; Comune di Roma, Prefettura di Roma, Provincia di Roma and Regione Lazio, 2011). The national government, in those years, was led by Silvio Berlusconi (2008–11), with a right-centre coalition. The next mayor, Ignazio Marino (2013–15), did not sign a further pact. Marino's political programme refused SPs that, according to the new mayor's view, represent a policy failure, since the city still has many problems related to crime and security despite the several SPs signed by his predecessor (Programma Marino Sindaco, 2013: 57–58). Thus, Rome shows continuity in signing pacts and a long tradition of cooperation with the national government which was interrupted only in the last two years of our study (2013–14). Marino might, following his initial reluctance in adhering to the national policing agenda, have represented a change in the convergence process; however, he then became so politically weak and his office was so troubled by many scandals involving local councillors and senior civil servants of the municipality, that his political action was paralysed for about two years. In this very peculiar situation, the national government – as we will demonstrate later on – remained extremely influential in the local policing agenda, even if no new SPs were signed.

The contents of all these pacts have large similarities between themselves, following the priorities indicated by the national pact of 2007. These priorities are: 'predatory crimes' and other forms of 'widespread' and 'aggressive crime'; problems of 'illegal occupation' and 'unauthorised camps', with particular reference to mobile populations and Roma people;[11] 'illegal itinerant trade and counterfeiting of goods'; and 'prostitution'. Moreover, as suggested by the national pact, all the local pacts in Rome claim that urban security is a 'right', which requires the coordinated action of 'multiple levels of government' and 'integrated policies'. The 'growing sense of insecurity' – especially in the suburbs – has to be addressed through a 'combined action to intensify the activities to control the territory and the investigation', and with the 'completion of technological tools suitable to monitor the areas at risk' (Pact for the Safety of Milan – see below – and PSR). Despite the different institutional actors (and their political affiliations) involved in the second and third SPs for Rome (PSR2 and PSR3), the contents addressed by the agreements seem to remain the same over time. Some few minor differences, however, are worth noting: the reference to mobile populations and Roma people disappears in the third pact for Rome, while it is present in the second one. In the PSR2, unlike the other two, robbery and organised crime are mentioned as priorities, going far beyond the conventional focus on street crime and incivility in urban security policies. Also, interestingly, in PSR3 two of the main concerns in the agenda are not strictly identifiable with crimes, but instead with broader social and economic processes, such as 'population growth' and 'economic crisis'.

The coalition of actors responsible for formulating the agenda in the case of Rome includes the municipality and the prefecture, plus the regional and the provincial governments. The role of the city mayor is clear, and for all three pacts under analysis municipalities, at least in agenda setting, have exclusive responsibilities in promoting 'a permanent conference of the institutions involved in volunteer work and assistance' (PSR2), and in increasing 'the degree of vigilance and security in the public transport services' (PSR3).

Municipalities, then, have shared responsibilities – first, with the police headquarters, the municipal force and the prefecture, and second, with other local institutions and agencies such as, in the case of Rome, the province and the region. These relate to diverse goals: to 'frame strategies for operational synergies between institutions aimed at the prevention of forms of crime that interact with the social and situational issues' (PSR), to 'recover environmental decay, through the reorganisation and enhancement of the urban space', and 'to strengthen video surveillance' (PSR2). Municipalities (with the provinces and the regions) are responsible for the allocation of the resources necessary to achieve the goals of these agendas, through a specific financial contribution often associated with the provision of a special fund (PSR, PSR2).[12] If funding is a responsibility of local governments, availability of human resources (Guardia di Finanza, Polizia di Stato and Carabinieri units) is the responsibility of the Ministry of the Interior.

In short, the prefect manages the budget, fed by the local governments, and decides how many national police agents will be dedicated to the goals of the pact, keeping its central position within policing agenda setting. Moreover, the prefecture is responsible for coordinating the other actors involved in implementing the programmes (PSR3), and for creating plans on the different urban areas (PSR2). A core role in setting the agenda for policing is also played by a 'working group' (PSR, PSR2, PSR3), whose duties are 'develop[ing] processing task and criticality analysis' (PSR2, PSR3), and performing a broader coordination role. The working group is one of the most important innovations introduced by the pacts of Rome (and of Milan, see below). The establishment of these new bodies also confirms the vanishing role of regional governments, which, as mentioned before, were once central actors in defining policing agendas at the local level. In the pacts signed in Rome, their role seems to be irrelevant in deciding priorities, and limited to provide funding for the different measures envisaged in the pacts. The pacts signed in Rome are very similar to many other national pacts signed in other big Italian cities (such as Bologna, Cagliari, Florence, Genoa, Turin, Venice, to name a few) in the same years (Calaresu, 2013, 2017). This seems to be evidence that Rome, in the indicated period, was aligned to the national tendency for both the institutional design and the content of local security policies and policing. One more piece of evidence of this dynamic is the fact that Rome also signed a different pact, which replicates a national pattern, the aforementioned 'Thousands of Eyes on the City', which involves the private sector, CCTV business and private policing (Ministero dell'Interno, 2014b).

We mentioned earlier that another important tool for policing and urban control adopted by the Italian cities after 2008 are the so-called administrative orders (AOs). In Rome, between 2007 and 2014, many AOs about urban security were issued. Of particular significance was Order N° 242 of 2008, which was enforced until 2012 and addresses the problem of prostitution. Prostitution (which in Italy is not a crime since 1958) is prohibited and sanctioned in these orders (as in many other orders across the country) as behaviour that threatens urban security. The result is a sort of re-criminalisation of this behaviour under a different legal regime from criminal law (Giovannetti & Zorzella, 2010).

The second important problem addressed by AOs in Rome is the combination of youth nuisance, nightlife and alcohol consumption, with the specific goal of avoiding 'pub crawling' and 'alcoholic trekking'. Before 2009 these orders were addressed only to consumers, but after that year the orders also punished the owners of pubs, bars and restaurants. After the election of the new mayor Marino in 2013, no more AOs related to urban security were issued and, generally speaking, relationships between the local and the national governments became more conflicted (Selmini in this volume).

5.2 Security pacts and administrative orders in Milan

Milan has a different history regarding SPs, at least for the last four years of our study (2011–14). This tool, whose role in designing and influencing the local agenda was, and still is, quite relevant, was adopted only once, in 2007, by Letizia Moratti, the mayor of the right-wing coalition that ruled the city between 2006 and 2011. The Pact, thus, was enforced for about three years. The 'Patto per Milano sicura' (Pact for the Safety of Milan, hereafter referred to as PSM) was approved on 18 May 2007 (Comune di Milano & Prefettura di Milano, 2007), within 60 days of the agreement of the national pact by the minister of the interior. The timing is the same as the signature of the first PSR. In the case of Milan, however, the pact was signed only by the city mayor with the prefecture.

The contents of the PSM shows large similarities to the pacts signed in Rome in the same period and with the national pact. As occurred in Rome, the main targets of the PSM were 'predatory crimes' and other forms of 'widespread' and 'aggressive crime', problems of 'illegal occupation' and 'unauthorised camps' (once again with particular reference to Roma people), 'illegal itinerant trade and counterfeiting of goods', and 'prostitution'. The PSM also addressed drugs and youth problems, and violence against women, minors and the elderly. Similar to the pacts in Rome and other local SPs signed in Italy at the time (Calaresu, 2013, 2016), the PSM emphasises the rhetoric of 'integrated security', which implies the involvement of different levels of government, and of urban security as a fundamental right of citizens. The PSM envisages a municipal responsibility for the establishment of intermediate bodies and working groups whose task is to make coordination and cooperation easier and smoother. In the case of Milan, this working group includes representatives of the municipal government, of the province and the region (which are not, however, among the institutional actors who signed the pact) and has the main functions to manage the phenomenon of 'nomadism', i.e. of Roma people, and of defining 'future agreements and forms of coordination among different police forces'. The prefect has general responsibility for the coordination of the actors involved through the PSM working group. The PSM also clearly states that the prefect can also coordinate the municipal police for some specific purposes, a fact that confirms the stronger role played by the national actors in designing the local policy agenda for policing.

The PSM follows a similar pattern for the allocation of resources, with local governments in charge of the whole funding of the pact.[13] In the case of Milan, the administration of Giuliano Pisapia, elected with a centre-left coalition in 2011 (and still in office in 2015), decided not to propose or join a new pact after the first one. This seems to be consistent with his political programme (Programma per Giuliano Pisapia Sindaco, 2011) which did not mention SPs as tools for policing and urban control, and was oriented to fight against corruption and economic crime and to adopt social and community prevention as better measures to improve urban security.

This divergence in Milan's metropolitan policing agenda is also evidenced in the particular use of AOs by Pisapia's administration (2011–time of writing), as contrasted with those adopted by Moratti's administration (2008–11). Whereas Moratti's administration followed Rome, with AOs issued mostly in the fields of prostitution and illegal selling of goods, under Pisapia's administration the majority of AOs were issued for problems unrelated to crime, such as weather alerts or road safety. The few orders that refer to urban security address alcohol consumption and urban decay related to overcrowded areas close to bars and pubs. Orders issued are usually restricted in time and space and emphasise the use of fines for the owners of bars and pubs that sell alcohol after a certain time of day. In February 2014, Pisapia issued an order against gambling that prescribed the closure of a gambling establishment. This is one of the few examples in Italy of AOs addressed to forms of organised crime and not, as is almost always the case, against vulnerable groups of people (Selmini in this volume; Calaresu, 2016). This confirms the mayor of Milan's greater autonomy in deciding priorities at the local level and the weaker influence of the national agenda.

6 Conclusions: convergence and divergence in Rome and Milan

The comparison of Rome and Milan concerning the SPs and the AOs shows different trajectories in their relationship to the national government's attempted centralisation of metropolitan policing agendas. The different timing and duration of these electoral mandates make our analysis quite fragmented and so it is useful to clarify further the changing political contexts in the two cities and their impact on metropolitan policing agendas.

Rome had a mayor from the Democratic Party (Walter Veltroni) and was ruled by a centre-left coalition between 2007 and 2008, and then again between 2013 to 2015 with Ignazio Marino, who, however, resigned in late 2015. Between 2008 and 2013, the city was ruled by Gianni Alemanno, affiliated with a right-wing party, and by a centre-right coalition: this created a context of good relationships with the right-wing national government that was in power until 2011.

Milan has a different political history. Between 2007 and 2011 the city was ruled by Letizia Moratti of the centre-right coalition, who was replaced by a left-wing mayor, Giuliano Pisapia, who is also a lawyer, an expert on criminal justice procedures, and well-known for his involvement in civil rights movements and his support of more radical political positions. His term was to end in 2016.

The two cities show clearly a convergent process only when both of them were ruled by a right-wing mayor. In the same city, Rome shows a convergent process also between the electoral mandate of the left mayor Walter Veltroni (2007–08) because the pact that he signed was not different from those signed later by his successor of the right wing. However, the period when Veltroni was mayor is so short that we cannot draw further conclusions. It seems, however, that right-wing mayors were more willing to cooperate with right-wing national governments. This pattern in Rome is different not only from Milan, but also from the national pattern that, in relation to both SPs and AOs, does not show any clear importance of the political ideology variable in influencing the adoption of national strategies, as some studies on AOs (Giovannetti, 2009, 2012) and SPs (Calaresu, 2013, 2017) show, not seeing a strong correlation between any particular territorial configuration of SPs and their political 'colour', and the priorities included in the same pacts. The agreements were signed – without any substantial changes – by both right-wing and left-wing administrations of city councils with other territorial levels of government that were not (not all and not always) homogeneous in terms of political affiliation (including the national government). This means that the greater autonomy of Milan is the result of more factors than just political consistency between local and national governments.

Rome was more active in signing SPs and in issuing AOs that replicated national priorities for metropolitan policing. In Milan, the mayor of the last four years seems to have been more reluctant to adhere to national strategies and has pursued more autonomous goals, as demonstrated by the kinds of AOs issued, and his rejection of SPs with the national government, even when the national government was ruled by a centre-left coalition, after 2013.

Generally speaking, mayor Alemanno of the right-wing coalition in Rome was extremely active, not only in issuing AOs but in maintaining relations with the national government. Analyses of official documents show that national and local agenda setting were characterised by the same priorities; the same features of the metropolitan policing agenda in Rome between 2008 and 2011 were also found in the comparative study carried out by Lucianetti (2011).[14] When law enforcement initiatives were undertaken by the national government in Milan, mayor Pisapia was not involved, as contrasted with Mayor Alemanno's administration in Rome during the same period. During the period 2008–13, there was a strong alignment between the municipality of Rome and the national government concerning definitions of problems and decisions about policing (see also Lucianetti, 2011). An analysis of documents of the minister of the interior shows that Rome was a focus of attention. For instance, in 2011, the minister announced an increase in the number of police agents in the capital city, during a meeting to which the mayor was invited, motivated by a general concern about 'violence'.[15]

With Ignazio Marino as mayor of Rome in more recent years, things changed, but still revealed the pre-eminent role of national government, which appears to have taken full control of policing, not because of a strong alignment of central-local policy priorities but primarily as a result of the political weakness of the new mayor. For instance, on 19 May 2014, the minister of the interior of the new centre-left national government launched his plan of action for the city, defined as Rome Safe Capital (Ministero dell'Interno, 2014b). The mayor was 'invited', but he does not seem to have played any role in the definition of priorities and actions to be taken. The agenda emphasises the following as major problems in Rome: prostitution again, illegal selling of goods, nightlife, domestic burglaries and robberies, and hooliganism. The measures proposed are based on a 'tough on crime and disorder approach' that mixes together traditional law and order approaches and new technologies of risk management, including CCTV, crime mapping and tighter control of 'street demonstrations'.

In Milan, relationships between the mayor and the national government are not as close as they were in Rome before the election of Ignazio Marino. In May 2013, the newly appointed minister of the interior chaired a meeting of the County Committee on Public Safety and Public Order[16] in which he announced an increase of 140 national police officers in Milan. The mayor was not mentioned. The selected documents show a situation of greater autonomy of the mayor in Milan concerning policing and urban control, and a looser relationship with the national government. In deciding priorities at the local level, the mayor seems not to be influenced by national rhetoric and rationalities about law enforcement and being 'tough on crime'. The programme on urban security of the municipality, for instance, includes three main activities: an ongoing project of mediation for victims of crime and offenders, some projects on women's safety, and CCTV programmes. Only the last is consistent with the national agenda. Moreover, community policing is strengthened through the project of the 'Vigile di quartiere', a tradition of Italian municipal police that in Milan is still implemented widely and competes with strategies of urban policing based more on law enforcement and control. Milan also diverged from Rome in not signing a 'Thousands of Eyes on the City' SP for public-private cooperation in urban security.

How can we explain the greater resistance of Milan to the centralisation of metropolitan policing agendas in Italy? Political affiliation plays an important role; however, as already mentioned, this is not the most important factor. It is also worth noting that Giuliano Pisapia is not a member of the Democratic Party; he is a more radical left-wing politician, who won the primary elections against the main candidate of the Democratic Party and then become mayor with a broad and stable coalition that also included some radical left organisations and civic associations. His personal biography and charismatic leadership of municipal politics in Milan are key to understanding the divergent policing agenda in this city during his period in office since 2011, and in comparison with Rome and with other Italian metropolises.

In Rome, the presence from 2013 to 2015 of a mayor from a left coalition did not make a difference because of his political weakness, the very limited time he was in office and allegations of corruption. Since 2013, municipal government in Rome has experienced a difficult period of scandals, political instability and persisting economic problems that culminated in the resignation of the mayor and his replacement by a 'special commissioner', the former prefect, and consequently direct rule from national government.

By contrast, Milan is regaining its role as the financial capital of the country, also thanks to stronger political stability, the absence of scandals and corruption, and improvements in many economic indicators (*Il Sole 24 Ore*, 5 May 2015). It can also be argued that Milan's distance from the national government's centres of power helped the city behave like a city-region. Last, but not least, in 2015 Milan hosted a successful exhibition that remarkably improved the city's visibility and power as a national and international centre of political and economic importance for the country as a whole, which in turn has enhanced the reputation and bargaining power that the mayor can use in resisting national government objectives.

In a country as fragmented as Italy is, with the lack of an institutional culture of real cooperation, tendencies toward centralisation as a means to re-establish a (coerced and therefore always fragile) stability and unity are common and sometimes successful, as occurred in Rome. In these conditions, personal biographies and the leadership qualities of politicians, together with the broader factors we have mentioned, can make a difference, and an important one. In the case of Milan, this also means that the city was able to develop a more socially inclusive approach and a less law and order-oriented policing style, showing a remarkable capacity of resistance to the punitive and exclusionary rationalities that seem to characterise national tendencies in metropolitan policing agendas within Italy and in other European countries.

Notes

1 This chapter is the result of joint research undertaken by the two authors. Marco Calaresu primarily wrote sections 2, 3, 4 and 5.1. Rossella Selmini primarily wrote sections 1, 5.2 and 6. Both authors reviewed and approved the final manuscript.
2 On this matter see volume 2, issue 1 of the *European Journal of Policing Studies* (Ponsaers et al., 2014).

3 Law N° 125/2008 and Law N° 94/2009 envisaged new penalties for street crime and new restrictions on immigration rules. Law N° 125/2008 changed the status of mayors for what concerns their powers of AOs.
4 With the Decree of the President of the Council of Ministers of 21 May 2008, Silvio Berlusconi declared a 'state of emergency in relation to nomad settlements', in the regions of Campania, Lazio and Lombardy. According to the decree, the state of emergency would be necessary for the presence of many non-EU citizens and irregular nomads who have settled permanently in urban areas. Also, according to the decree, the above situation would be 'unfaceable with the tools provided by ordinary legislation'. On 30 May 2008, the president of the council also issued three orders for the implementation of the aforementioned decree with which the prefects of Milan, Rome and Naples have been appointed as commissioners to overcome the state of emergency. On 16 November 2011, with judgment N° 6050 the Council of State declared the illegitimacy of the decree, mainly because of the lack of a requirement of emergency.
5 Decree-Law N° 11 of 23 February 2009.
6 The trip that Minister of the Interior Roberto Maroni took to New York City at the beginning of his work in 2008 is a clear example of 'policy transfer'. Interviewed after his trip, the minister affirmed: 'Zero Tolerance is a model that we want to implement in all Italian cities' (Ministero dell'Interno, 2008).
7 About the role of municipal police in Italy, see Devroe and Ponsaers in this volume, Braccesi and Selmini (2005), and Carrer (2009).
8 That excludes regional governments, once a pivotal actor in policing and urban control.
9 GDP is the value of all final goods and services produced within a state in a given year, derived in this case from purchasing power parity (PPP) calculations.
10 Rome has fallen from the 43rd to 53rd position, whereas Milan has fallen from 46th to 65th.
11 The PSR contemplated the construction of four 'villages of solidarity' in equipped areas able to accommodate about 1,000 Roma people each.
12 In the PSR the Lazio Region promises €11 million, while the municipality contributes with €4 million. In the PSR2, the region confirms €11 million in three years, the Province of Rome ensures €3 million, while the municipality warrants €10 million. In the PSR3, the region assures €1 million for the first year of the agreement, the province €400,000 and the municipality of Rome €1 million.
13 In the PSM, the Lombardy Region and the Province of Milan declared their willingness to bestow financial resources in the special fund created at the Prefecture of Milan, without, however, specifying a concrete amount. The municipality declares itself willing to grant loans that will be gradually earned towards the state during the whole period of the enforcement of the pact.
14 This study, however, compares convergence and divergence, in both discourses and policy implementation, at an international level, namely in Rome and London.
15 Considering that the same document confirms the drop in violent crimes, it seems that the 'violence emergency' is actually only related to public protest and urban violence. The announcement, in fact, follows some disorders that occurred during a protest of anti-austerity movements (Ministero dell'Interno, 2011)
16 The 'Comitato provinciale per l'ordine e la sicurezza pubblica' is a collective body of the Italian state with advisory functions, set up in each prefecture, and chaired by the prefect.

Bibliography

Bowling, B., Sheptycki, J. (2012) *Global Policing*, London: Sage.
Braccesi, C., Selmini, R. (eds) (2005) *Sicurezza urbana e ruolo della polizia locale*, Sant'Arcangelo di Romagna: Maggioli.
Bremner, C. (2015) *Top 100 City Destinations Ranking*, Euromonitor International. Online. Available blog.euromonitor.com/2015/01/top-100-city-destinations/ranking.html (accessed 10 November 2015).
Brunsson, N. (1989) *The Organization of Hypocrisy: Talk, Decisions and Actions in Organizations*, Chichester: John Wiley & Sons.
Calaresu, M. (2012) 'La politica di sicurezza urbana in Italia. L'esperienza dei "patti per la sicurezza" nel triennio 2007–2009', *Rivista Italiana di Politiche Pubbliche*, 3(7): 387–418.
Calaresu, M. (2013) *La politica di sicurezza urbana. Il caso italiano (1994–2009)*, Milano: Franco Angeli.
Calaresu, M. (2016) 'The top-down instruments for governing crime and disorder: What lessons can be drawn from the Italian experience (2007–2011)?', in N. Peršak (ed.), *Regulation and Social Control of Incivilities*, London: Routledge.
Calaresu, M. (2017) *Security Pacts: The Italian Experience*, The Hague: Eleven International Publisher.
Calaresu, M., Tebaldi, M. (2015) 'Local security policies and the protection of territory: An analysis of the Italian experience (2007–2009)', *City, Territory and Architecture*, 2(1): doi:10.1186s40410-40014-0017-y
Carrer, F. (eds) (2009) *Le politiche della sicurezza. Dalla 'polizia comunitaria' alla 'tolleranza zero'*, Milano: FrancoAngeli.
Comune di Milano and Prefettura di Milano (2007) *Patto per Milano Sicura*. Online. Available www.prefettura.it/lecco/contenuti/162278.htm (accessed 30 November 2015).
Comune di Roma, Prefettura di Roma, Provincia di Roma and Regione Lazio (2007) *Patto per Roma Sicura*. Online. Available www.prefettura.it/lecco/contenuti/162278.htm (accessed 30 November 2015).
Comune di Roma, Prefettura di Roma, Provincia di Roma and Regione Lazio (2008) *Secondo Patto per Roma Sicura*. Online. Available www.prefettura.it/lecco/contenuti/162278.htm (accessed 30 November 2015).
Comune di Roma, Prefettura di Roma, Provincia di Roma and Regione Lazio (2011) *Terzo Patto per Roma Sicura*. Online. Available www.prefettura.it/lecco/contenuti/162278.htm (accessed 30 November 2015).
Corbetta, P. (1999) *Metodologia e tecniche della ricerca sociale*, Bologna: Il Mulino.
Crawford, A. (1999) *The Local Governance of Crime: Appeals to Community and Partnerships*, Oxford: Clarendon Press.
Cutrufo, M. (2010) *La quarta capitale*, Roma: Gangemi Editore.
Devroe, E., Ponsaers, P. (2016) 'European national police systems and metropolitan realities', in A. Edwards, E. Devroe, P. Ponsaers (eds), *Policing European Metropolises*, London: Routledge.
Di Ronco, A., Peršak, N. (2014) 'Regulation of incivilities in the UK, Italy and Belgium: Courts as potential safeguards against legislative vagueness and excessive use of penalising powers?', *International Journal of Law, Crime and Justice*, 42(4): 340–365.
Edwards, A. (2016) 'Comparing the governance of policing in European metropolises: Researching city-region regimes in a world urban system', in A. Edwards, E. Devroe, P. Ponsaers (eds), *Policing European Metropolises*, London: Routledge.

Edwards, A., Hughes, G. (2012) 'Public safety regimes: negotiated orders and political analysis in criminology', *Criminology and Criminal Justice*, 12(4): 433–458.

Edwards, A., Prins, R. (2014) 'Policing and crime in contemporary London: A developmental agenda?', *European Journal of Policing Studies*, Special Issue Policing European Metropolises, 2(1): 403–435.

EUROSTAT (Statistical Office of the European Communities) (2012) *EUROSTAT: Population Distribution and Demography*. Online. Available ec.europa.eu/eurostat/web/gisco/geodata/reference-data/population-distribution/demography (accessed 10 November 2015).

Garland, D. (1996) 'The limits of the sovereign state: Strategies of crime control in contemporary society', *British Journal of Criminology*, 36(4): 445–471.

Giovannetti, M. (2009) 'Le politiche di sicurezza e prevenzione della criminalità in Italia', in CITTALIA – Fondazione ANCI Ricerche, *Oltre le ordinanze: i sindaci e la sicurezza urbana*, Roma: Fondazione IFEL.

Giovannetti, M. (2012) 'Le ordinanze dei sindaci sulla sicurezza urbana', in CITTALIA – Fondazione ANCI Ricerche, *Per una città sicura*, Roma, 25–60.

Giovannetti, M., Gramigna, A. (2013) 'Le persone', in CITTALIA – Fondazione ANCI Ricerche, *Rapporto Cittalia 2013. Le città metropolitane*, Rome: Digitalia Lab srl.

Giovannetti, M., Zorzella, N. (2010) 'Lontano dallo sguardo, lontano dal cuore delle città: la prostituzione di strada e le ordinanze dei sindaci', *Mondi Migranti*, 1: doi 10.3280/MM2010-001003

Hallsworth, S., Lea, J. (2011) 'Reconstructing Leviathan: Emerging contours of the security state', *Theoretical Criminology*, 15(2): 141–157.

Hough, M. (2013) 'Procedural justice and professional policing in times of austerity', *Criminology & Criminal Justice*, 13(2): 181–197.

IMF (International Monetary Fund) (2015) *World Economic Outlook Database*. Online. Available www.imf.org/external/pubs/ft/weo/2015/02/weodata/weorept.aspx? (accessed 10 November 2015).

Infocamere – Movimprese (La società di informatica delle Camere di Commercio italiane) (2013) *Dati totali imprese 1995–2015*. Online. Available www.infocamere.it/movimprese1 (accessed 10 November 2015).

ISTAT (Istituto Nazionale di Statistica) (2014) *ISTAT: Popolazione e famiglie*. Online. Available www.istat.it/it/popolazione (accessed 10 November 2015).

Johnston, L., Shearing, C. (2003) *Governing Security. Explorations in Policing and Justice*, London: Routledge.

Lucianetti, L. (2011) 'Crime prevention and community safety policies from a dynamic and comparative perspective: The cases of Rome and London', *Crime Prevention and Community Safety*, 13(4): 260–272.

Mangiardi, R. (2009) 'Il ruolo della polizia locale nella sicurezza urbana', in F. Carrer (ed.), *Le politiche della sicurezza. Dalla 'polizia comunitaria' alla 'tolleranza zero'*, Milano: FrancoAngeli.

Millie, A., Bullock, K. (2013) 'Policing in a time of contraction and constraint: Re-imagining the role and function of contemporary policing', *Criminology & Criminal Justice*, 13(2): 133–142.

Ministero della Difesa (2015) *Operation Safe Streets*. Online. Available www.difesa.it/OperazioniMilitari/NazionaliInCorso/StradeSicure/Pagine/default.aspx (accessed 30 November 2015).

Ministero dell'Interno (2007) *Patto per la sicurezza delle città metropolitane con ANCI*. Online. Available www.interno.gov.it/it/temi/territorio/patti-sicurezza/patto-sicurezza-ministero-dellinterno-e-lanci (accessed 30 November 2015).

Ministero dell'Interno (2008) *Press Releases. News. Safety. 13.12.2008*. Online. Available www1.interno.gov.it/mininterno/export/sites/default/it/sezioni/sala_stampa/notizie/sicurezza/0670_2008_12_13_Maroni_2_giorni_a_New_York_.html_516981391.html (accessed 30 November 2015).

Ministero dell'Interno (2011) *Press Releases. News. Safety. 31.08.2011*. Online. Available www1.interno.gov.it/mininterno/export/sites/default/it/sezioni/sala_stampa/notizie/sicurezza/0000091_2011_08_31_sicurezza_Roma.html_1362891800.html (accessed 30 November 2015).

Ministero dell'Interno (2014a). *Performance Plans, 2015–2017*. Online. Available www.interno.gov.it/it/amministrazione-trasparente/performance/piano-performance (accessed 30 November 2015).

Ministero dell'Interno (2014b). *Press Releases. News. Safety. 19.05.2014*. Online. Available www1.interno.gov.it/mininterno/export/sites/default/it/sezioni/sala_stampa/notizie/sicurezza/2014_05_19_piano_capitale_sicura.html_2124499340.html (accessed 30 November 2015).

Ministero dell'Interno and ANCI (National Association of Municipalities) (2010) *Thousands of Eyes on the City*. Online. Available www1.interno.gov.it/mininterno/export/sites/default/it/sezioni/sala_stampa/notizie/2100_500_ministro/00938_2010_02_11_milleocchi_firma.html (accessed 30 November 2015).

Moroni, S., Chiodelli, F. (2014) 'Municipal regulations and the use of public space: Local ordinances in Italy', *City, Territory and Architecture*, 1(11): doi:10.1186/2195-2701-1-11.

OECD (Organisation for Economic Co-operation and Development) (2006) *OECD Territorial Reviews: Milan, Italy*. Online. Available www.oecd.org/italy/oecdterritorialreviewsmilanitaly.htm#chapter_1 (accessed 10 November 2015).

Parilla, J., Trujillo, J.L., Berube, A., Ran, T. (2015) *Global Metromonitor 2014. An Uncertain Recovery*, Metropolitan Policy Program at the Brookings Institution. Online. Available www.brookings.edu/~/media/Research/Files/Reports/2015/01/22-global-metromonitor/bmpp_GMM_final.pdf?la=en (accessed 10 November 2015).

Pavarini, M. (2006) 'L'aria delle città rende (ancora), liberi? Dieci anni di politiche locali di sicurezza', in M. Pavarini (ed.), *L'amministrazione locale della paura. Ricerche tematiche sulle politiche di sicurezza urbana in Italia*, Roma: Carocci.

Pizzetti, F. (2012) 'Conclusioni. Sicurezza urbana e ordinanze sindacali tra diritto e realtà', in A. Galdi, F. Pizzetti (eds), *I sindaci e la sicurezza urbana, Le ordinanze sindacali e i loro effetti*, Roma: Donzelli.

Pollitt, C. (2001) 'Clarifying convergence. Striking similarities and durable differences in public management reform', *Public Management Review*, 3(4): 471–492.

Ponsaers, P., Edwards, A., Verhage, A., Recasens i Brunet, A. (eds) (2014) 'Policing European metropolises', *European Journal of Policing Studies*, Special Issue Policing European Metropolises, 2(1): 345–354.

Programma Marino Sindaco (2013) Available at www.ignaziomarino.it/wp-content/uploads/Programma_MarinoSindaco.pdf (accessed 20 November 2015).

Programma per Giuliano Pisapia Sindaco (2011) Available at www.pisapiaxmilano.com/wp-content/uploads/2011/04/programma-coalizione.pdf (accessed 20 November 2015).

Provincia di Roma (2014) *Rapporto annuale. La situazione dell'area metropolitana romana 2013–2014*. Online. Available www.provincia.roma.it/percorsitematici/statistica-e-studi/approfondimento/42222 (accessed 10 November 2015).

PwC (PricewaterhouseCoopers UK) (2009) *Economic Outlook – Largest City Economies in the World in 2008 and 2025*. Online. Available. www.ukmediacentre.pwc.com/imagelibrary/downloadMedia.ashx?MediaDetailsID=1562 (accessed 10 November 2015).

Recasens i Brunet, A., Cardoso, C., Castro, J., Nobili, G.G. (2013) 'Urban security in Southern Europe', *European Journal of Criminology*, 10(3): 368–382.

Recasens i Brunet, A., Ponsaers, P. (2014) 'Policing Barcelona', *European Journal of Policing Studies*, Special Issue Policing European Metropolises, 2(1): 452–470.

Ruga Riva, C. (2008) *Regioni e diritto penale. Interferenze, casistica, prospettive*, Milano: CUEM.

Ruga Riva, C. (2010) 'Diritto penale e ordinanze sindacali. Più sanzioni per tutti, anche penali?', *Le Regioni*, 1–2: 385–396.

Sassen, S. (2001) *The Global City* (2nd edn), Princeton, NJ: Princeton University Press.

Selmini, R. (2005) 'Towards Città sicure? Political action and institutional conflict in contemporary preventive and safety policies in Italy', *Theoretical Criminology*, 9(3): 307–323.

Selmini, R. (2013) 'Le ordinanze sindacali in materia di sicurezza: una storia lunga, e non solo italiana', in S. Benvenuti et al. (eds), *Sicurezza pubblica e sicurezza urbana. Il limite del potere di ordinanza dei sindaci stabilito dalla Corte costituzionale*, Milano: Franco Angeli.

Selmini, R. (2016) 'Urban policing in Italy: Some reflections in a comparative perspective', in A. Edwards, E. Devroe, P. Ponsaers (eds), *Policing European Metropolises*, London: Routledge.

Stenson, K. (2008) 'Surveillance and sovereignty', in M. Deflem, J.T. Ulmer (eds), *Surveillance and Governance: Crime Control and Beyond*, Bingley: Emerald Group Publishing Limited.

Triventi, M. (2008) 'Segni di inciviltà sul territorio e paura del crimine. Un'analisi dei dati dell'Indagine sulla sicurezza dei cittadini', *Quaderni di Sociologia*, 48(3): 73–102.

Chapter 8

Britain

Metropolitan policing agendas in
Britain: Divergent tendencies in a
fragmenting state?

*Adam Edwards, Sophie Chambers, Nick Fyfe and
Alistair Henry*

1 Introduction

This chapter draws on case study research into governing arrangements and agendas in Bristol, Cardiff, London and Edinburgh to question assumptions about the interplay of global and local social relations, elsewhere referred to as 'glocalisation' (Swyngedouw, 1997), in driving metropolitan policing agendas in Britain. It has been argued this interplay generates greater subnational variegation in broader processes of social and economic change, as city-regions thrive or struggle to adapt in a world system characterised by the greater mobility of capital, labour, goods and services across national borders (Sassen, 2001; Massey, 2007; Moulaert et al., 2007; Warwick Commission, 2012). In turn it is argued, not least by institutions of the European Union (EU), that this mobility can weaken the sovereign powers of nation-states, including their capacity to ensure internal security within their own borders, and consequently necessitates transnational responses to transnational threats (European Commission, 2015). However, allied arguments about the establishment of a 'transnational state system' (Bowling & Sheptycki, 2012) and related 'post-national state formations' (Jessop, 2004), seem premature given the current resurgence of nationalist political movements in Europe. The most obvious expression of this, of fundamental concern for the subject matter of this chapter, is the outcome of the UK referendum on membership of the EU, held on 23 June 2016, in favour of leaving. Whether the vote for so-called 'Brexit' is actually accepted by the UK Parliament and, if so, what kind of nation-state emerges from the subsequent and prolonged renegotiation of the UK's international relations, including its commitment to policing and judicial cooperation in Europe, this development re-emphasises the continued analytical importance of nation-state power, a theme that has also been pursued in recent accounts of sovereignty and the national security state (Lea & Stenson, 2007; Hallsworth & Lea, 2011; Stenson, 2012).

The chapter uses the cases of metropolitan policing agendas in Bristol, Cardiff, Edinburgh and London to question how the differential insertion of city-regions into this world system might generate divergent trajectories for policing, for example the particular policing problems that capitals, as contrasted with regional cities, encounter as the focal points for national and international protest as well as mundane problems of crime and civil unrest. It also uses contrasts and comparisons of governing arrangements and policy agendas for policing in these four city-regions to question the presumption that glocalisation necessarily generates greater sub-national variegation or whether, insofar as meaningful divergences exist, they are better explained as contingencies, particularly of the political agency of key actors such as police chiefs, elected mayors and, in England and Wales, the recently established Police and Crime Commissioners (PCCs).

The chapter contrasts this presumption with two countervailing arguments. First, that irrespective of any governing arrangements devolving policy making for metropolitan policing to sub-national authorities, policing agendas are converging, as authorities copy one another's responses to commonly perceived problems, such as organised crime, terrorism, migration and social cohesion. Second, that nation-states retain considerable influence over the trajectories of local governance within their sovereign territory and that insofar as any divergences can be identified across Europe these are better understood in terms of *inter*national rather than *intra*-national comparisons.

Addressing these countervailing arguments necessitates some engagement with the meaning of nation-state power in the United Kingdom and its role in shaping policing. To this end, certain particularities of the constitutional-legal settlement in the United Kingdom need to be acknowledged, including the ongoing process of devolving political authority to the constituent nations of the Union and, within England and Wales, to sub-national actors such as the directly elected mayors and PCCs. In this context, pressures for greater self-determination within the four constituent nations of the 'United Kingdom' render abstract concepts of the national security state problematic. Following the devolution of powers to these constituent nations, commencing in the late 1990s with the establishment of the Scottish Parliament, the Welsh Assembly and the Northern Ireland Assembly, the United Kingdom is better conceptualised as a fragmenting, if not a federalising, state rather than a coherent unitary political actor. Grounds for thinking about the fragmentation of the UK include the composition of the Brexit vote, which was primarily concentrated in provincial England and Wales, whereas voters in Scotland and Northern Ireland voted overwhelmingly to remain within the EU. In turn this provoked Nicola Sturgeon, the First Minister of the Scottish Parliament and leader of the Scottish National Party (SNP), to argue the case for another referendum on Scottish independence from the United Kingdom, claiming this was now back on the agenda less than two years after the last vote, which the Scottish independence movement narrowly lost.

Further peculiarities in the constitution of the United Kingdom complicate simple references to nation-state power, especially in relationship to policing. Scotland has always had its own legal system and separate governing arrangements for policing and criminal justice to those of England and Wales. In turn, governing arrangements for policing and criminal justice in Northern Ireland have evolved separately and in reaction to the particular conditions generated by the longstanding conflict between unionists and Irish republicans and by the subsequent peace process. Yet a further layer of complexity exists as a consequence of devolution in Wales where some competences for contemporary policing, including the role of schools, health authorities and local government working together in multi-agency 'partnerships' for 'community safety',[1] have been devolved to the Welsh government whilst others, specifically relating to the police, the courts and the management of offenders by probation and prison services, have not. Finally, in part as a response to the anomalies of this earlier phase of devolution, in particular the absence of a specifically English assembly within the UK, a number of 'devolution deals' have been made with city-regional authorities in England, in particular the pilot case of the Greater Manchester Combined Authority, which includes responsibility for the strategic leadership of policing. It will be argued that opportunities arise for sub-national discretion and political agency in setting metropolitan policing agendas precisely as a consequence of this constitutional mess, itself a product of an unstable compromise to retain the integrity of the United Kingdom. In this sense it may seem counter-intuitive to respond to pressures for fragmentation with constitutional reforms that devolve rather than reassert nation-state power but in this regard various devolution deals within and between the constituent nations of the UK can be understood as a means of averting the collapse of the UK into secessionist conflicts. Fragmentation is one thing, secession is another. In promoting the former to avoid the latter, however, new circuits of power are established which can facilitate divergent policing agendas.

2 Comparing metropolitan policing agendas in the context of devolution

The vote in favour of 'Brexit' occurred during the final drafting of this chapter and, whilst it is clearly too early to ascertain what the implications will be, it is an exemplar of the kind of national politics discussed in other recent accounts of policing change (Hallsworth & Lea, 2011; Lea & Stenson, 2007; Stenson, 2012), particularly given the prominence of policing, immigration and national sovereignty in the Leave campaign. Even so, there is an important difference between the *de jure*, constitutional-legal, powers claimed by nationalist politics and the *de facto* powers of nation-states to govern within their territories. Transnational challenges that are unlikely to respect territorial boundaries, whilst fundamentally shaping or disrupting social order within them, abound, notably those facilitated by the internet and the proliferation of digital communications. In any case, what, in post-Brexit conditions, will constitute the UK's territory for internal security? In addition to rekindling calls for a referendum on Scottish independence, Brexit has disrupted the peace process in Northern Ireland, given the prospect of re-establishing a land border between the six counties of the North and the Republic of Ireland.

If understanding the powers and analytical significance of metropolitan policing, including the very existence of distinctive sub-national policing agendas, entails an understanding of the relationship of these agendas to 'national' policy making, what constitutes national policy in the 'United Kingdom of Great Britain and Northern Ireland'? The full title of this constitutional-legal settlement indicates its complexity – a product, in turn, of the ongoing political conflicts and compromises between the historic nations of England, Ireland, Scotland and Wales which, in their latest phase, can be traced back to the various devolution agreements of the late 1990s. Specifically in relation to policing policy, this complexity has three key dimensions that set the context for the case studies discussed later: the asymmetrical devolution of powers, the process of centralisation pursued in Scotland, and the purported decentralisation of policy making in England and Wales given the establishment of the elected PCCs covering 41 constabularies (state police forces) in England and Wales, the adoption of this role by the elected mayor for London and, prospectively, by other elected mayors in newly established city-regions. For the analytical purposes of this edited collection and given the very distinctive experience of policing during and following the conflict in Northern Ireland, the remainder of the chapter focuses on the comparison of metropolitan policing in Britain.[2]

As discussed in the introduction to this edited volume, the second phase of the Policing European Metropolises Project defines the objects of comparison as the formulation of policy agendas for metropolitan policing. It does this in order to establish any convergent and divergent trends in the strategic priorities of metropolitan policing and to question the very existence of sub-national policing agendas. In England and Wales, this comparative task has been simplified following the Police Reform and Social Responsibility Act 2011, which provided for the election of PCCs in each constabulary area, who have the statutory duty to set the strategic priorities and allocate funding for policing in their areas (Edwards & Prins, 2014). To this end, each PCC is required to formulate and publish a Police and Crime Plan covering their four-year term of office. Whilst these plans provide an initial empirical focus for investigating metropolitan policing agendas, the plans cover entire constabulary areas which include within them several districts or boroughs which are the basic units of municipal government in England and Wales. In effect the PCCs introduced a regional tier of government in which several boroughs compete for prioritisation on the relevant PCC's agenda. As a consequence, further case study research has been undertaken to clarify the relationship of the plans to the policing agendas for Cardiff, the capital of Wales and largest city within the region covered by the PCC for South Wales, and Bristol, the largest city in the region covered by the PCC for Avon and Somerset in the south-west of England.

In London the situation is different as the elected mayor undertakes the statutory obligations of the PCCs including the publication of the Police and Crime Plan for Greater London by the Mayor's Office for Police and Crime (MOPAC). As with other PCCs, MOPAC are obliged to engage in public consultations about their proposed plans, which although variable in quality and content, also provide an important source of empirical data on policing policy and politics (Edwards & Prins, 2014: 72). The statutory obligation for PCCs to consult the public about their plans was a key factor in the 2010–15 coalition government's 'Big Society' Agenda, aiming to devolve power to the local level and to better engage the public in policy making, particularly in an era of austerity and controversial decisions about cuts to expenditure on public services.

Explaining the distinctiveness of policing governance in London requires further clarification of the peculiarities of constitutional power in the UK. Until the election of the mayor for London in 2000 there were no directly elected mayors in England or Wales; instead mayors performed a ceremonial, non-party political role. The case for directly elected mayors gained momentum during the 1990s amongst those wishing to enhance the strategic leadership of local government in social and economic affairs and to improve the democratic accountability of that leadership to local electorates who, research suggests, often do not know who their local elected representatives are, what governing programmes they are pursuing or whom to contact should they wish to complain. In this context it is argued that directly elected mayors provide a clear, responsive and accountable focus for local political and economic leadership (Warwick Commission, 2012). Opinion remains divided, however, over the strengths and limitations of this more 'presidential' style of government relative to the more collective, albeit complicated and obscure, 'leader and cabinet-based' structure of local government that currently persists in most local authorities in England and in all local authorities in Wales. However, such was the perceived need for strategic leadership across the region of Greater London that a directly elected mayor was established by the Greater London Authority Act 1999 and the first incumbent of this office, Ken Livingstone, was subsequently elected in 2000. It is important to emphasise that directly elected PCCs are, in effect, regional political actors overseeing the strategic direction of policing across a whole police service area which will encompass a number of local authorities. Indeed, as discussed in the case studies in this chapter, one of the key tensions driving the politics of metropolitan policing is between these regional actors and the various local authorities that fall within their administration. In the case of Greater London the office of elected mayor pre-dated the establishment of the PCCs in 2012 and so the capacity for strategic leadership of the Metropolitan Police Service already existed without duplicating it through the establishment of a PCC for Greater London. Hence, the office of the mayor of London assumed the strategic responsibilities for policing that elsewhere in England and Wales were given to the PCCs.

At the time of writing, the incumbent Conservative UK government had expressed its intention to extend the London model of city-regional governance to other places. To this end it passed the Cities and Local Government Devolution Act 2016 which provides for the establishment of directly elected mayors in regions of combined local authorities. This Act also empowers the UK government to agree devolution deals with a combined city-regional authority that include responsibility for policing. Where such deals are reached, as they have been with the establishment of the Greater Manchester Combined Authority (GMCA), responsibility for policing will transfer from the relevant PCC to any newly elected city-regional mayor. Although the provisions of this Act are generic it is expected they will, in the first instance, apply to the 'Core Cities Group'[3] of large urban conurbations in the UK, including Bristol and Cardiff. The first devolution deal to be negotiated has been with the GMCA, the mayor for which will be directly elected in May 2017. This emerging geometry of city-regional power provides the political conditions both for distinctive and divergent governing 'regimes' which may maintain the conventional prioritisation of criminal justice responses to security threats, 'develop' this agenda augmenting law enforcement with forms of risk management or else 'reform' or 'transform' this conventional agenda through the promotion of alternative, restorative and social, justice policies (Edwards & Hughes, 2012). This new geometry also has the prospect of intensifying 'civic boosterism' including the competition for resources within and between combined authorities and with other areas of local governance in the UK, in particular rural areas and smaller towns which some fear will be neglected as a consequence of this increasing metropolitan emphasis (BBC News, 2015).

The situation is again quite different in Scotland. Just as PCCs were being established locally throughout England and Wales, Scotland underwent a quite divergent process of reform, the drivers of which were less about local democracy and more about good governance and economic efficiency (Fyfe & Henry, 2012). The Police and Fire Reform (Scotland) Act 2012 amalgamated Scotland's eight regional police forces into a single Police Service for Scotland, now named Police Scotland, which came into being on 1 April 2013. Powers previously associated with local Police Boards around funding, strategic policy development, and the appointment and dismissal of senior ranks were centralised at a national level with the establishment of the Scottish Police Authority (SPA). However, the 2012 Act did give statutory force to the importance of 'local policing', although without ever defining what this phrase means, by maintaining two key links with local government, both of which are relevant to any consideration of emergent policing strategies or agendas specific to the City of Edinburgh. On the one hand Local Scrutiny and Engagement Committees (replacing the Police Boards but not themselves defined in the legislation itself) were established by each of the 32 local authorities in Scotland, with a direct link to a local area commander in Police Scotland to be consulted on the drafting of Local Police Plans reflecting local interests (which is required in the legislation). Police Scotland has since been structured into 14 Divisions with a divisional commander at the rank of chief superintendent, some of whom serve multiple local authorities (see Terpstra & Fyfe, 2015). However, the Edinburgh Division of Police Scotland is coterminous with Edinburgh City Council, making agreed plans and policies a good approximation of such at the city level. The second local government link was the maintenance of Police Scotland's statutory duty to participate in Community Planning, the model of local partnership working formally established in Scotland in 2003. Although Community Planning covers the governance of public services more generally, the strategic policies and agendas of the Edinburgh City Partnership potentially provide further insight into how Edinburgh seeks to negotiate current challenges of urban governance.

Given the advent of these new governing arrangements for policing, it is possible to clarify and justify the scope of applicability, objects and predicates for comparing metropolitan policing agendas across the constituent national contexts of Britain.

2.1 Scope of applicability

As Sztompka (1990) notes, defining the logic and foci of comparative research is a theoretically driven exercise. As the title to this chapter suggests, the logic of comparing policing agendas in Bristol, Cardiff, Edinburgh and London is to question whether the increasing devolution of governing competences has resulted in any major divergence in policing agendas. The decentralisation of governing arrangements through devolution, which commenced in earnest during the UK New Labour administration (1997–2010), has been complemented in England by the 'new localism' advocated by the UK coalition government (2010–15), which emphasised the rights of municipal authorities to set their own policy agendas but also their responsibilities for finding the resources for these agendas in an era of 'austere' public expenditure. As noted above, the new localism has been intensified by the Conservative administration elected in 2015 through the Cities and

Local Government Devolution Act 2016. It is in the context of this constitutional change that the UK, once a highly centralised, unitary polity, is becoming an increasingly decentralised and fragmented state. However, within the devolved region of Scotland, Westminster's wider policy of decentralisation is less in evidence. Here, policing exemplifies a divergent tendency towards the greater centralisation of public administration under the strong direction of the Scottish government at Holyrood. A key component of this centralisation is the use of 'single outcome agreements' by the Scottish government to define the priorities of the police and other public authorities and to relate the provision of increasingly stringent budgets to compliance with these priorities. There is somewhat of a tension, however, between this process of centralisation and the establishment of the Scottish Cities Alliance, in 2011, to promote Scottish city-regions as engines of economic development and social well-being.

Apropos the introduction to this edited volume and its discussion of multiple, overlapping, internal security fields, the UK 'security field' is shared by all four particular metropolises selected for comparison here. Specifically, the UK field is a primary focus for policy responses to serious and organised crime and for counter-terrorism. Whilst metropolises, particularly the capitals of the constituent nations of the UK, are both lucrative and symbolic targets for serious crime and terrorism, these are perceived in the UK National Intelligence Model (NIM) for policing,[4] to be threats that have a transnational dimension that cannot be adequately addressed by metropolitan authorities. Even so, Cardiff has, at least rhetorically, distinguished its policing and crime control agenda from that pursued in England. There is a purported 'dragonisation'[5] of policing which defines a distinctively Welsh security field (Edwards & Hughes, 2009) of policies for volume crime and disorder reduction, most obviously in approaches to youth offending. It is argued, for example, that the All Wales Youth Offending Strategy reflects the determination of the Welsh government to define youth crime as a problem of social justice, of failures on behalf of the state to adequately extend to young people their entitlements to health, education and employment, as distinct from the 'low trust' and punitive politics of youth justice that is perceived by some to prevail in England (Drakeford, 2010).

Similarly to Wales, in Scotland both the political rhetoric of the Scottish National Party (SNP) government since 2007 and the pre-existing institutional design of the Children's Hearings system formally present youth crime and associated inequalities as primarily issues of social justice. In the specific case of policing, the aforementioned 2012 Act also adopts a progressive tone in setting out the purposes of the police in Scotland around issues of securing community well-being and engagement through working in partnership with others (The Police and Fire Reform (Scotland) Act 2012, section 32). So the language of social justice certainly does seem to have some political currency in the Scottish security field at present, even if it does not necessarily shape actual practice in either youth justice or policing (McAra, 2014).

Within the English security field, however, London is such an exceptional policing context given its status as a 'global city' (Edwards & Prins, 2014), that an understanding of any English effect on metropolitan policing agendas also requires the study of provincial cities. In this regard, Bristol was selected because it has, in the past, been regarded as a locality with commensurate policing and crime problems to those of Cardiff, as contrasted with the higher magnitude of problems encountered in the big English conurbations such as the West Midlands, Greater Manchester and Merseyside. Finally, these metropolises also inhabit the EU security field but in ways that reflect the very particular and post-Brexit conditions of the UK's membership of the European Union. So, these cities are all subject to the major, unanticipated, legal migration of EU citizens, notably from Eastern and Central European countries following the Eastward expansion of the EU in 2004 and 2007, but they are not a part of the Schengen Agreement Area of cross-border freedom of movement. This, it has been argued, is a major contrast with the security challenges that confronted the Parisian authorities, ahead of the terrorist attack on Friday 13 November 2015, as a consequence of the ease of movement of the attackers across the French and Belgian borders within the Schengen Area (see section 3.2, below).

In summary, we have taken major constitutional reform in the UK since the late 1990s as the temporal scope of our comparison, to consider the proposition that such reform will facilitate divergence in metropolitan policing agendas and, therefore, opportunities for learning from this divergence in understanding how UK metropolises can be policed otherwise. We have also defined the applicable scope of comparison in terms of the various internal security fields these metropolises inhabit as a consequence of their particular location in overlapping EU, UK, English, Scottish and Welsh contexts of policing. The concern with these multiple, overlapping, internal security fields is also driven by a theoretical assumption, that the particular configuration of these fields will facilitate divergence in policing agendas given the ways in which metropolitan, national and European security fields interact and how these can alter the standing conditions and dispositions of policing agendas (see 'scope of predicates', below). A rival proposition, however, is that the interaction of these different security fields will facilitate increased convergence in policing agendas akin to the thesis that organisations tend to copy the most successful in their field as a means of maximising their own success and minimising the risks of failure and reputational damage associated with radical innovation, that of so called 'mimetic institutional isomorphism' (DiMaggio & Powell, 1983). In turn, this is akin to McAra's (2008) account of the apparent contradiction between devolution in Scotland and the pursuit, by the Labour Party administration during the first Scottish Parliaments post-Devolution, of policing and criminal justice policies much closer to those pursued at that time by the New Labour administration in England, a process McAra describes as 'de-tartanisation'.[6] It is through this comparative logic of seeking uniqueness in metropolitan policing agendas and failing to find it, that convergence can be established.

2.2 Scope of objects

As also noted in the introduction to this edited collection, the comparative work undertaken for the second phase of the Policing European Metropolises Project delimits the objects of analysis to:

- 'public' policing (not commercial, voluntary or informal);
- 'policy formulation' (not implementation or evaluation of outcomes); that is
- 'strategic' and concerned with medium-term planning and agenda setting (not operational policing).

This is not to deny the significance of these other objects for comparison but to privilege, in the first instance, a concern with the capacity of metropolitan authorities to set their own policing agendas before any further research into the capacity of metropolitan actors to translate these agendas into practice is undertaken. In some instances, such as the regional Police and Crime Plans formulated by the PCCs, there is an obvious empirical focus for comparison. In others, further case study research is required to elicit municipal-level policing agendas, as in the 'What Matters' strategy for governing Cardiff from 2010–20, which is formulated by an 'integrated partnership board' of all the authorities responsible for delivering public or statutory services in that metropolis, including the police, and which identifies strategic priorities for policing as part of its 'Safer and Cohesive Communities workstream'.

Further material is also available on the thinking, consultation and arguments behind the formulation of these agendas as registered in the minutes of key decision-making arenas, such as municipal authority 'oversight and scrutiny committees', which are charged with scrutinising the formulation, implementation and outcomes of policing agendas, and Police and Crime Panels which provide an opportunity to hold PCCs to account for their priorities and performance. These decision-making arenas are part of the complex apparatus of the 'partnership approach' to policing and crime reduction which has, since the mid-1980s formally extended responsibility for policing in England and Wales beyond the (state) police to other responsible authorities (Hughes, 2007). The methodological corollary of this shift to multi-agency policing is that metropolitan policing agendas are set by partnership boards in concert with PCCs rather than by senior police officers, and it is the decision-making arenas of partnerships that provide a key empirical focus for comparative research (Edwards & Prins, 2014: 72).

2.3 Scope of predicates

Understanding policy formulation implies a theory of power and, in these terms, our comparison has employed concepts from Clegg's (1989) 'circuits of power' framework. This proceeds from the basic assumption that power is a strategic relation, in Machiavelli's sense of a campaign that needs to be won through the careful negotiation of alliances, rather than a possession, epitomised in Hobbes's image of Leviathan's sword, which is held and wielded by some over others. In these terms, what is of interest is the 'standing conditions' of the negotiation in which causal power is exercised and how certain agents ('As') get others ('Bs') to do things they otherwise would not. These conditions set out the means and resources available to certain policy actors, for example the constitutional-legal powers that PCCs and the mayor of London have, to set the strategic priorities and allocate funding for policing in their constabulary areas, the electoral mandate they have to set certain priorities rather than others, their dependence on the organisational capacities and intelligence of municipal authorities, including the police, needed to realise strategic goals, and so forth.

In turn, however, understanding this circuit of causal power cannot be divorced from the circuit of 'dispositional' power, all those meanings and membership categories that define governing programmes and obviate alternatives, setting the rules of negotiation within particular standing conditions. Most notably in policing the categories of warfare and criminal justice have dominated public policy priorities in, for example, the wars on drugs, terrorism, delinquency, even 'incivility' and 'anti-social behaviour'. More recently the language of 'risk management', augmenting failing criminal justice strategies, has assumed a greater prominence epitomised in the hegemony of pragmatic, situational, crime prevention initiatives that have proliferated in metropolitan policing in Britain. It is argued the dispositions of 'punitive display' and mundane risk management have obviated or 'eclipsed' (Garland, 1996) longer-standing social democratic dispositions. Yet, as noted above, the language of social justice underpins much of the policing agenda for youth crime in the Scottish and Welsh contexts and, in Wales, the allied rejection of anti-social behaviour orders, child curfews and other draconian methods of enforcement as policy priorities (Edwards & Hughes, 2008). To subsume this within some over-determinant authoritarian agenda would be to ignore a significant divergence in policy talk and decisions traducing, in turn, the political competition that continues to produce variegated policing agendas and therefore insight into the success of policing alternatives. Analytically this is important because the recognition of alternative agendas identifies sources of innovation and further questions for comparative analysis: what, for example, are the conditions for social justice agendas that disrupt the predominance of criminal justice and risk management?

Posing this question provokes a concern with Clegg's final, 'facilitative', circuit of power, the innovations in technologies of production and discipline that can disrupt or reproduce particular policing agendas. Most obviously, in the contemporary contexts of metropolitan policing in Europe, there are the consequences of the financial crisis of 2008 and the subsequent sovereign debt crises affecting a number of European countries including the UK. The latter subsequently embarked upon an 'austerity' programme of severe cutbacks in public expenditure, including reductions of 20–30% in spending on policing (Edwards & Hughes, 2012). A concern with facilitative power provokes further questions about the impact of austerity on the disruption or further reproduction of deep-rooted, but relatively expensive, criminal justice dispositions in policing. It also provokes questions about the impact of other 'exogenous shocks' on entrenched policing dispositions, such as the migration crisis of summer 2015, the threat of transnational terrorism as witnessed in the attack on Paris in November 2015, and innovations in digital technologies of production and discipline, such as the surveillant powers of 'big data' (Edwards, 2016) that may facilitate 'smarter' criminal justice and risk management agendas or promote the case for social and economic policy responses to metropolitan policing problems.

3 Comparing policing policy agendas in Bristol, Cardiff, London and Edinburgh

These concepts of causal, dispositional and facilitative power can be used, in turn, to clarify processes of convergence or divergence in metropolitan policing agendas and are used here to organise and precis the discussion of policing agendas in Bristol, Cardiff, London and Edinburgh. Given the strong affinities in the governing arrangements for policing in Bristol and Cardiff, it is useful to discuss these in tandem before a consideration of the London and Edinburgh cases.

3.1 Bristol and Cardiff

As noted above, a principal reform to local policing governance in England and Wales, and therefore the 'standing conditions' of metropolitan policing, is the establishment of directly elected PCCs in 2012 in each of the police force areas outside London. The main responsibilities of the PCCs are to allocate the force budget, set the strategic direction and policy priorities for policing, and to hold the chief constable to account.

Each PCC in England and Wales has the statutory obligation to publish their priorities in a Police and Crime Plan, which can be reviewed and amended at any time. In Avon and Somerset and in South Wales, the police force areas in which Bristol and Cardiff are respectively situated, both PCCs publish annually a plan that covers their term of office (for example the first plan was 2013–17, the second 2014–17, and so on). However, there is a potential for conflict between the force-wide priorities of the PCC and those set by the statutory partnerships in both Cardiff and Bristol, which have a role to 'protect local communities from crime and help people feel safer' (Crime and Disorder Act 1998). Composed of various responsible authorities, including, in addition to the police, local government, fire and rescue, health and probation services, the partnerships in both cities have strategies strongly related to policing. Cardiff Integrated Partnership Board has an objective of ensuring, '[p]eople in Cardiff are safe and feel safe' within their 'What Matter's Strategy', which is the overall strategic plan for governing the city between 2010 and 2020. In turn, the statutory partnership in Bristol, entitled, 'Safer Bristol', has an objective of, 'a city of strong and safe communities' which also forms part of the city-wide strategic plan, 'Bristol 20:20'.

Scrutinising the actions of the statutory partnerships in each city is a council-based Oversight and Scrutiny Committee. Prior to the election of PCCs, the Cardiff Overview and Scrutiny Committee voiced concerns that a PCC could disregard local community safety strategies.[7] This concern was based on the vague legislation outlining the powers of PCCs, and was said to be exacerbated by the fact that the PCC would receive the funding from which to commission community safety projects that had previously been managed by the partnerships themselves.[8] This, it was argued by the committee, has the potential to undermine the capacity of partnerships to set their own agenda for community safety and to generate conflict with the PCC's regional agenda. Similar concerns were raised in Bristol and, in the London context, between MOPAC and the community safety partnerships in each of the 32 London Boroughs constituting the Greater London region.

A significant contrast in the standing conditions of metropolitan policing in the two cities is provided by the Welsh government and its interests in community safety in Cardiff and other Welsh localities. Following its establishment in 1999, the Welsh Government has competences in a number of the, areas covered by the responsible authorities in the statutory partnerships for community safety, in particular local government and health services. Significantly and symbolically, community safety policy making is located in the Welsh Government's Department for Local Government and Social Justice, emphasising the Welsh Government's promotion of social and economic policy responses to problems of crime and civil unrest. A key vehicle for this approach has been the All Wales Youth Offending Strategy. This emphasises the responsibilities of the state to ensure that the entitlements that young people have to health, housing, education, training and employment opportunities are effectively extended to all young people. In this social justice framework, youth offending is understood primarily in terms of the failures of social and economic policy to effectively support the young people in question rather than in terms of the risky behaviours these young people have chosen to indulge in and for which they are, in the terms of criminal justice, culpable. In support of this approach the Welsh Government has provided funds to community safety partnerships through its Safer Communities Fund and its Substance Misuse Action Fund (Welsh Assembly Government, 2009). Since the introduction of PCCs this funding has been substantially reduced, and has a narrower focus, renamed as the Youth Crime Prevention Fund, yet the Welsh government remains a key funding provider of community safety, including the provision of £16.8 million for 500 additional Police and Community Support Officers (Chambers, 2016).

The influence of the Welsh Government in these standing conditions of policing governance in Cardiff adds another potential source of tension between its social justice agenda, the strategic agenda of the PCCs and the priorities of Cardiff Council. However, these tensions may be as much about the competition for resources as they are about the dispositions, the kinds of policing problems and policy responses, that are prioritised. This certainly seems to be a key finding of case study research into the respective priorities of the PCCs in Avon and Somerset and in South Wales, and the community safety partnerships in Bristol and Cardiff (Chambers, 2016). This research identifies a striking convergence in the priorities given by all these actors to reducing domestic and sexual violence, promoting community cohesion, improving offender management, reducing first time entrants to the youth justice system and making people 'feel safer'. Rather, the principal sources of tension occur over the competition for resources, in support of action on these shared priorities, amongst the various municipal authorities within the police force-wide areas covered by the PCCs. In Avon and Somerset, Bristol competes with five other local governments for a share of the PCC's budget. In South Wales, Cardiff is one of seven local governments competing for PCC funds including Newport and Swansea, the other main cities in Wales, and the multiply deprived former mining towns in the South Wales valleys. This struggle for resources has been accentuated by the impact of the UK Government's austerity programme and the associated severe reductions in funding made available to the Welsh Government (which, unlike the Scottish Parliament, does not have tax-raising powers and is consequently dependent on the UK Government in London for core funding) and to local authorities in England and Wales. Over the period in which this austerity programme has been pursued, first by the UK Coalition Government in office from 2010–15 and then by the Conservative Government elected in May 2015, local authority budgets have been cut by just over a third (Centre for Local Economic Strategies/Trades Union Congress, 2014: 2). Case study research into the consequences of these severe financial cuts for the community safety priorities pursued by Cardiff Integrated Partnership Board identifies a major reduction in governing capacity, to the point that the resources simply do not exist to deliver on the rhetorical objectives of the City's 'What Matters' strategy to establish Cardiff as a socially just and 'restorative' city. It is argued these cuts have not been compensated by the relatively limited budgets controlled by the PCC or even of the Welsh Government which initially sought to insulate Welsh local government from the full impact of austerity budgets experienced by their English counterparts (Cartwright, 2016).

In summary, a comparison of the governing arrangements and policy agendas for policing in Bristol and Cardiff reveals a common preoccupation with volume crimes and issues of social cohesion, a significant contrast in the social justice disposition of community safety policy in Cardiff, primarily under the influence of the Welsh Government, but in both cities an acute struggle for resources to deliver policing policy agendas in a context of severe financial cuts imposed by the UK government's austere public expenditure policy.

3.2 London

In London, the responsibilities of the PCC are assumed by the directly elected mayor. Given the other substantial duties of the mayor of London, the practice has been to delegate these responsibilities to a deputy mayor for policing and crime (DMPC). This first occurred during the administration of Mayor Boris Johnson, of the Conservative Party, who first assumed responsibility for setting the strategic direction and budgeting of the Metropolitan Police Service for London in January 2012 and who appointed Stephen Greenhalgh as DMPC to lead MOPAC. In May 2016 the opposition Labour Party's candidate, Sadiq Khan, was elected mayor of London and, in turn, he appointed Sophie Linden as his DMPC. At the time of writing the new administration were in the process of composing their Police and Crime Plan but the cross-examination of Linden at her appointment hearing at a meeting of the Police and Crime Committee in City Hall on 9 June 2016[9] suggested a significant shift in the agenda from that pursued by the former Johnson/Greenhalgh administration.

This former administration has been characterised as a 'developmental regime', augmenting a criminal justice agenda for policing London through measures aimed at managing the risks of offending and victimisation (Edwards & Prins, 2014). In contrast, Linden defined the broad principles of her agenda by arguing, '[i]t's about justice but also about pursuing social justice'. Drawing upon her previous experience as deputy leader of Hackney Council, one of the 32 Borough Councils comprising the Greater London area covered by the mayor's city-wide administration, and her leadership of community safety policy in that Borough, Linden referenced her use of social and economic policy interventions to divert young people from gang-related violence, using youth services and non-governmental organisations as well as police and criminal justice agencies. The full articulation of this agenda must await the production of the new administration's Police and Crime Plan for Khan and Linden's four-year term of office, through to 2020, but some of the tensions and challenges this agenda is likely to encounter can be clarified through reference to the experience of the previous Johnson/Greenhalgh administration.

The Greater London area covered by the mayor of London's administration is more of a region than a city, certainly when compared to the other capital cities in Britain and provincial English cities such as Bristol. It is also the largest metropolis in Europe with a population exceeding 8 million registered residents who, for the purposes of public administration, are served by 32 Borough administrations. The London Boroughs are district-rather than regional-level authorities, equivalent in status to the city administrations of Bristol, Cardiff and Edinburgh and, for policing purposes, each has its own statutory community safety partnership. These standing conditions for policing policy making generate particular competitive tensions and interests. MOPAC sets the strategic direction and budgets for the Metropolitan Police Service (MPS) across London but, beneath this city-wide strategy, the MPS works 'in partnership' with the Boroughs and with other authorities perceived to have a responsibility for community safety, including health authorities, fire and rescue services, and probation or offender management services. A major feature of the Johnson/Greenhalgh administration was the conflict that arose over MOPAC's decision to set city-wide priorities irrespective of the particular concentration of problems in the different Boroughs (Edwards & Prins, 2014: 81–82).

Central to that administration's Police and Crime Plan was the '20:20:20 Challenge' to reduce, by 20%, seven priority crimes, 'The MOPAC 7' (violence with injury, robbery, burglary, theft of a motor vehicle, theft from a motor vehicle, theft from the person, and vandalism), whilst simultaneously reducing public expenditure on policing by 20% and boosting public confidence in policing by 20%. A common reaction to this strategy amongst the Boroughs was epitomised in the London Borough of Southwark's response to the public consultation over the 20:20:20 challenge. This Borough argued that Southwark accounted for the highest levels of knife crime in the city and, at the time, increasing rates of youth-related crime and robbery against a backdrop of a London-wide overall reduction in these crime rates. It was argued this more Borough-specific pattern was obscured by the use MOPAC made of aggregated, city-wide, data on the declining rates of crime to bolster their claim that it was possible to reduce both crime and expenditure on crime reduction by a fifth. In summary, this Borough argued, '[t]he crime levels in Southwark, combined with its high density and footfall demand a much greater allocation of resources' (cited in Edwards & Prins, 2014: 81).

This problem of tailoring policing to the particular contexts found within cities whilst pursuing city-wide policies is accentuated in London, given its particular position within the national, European and global security fields. As the capital of the UK and the principal centre of global financial services, it is a symbolic target for mass political demonstrations over the economic and foreign policies pursued by the UK Government. The city has also been a target for political violence including the bombing campaign pursued by the Provisional Irish Republican Army prior to the Northern Ireland peace process and, more recently, the suicide bombing of the public transport system on 7 July 2005 by critics of the UK's foreign policy in the Middle East and, allegedly, to all those of the Muslim faith. In a valedictory video recorded prior to his participation in these bombings, Mohammad Sidique Khan argued: 'Your democratically-elected governments continuously perpetrate atrocities against my people all over the world. And your support of them makes you directly responsible, just as I am directly responsible for protecting and avenging my Muslim brothers and sisters' (cited in Edwards & Prins, 2014: 77).

The '7/7' bombings exemplify London's particular vulnerability to the import of global security threats which necessarily stretch policing priorities and resources. In the policy argot of the NIM, such terrorist incidents are defined as 'Level 3' threats which have an international dimension. Another Level 3 threat stretching policing priorities and resources is that of organised crime. Given its lucrative markets for illicit goods and services, from racketeering and unregulated gambling to prostitution and narcotics, the city has long been a magnet for criminal enterprises from the iconic 'firms' of the Kray and Richardson twins to the more mobile 'transnational' enterprises of the present (Hobbs, 2013). In addition to the city's role in hosting major international and national cultural and sporting events, such as the 2012 Olympic Games, policing in London is also stretched by 'Level 2' threats, which refer to inter-regional problems within the UK, primarily the distribution of narcotics. After Amsterdam, London is a principal focus for the wholesale markets in illicit drugs. From London these are then distributed to the other major wholesale drug centres in the UK, the West Midlands, Greater Manchester and Merseyside, before further distribution out to local drugs markets. Consequently, the MPS plays a significant role in policing and seeking to disrupt this distribution chain, albeit a role that has been further complicated by the establishment of the UK National Crime Agency in 2013 with which the MPS and other police services cooperate on Level 2 and 3 threats.

Simultaneously, however, policing in London is stretched by substantial 'Level 1' threats, the mundane volume personal and property crimes and 'anti-social behaviour' that preoccupy the public and, more specifically, the electorate for the Mayor and for politicians in the 32 Boroughs. As indicated by Southwark Borough's response to MOPAC's Police and Crime Plan, patterns of victimisation and disadvantage vary enormously between Boroughs, including Borough-specific problems of gun, knife and gang-related crime (Hallsworth & Young, 2008), but also within them, reflecting the increasing social inequalities and allied relative deprivation in London. Commentary on the transition of London's economy from an industrial city to the 'command centre' for global financial services has catalogued the consequences of this for social polarisation in its labour and housing markets, the implications of this for social exclusion, particularly amongst the young, and the relationship of this inequality to patterns of mundane crime and civil unrest (Edwards & Prins, 2014: 75). Whilst the relationship between social class composition, (im)mobility in labour and housing markets, and allied patterns of mundane crime and disorder is a well-established theme in studies of policing London (Cohen, 1979), the additional pressures on policing the city arising from its role in the greater transnational mobility of illicit as well as licit capital, labour, goods and services represents a new social condition intensifying the competing interests in prioritising Level 3, 2 or 1 threats.

These competing pressures confront mayors of any political party and policing disposition in London. The developmental policing regime pursued by the Johnson/Greenhalgh administration was vulnerable to the criticism that it was degrading policing capacity in multiply deprived Boroughs, such as Southwark, with particularly challenging problems of mundane crime, a problem of capacity that had been exposed earlier in Johnson's first term of office as mayor during the city-wide riots of August 2011. Unlike previous bouts of major civil unrest in the city, as in Brixton in 1981 or Tottenham in 1985, in 2011 rioting was not contained within particular Boroughs but spread rapidly and was coordinated with the aid of mobile smartphones and social media services, effectively outflanking the police for the first 48 hours of the unrest (*The Guardian*/LSE, 2011). Early signs are that the new Khan/Linden administration intends to pursue a more transformative social justice agenda for policing which may result in a more nuanced tailoring of policing to Borough-specific contexts, possibly aided by innovations in the analysis of 'big data' and so-called 'smart' or 'predictive' policing (Edwards, 2017). However, the Khan/Linden administration will inherit an MPS degraded through 20% reductions in investment but also, and more critically for its social justice agenda, a local government system of Boroughs decimated by austere budget settlements since 2010. The practical realities of this enormous shock to public administration in London include the closure of out-of-school educational and leisure facilities for young people, the loss of whole cohorts of local civil servants with expertise in social and economic policy responses to crime, and the consequent and enormous pressure placed on the police as first and last line of defence against security threats.

This has a direct bearing on the kinds of community-oriented policing strategies that are central to the social justice agenda and which, it is claimed, have been central to the successful anticipation and disruption of further acts of political violence in London as well as preventing 'radicalisation' and enhancing 'community cohesion'. Following the series of terrorist incidents experienced in French cities in 2015 and 2016, there has been a certain tendency to favourably compare London's greater resilience to similar attacks, post-7/7, and to explain this in terms of the capacity of policing in the UK capital to effectively connect Level 3 to Level 1 policy responses.[10] It is, however, precisely this capacity to stretch policing in London across Level 3, 2 and 1 threats that is in jeopardy as a consequence of the developmental regime pursued by Johnson and Greenhalgh.

3.3 Edinburgh

As the capital city of Scotland, Edinburgh is home to the Scottish Parliament and the government buildings, offices, international consulates, an international airport, and financial services headquarters associated with this status. This alone ensures that Edinburgh is often the chosen venue of political marches and events that require to be stewarded, notwithstanding the ongoing security needs of such institutions. It is also a capital city that thrives on the dynamism of attracting distinct transient populations through it on a seasonal basis. It hosts high-profile international arts and sciences festivals – The Edinburgh International Festival and the Edinburgh Fringe being the most significant – which bring around a quarter of a million visitors to the city for the late summer months. Three universities mean that the city is also home to a substantial, relatively transient and diverse population of students for large parts of the year, a population that also helps to sustain a vibrant night-time economy. Under the surface of this image of Edinburgh as lively and prosperous it is also shaped by inequality and disadvantage, containing some of the most deprived neighbourhoods in the country (see HMICS, 2015 for a useful overview of the challenges of policing Edinburgh).

The standing conditions, dispositions and facilitative powers shaping the metropolitan policing agenda for Edinburgh are made in the context of the recent (2013) reforms to the policing of Scotland. In terms of standing conditions, Edinburgh (like other local authorities) has a Local Policing Plan as required under the police reform legislation which must be drawn up by the local police commander in consultation with local partners and approved by the local council (the police reform legislation is silent on what would happen if the Local Policing Plan were not approved). In addition the policing environment is also shaped by the strategic work carried out through the Edinburgh Partnership with which the police retain a statutory obligation to participate. These standing conditions within which actors negotiate a discernible Edinburgh vision of policing and security have been much affected by the creation of Police Scotland, although the arrangements have recently been reviewed by the chair of the Scottish Police Authority given wider concerns about the emerging tensions between centralism and localism within the new policing landscape (Scottish Police Authority, 2016). As briefly noted, the 2012 Act might be seen as embodying contradictory impulses towards local policing.

On the one hand, the Act has placed local policing on a statutory footing emphasising its importance within the new national structure (chapter 7 of the Act) and set a context for an approach to local policing by setting out normative policing principles (with deliberate echoes of the Peelian principles of policing drawn up for London's Metropolitan Police of 1829) that offer a narrative of policing based on partnership working, community well-being, and focused on measures to prevent harm, crime and disorder (para. 32). On the other hand the Act has reconfigured the police relationship with local government as a consultative one, moving powers over finance and the appointment and dismissal of senior ranks to the Scottish Police Authority, a central governance body covering the whole of Scotland. In addition, responsibility for overall policing strategy in Scotland now lies jointly with the Scottish Police Authority and the executive team within Police Scotland. One consequence of this has been growing public and political unease about the asymmetrical power relations between 'central' and 'local' institutions within the new policing arrangements which has been exemplified by the experience of Edinburgh. The first six months of the new national police force saw the abolition of Edinburgh's specialist housebreaking unit (because of a national strategic decision to lower the priority given to property crime in order to focus on inter-personal violence), greater use of enforcement powers in relation to the city's saunas (used by the sex industry), and a 100% increase in the recorded use of stop and search, all developments seen as running counter to the pre-reform policing approach in the city and as illustrative of Police Scotland, and not the Edinburgh Division, setting the agenda in terms of priorities and policing styles.

These developments speak directly to the broader issues of dispositional and facilitative power within contemporary Scottish policing. In terms of dispositional power, Police Scotland has been keen to assert an identity strongly oriented towards policing as crime fighting and law enforcement. This was clearly signalled in a public lecture delivered by the chief constable less than six months into his new role. Although he spoke very positively about partnership, emphasising that '[p]artnership is not under threat from Police Scotland', in defining more precisely the role of the police in such partnerships, the chief constable made clear his view about the police mission, asserting that '[w]e are not a solutions agency, we are a restraint agency. We can control behaviour, we can rarely change it ... I will insist that we remember our unique area, the unique selling point that we should have is that we are an enforcement agency' (House, 2013: 9).

The operation carried out by the new national force on saunas in Edinburgh exemplified this thinking and prompted the convenor of the Scottish Parliament's Justice Committee to observe that these raids provided 'quite a dramatic example of the fears that local policing – which seemed to be succeeding in a different way in a different place – was being overridden by a national attitude that came from the top'. This view was endorsed by one of Police Scotland's most senior officers, who noted that '[t]he sauna raids in Edinburgh challenged a way of policing that had existed for a decade or more in terms of style and methods. The new policy pursued by Police Scotland challenged the approach that police had taken there which was about tolerance and harm minimisation' (*The Scotsman*, 2014).

This exercise of dispositional power by Police Scotland, allowing it to impose a national policing agenda of crime fighting and law enforcement in Edinburgh, has been underpinned by two 'facilitative' mechanisms. The first has been the creation of a national police itself, an innovation that has overturned nearly 200 years of local, municipal policing in Scotland and which was driven explicitly by the financial crisis of 2008. The ensuing cuts to public spending prompted the Scottish Government to search for a financially sustainable policing model, resulting in the decision to merge the country's eight local forces to create a single police service and therefore allow a centralisation of power over the policing of local areas. The second facilitative mechanism has been the introduction of a performance regime within the national police force based around a set of key enforcement-focused indicators. With strong parallels with the Compstat performance technologies deployed in New York City in the 1980s, Police Scotland has adopted a model of performance management in which a local police commander in Edinburgh must focus their resources on targets set centrally by the force executive. The consequence has been spiralling rates of 'stop and search' and the marginalisation of 'softer' policing approaches, such as partnership working and other engagement activities, not readily accommodated within quantitatively based performance metrics. Thus, although the Edinburgh Division has clearly made efforts to reflect particular local concerns, any articulation of a distinctive 'Edinburgh approach' to policing has been significantly constrained by the broader policing environment within Scotland that has allowed much greater central influence over local policing.

4 Convergent or divergent agendas?

In the light of these case studies it is possible to reach some conclusions about the existence and significance of divergent tendencies in metropolitan policing agendas in Britain. The predicates we have used for comparing agendas in Bristol, Cardiff, London and Edinburgh, those of the circuits of power, reveal a significant divergence in the standing conditions and dispositions of policing agendas in these city-regions. They also suggest that major external shocks to the policing policy environment in Britain, including devolution, austerity and potential withdrawal from the EU, facilitate a further intensification of the 'local reality' of metropolitan policing whilst disrupting the meaning and efficacy of sovereign power and its projection through a national security state. By way of conclusion, our thesis on divergence can be summarised in terms of these three circuits of causal, dispositional and facilitative power.

PCCs and the mayor of London clearly have the power to cause shifts in policing agendas notwithstanding resistance from the statutory community safety partnerships within their regional administrations. However, this political agency is exercised within certain standing conditions that constrain and enable the capacity of these actors to formulate and defend their agendas. These conditions include a constitutional-legal framework which, following the establishment of the PCCs and as part of the UK government's broader city-regions programme, now explicitly devolves strategic leadership of policing to directly elected policy makers. These conditions also include the tensions between the local, regional and transnational policing priorities identified in the UK National Intelligence Model. In these terms, divergence in policy agendas reflects the specific configuration of local, regional and transnational problems confronting a global city like London as contrasted with the other capital cities of Britain and provincial cities like Bristol. It could be argued these actors fail to act on the discretion given to them by various devolution deals as they choose, instead, the risk-averse option of copying others' 'best practice'. The critical issue is whether these powers and liabilities are comprehended and acted upon by policy makers. The failure to act upon context-specific challenges can be a product both of centralised performance management, compelling local authorities to prioritise problems that have limited local relevance, and of the impulse to copy in which the plagiarism of other metropolitan policing agendas appeals to those with limited resources or no inclination to formulate their own bespoke policies. These policy drivers may result in a convergence of policy agendas amongst the less resourceful or imaginative, but they should not blind social scientists to the specificity of metropolitan policing. In questioning the rival thesis of policy convergence we have found it useful to consider the effects of dispositional power.

Policing dispositions, specifically the meanings and membership categories which integrate actors into, and exclude others from, particular policy agendas, help to clarify tendencies toward convergence or divergence. The implications of our case studies suggest that devolution has witnessed convergence, as in the 'de-tartanisation' of youth justice in Scotland during the early years of the Scottish Parliament, but also its 're-tartanisation' following the electoral success of the SNP. It has also been argued that the consistent leadership of the Welsh Government by the Labour Party has facilitated an explicit social justice agenda for responding to youth crime and a related rejection of anti-social behaviour orders. The latter have been dismissed by the Welsh Government as a form of 'low-trust' governance that may have prevailed in some of the English city-regions, most notoriously in Greater Manchester, but which is antipathetic to the more inclusive agenda for safer communities that has been promoted by the Labour administration in Wales (Edwards & Hughes, 2008; Drakeford, 2010). Our case studies also identify divergent tendencies amongst city-regional policing agendas, such as the developmental agenda in Bristol, which under the new PCC has prioritised criminal justice and risk management responses to volume crimes and public disorder, and the transformative agenda in Cardiff, which has prioritised social and economic policy responses and investment in restorative justice for safer and cohesive communities. As noted, our case studies also registered a significant shift in London from a developmental to a transformative policing agenda following the election of the Khan/Linden administration.

A comparative understanding of the stabilisation or disruption of these agendas requires further research to investigate any 'implementation gaps' between the formulation and outcomes of policing agendas 'in action' (see Edwards, Devroe and Ponsaers, this volume). Research into Cardiff's agenda for community safety suggests, however, that its dependence on funding from the UK Government left it vulnerable to the severe reductions in public expenditure imposed by this government through its austerity programme, and this, in turn, subverted the implementation of Cardiff's social justice agenda (Cartwright, 2016). This experience reinforces a key insight of the circuits of power framework that rival centres of political authority are nonetheless inter-dependent and cannot, certainly in advanced liberal democracies, unilaterally command their will to be done. The implication of this is that where rival authorities fail to bargain and negotiate, they are liable to disrupt each others' objectives. As such, the UK government may have facilitated the formulation of a social justice agenda in Cardiff through its various devolution deals, first with the Welsh Government and subsequently with authorities in the Cardiff city-region, only then to disrupt this agenda through withdrawal of the financial support required for its implementation.

The power to disrupt is nonetheless qualitatively different from the power to project policy agendas and, in this regard, the UK Government's own security agenda requires the active support of the various authorities with which it has struck devolution deals. This has been less of a problem for recent UK government administrations which have, since the election of the Coalition Government in 2010, pursued a policy of aggressively restructuring public administration in an attempt to reduce its size and capacities for social intervention whilst simultaneously devolving responsibility for governance to various sub-national actors, 'the new localism', and also to private citizens and their voluntary associations, the 'Big Society'. As argued in an earlier reflection on this restructuring, the principal implication for policing is the abandonment of vulnerable populations to various forms of predatory self-governance rather than any further enhancement of an authoritarian, national, security state (Edwards & Hughes, 2012). Again, this experience of abandonment is liable to be highly uneven, reflecting inequalities in policing capacity between relatively prosperous city-regions with wealthier tax bases and those that have been in long-term economic decline and which are disproportionately dependent on the very public services that have been radically reduced through the austerity programme.

These divergent tendencies are likely to be further intensified by Brexit and, should it come to pass, the actual withdrawal of the UK from membership of the EU. Withdrawal from the EU and, consequently, access to its regional development funds also puts the viability of thriving city-regions into doubt, unless they can all successfully reintegrate themselves into the wider global economy without the economic stimulus of participation in the European single market. Such reintegration is likely to be more feasible for some city-regions, such as London, which are already integrated into the global economy, than others, such as Cardiff or Bristol, whose fortunes have been more closely tied to the EU. This, to return to the starting point of our argument, is the fundamental implication of processes of 'glocalisation': they subvert national sovereign power to govern localities whilst privileging the fortunes of certain city-regions at the cost of others.

The implication of this for policing is that metropolitan-specific configurations of local, regional and transnational security will intensify whether or not policy makers acknowledge and respond to these with appropriately tailored policy agendas. For advocates of Brexit, it is precisely the capacity to 'take back control' of borders and thus control the import and export of illicit as well as licit capital, labour, goods and services that makes withdrawal from the EU appealing. In the Brexit imagination, withdrawal from the EU facilitates the reconstitution of a powerful national sovereignty that could, from the perspective of British social democracy, be used to 're-balance' the national economy in ways that reduce the predominance of finance capital in London and the south-east of England and the gross, criminogenic, social inequalities within and between city-regions that has accompanied this political-economy. However, amongst the advocates of Brexit, this kind of social democratic isolationism has been a minority voice, whilst the more powerful refrain, certainly of the current Conservative UK Government, is that Britain 'remains open for business'. Logically, this implies the exposure of British city-regions to even more intensive global market competition and thus even greater social inequality. In this scenario, configurations of local, regional and transnational security threats are liable to become even more unevenly experienced and metropolitan-specific than at present, further emphasising the analytical importance of comparing the politics of security in city-regions.

Notes

1 Multi-agency partnerships for community safety are not specific to Wales, although they explain the particular interest in, and influence over, policing by the Welsh government even though police and criminal justice policy making is not, as yet, devolved to Wales. Initially these partnerships evolved on an ad hoc basis throughout England and Wales and in Scotland as a consequence of forward-looking, innovative local authorities and chief constables who voluntarily cooperated as a means of tackling problems of crime and civil unrest through preventive interventions not just reactive criminal law enforcement. Such was the perceived success of this approach that forming multi-agency partnerships became a statutory duty, placed on all local authorities and police services in England and Wales, by the Crime and Disorder Act 1998. During this 'national mandatory period', public policing was statutorily required to be an exercise in partnership between the police, local authorities and other 'responsible authorities', in particular health, fire and rescue, and offender management services, and something that could not, therefore, be reduced simply to the actions of the (state) police. Gilling et al. (2013) argue that this period has since been superseded by the 'new localism' promoted by the Coalition Government, 2010–15, and the Conservative administration elected in 2015. In this period responsible authorities have been freed from detailed performance management by national government in England and Wales (but not in Scotland, see below) and invited to formulate their own partnership approach, but have also had their resources severely reduced in line with the 'austerity programme' pursued by these administrations.
2 For a comparison of policing in the UK and Eire, see Gilling et al. (2013); for a recent review of policing in Northern Ireland see Topping (2016) and Ellison and O'Reilly (2008).
3 www.corecities.com (accessed on 18 August 2016).
4 The UK National Intelligence Model (NIM) was first introduced by the National Criminal Intelligence Service (NCIS) in 2000 and endorsed by both the Association of Chief Police Officers for England, Wales and Northern Ireland (ACPO) and the Association of Chief Police Officers in Scotland (ACPOS) (see NCIS, 2000). Subsequently NCIS, which provided intelligence support to police services in ACPO and ACPOS on matters of transnational crimes such as drug trafficking and regional cross-police service threats such as football hooliganism, was replaced by the Serious Organised Crime Agency in 2006, which, in turn, was replaced by the UK National Crime Agency in 2013. Also, in 2013 ACPOS was disbanded following the establishment of the single national Police Service of Scotland, entitled 'Police Scotland'. Whilst this institutional and constitutional reform reflects the very tensions and processes of fragmentation that are the focus of this chapter, the NIM remains in use as a conceptual framework which policing policy makers can use to distinguish between, and subsequently prioritise, threats that are primarily local (Level 1), from those that are regional and necessitate cooperation between different policing agencies (Level 2), and those that are transnational, including terrorism (Level 3). Much of the current politics of policing in the UK, including that of metropolitan policing, reflects disputes over the appropriate conceptualisation of security threats in terms of the three levels of the NIM, their subsequent prioritisation and the consequent implications for funding. It is argued here that abstractions about national sovereign power and the national security state may capture certain tendencies in this politics but they cannot account for the range of disputes over the politics of policing in the UK

nor facilitate an understanding of their significance in the increasingly fragmented institutional and constitutional contexts of policing in the UK.
5 A reference to the national symbol of Wales, 'Y Ddraig Goch', 'The Red Dragon'.
6 An analogy with the distinctively Scottish 'tartan' cloth.
7 Cardiff Overview and Scrutiny Committee meeting, 23 October 2012.
8 Following distribution by the Welsh government.
9 For a full webcast of this hearing, see: www.london.gov.uk/police-and-crime-committee-2016-06-09
10 See *Independent*, 'Paris attacks analysis: what more can the authorities do to protect the British public?', Sunday 15 November 2015, see: www.independent.co.uk/news/uk/politics/paris-attacks-how-britain-is-responding-to-prevent-a-similar-atrocity-on-uk-soil-a6735606.html (accessed 5 August 2016).

Bibliography

BBC News (2015) 'Queen's Speech 2015: "Metro mayors" able to replace PCCs', 27 May, see: www.bbc.co.uk/news/uk-england-32897288 (accessed 18 August 2016).
Bowling, B., Sheptycki, J. (2012) *Global Policing*, London: Sage.
Cartwright, T. (2016) *Community Safety in an Age of Austerity: An Urban Regime Analysis of Cardiff, 1999–2015*, unpublished PhD thesis, Cardiff University.
Centre for Local Economic Strategies/Trades Union Congress (2014) *Austerity Uncovered*, London: Centre for Local Economic Strategies.
Chambers, S. (2016) *The Impact of Police and Crime Commissioners on Community Safety Agendas in England and Wales: A Comparative Study of South Wales and Avon and Somerset, 2012–2016*, unpublished PhD thesis, Cardiff University.
Clegg, S. (1989) *Frameworks of Power*, London: Sage.
Cohen, P. (1979/1981) 'Policing the working class city', in M. Fitzgerald et al. (eds), *Crime and Society*, London: Routledge & Kegan Paul.
DiMaggio, P., Powell, W. (1983) 'The iron cage revisited: Institutional isomorphism and collective rationality in organizational fields', *American Sociological Review*, 48(2): 147–160.
Drakeford, M. (2010) 'Devolution and youth justice in Wales', *Criminology and Criminal Justice*, 10(2): 137–154.
Edwards, A. (2016) 'Multi-centred governance and circuits of power in liberal modes of security', *Global Crime*, 17(3–4): 240–263.
Edwards, A. (2017) 'Big data, predictive machines and security: The minority report', in M. McGuire and T.J. Holth (eds), *Routledge Handbook of Technology, Crime and Justice*, London: Routledge.
Edwards, A., Hughes, G. (2008) 'Resilient Fabians? Anti-social behaviour and community safety work in Wales', in P. Squires (ed.), *ASBO Nation: The Criminalization of Nuisance*, Bristol: Policy Press.
Edwards, A., Hughes, G. (2009) 'The preventive turn and the promotion of safer communities in England and Wales', in A. Crawford (ed.), *Crime Prevention Policies in Comparative Perspective*, Cullompton: Willan Publishing.
Edwards, A., Hughes, G. (2012) 'Public safety regimes: Negotiated orders and political analysis in criminology', *Criminology and Criminal Justice*, 12(4): 433–458.

Edwards, A., Prins, R. (2014) 'Policing and crime in contemporary London: A developmental agenda?', *European Journal of Policing Studies*, 2(1): 61–93.
Ellison, G., O'Reilly, C. (2008) '"Ulster's policing goes global": The police reform process in Northern Ireland and the creation of a global brand', *Crime, Law and Social Change*, 50(4): 331–351.
European Commission (2015) *The European Agenda on Security*, Strasbourg, 28 April, COM(2015) 185 final.
Fyfe, N.R., Henry, A. (2012) 'Negotiating divergent trends of police reform within the UK', *Journal of Police Studies*, 4, 171–190.
Garland, D. (1996) 'The limits of the sovereign state: Strategies of crime control in contemporary society', *British Journal of Criminology*, 36(4): 445–471.
Gilling, D., Hughes, G., Bowden, M., Edwards, A., Henry, A., Topping, J. (2013) 'Powers liabilities and expertise in community safety: Comparative lessons for "urban security" from the United Kingdom and the Republic of Ireland', *European Journal of Criminology*, 10(3): 326–340.
The Guardian , LSE (London School of Economics and Political Science) (2011) 'Reading the riots: Investigating England's summer of disorder', at: www.theguardian.com/uk/series/reading-the-riots (accessed 6 June 2014).
Hallsworth, S., Lea, J. (2011) 'Reconstructing Leviathan: Emerging contours of the security state', *Theoretical Criminology*, 15(2): 141–157.
Hallsworth, S., Young, T. (2008) 'Gang talk and gang talkers: A critique', *Crime, Media, Culture: An International Journal*, 4(2): 175–195.
Hamnett, C. (2003) *Unequal City: London in the Global Arena*, London: Routledge.
HMICS (Her Majesty's Inspectorate of Constabulary in Scotland) (2015) 'Inspection of Edinburgh Division', in *Local Policing + Inspection Programme*, Edinburgh: Her Majesty's Inspectorate of Constabulary in Scotland.
Hobbs, D. (2013) *Lush Life: Constructing Organized Crime in the UK*, Oxford: Clarendon Press.
House, S. (2013) 'Collaborative working and shrinking budgets: Can we get better value by behaving smarter?', in *Apex Scotland Annual Lecture*, Edinburgh: Apex Scotland.
Hughes, G. (2007) *The Politics of Crime and Community*, London: Palgrave.
Jessop, B. (2004) 'Hollowing out the "nation state" and multilevel governance', in P. Kennett (ed.), *Handbook of Comparative Social Policy*, Cheltenham: Edward Elgar Publishing.
Lea, J., Stenson, K. (2007) 'Security, sovereignty, and non-state governance "from below"', *Canadian Journal of Law and Society*, 22(2): 9–27.
Massey, D. (2007) *World City*, Cambridge: Polity.
McAra, L. (2008) 'Crime, criminology and criminal justice in Scotland', *European Journal of Criminology*, 5(4): 481–504.
McAra, L. (2014). 'Crime and justice: A vision for modern Scotland', in *Apex Scotland Annual Lecture*, Edinburgh: Apex Scotland.
Moulaert, F., Martinelli, F., Gonzalez, S., Swyngedouw, E. (2007) 'Introduction: Social innovation and governance in European cities: Urban development between path dependency and radial innovation', *European Urban and Regional Studies*, 14(3): 195–208.

NCIS (National Criminal Intelligence Service) (2000) *The National Intelligence Model*, London: NCIS, see: www.intelligenceanalysis.net/National%20Intelligence%20Model.pdf (accessed 18 August 2016).

Sassen, S. (2001) *The Global City*, second edn, Princeton, NJ: Princeton University Press.

The Scotsman (2014) 'Edinburgh sauna raids show police "culture clash"', *The Scotsman*, 30 May, www.scotsman.com/news/edinburgh-sauna-raids-show-police-culture-clash-1-3427402 (accessed 28 August 2016).

Scottish Police Authority (2016) *Review of Governance in Policing*, Glasgow: SPA, see: www.spa.police.uk/assets/128635/337350/337362 (accessed 18 August 2016).

Stenson, K. (2012) 'The state, sovereignty and advanced marginality in the city', in P. Squires, J. Lea (eds), *Criminalisation and Advanced Marginality, Critically Exploring the Work of Loic Wacquant*, Bristol: The Policy Press.

Swyngedouw, E. (1997) 'Neither global nor local: "Glocalization" and the politics of scale', in K.R. Cox (ed.), *Spaces of Globalization: Reasserting the Power of the Local*, London: Longman.

Sztompka, P. (1990) 'Conceptual frameworks in comparative inquiry: Divergent or convergent?', in M. Albrow and E. King (eds), *Globalization, Knowledge and Society: Readings from International Sociology*, London: Sage.

Terpstra, J., Fyfe, N.R. (2015) 'Mind the implementation gap? Police reform and local policing in the Netherlands and Scotland', *Criminology and Criminal Justice*, 15(5): 527–544.

Topping, J. (2016) 'Accountability, policing, and the police service of Northern Ireland: Local practice, global standards?' in *Accountability of Policing*, Abingdon: Routledge, pp. 150–171.

Warwick Commission (2012) *Elected Mayors and City Leadership, Summary Report of the Third Warwick Commission: What is the Role of Elected Mayors in Providing Strategic Leadership in Cities*, Warwick: Warwick University, see: www2.warwick.ac.uk/research/warwickcommission/electedmayors/summaryreport/the_warwick_commission_on_elected_mayors_and_city_leadership_summary_report.pdf (accessed on 18 August 2016).

Welsh Assembly Government (2009) *Evaluation of the Effectiveness of the Safer Communities Fund, 2006–2009*. Final Research Report Submitted by Cardiff University, Swansea University and ARCS Ltd, http://gov.wales/docs/caecd/research/100205-effectiveness-safer-communities-fund-2006-09-en.pdf (accessed 28 August 2016).

Chapter 9

Germany
Policing metropolises in a system of cooperative federalism: Berlin as the German capital and a city-state compared to Cologne as the biggest city in North Rhine-Westphalia

Hartmut Aden and Bernhard Frevel

1 Introduction

This chapter compares the political agenda for policing in two of Germany's biggest cities: Berlin and Cologne. These cities have been selected for comparison because they share a number of characteristics of all metropolises, while at the same time they differ considerably. Berlin is not only the biggest city in Germany, but also the capital of the Federal Republic, and it has the status of a so-called 'city-state'. This means that Berlin has state status (like Hamburg and Bremen) in the German federation. Cologne is 'just' a city (without state character), it is the fourth biggest city in Germany (after Berlin, Hamburg and Munich) and the biggest city in North Rhine-Westphalia (NRW). Berlin is located in the eastern part of Germany, divided during the Cold War, while Cologne is located in the centre of the most densely populated area of the former (West) German Federal Republic. Both cities face some similar security and safety challenges, for example in the fields of crime and traffic, hosting First League (Bundesliga) football matches (and their associated hooligan problems), dealing with segregation and the conflicts between wealthy and deprived neighbourhoods, or native and migrant inhabitants, with problems of alcohol and drug abuse concentrated in certain locations. Berlin, as the German capital, has some specific security problems like a high number of political demonstrations, the protection of federal ministries and authorities, the presence of embassies and consulates, dealing with state visits and handling major events.

Both cities have many more people present than they have inhabitants. This is due to tourism, the important role of these cities in regional economics, including employment opportunities, and therefore the high commuter population. Both cities consequently function as 'major centres' with large infrastructures, including hospitals, universities and theatres, etc., that are used by people from the wider region.

This comparison will consider the different police systems and the specific framework of a cooperative version of federalism in Germany. Against this backdrop, the chapter explores two central research questions. 1 To what extent can similarities of the political agenda for policing in Berlin and Cologne be explained by the specific patterns of cooperative federalism and to what extent can they be explained by parallel trends, for example the pluralisation of policing and police strategies (cf. Jones & Newburn, 2006)? 2 How can differences between the agenda for policing in these two metropolises be explained? Path dependency (cf. Mahoney, 2000; Werle, 2007) will be identified as a major factor.

2 Policing in the context of cooperative federalism and 'unity in diversity'

Germany has a semi-(de)centralised police system. The 16 German states, the 'Länder', are the dominant political authority for making policy on security issues (Aden, 2004; Aden et al., 2004; Aden & De Pauw, 2014; Groß et al., 2008). The Federation (Bund) has only restricted power over policing according to Articles 70 and 73 of the 'Grundgesetz' (German Basic Law = Constitution). This is a consequence of the path dependency created by the situation in Germany when occupied by the Allied Forces after World War II. The Allied Forces took care to prevent Germany from becoming a centralised authoritarian state as it had been between 1933 and 1945. Therefore, the 16 Länder today enjoy a high level of autonomy in the organisation and steering of their security agencies. The Länder are also the driving force for establishing new security strategies, i.e. local crime prevention initiatives involving different state actors and non-governmental organisations (NGOs) (Aden, 2002; Frevel, 2007). While Berlin as a city-state does not have autonomous local authorities, cities such as Cologne and other NRW local authorities enjoy a high degree of autonomy. However, as policing is a state task, the scope of local decision making for security issues is limited, for example to supporting crime prevention through the urban planning competences that local authorities have. This means that the German police system is more centralised compared, for example, with the US system that is predominantly based on autonomous local police agencies, but more decentralised compared with police systems in unitary states, for example France.

Each 'Land' (and also the 'Bund' for the Federal Police and the Federal Criminal Police Office) has its own police law, organisational structure (with slightly different nomenclature of units and departments), system of oversight and system of police training and career paths for officers. In this system of federalism the Länder have scope for the setting of the political agenda for policing and security. This includes aspects of police 'philosophy', financial endowment, political priorities of the parties involved in coalition governments and ideas of how to steer public administration. The consequences are obvious: a range of differences in several areas of police organisation and policing.

However, decentralisation does not mean that police and policing in the 16 Länder are completely different. The German political system is characterised by a cooperative variation of federalism and a set of instruments, which make similarities not only possible, but in some way guarantee 'unity in diversity'. The nationwide criminal law and penal procedure code and also the nationwide traffic regulations have an integrating effect on policing. These acts have to be applied and enforced by all police officers in Germany. Similarly to what has been observed in the United States and other countries (cf. Garland, 2001), German federal politics, sometimes driven by European Union (EU) politics or the Council of Europe, tend to use criminal law as a reflex to react to new problems and challenges (cf. Schlepper, 2015; and Aden, 2015). In this respect, the federal and the European political agenda directly influence what the semi-(de)centralised police agencies have to enforce.

A second integrating factor comes from the 'Standing Conference of Ministers and Senators of the Interior' (Innenministerkonferenz – IMK) and its 'Arbeitskreis II' (working group II – Internal Security). The conference meetings are not public, but some of the results and decisions are published online (www.innenministerkonferenz.de). Most of the work is done by high-ranking officials and seldom noticed by the public. However, twice a year the meetings of the ministers are in the focus of the media, especially if topics such as terrorism or refugees are on the agenda. This IMK and its working group agreed on some central and convergent aspects which are elements of all police laws: it generates internal Police Service Regulations (Polizeidienstvorschriften) which are mostly applicable for all police forces, and every few years the conference adopts the 'Programme for Internal Security'. These programmes define priorities, especially for nationwide law enforcement and for investment into common police and security technology such as a nationwide IT and communication infrastructure for security agencies.

The third factor that fosters convergence is the fact that all senior police officers of all police forces receive their initial and ongoing education at the German Police University (Deutsche Hochschule der Polizei, the former Polizeiführungsakademie, or Police Leadership Academy). Therefore, German senior police officers share knowledge about policing and are part of a nationwide network (Groß et al., 2008: 36–37), despite the organisational divergence of the police forces to which they belong. In addition, cooperation among the 16 German state administrations is intense and a central feature of governing the decentralised country effectively. Studies comparing metropolises have shown trends of convergence, but also differences due to path dependencies created by institutional settings and the specific historic context of the city and the country in which it is located (cf. Röber & Schröter, 2002). These two overlapping and sometimes contradictory trends, convergence and remaining differences, can also be observed for policing in Berlin and Cologne.

3 Setting the agenda for policing in Berlin and Cologne: political context and institutional structures compared

In most countries, policing functions are not bundled in a single administration, but attributed to a number of public and private actors sharing a broad range of tasks (Bayley, 1994; Aden, 1998; van Sluis et al., 2013). This is also the case in Germany where state police forces carry out most police tasks, supplemented in some areas by federal police forces and a growing number of private security companies.

3.1 Police forces present in Berlin and Cologne

The Federal Police is the successor of the former Federal Border Police (Bundesgrenzschutz), renamed in 2005 due to the diminishing role of border controls in the Schengen Area. By 1992, the former Federal Railway Police had already been integrated into the Federal Border Police. Therefore, the Federal Police is now composed of police units and forces specialising in railway and airport security (Peilert & Kösling, 2008). In Berlin and Cologne, as in all German cities, the Federal Police are mainly present at the railway stations, along the railway lines and at the airports. As all railway stations and the light railway system (S-Bahn) belong to the state-owned Federal Railway Company (Deutsche Bahn), the Federal Police are present in everyday life in both cities. The Federal Criminal Police Office (Bundeskriminalamt), which has its headquarters in Wiesbaden (Hesse), maintains a satellite office in Berlin where it is involved in the protection of government institutions and the coordination with other security agencies, e.g. for anti-terrorism intelligence. The Federal Parliament also has its own small police force in Berlin (Polizei des Deutschen Bundestags) with limited authority in the Parliament buildings.

Berlin, with a territory of 892 square kilometres (km^2), has about 3.42 million inhabitants according to the official federal statistics (Statistisches Bundesamt, 2015: 26). In recent years, the city has been in a process of expansion with 100,000 additional inhabitants arriving between 2005 and 2011 (Amt für Statistik Berlin-Brandenburg, 2012). Further growth is expected in coming years. However, the city had its highest population in 1942 (4.48 million). Towards the end of World War II and in the period of division by the Berlin Wall and the 'iron curtain', the number of inhabitants decreased. The Berlin Police has approximately 21,000 employees in total, including approximately 16,000 police officers (480 per 100,000 inhabitants). The Berlin State Police officers are paid by the city-state.

Cologne has a territory of 405 km² and some 1.04 million inhabitants. It is integrated in a high-density region by the river Rhine and has several other big cities in close proximity, such as Bonn and Leverkusen, and is also quite near Düsseldorf, the capital of North Rhine-Westphalia. Cologne is a major centre for the region with several rural and industrialised counties. The city is famous for its Roman history, a thriving cultural scene, and is important as an education location with more than 80,000 students in 18 universities and academic schools.

The Cologne Police are the biggest regional police force in the state of North Rhine-Westphalia. They have approximately 3,800 officers (312 per 100,000 inhabitants), who are paid by the state. They are not only responsible for the city area of Cologne but also for the city of Leverkusen (with 160,000 inhabitants in 79 km²). As a so-called 'main crime office' (Kriminalhauptstelle) for the Rhine region, the Cologne Police also have special responsibilities outside the police district in fighting serious crime such as murder, hostage taking, organised crime, disruption of social order, crime against the state, etc. The force also polices the motorways in the region and hosts three units of formed police (anti-riot police) and special forces (squad teams, mobile task forces, a negotiation team, a technical unit).

Table 9.1 Facts and figures (Berlin, Cologne)

	Berlin	Cologne
Inhabitants	3,421,829	City: 1,034,175 Police district: 1,195,715
Size	892 km²	City: 405 km² Police district: 484 km²
Number of police officers	16,000	3,833 (in 2013)*
Police officers per 100,000 inhabitants	480	312
Selected crime data (total/ offences per 100,000 inhab.), 2014		(only the city of Cologne)
All registered crimes	543,157/15,873	157,113/15,192
Clearance rate (%)	44.9	43.4
Murder (incl. attempted murder)	131/3.8	25/2.4
Grievous bodily harm	9,946/290.7	3,406/329.3
Robbery	5,697/83.3	1,774/101.4
Theft under aggravating circumstances	12,159/355.3	5,057/489.0

(Bundeskriminalamt, 2015; *Polizei Köln, 2014)

3.2 Policing and security policies in Berlin and Cologne

The impact of policy making on policing metropolises depends on several factors, which are related to, for example, historical developments and their effect on path dependencies, the organisational position of the police in the public administration of the state, the political 'colour' of the government or the – more or less – institutionalised inclusion of the police into local networks with other authorities, NGOs and other partners. Often events such as major disasters or crimes in which shortcomings of the security system have been identified influence the political agenda for policing (cf. Aden, 2008). Politics may encourage the police, for example, to be more present in certain areas or to cooperate with local NGOs in certain crime prevention issues. Some significant differences, but also some similarities, can be found that influence policing strategies in Berlin and Cologne.

Berlin city politics and policies, public security included, are still largely dominated by the consequences of reunification. The need for investment in public infrastructure is still high – for streets and public transport, schools and universities, police buildings and equipment, etc. As in other metropolises, industrial production in Berlin has been in decline for many years (cf. Röber & Schröter, 2002: 320). For Berlin, this effect has been accelerated by two factors. Old East German industries were not prepared for international competition, and subsidies for industrial production in the western part of Berlin were reduced after reunification. Tax revenues are low and unemployment rates high compared to other German regions. The city is therefore dependent upon financial transfers from the wealthier regions and from the federal government. Budget restrictions have repeatedly raised the question of which kinds of public services the city can afford. The budget of the Berlin Police has been under permanent pressure since the 1990s.

The specific situation of a divided city that has now been reunified, the establishment of federal government institutions in the city and the growing and increasingly diverse population caused rapid transition in the 25 years after German reunification. Berlin's specific history since the 1950s has created a number of path dependencies that influence public policies, including public security and the organisation of policing. These path dependencies overlap with influences of the broader German political and administrative system. In 1948, the Berlin Police was separated into two parts: the police of the western sectors of the city and the police of the Soviet sector (cf. Steinborn & Krüger, 1993: 37–87). The police of the Soviet sector became part of the East German People's Police (Volkspolizei). In parallel, the East German state established a powerful political secret service (Staatssicherheit, or Stasi). In view of the East–West conflict, paramilitary tasks characterised the development of the police in the western sectors in the 1950s. Towards the end of the 1960s, in a period of emerging political protest, this kind of policing became more and more contested (cf. Steinborn & Krüger, 1993:

88–216). In 1974, a major reform promoted a more pluralised concept of policing in which beat officers and problem solving in the interest of citizens became more important. Some administrative tasks were transferred to other public administrations (cf. Diederichs, 1997; Hübner, 1998). After German reunification in 1990, the East Berlin People's Police was integrated into the Berlin Police in a long process of cultural adaptation and selection of staff qualified to work in a democratic polity (cf. Glaeser, 2000: 125–140; Schertz 1998).

Since reunification Berlin has been governed by different constellations of coalitions composed of two parties. The majority of the state parliament elects the governing mayor. While the reunified city was governed by Christian Democratic mayors (Christlich Demokratische Union, CDU) with different coalition partners in the 1990s, Social Democratic Mayor Klaus Wowereit (Sozialdemokratische Partei Deutschlands, SPD) governed the city from 2001. Until 2011 he governed in a coalition with the Left Party (Linkspartei) and since 2011 with the CDU. In 2014 he resigned and was replaced by Michael Müller, a member of the SPD as well. Therefore, the past two decades have been characterised by a high degree of continuity for internal security policy and for policing.

The mayor nominates the members of the government (in Berlin: Senat). Security issues are usually bundled into the portfolio of the member of government responsible for the interior (Innensenator). Erhard Körting (SPD) who had been Senator of the Interior from 2001, was replaced in 2011 by Frank Henkel (CDU). This did not lead to major changes for policing and internal security. The governmental parties' electoral programmes and the coalition agreements are the most important programmatic documents, not only for policing and security issues. The coalition agreement for the legislature 2011 to 2016 includes three pages on policing and security (out of 104 pages in total). The CDU and the SPD announced their intention to hire more police officers originating from migrants' families. They also promised to hire 250 additional police officers in order to enable the police to be more present in public spaces, to strengthen crime prevention and to extend the legal framework for policing, especially for video surveillance (SPD & CDU Berlin, 2011: 66–68).

In Berlin, all state police forces, officers in uniform, as well as the criminal police, are bundled into a single administrative structure directed by the President of the Berlin Police (Polizeipräsident), who is nominated by the Senat. Professional skills and loyalty towards the political leadership usually play a role when it comes to selecting the President of the Berlin Police. The current president, Klaus Kandt, is a longstanding police officer who started his career in the Federal Police. Like Senator Henkel, he is a member of the CDU. His predecessor, Dieter Glietsch, a longstanding police officer as well, started his career in the NRW police and is a member of the SPD. Even if their tasks are often close to politics, the police presidents do not tend to publish policy statements, but mostly leave policy making to the senators of the Interior. The police president is in a 'sandwich position' between the political leaders (Governing Mayor and Senator of the Interior) and the operative police force. Political guidelines and requirements therefore are easily translated into police practice.

The members of the Berlin State Parliament (Abgeordnetenhaus), who are directly elected by the citizens for five years, play an active role in the steering of local security, not only when it comes to law making. The parliament's Standing Committee for the Interior, Public Security and Order (Ausschuss für Inneres Sicherheit und Ordnung) closely follows local security issues. Much more than their colleagues in other state parliaments, for example the NRW 'Landtag', the members of the standing committee in Berlin closely follow local issues such as policing of political demonstrations or crime rates in specific areas of the city. In the committee, the Senator of the Interior and the Police President have to respond mainly to questions by members of parliament belonging to opposition party groups, for example if the opposition parties think that police officers have used excessive force against political demonstrators or did not react adequately to a security problem. This kind of case-by-case evaluation contributes to a policy-making style for policing and security that is characterised by the reaction to specific incidents (cf. Aden, 2008) rather than by rationally elaborated long-term strategies.

Everyday police work is delivered by officers who belong to the six local police directorates, which are subdivided into a staff unit, a department for crime fighting and 37 local neighbourhood police stations (Abschnitte).

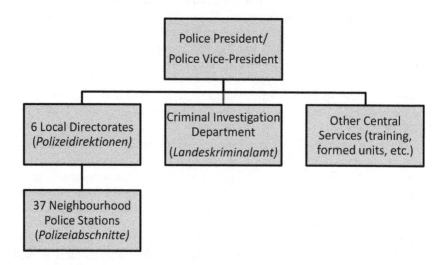

Figure 9.1 Reduced organisational chart of the Berlin Police

Citizens can go to these police stations to report crime, and most of the patrol officers are based in one of these stations from where they can quickly respond to emergency calls or start their patrol. Each police station also has a crime prevention unit that has some scope to organise the involvement of the police in preventive activities in the neighbourhoods. Their tasks also include networking with local NGOs. In areas with a high proportion of migrants, they have to coordinate this with police units specialising in migration issues that are located at the central and at the directorate level. Therefore, in a political framework that only broadly defines prevention as a priority, the decentralised directorates and police stations have considerable scope to define their own policies and strategies when it comes to cooperating with local NGOs and citizens (cf. Gauthier, 2012: 215 ff.).

The Berlin Police also have a number of centralised services such as the State Criminal Investigation Department (Landeskriminalamt), formed police units (anti-riot police, Bereitschaftspolizei) and training units. Recently, Police President Klaus Kandt and his deputy Margarete Koppers have significantly restructured these centralised services in order to make them work more effectively.

Cologne's position is in some respect different to Berlin's. It has not had such serious upheavals and has had continuous growth with economic and demographic evolution. The city belongs to the state North Rhine-Westphalia. NRW was founded in 1946 in the west of Germany and is the German state with the highest number of inhabitants (about 17.6 million, cf. Statistisches Bundesamt, 2015: 26). The State Government and Parliament reside in Düsseldorf, about 50 km from Cologne. With a short interruption between 2005 and 2010, NRW has been continuously governed by the Social Democrats (SPD) since 1966, mostly in coalitions with the Green Party or the Liberals (FDP).

The police in NRW belong to the portfolio of the Minister of the Interior and Local Government. The current Minister of the Interior is Ralf Jäger (SPD). The 2012 coalition agreement does not say much about policing policy or urban security and just announces a fight against right-wing extremism, the importance of better victim support, and the necessity of crime and social prevention, especially for young people, according to the motto, 'No young person will be left behind' (NRWSPD und Bündnis 90/Die Grünen NRW, 2012). Minister Jäger initialised some prevention programmes against speeding, burglary, pickpocketing, risky driving by young drivers and for early intervention against juvenile delinquency (see www.polizei.nrw.de).

NRW is divided into 30 counties, 22 district-free cities and the City Region of Aachen. The counties (governed by a directly elected Landrat, or district chief executive) and cities (governed by a directly elected mayor) have a constitutional right to self-administration (Article 28 of the Federal Constitution).

The NRW police are divided into 47 regional police authorities, which are headed by appointed police presidents (mainly) in the district-free cities or the elected Landrat in the counties. The regional police authorities are subject to the legal and professional supervision of the ministry and are also obliged to follow the political aims of the minister, but have status as an authority with some freedom of self-administration.

The organisational chart of the Cologne Police shows that the tasks of protection against threats belong to a directorate that is separate from the local crime inspectorates, which are themselves part of the Directorate for Crime. This separation was introduced with an organisational reform in 2007. Before this, the uniformed police officers (Schutzpolizei) and some criminal investigation officers (Kriminalpolizei) worked closely together in regional inspectorates and dealt with different tasks including 'everyday crime'. More serious crime and/or priority crimes were dealt with by the former Central Law Enforcement Department. Nowadays police inspectorates cover a local area, while crime inspectorates deal with specific offences such as murder, fraud and theft (see Frevel & Kuschewski, 2013).

The Cologne police are – as an authority within the state police – independent from local government. Therefore, and differently from Berlin, the mayor of Cologne cannot (directly or indirectly) instruct the police what to do or not to do. The police president is not accountable to the city's administrative representatives or to the city parliament, but only to the state minister and to the state parliament. In short, there is no direct link between the policy of the city and of the local police, and there is no explicitly stated concept of urban policing in NRW which would guide the policy of the police president of Cologne. This gives some discretion to the local police, but also leads to the risk of incoherent policing in the metropolises of NRW.

In Berlin, the policing of the metropolis can be steered and coordinated through close collaboration between the police and the city's government and other institutions that are relevant for security and/or safety. These are all supervised by the governing mayor and the senator of the interior. The situation is different in Cologne where the Cologne Police are independent from the local authorities, under the supervision (and political guidance) of the state government in Düsseldorf. Therefore, policing in Berlin is (or at least can be) done with an integrated approach, while in Cologne a more segregated or separated approach prevails. Either way, the police have to work within a network with other agencies, authorities and institutions; they have to coordinate their activities with them and try to create synergies.

3.3 Agenda setting, talk and strategies

The Cologne Police, as all regional police authorities in NRW, have to plan their strategic and tactical aims. Since 2005, according to a decree from the ministry, the authorities have to adopt a 'Sicherheitsprogramm' (Safety and Security Programme), which has to be updated every three to five years. In

Germany: policing in cooperative federalism 239

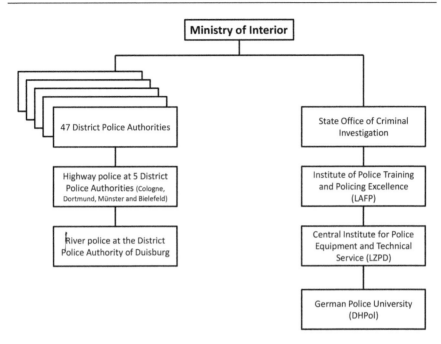

Figure 9.2 Structure of the Police in North Rhine-Westphalia
Source: Frevel & Kuschewski, 2013: 135.

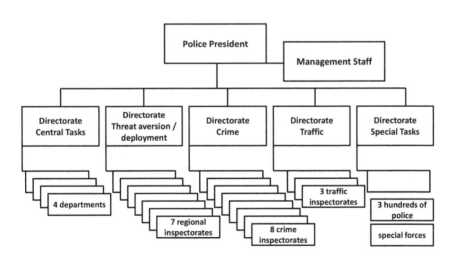

Figure 9.3 Reduced organisational chart of the Cologne Police
Source: The authors' own representation following the official organigram[1].

this programme, police tasks are prioritised and described with qualitative and quantifiable aims. The planning of the programme has (ideally) to be based on an analysis of the local security situation and has to regard the differentiated, but not site-specific, strategies and requirements from the ministry (Felske, 2014: 11). After a few years the programme will be evaluated and the results are summarised in a 'Sicherheitsbilanz' (Security and Safety Balance Sheet). Both papers are only for use within the police and therefore are not published. Only a short reference is available online (e.g. www.polizei.nrw.de/koeln/artikel__8544.html). The Sicherheitsprogramm 2015 of the Cologne Police describes in 61 pages the 'aims and strategy of the police authority' (Behördenstrategische Ziele) and the 'aims and strategy for the core police tasks' (Fachstrategische Ziele).

The overall strategic aims are:

> In the action area 'street': the case numbers of burglary and street crime will be reduced and the clearance rate increased. In the fields of burglary and pickpocketing, the amount of casualties, and the cyclists and pedestrians given violations for crossing red lights and right-of-way infringements, will be decreased. The police act in a timely manner in cases of a 'perpetrator at the scene'. The maintenance of employees' health will be supported. Networking is a strategic aim. The expectations of citizens, particularly of migrants and disabled people, and the plurality of cultures will be considered in all our activities.
> (Polizei Köln, 2015: 6, translated by B.F.)

More specific aims are, for example, the 'exploitation of possibilities of securing evidence', the 'focus on causes of traffic accidents with personal injury, especially in the context of speeding, alcohol or drugs', the 'exploitation of the possibilities to combat habitual offenders', and a 'targeted presence of officers in hot spots and places of fear'.

The single aims are differentiated and named, responsibility for them is given to a senior and/or dedicated officer in the organisation and key figures are listed in a (short) longitude table (2012–15), often with a target/actual comparison. The situation and the strategic approach are sketched out, activities refined and data for personnel calculated. The standardised assessment and the fine-tuned activities underlined with figures are static but show quite clearly the requirements and the idea of policing activities. The data of all police forces are collected by the ministry and compared against a standardised benchmark.

Besides the Sicherheitsprogramm, several other formats for planning and adjustment of policing activities are implemented. Quite important are the regular but informal meetings of 'heads of agencies' with the mayor, the police president, director of the court, chief prosecutor and others, in which the local situation is discussed and activities are coordinated at the leadership level. Further, in several city districts 'crime prevention councils' are installed in which representatives of the municipality and its departments, the local police and several representatives of civil society (welfare organisations, schools, social services, local integration council and several NGOs) discuss 'small-scale' security and its tackling by different stakeholders. In these councils the police are often seen as having equal weight with other stakeholders, but in practice they have a central and often decisive role (Frevel, 2012).

In contrast to Cologne, there are no general programmatic documents for policing and security in Berlin beyond the governmental parties' electoral programmes and their coalition agreements mentioned above. Beyond this, policy makers in Berlin mostly do not use programmes for the steering of policing and other security issues in the city. This might be explained as a result of the integration of local and state politics in a single structure, due to the specific path of Berlin as a city-state. Therefore, policy makers do not have to explain their policies and priorities in programmatic documents, but can transfer them directly to the police leadership that has to implement the policies. However, on occasion, security policies are in fact based on programmatic documents in Berlin as well. A specific programmatic document exists for traffic safety including measures developed in order to prevent vulnerable groups such as children, cyclists and pedestrians from becoming victims of traffic accidents. Interestingly, this document was not drafted and published by the Senator for the Interior, but by the Senator for City Development and the Environment (Senatsverwaltung für Stadtentwicklung und Umwelt, 2014).

3.4 Formed units: being prepared for all major events

Dealing with political protests and other major events is another issue where coordination in the German system of cooperative federalism prevails. All 16 Länder and the Federal State have their own formed units (Bereitschaftspolizei; mostly named Einsatzeinheiten, Einsatzhundertschaften or Polizeihundertschaften). If necessary, for example for policing major events, the state police forces support each other by sending formed units.

While political protest has been an important issue in the western part of Berlin since the late 1960s, the transfer of the Federal government to Berlin has made political protest much more important and visible in the city. For Berlin as the new German capital it has become a central aspect of policing policy to deal with political demonstrations in an open-minded way, but also to intervene against violence that sometimes occurs in connection with political protest in the city (cf. SPD & CDU Berlin, 2011: 67). In recent years the number of demonstrations has risen to over 4,000 per year. Other events such as sports championships, concerts and major parties in public spaces all require some kind of protection by the police and have become more frequent in recent years. Therefore, the Federal Police and police forces from other Länder such as North Rhine-Westphalia often provide assistance to the formed units of the Berlin Police.

Cologne does not have the role of a capital, even for the Land North Rhine-Westphalia. However, the size and attractiveness of this metropolis lead to many events that demand the deployment of formed units. In particular, political demonstrations with conflicts between right- and left-wing groups, state visits or religious events (e.g. the visit of the Pope in 2005) require the deployment of formed units for crowd and riot policing. Therefore, the Cologne Police maintains three Polizeihundertschaften (units with about 100 officers each), which are supported by other formed units from NRW, other Länder or the Federal Police in case of major events.

For the politics related to protest policing, it is not only coordination among the police forces that leads to similarities in the system of cooperative federalism. The freedom of assembly is a fundamental right guaranteed by the German Constitution (Article 8 Grundgesetz). Therefore, the Constitutional Court's (Bundesverfassungsgericht) judgments are another harmonising factor for policy making related to demonstrations. In many cases, the Constitutional Court has defined rules and limits for the way in which the police have to enable political protest and how they can limit it if necessary. This governs, and leads to a convergence in, the ways in which the police deal with protest in Berlin and in Cologne. This example shows that sometimes court decisions can replace political programmes.

3.5 Policing by and with non-police agencies

A growing importance of private security firms (PSFs) in the field of policing metropolises can be observed in Germany (but remarkably less important than, for example, in the UK). The market for private security business has steadily grown in recent years, and PSFs are commissioned by a heterogeneous set of clients. While enterprises traditionally engage PSFs to secure their premises and citizens to protect their houses, the role of PSFs is different in semi-public spaces, for example by securing shopping malls, shops, railway stations, cinemas or in the context of events like concerts, sport championships or city festivals. The guards and watchmen exercise the property rights of their clients. They can deny access, exclude undesirables or seize offenders for a short period until the police can record a charge (Frevel, 2015).

Generally, on the basis of contracts or codified agreements, PSFs are integrated in plural policing in public-private partnerships and/or police-private partnerships. If the co-contractors are the local authorities, the PSF activities concentrate on public order aspects, for example in the context of city festivals, parking enforcement, supervision and surveillance of public property. Almost all public administrations in Cologne and Berlin contract a private security firm to protect the premises and to control entrances, including even the police headquarters in Cologne. In police-private partnerships the PSFs help the police with 'observe – discover – report' (Koch, 2002). If PSF personnel see anything that seems problematic to them in the context of public order, safety and security, they report to the police and/or to the municipality.

In Berlin, the police and the association of private security companies have reached a general agreement (Polizeipräsident in Berlin & Bundesverband Deutscher Wach- und Sicherheitsunternehmen, 2006). Through this association, 11 mainly medium-sized PSFs with about 7,000 employees were integrated into an information and communication network with the police (Hirschmann & Groß, 2012: 112 f.). Close cooperation between PSFs and the police has also become a reality for major events such as football matches and concerts where usually PSFs are responsible for security inside the premises while the police are responsible for all security issues outside the premises.

In Cologne there is no such institutionalised police-private partnership. However, the PSFs are often integrated into the policing of major events and the activities are coordinated with the police. After the disaster at the 'Loveparade' in the City of Duisburg (NRW) in 2010, the police and the public order department of the municipality are now obliged to develop security plans for every big event. This includes involving PSF and attributing specific tasks to them, especially entrance and crowd control. At the Duisburg 'Loveparade' techno-music event on 24 July 2010, there was a panic and stampede in which 21 people died and more than 540 were injured. Researchers have shown that shortcomings in the planning process and poor cooperation among the stakeholders involved contributed to the causes of this disaster. With the lessons drawn from this disaster, PSFs have gained an even more important role in ensuring security in the (semi-)public spaces of the German metropolises.

4 Conclusion: setting the political agenda for policing German metropolises – convergence of path dependencies and remaining plurality

This chapter has shown that specific national and local path dependencies in policing overlap with national and international trends and coordination when it comes to explaining how policing in Berlin and Cologne, and the programmatic documents related to this policing, have developed over recent decades. Specific path dependencies have been created by the semi-(de)centralised German police system which was established in the western parts of Germany in the 1950s. These patterns still characterise policing in Berlin and Cologne today. The 16 states enjoy a high level of autonomy when it comes to defining priorities for policing, which explains far-reaching differences that can be observed between policing in Berlin and Cologne. At the same time, policing these cities is influenced by a number of international trends, in particular towards a pluralisation of policing (cf. Jones & Newburn, 2006). Prevention, in a broad sense, has contributed to a diversification of everyday police work. Private security companies have gained importance. Restrictions in public budgets and the influence of market models and New Public Management models have forced the municipalities and the police to adapt the provision of security tasks to a changing environment.

Besides the security problems that all globalised metropolises have in general, often linked to a diverse, multicultural population, the Berlin police system has had to deal with a completely new political and administrative context since the 1990s as a consequence of reunification and the transfer of government institutions to the city. The city and its police were 'divided in unity' (Glaeser, 2000) in the period of transition after reunification – something that has still not been completely accomplished.

The situation in Cologne differs from Berlin, as it is not a capital with the connected security challenges, such as protecting authorities, dealing with state visits or a high number of demonstrations. However, the other challenges for policing the metropolis are similar: high attractiveness of the city, an increasing number of inhabitants, tourism, etc.

The policing strategies in Berlin and Cologne are characterised by the different ways in which the police are integrated into the political system in both cities. These different paths mean that the police – as the most important player – are organised differently in Berlin and North Rhine-Westphalia. In the city-state Berlin, the police and local government are more closely dependant on each other: both belong to the same government and the political steering is more direct. By contrast, in Cologne, the police are an independent authority belonging to the state NRW. The linkage to the city and its mayor is therefore not as tight. Communication and negotiation between the institutions are not based on hierarchy, but police leaders and city government leaders meet on an equal footing in Cologne.

However, the chapter has also shown that another path of the German political system leads to numerous similarities of policing in both cities: the strong tradition of cooperative federalism. The fact that former Berlin Police President Glietsch started his career in North Rhine-Westphalia shows that cooperative federalism even leads to a nationwide market for leading police positions. For policing major events, formed units from Berlin may be sent to Cologne and vice versa.

In the cases of Berlin and Cologne, the fact that the states of Berlin and North Rhine-Westphalia have mostly been governed by the Social Democrats over the past decades is also a factor contributing to convergence. The priority that preventive approaches and a close cooperation with NGOs and other actors outside the security sector have gained for policing policies in both cities is probably the most visible outcome of party politics' priorities as a converging factor. These cooperative prevention policies developed later in Germany, compared to other European countries such as France and the UK. In the 1990s, Länder governed by the Social Democrats, sometimes in coalitions with the Green Party, tried to shift away from a conservative law-and-order security policy. Therefore, they implemented round-table approaches for crime prevention, based on experiences in other European countries, bringing together local administrations, the police, social workers, shopkeepers, NGOs and churches, among other groups (cf. Aden, 2002: 138). In NRW, this policy was centrally implemented by a decree by the Minister of the interior in 1998 on Public Order Partnerships in which the cooperation of police, municipality, civil society groups and also local business was demanded (see Frevel, 2007: 54–55). In Berlin and Cologne, crime prevention councils were only implemented at decentralised levels (Bezirke); for Cologne a city-wide council was announced in 2016 (Kölnische Rundschau, 2016). Depending upon the interests of the local policy makers and NGOs involved, these activities may prioritise either situational or social crime prevention. By contrast, the Berlin Police concentrate on situational crime prevention at the state level (cf. Landeskriminalamt Berlin, 2016).

Cooperative crime prevention is also part of the strategy to establish an 'activating state', promoted by the SPD since the 2000s. Sharing responsibilities between state and civil society actors is a core element of this 'activating state'. Since the beginning of the 21st century, social-democratic security policy follows the motto 'tough on crime and violence, but also tough on the reasons for crime' (SPD, 2009: 69), combining preventive and repressive approaches.

Policing metropolises in Germany has to consider the restricted resources due to growing challenges and expectations of the inhabitants. Under these circumstances policing is and probably will be increasingly organised in forms of plural policing.

Note

1 cfr. www.polizei.nrw.de/media/Dokumente/Behoerden/Koeln/OrganisationsplanPPK.pdf

Bibliography

Aden, H. (1998) *Polizeipolitik in Europa. Eine interdisziplinäre Studie über die Polizeiarbeit in Europa am Beispiel Deutschlands, Frankreichs und der Niederlande*, Opladen/Wiesbaden: Westdeutscher Verlag.

Aden, H. (2002) 'Preventing crime, mobilizing new actors and tendencies towards a repressive roll-back: German security and crime prevention policies in the 1990s', in P. Hebberecht, D. Duprez (eds), *The Security and Prevention Policies in Europe*, Brussels: VUB Brussels University Press, 133–116.

Aden, H. (2004) 'Fédéralisme et sécurité publique: Spécificité des politiques de sécurité en Allemagne', in S. Roché (ed.), *Réformer la police et la sécurité: Les nouvelles tendances en Europe et aux États-Unis*, Paris: Odile Jakob, 169–187.

Aden, H. (2008) 'Problemdefinition und Agendagestaltung in der Kriminalpolitik', in H.J. Lange (ed.), *Kriminalpolitik*, Wiesbaden: Verlag für Sozialwissenschaften, 121–136.

Aden, H. (2015) 'Ausweitung des Strafrechts durch europäische Vorgaben', *Vorgänge*, 212(54, 4): 20–28.

Aden, H., De Pauw, E. (2014) 'Policing Berlin. From separation by the "iron curtain" to the new German capital and a globalised city', *European Journal of Policing Studies*, 2(1): 13–29.

Aden, H., Domingo, B., Maguer, A., Stephens, M. (2004) 'Policing and internal security', in H. Compston (ed.), *Handbook of Public Policy in Europe: Britain, France and Germany*, Basingstoke: Palgrave-Macmillan, 39–48.

Amt für Statistik Berlin-Brandenburg (2012) 'Entwicklung der Bevölkerungszahl in Berlin im Jahr 2011', *Zeitschrift für amtliche Statistik Berlin-Brandenburg*, 5(2012): 24–27. Available at: www.statistik-berlin-brandenburg.de/Publikationen/Aufsaetze/2012/HZ_201205-01.pdf (accessed 20 February 2016).

Bayley, D.H. (1994) *Policing the Future*, Oxford: Oxford University Press.

Bundeskriminalamt (2015) *Polizeiliche Kriminalstatistik 2014*, Wiesbaden: Bundeskriminalamt.

Diederichs, O. (1997) 'Berliner Polizeireformen – Organisationsveränderungen durch Unternehmensberatung', *Bürgerrechte & Polizei/CILIP* 56(1/1997): 31–38. Also available at: online: www.cilip.de/ausgabe/56/mummert.htm (accessed 20 February 2016).

Felske, M. (2014) *Erfolgsrezept Sicherheitsprogramm. Welchen Beitrag kann das Sicherheitsprogramm des Polizeipräsidiums Oberhausen zur Effizienz- und Effektivitätssteigerung polizeilicher Arbeit leisten?* Bochum: Ruhr-Universität.

Frevel, B. (2007) 'Kooperative Sicherheitspolitik in Mittelstädten. Vergleichende Fallstudien zu den Grundlagen, der Gestaltung und den Wirkungen von Ordnungspartnerschaften und Kriminalpräventiven Räten', in B. Frevel (ed.), *Kooperative Sicherheitspolitik in Mittelstädten. Studien zu Ordnungspartnerschaften und Kriminalpräventiven Räten*, Frankfurt am Main, 13–212.

Frevel, B. (ed.) (2012) *Handlungsfelder lokaler Sicherheitspolitik. Netzwerke, Politikgestaltung und Perspektiven*, Frankfurt am Main: Verlag für Polizeiwissenschaft.

Frevel, B. (2015) 'Pluralisation of local policing in Germany. Security between the state's monopoly of force and the market', *European Journal of Policing Studies*, 2(3): 267–284.

Frevel, B., Kuschewski, P. (2013) 'The police system of Germany: Police organization, management and reform in North Rhine-Westphalia', in A. van Sluis et al. (eds), *Contested Police Systems. Changes in the Police Systems in Belgium, Denmark, England & Wales, Germany and the Netherlands*, Amsterdam: eleven, 119–148.

Garland, D. (2001) *The Culture of Control. Crime and Social Order in Contemporary Society*, Oxford: Oxford University Press.

Gauthier, J. (2012) *Origines contrôlées. La police à l'epreuve de la question minoritaire à Paris et à Berlin*. Thèse en Sociologie, Université de Versailles-Saint Quentin en Yvelines. Available at: https://tel.archives-ouvertes.fr/tel-00778649/document (accessed 20 February 2016).

Glaeser, A. (2000) *Divided in Unity. Identity, Germany, and the Berlin Police*, Chicago, IL: University of Chicago Press.

Groß, H., Frevel, B., Dams, C. (eds) (2008) *Handbuch der Polizeien Deutschlands*, Wiesbaden: VS Verlag für Sozialwissenschaften.

Hirschmann, N., Groß, H. (2012) *Polizierende Präsenz. Kommunale Sicherheitspolitik zwischen Polizei, Verwaltung, Privatwirtschaft und Bürgern*, Frankfurt a.M.: Verlag für Polizeiwissenschaft.

Hübner, K. (1998) 'Die Polizeireform von 1974', in v.-Hinckeldey-Stiftung (ed.), *Berliner Polizei. Von 1945 bis zur Gegenwart*, Berlin: Jaron Verlag, 96–123.

Jones, T., Newburn, T. (eds) (2006) *Plural Policing: A Comparative Perspective*, London: Routledge.

Kienbaum Unternehmensberatung GmbH (1991) *Funktionsbewertung der Schutzpolizei. Studie im Auftrag des Innenministers des Landes Nordrhein-Westfalen*, Gummersbach: Kienbaum.

Koch, U. (2002) 'Zusammenarbeit von Polizei und privaten Sicherheitsdiensten', Sicherheitsmelder.de – Wissens-Update in Fachbeiträgen. Available at: www.sicherheitsm elder.de/xhtml/articleview.jsf;jsessionid=143D3364A1D8CD6B9B091974533AD8CF.B oorbergSolrappLive?id=2DE4D2BA4A2F.htm (accessed 20 February 2016).

Kölnische Rundschau (2016) *Polizeipräsident Mathies will zukünftig mit Stadt zusammenarbeiten*, Cologne: Kölnische Rundschau (2 February 2016). Available at: www. rundschau-online.de/koeln/gemeinsam-fuer-sicherheit-in-koeln-polizeipraesident-mathie s-will-zukuenftig-mit-stadt-zusammenarbeiten,15185496,33700502.html (accessed 27 February 2016).

Landeskriminalamt Berlin (2016) *Zentralstelle für Prävention*, Berlin. Available at: www.berlin.de/polizei/dienststellen/landeskriminalamt/lka-praevention/ (accessed 27 February 2016).

Mahoney, J. (2000) 'Path dependence in historical sociology', *Theory and Society*, 29(4): 507–548.

NRWSPD und Bündnis 90/Die Grünen NRW (2012) *Koalitionsvertrag 2012–2017. Verantwortung für ein starkes NRW. Miteinander die Zukunft gestalten*, Düsseldorf. Available at: www.spd-fraktion-nrw.de/fileadmin/SPD/user_upload/Dokumente_allgemein/ Koalitionsvertrag_Rot-Gruen_NRW_2012-2017.pdf (accessed 20 February 2016).

Peilert, A., Kösling, W. (2008) 'Bundespolizei – vormals Bundesgrenzschutz', in H. Groß, B. Frevel, C. Dams (eds), *Handbuch der Polizeien Deutschlands*, Wiesbaden: VS Verlag für Sozialwissenschaften, 555–590.

Polizei Köln (2014) *Sicherheitsbilanz 2013 der Polizei Köln*, Köln: Der Polizeipräsident.

Polizei Köln (2015) *Sicherheitsprogramm PP Köln 2015*, Köln: Der Polizeipräsident.

Polizeipräsident in Berlin & Bundesverband Deutscher Wach- und Sicherheitsunternehmen, Landesgruppe Berlin (2006) *Vereinbarung über eine Zusammenwirkung zur Stärkung der öffentlichen Sicherheit und Ordnung in der Bundeshauptstadt Berlin*, Berlin. Available at: www.befreite-dokumente.de/www.befreite-dokumente.de/bea ntragte-akten/kooperation-polizei-privaten/attachment_download/publication_dow nload.pdf (accessed 20 February 2016).

Röber, M., Schröter, E. (2002) 'Metropolenvergleich in europäischer Perspektive', in M. Röber, E. Schröter, H. Wollmann (eds), *Moderne Verwaltung für moderne Metropolen. Berlin und London im Vergleich*, Opladen: Leske + Budrich, 319–333.

Schertz, G. (1998) 'Auf dem Weg zu einer einheitlichen Polizei (1990–1992)', in v.-Hinckeldey-Stiftung (ed.), *Berliner Polizei. Von 1945 bis zur Gegenwart*, Berlin: Jaron Verlag, 169–183.

Schlepper, C. (2015) 'Immer mehr Strafrecht? Empirische Befunde zur Punitivität', *Vorgänge*, 212(54, 4): 9–19.

Senatsverwaltung für Stadtentwicklung und Umwelt (2014) *Verkehrspolitik. Berlin sicher mobil 2020. Kontinuität und neue Akzente*, Berlin. Available at: www.stadtentwicklung.berlin.de/verkehr/politik_planung/sicherheit/download/berlin_sicher_mobil2020_broschuere.pdf (accessed 20 February 2016).

SPD (Sozialdemokratische Partei Deutschlands) (2009) *Sozial und demokratisch. Anpacken. Für Deutschland. Regierungsprogramm der SPD*, Berlin: SPD. Available at: www.spd.de/fileadmin/Dokumente/Beschluesse/Bundesparteitag/regierungsprogramm_bundesparteitag_berlin_2009.pdf (accessed 24 February 2016).

SPD/CDU Berlin (Sozialdemokratische Partei Deutschland, Landesverband Berlin & Christlich Demokratische Union, Landesverband Berlin) (2011) *Berliner Perspektiven für starke Wirtschaft, gute Arbeit und sozialen Zusammenhalt. Koalitionsvereinbarung für die Legislaturperiode 2011 bis 2016*, Berlin. Available at: www.berlin.de/rbmskzl/regierender-buergermeister/senat/koalitionsvereinbarung/ (accessed 20 February 2016).

Statistisches Bundesamt (2015) *Statistisches Jahrbuch 2015. Deutschland und Internationales*, Wiesbaden: Statistisches Bundesamt. Online: www.destatis.de/DE/Publikationen/StatistischesJahrbuch/StatistischesJahrbuch2015.pdf?__blob=publicationFile (accessed 20 February 2016).

Steinborn, N., Krüger, H. (1993) *Die Berliner Polizei 1945 bis 1992. Von der Militärreserve im Kalten Krieg auf dem Weg zur bürgernahen Polizei?* Berlin: Berlin Verlag Arno Spitz.

van Sluis, A. et al. (eds) (2013) *Contested Police Systems. Changes in the Police Systems in Belgium, Denmark, England & Wales, Germany and the Netherlands*, Amsterdam: eleven.

Werle, R. (2007) 'Pfadabhängigkeit', in A. Benz, S. Lütz, U. Schimank, G. Simonis (eds), *Handbuch Governance*, Wiesbaden: Springer VS, 119–131.

Chapter 10

Belgium

Governance of security in Antwerp and
Brussels: Two of a kind?

Evelien De Pauw and Marleen Easton

1 Introduction

To get a grip on the governance of security in Antwerp and Brussels, we want to address the unique governance structure of our country on the one hand and the implications of this structure for the security policy and the organisation of public policing in Antwerp and Brussels on the other hand.

In this contribution we ask ourselves if the governance of security in Antwerp and Brussels are two of a kind. Antwerp and Brussels deal with similar urban challenges such as 'glocal' threats to local safety and public order, large and multiple ethnic background populations and huge socio-economic differences. Nevertheless both metropolises develop their own approach to deal with the impact of these challenges on their urban safety. These differences are rooted in Belgium's national dispositions consisting of a complex state structure with multiple levels (municipalities/cities, provinces, regions, communities and the national government), contracts between local and supra-local authorities, and strong municipal autonomy and politics. This leads to a tendency towards convergence from supra-local government on the one hand and a tendency towards divergence, given robust local management and autonomy. In this contribution we illustrate these tendencies in both metropolises by pointing out differences and similarities in the security policy agendas and some of the implications for public policing.

After all, this book is linked to the Policing European Metropolises Project (PEMP) which studies the degree to which 'plural policing' takes place in European metropolises. Plural policing is a process in which various players in public spaces are involved in policing (supervisory, monitoring and enforcement tasks) (Edwards & Prins, 2014; Devroe et al., 2014). In Belgium, the classic concept of plural policing in which security is no longer the exclusive task of the police but shifts to a shared responsibility between a large number of public and private stakeholders (Ponsaers et al., 2006; Crawford, 2006; Loader, 2000; Jones & Newburn, 2002, 2006; Stenning, 2009; Reiner, 2013) has been anchored to the philosophy of 'integral security policy' (Integraal Veiligheidsbeleid) in which cooperating in networks is key

(Ponsaers et al., 2006; Devroe, 2013, 2015). The philosophy is built up from the idea of 'global social policy'. The fact that the circular letter[1] of the government, regarding the function of the community guard,[2] had a dual aim, namely job creation for the long-term unemployed and more supervision on the streets, is one illustration of this.

The methodology used to underpin our arguments in this chapter is a study of literature and a content analysis of policy documents in Antwerp and Brussels. Two main research questions were guiding this analysis. The first research question is regarding who defines the security agendas in Antwerp and Brussels. What is the role of the national state (Bowling & Sheptycki, 2012) and other administrative levels (such as regional and municipal authorities) in this process? The second research question is regarding how these security agendas can be characterised. Are they socially oriented or does law enforcement take precedence? What role does politics play in this process? What is the influence of crisis situations like the terrorist assaults in November 2015 in Paris and March 2016 in Brussels?

The agenda setting has been screened throughout various policy documents such as the council agreements from the 2006–12 and 2013–18 legislatures in Antwerp and Brussels, council agreements from the Brussels-Capital Region, zonal security plans from the police zones involved, a large 'security' study by the Brussels Institute for Prevention and Security, and scientific studies on security policy within these metropolises.[3] The limitation of our methodology is that we cannot draw any conclusions on implementation, the vision behind the choices, or any gaps between decisions and actions. That would require further in-depth research.

To study local security agendas in both cities we used the 2006 (period of office 2007–13) and 2012 (period of office 2014–18) local elections as the period of reference. Local elections are held every six years and the political outcome to a large extent determines the nature of the security policy. This emphasises the principle of strong municipal autonomy in Belgium that has been previously expounded upon in this volume (Devroe and Ponsaers, this volume). Furthermore, we looked at the influence of the national and regional policies on the security agendas in both metropolises to answer our first research question.

Second, we looked at the local agenda setting as such. We are interested in the relationship between governing arrangements and the metropolitan security agendas. The period 2007–13 was characterised in both cities by a mainly Socialist policy.[4] Since 2013, after 80 years of Socialist mayors in both cities, we see an electoral defeat of the Socialists in Antwerp. The city policy is nowadays in the hands of a new coalition between the Flemish Nationalist Party (N-VA), together with the Flemish Liberal Party (Open VLD) and the Flemish Christian Democrats (CD&V). The question rises whether this shift in power had an influence on the security agendas of city authorities in terms of social justice, criminal justice or risk management approaches (Edwards & Prins, 2014: 9). Furthermore, we are interested in the possible shift in these approaches after the terrorist assaults of 2015 and 2016.

To contextualise the results of our analysis we need to point out a number of national dispositions that make Belgium unique and which play a role in making the security policy of Antwerp and Brussels so very different. This makes up the first part of our contribution. The Belgian State structure, in which the municipalities/cities, provinces, regions, communities and the national government play a role, generates complex governing arrangements for urban security. Through various subsidies and plans, these multiple actors have an impact on the governance of security in Belgian metropolises. Nevertheless, the elected mayor and his or her policy play a major role setting the city security policy agenda. The latter argument is built up in the second part of our contribution, where we analyse the similarities and differences in the security policies of Antwerp and Brussels and the implications for the organisation of the public police. In our conclusion we reflect upon the complexity of these findings.

2 National dispositions that have an influence on metropolitan agenda setting

In this section we describe the strong municipal autonomy, the use of contracts between national and sub-local authorities, and the impact of politics in Belgium as dispositions that influence the governance of security in Antwerp and Brussels.

2.1 Strong municipal autonomy

The municipalities existed even before the Belgian State itself, and were recognised by the 1831 Constitution of Belgium and consolidated by the Law of 1836. There has always been a strong sense of municipal autonomy, which means that the municipalities form local entities that are self-governing, though still under the supervision of the Federal government.

After the state reform of 1988 and the New Communal Law,[5] the autonomy that municipal authorities had from national government was further strengthened, including their increased competences in metropolitan policing (Devroe, 2015). As a consequence of this reform, municipalities were empowered to draw up general police regulations with various rules and provisions concerning the preservation of public order and public safety. Until the end of the 20th century, violations of such provisions were criminal offences that were enforced by the police, for which charges could be brought before the public prosecutor for prosecution and for which the judge could impose a penalty for a summary offence.

In 1998[6] Belgium integrated its former Gendarmerie, municipal police forces and judicial police in a new police system. It implied a structural reorganisation in which these three formerly constituted separate independent agencies were integrated. Since then, the newly created Integrated Police Force consists of a Federal Police component and a Local Police component, which are functionally (not hierarchically) linked to each other. The Local Police component consists of 189 local police zones that cover one or more local municipalities. This structural reorganisation was inspired by the philosophy of community policing that was considered to be the cultural reorganisation of the Belgian policing landscape (Easton & Ponsaers, 2010). The principle of local autonomy was reinforced as the Law reaffirmed the mayors in their steering role towards their local police force and in their authority to determine the content of local security policy.

In 1999, the competences of municipalities were increased even further through the law implementing Municipal Administrative Sanctions (MAS)[7] for low-impact crimes. Since then an alternative administrative procedure has been made possible. When establishing their regulations, municipal authorities can choose whether to impose a classic criminal penalty for a summary offence or a municipal administrative penalty for certain violations. The latter choice grants the municipalities complete control over the chain of enforcement.

2.2 Contracts with supra-local authorities

The period of state reform in Belgium between 1980 and 2012 caused the country to evolve from a federal state to a country with various sub-states (three economic regions and three linguistic communities). Today, Belgium has 11 million inhabitants with three language communities (60% Flemish-speaking, 40% French-speaking and a minuscule population of German-speaking) and three regions (the Flemish Region, the Walloon Region and the Brussels-Capital Region). The competences of each of these governmental levels generate a complexity in the domain of security.

The Belgian federal state is competent regarding internal security, such as police, justice, prisons and civil security. The main actors are the Ministry of the Interior and the Ministry of Justice. The regional governments of Flanders, Wallonia and Brussels-Capital are competent for subjects that are directly connected to the topic of security, such as public order, welfare and the environment. The regional governments make the policy strategy concerning youth welfare, for example, but need to collaborate with the Federal government concerning youth crime. The municipal authorities take responsibilities for the local affairs, for example youth training programmes. This example illustrates the complexity of the Belgian state structure and the challenges of coordination it generates. Furthermore, it shows that different governmental levels of the Belgian State are involved in setting the goals of an integral security policy in which social, economic and security risks are taken into account.

In the period 1988–99, Christian Democratic and Social Democratic parties were in power in the Federal government of Belgium. The adoption of a preventive policy policing agenda was related to the Federal government's broader social and economic policy agenda to combat disadvantage, social exclusion, discrimination and racism (Hebberecht, 2004). In 1992 the Federal government established security and prevention contracts with municipalities for the first time along the same lines as France (see de Maillard and Mouhanna, this volume). The focus was mainly on social prevention projects. In 1999 the Federal government also appointed the first minister of metropolitan policy (Devroe, 2012). The intent was to strengthen social cohesion in the cities in response both to growing popular concerns about the impact of immigration on social integration and civil unrest, and as a response to the manipulation of these issues by right-wing political parties for their electoral advantage. For metropolitan policy, security was only one of the goals towards making a city liveable. With the transfer of a part of the competences of home affairs to metropolitan policy, the security discourse was redirected, according to Devroe, to a social integration discourse (Devroe, 2012). Neighbourhood development was financed through the metropolitan policy and the cities concluded contracts for 'urban renewal'.

This urban security policy has to be interpreted in the broad sense of encompassing social and economic policy responses to problems of crime and civil unrest in addition to police and criminal justice responses. The Federal government initially supported this through 'security and society contracts' with cities and municipalities. From 1999 this approach was gradually cut back in favour of the Federal government's more liberal political policy approach.[8] Projects focusing on liveability and urban renewal with an impact on security were managed and subsidised by the regional governments and no longer supported by the Federal government.

We notice differences here between the different regional governments. The Brussels-Capital Region plays a much larger role than the Flemish Region (which includes Antwerp). Through its 2011–14 prevention and neighbourhood policy, the Brussels-Capital Region attempted to improve security in the cities and tackle the increasing feeling of insecurity in certain neighbourhoods. Urban revitalisation (through neighbourhood contracts) and the protection of social housing are examples of Brussels regional impulse to stimulate security in the broadest sense of the word (De Pauw et al., 2012). This kind of pressure for social prevention of crime has been less prominent in Flanders.

2.3 Impact of politics

In 2012 elections generated a 'revolution'. For the first time in many years, the Socialist Party disappeared into the opposition and a Federal government was formed with the Flemish-speaking Nationalist party (N-VA), the

Liberal parties (French-speaking, MR; and Flemish-speaking, Open VLD) and the Flemish-speaking Christian Democrats (CD&V): the so-called 'Swedish'[9] coalition. The coalition agreement shows that prevention remains a priority and that municipalities must play a prominent role.[10] The new plans were concluded for 2014 to 2017 with the focus still on social prevention through contracts. This is rather remarkable as these contracts were questioned during the transition to the Swedish coalition in Belgium and a cut back on social prevention can be observed in nearly all other European countries. This also means that the shift in the ideological stance of the Federal government did not immediately influence the policy agenda for metropolitan policing, which continued to prioritise a social and preventive policy agenda through contracts.

Nevertheless, some changes on the national level can be observed. For the first time, a federal minister of security was appointed, Flemish Nationalist Jan Jambon, who is charged with homeland affairs and security. His policy document is of neo-liberal nature and promotes the privatisation of a number of security tasks, particularly in response to the vulnerabilities revealed by the terrorist assaults in Paris (13/09/2015) and Brussels (22/03/2016). These assaults have also legitimised the routine deployment of soldiers in Belgian cities. On 17 January 2016, the Council of Ministers decided to deploy the Army for specific security assignments to reinforce the police (Justaert & Vanhecke, 2015). The deployment also has a legal base;[11] moreover, the possibility remains open for local mayors to commandeer the military.

Furthermore, since the 2012 elections the way has been paved for a more significant role for the Brussels-Capital Region in defining security agendas (Government Policy Statement, 2014). As a direct consequence of the Sixth State Reform in 2014, Brussels established a new department for the coordination of prevention and security policy in the Brussels-Capital Region. The 'Brussels Security and Prevention Institute' is a public service institute intended to evolve into a benchmark for the other regions. Although its structure was established[12] at the time this chapter was written, several implementing provisions remain to be decided upon before the department can actually start working. Every aspect of the prevention and security policy in Brussels will be centralised here, with the purpose of creating more coherence in the execution of policy (Bailly et al., 2015). This plan is a guideline, whereas actual power to make decisions about metropolitan policing remains with the 19 municipal mayors who can decide what to adopt. Nevertheless, the main idea is to give a signal to the municipalities and create more coherent policy in Brussels.

The new Brussels Security and Prevention Institute is responsible for both the preparation and the execution of the decisions of the Brussels government, while the prime minister and the senior official are responsible for coordinating the security and prevention plans at a regional level. Among others, this regards the development of the Brussels Prevention and Security Plan, subsidising security initiatives and preparations of the Local Prevention and Neighbourhood Plans.[13] It is important to note that this kind of initiative has not been installed in Flanders and Wallonia.

2.4 Tendencies in the governance of security

We can conclude that the governance of security in Belgium is characterised by two tendencies. On the one hand a tendency towards convergence from supra-local governments and, on the other hand, a tendency to diverge, given robust local management and autonomy.

The tendency towards convergence is strongly supported by the Federal government and metropolitan policy. In a municipal context, there is a desire to focus on anti-social behaviour as well as to promote neighbourhood development and liveability. This is supported by contracts and subsidies provided by the Federal and regional governments. Despite the fact that the new federal coalition has embraced the European trend towards security policy privatisation, the social aspect has been more or less retained. A consistent shift from a welfare-oriented approach towards a law enforcement and a risk assessment approach cannot be observed throughout the documents being analysed here.

The tendency towards divergence in the governance of security is mainly underpinned by the strong local autonomy in Belgium as described above. This is embedded (also in terms of the law) in the organisation of municipalities and cities and in the police zones they contain. It generates a significant amount of freedom in the local governance of security.

Furthermore the installation of the Brussels Security and Prevention Institute in the Brussels-Capital Region fits into both tendencies. It fits into the tendency to converge within the region as it aims to coordinate the policy of the 19 municipalities. The installation of the institute reflects a belief in a stronger regionalisation as the optimum scale of governing arrangements for security and addresses emerging issues such as terrorist plots and increasing tensions between settled and migrant populations. At the same time it fits into a tendency to diverge on a Belgian level as the other regions did not take a similar initiative and in this respect it generates differences.

3 Antwerp and Brussels as Belgian metropolises

Keeping the above-mentioned contextualisation in mind, in this section we will explore the dynamics this generates on the level of security policies in Antwerp and Brussels and some of its implications for public policing. Brussels and Antwerp are the two largest metropolises in Belgium. Both are confronted with similar urban challenges, such as unemployment, ageing, migration and poverty. In addition to liveability, the fight against crime and maintaining public order are important points on the agenda of both city councils.

3.1 Antwerp, from 'living together' (coexistence) to 'risk management'

Antwerp is a city situated in Flanders. It is the capital of Antwerp Province and has a population of 516,009 (Buurtmonitor Antwerp, 2015). Antwerp consists of nine districts, which is unique in Belgium. The districts consist of a district council and a district collegiate body. The district council members are appointed directly and they determine the local policy in the district. Originally, the districts had a purely advisory function to the urban council of the city of Antwerp, but since 2000 they also have had an administrative role. They determine policy in the areas of sport, youth, culture and senior citizens and rule on the development of public space (Flanders, 2015). In other matters, they maintain their advisory function with regard to Antwerp's city council and its college of mayor and aldermen. Concerning safety and security matters they can only advise the city council of Antwerp.

Antwerp consists of one city administration, led by a mayor, and nine districts that decide autonomously on various matters. Regarding the police organisation, Antwerp has a single police zone, which means that the local police are organised as one police zone with one chief of police. The local police of Police Zone Antwerp is responsible for Antwerp and all its districts.[14]

Concerning the metropolitan security agenda setting in the city of Antwerp, four governance levels have an influence on the process of policy making in the domain of security. The Federal government's security and prevention programme and its metropolitan programme set certain policy objectives for securing the metropolis and support this social policy through contracts (mentioned earlier). The regional government of Flanders support some welfare projects but they do not have a prominent role like the regional government of Brussels which installed an institute to promote this role (see above). The role of the districts is unique to Antwerp but limited to giving advice. The most prominent role is taken up by the city council of Antwerp.

Until 2012, the city of Antwerp's policy was determined by a socialist regime that focused mainly on a preventive and metropolitan policy with a sanctioned conclusion in the form of MAS as a last resort (Devroe, 2012). This was paired with the establishment of 'Living Together', an artificial division between a social policy (geared towards rights) and a security policy (geared towards obligations) (Meeuws, 2012). In collaboration with the police and the prosecutor, the city chose an integrated approach, the so-called BBB method, which stands for 'break – bend – build'.

'Break' stands for restraint by the police and judiciary system. 'Bend' stands for the administrative approach based on determinations within the framework of MAS as a starting point for interventions and social trajectories targeting progress for clients regarding living, working and welfare. Finally, 'build' stands for providing sufficient physical and social infrastructure (Meeuws, 2012). The latter translates into urban development projects, such as the renovation of the railway station in the city of Antwerp. The BBB method stands for a cycle of 'tearing down' and rebuilding with a focus on the integration of a security policy and a social policy.

Financially the city plan 'Security' in Antwerp relies at a federal level on the security and prevention agreement from the Ministry of Internal Affairs, but is also funded by the Federal government service's Metropolitan Policy (35%) and, moreover, 40% is financed by the city of Antwerp itself (Meeuws, 2012). In other words, the policy is based in part on the priorities and policy lines of the Federal government (city development, prevention projects, etc.), but is also given its own content (cf. BBB method) by the city of Antwerp.

From 2013 onwards, the current mayor and Flemish-speaking Nationalist Bart De Wever (N-VA) took over the helm from the Flemish-speaking Socialist Patrick Janssens (SPA). Since the local elections in 2012, Antwerp (until 2018) has been governed by a triple coalition. The N-VA (the largest party) joined forces with the CD&V and the Open VLD.

With the start of Mayor Bart De Wever's coalition agreement in 2013, a small shift in the primary objectives of the city has become visible. The trend towards risk management, started during the previous period, has been given an extra boost. The coalition agreement states that the goal is '[a] safe city where respect for the rules is educated and if necessary enforced' (Council Agreement, 2013: 3).

The shift from a more social policy to risk management can be illustrated by a number of trends that we have observed. The current social projects were indeed retained, but transferred to the private sector. In the previous administrative period ruled by the Socialist Party activities in the squares were organised by city services. Now activities are no longer organised by the city but by non-profit organisations.

In the city's coalition agreement, guaranteeing the safety of everyone is described as a top priority. Dealing with drugs, not just trafficking but also the anti-social behaviour connected to it, is described as priority number one. Also, dealing with burglaries is high on the political agenda (Council Agreement, 2013). The MAS is additionally being used to combat illegal dumping of waste. There is also an increase in the more offender-oriented tertiary strategies targeting prolific and priority offenders to expedite deterrence from criminal careers. The U-Turn project in Antwerp, for example, helps young adults with a troubled background who have committed multiple serious offences (Gilleir et al., 2010).

Furthermore, the city of Antwerp's coalition agreement, for the period 2013–18, talks about the role of the local police within this security plan. It guides the local police in Antwerp in two directions (Council Agreement, 2013). On the one hand, the agreement argues in favour of the optimisation of the operational capacity based on centralisation of the intervention service of the local police. This centralisation movement means a scale increase with one central dispatch (from the six departments[15]), aimed at greater availability, visibility, approachability and strength of the local corps. Additionally, investment in a more professional reception and a decrease in response times are applied. On the other hand, the plea has been made for a stronger neighbourhood watch and community policing. The department officer is the departments' anchor for more availability, either on foot or bicycle. Technology such as a camera surveillance system and a mobile office is considered essential for making this possible in both tracks. The security plan for this police zone is based on the coalition agreement of the city and focuses on the implementation of all previous policy options (Zone Security Plan, Police Zone Antwerp, 2013–17; Jaarboek Lokale Politie Antwerpen, 2014).

Both tracks have implications as to the nature of police work and the degree of *plural policing* in the city of Antwerp. A centralisation of the intervention in combination with heavy policing in the neighbourhood is indeed being made possible by transferring specific tasks to other actors within the city. Preventive and educational tasks could be left to the city services and there could be an increased cooperation with the private security sector. Moreover, collecting bicycles, monitoring absence and mediating conflicts between neighbours would no longer be viewed as the department officer's task. This development has been significantly scrutinised. Ponsaers (2015) sees this as a decline in the community-oriented police model and a regression to a 'crime fighting' or 'law and order' police agenda with a major focus on these areas. According to him, this approach threatens to lead to a police force that is far removed from the population.

3.2 Brussels, from diversity to regional policy

Brussels is the capital of Belgium and Europe. Compared to other major European metropolises, Brussels is something of an outsider. The metropolitan area consists of 19 municipalities, a region with a state capital function, of which *the City of Brussels* is just one (Meerschout & De Hert, 2008). In other words, the competences of the region and the City of Brussels are not the same. This means that Brussels differs from, for example, Berlin. Berlin is a city-state in which the competences of the 'Bundesstaat' (Federal state) are the same as the competences of the mayor (Aden & De Pauw, 2014).

Concerning the metropolitan security agenda setting in the city of Brussels, three governance levels have an influence on the process of policy making in the domain of security. The Federal government's security and prevention programme and its Metropolitan programme sets certain policy objectives for the policing of the metropolis and supports this social policy through contracts (mentioned earlier). The regional government of Brussels gained power with the Sixth State reform and with the establishment of the Brussels Security and Prevention Institute which developed a plan (mentioned earlier). This institute aims to provide a coherent regional city project in Brussels but for the time being this plan is just guidance, whereas actual decision-making power about metropolitan policing remains with the 19 municipal mayors who can and do adopt very different policing agendas.

Brussels has 1,154,635 inhabitants over a surface area of 161.38 square kilometres (ADS, 2015). These inhabitants are spread out over 19[16] municipalities, each with their own mayor and local policy. This means there are 19 different mayors and, taking into account their local self-government, in some cases also 19 different types of policies.

In comparison with Antwerp's 'right-of-centre coalition' in the administration period 2014–17, Brussels municipalities are oriented more to the left of centre. The main role in these municipalities is taken up either by the French-speaking Parti Socialiste (PS) or the liberal French-speaking Mouvement Réformateur (MR).

A detailed discussion of the agenda setting of each of the 19 municipalities would lead us too far in this chapter. It is, however, immediately obvious that the administrative embedding of Brussels does, on the one hand, give rise to significant diversity of security policies as each of the 19 municipalities and their mayors have local autonomy in determining the local security policy. On the other hand, the Brussels-Capital Region influence on security policy in Brussels is gradually increasing, which could lead to more unity in the future. The Brussels Prevention and Security Institute notes that, with regard to drawing up the local security diagnostics and consequently priority determination in the policy, the different municipalities address prevention in different ways. Some municipalities focus on prevention of the determined priority criminal phenomena; others focus solely on social prevention, such as the fight against social exclusion (Bailly et al., 2015: 64).

The administrative embedding of Brussels also has an influence on the subsidies that the 19 municipalities receive for their policy. The Brussels municipalities receive federal subsidies for their local security policy via the Strategic Security Plan of the Ministry of Internal Affairs and, like Antwerp, they receive a budget via the Department for Metropolitan Policy. Lastly, the Brussels-Capital Region[17] provides a wide range of subsidies via the Brussels prevention and neighbourhood plans to support European summits, to draw up prevention policies regarding school absenteeism, for a socially secure living policy, to draw up the MAS and to support urban renewal.

It is remarkable that various municipalities maintain different policies regarding anti-social behaviour. Parking fines, for example, can differ between municipalities and some offences can be punishable with a MAS in one municipality but not in another. For some time now various scientists have been advocating a redesign of the political landscape, and they believe in a more prominent role for the Brussels-Capital Region which, in their opinion, must provide for a coherent regional city project in Brussels that focuses on urban renewal and welfare (Mincke et al., 2009; Meerschout & De Hert, 2008).

Despite the fact that Brussels consists of 19 municipalities, each with its own policy, the Brussels-Capital Region has been divided into six police zones (Brussels-Capital, Brussels West, South, Ukkel/Watermaal-Bosvoorde/Oudergem, Montgomery, Polbruno).[18] These six local police zones are all multi-municipality zones. Each zone has a chief of police who determines policing policy together with his or her mayors of the municipalities. The major difference from the city of Antwerp is the manner in which local policing and intervention are managed at an organisational level. The city of Antwerp has opted for strong centralisation while in Brussels decentralisation is predominant. This decentralisation has been employed even further in the Brussels-Capital Elsene zone by dividing the zone into five local commissioners' offices from which policing is provided (Zone Security Plan, Police Zone Brussels-Elsene, 2013–17).

The lack of central management for the six local police zones in Brussels is an important point of discussion that has been brought up repeatedly, most recently due to the link between the municipality of Molenbeek and the terrorist attacks in Paris (13/11/2015) and the aftermath of the attacks in Brussels (22/03/2016). The merger of the six police zones is seen as a potential means of achieving a more coherent approach to policing in light of the current security challenges. One of the arguments is that there are other metropolises (Berlin, London) in which the police are supervised by one mayor and with the objective of guaranteeing adherence to city-wide policies (Ponsaers, 2015; Aden & De Pauw, 2014; Edwards & Prins, 2014). Furthermore, a possible downside to this merger is pointed out: 'Creating one large Brussels police zone, without changing the 19 separate municipalities, can however only lead to greater distance between the administration and the police and at the same time lead to less focus on community issues', according to Ponsaers (2015).

In other words, the administrative organisation of Brussels in 19 municipalities has major consequences for the city's security policy and the functioning of the public police within this metropolis. Nonetheless, additional research is needed to substantiate the (optimum) link between the administrative and police organisation of Brussels with scientific and operational arguments.

3.3 The outlines are clear, but there are still differences

Inspired by our analysis above, Figure 10.1 captures the main differences between Antwerp and Brussels in terms of their security agenda setting.

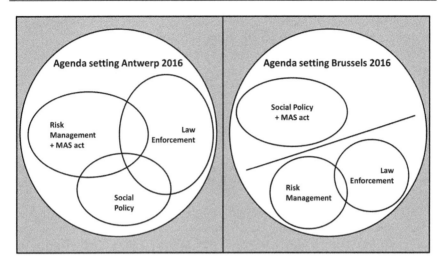

Figure 10.1 Comparison of agenda setting in Antwerp and Brussels, 2016

In the agenda setting of Antwerp, we observe a shift from a more welfare-oriented approach to a 'risk management' approach with the MAS law also being implemented in that risk management. This has merged several urban renewal projects, while retaining focus on a number of projects with a social perspective, as the city also focuses on law enforcement. This process is not the outcome of the shift from a Socialist policy towards a Flemish Nationalist policy. The focus on risk management started before with the BBB method. As explained in section 3.1, this method combines law enforcement (closing premises, prosecuting dealers), risk management (fining incivilities with administrative sanctions using the MAS, projects like U-Turn), and social policy (focus on liveability of the city and social events). The risk management approach has become more important since the council agreement of 2013, but the city still has some social policy projects (with support of the Federal government) and law enforcement.

The agenda setting in Antwerp is a complex of local decisions and influences of the Federal government. The fact that the mayor of the city is also the party chairman of Belgium's largest national party in the Federal government might be one explanation for this alignment.

A more disintegrated tendency has become clear in the agenda setting of Brussels. Most projects are subsidised by the Brussels-Capital Region, which is still governed by a Socialist regime. Therefore, most of the Brussels municipalities opt for a social policy with MAS as the major deterrent. For example, the municipality of Anderlecht has several projects to help youngsters. An example is the FIFA (Fédération Internationale de Football Association) project that focuses on social integration and the development of young people through football. Nevertheless, the MAS fine can be used if youngsters are still gathering together on the street.

Recently, in response to the terrorist attack and threats in Brussels, risk management and an enforcement policy were partly implemented. We see a line in Figure 10.1 to show these policy agendas were implemented in another way. In Antwerp, the approaches are part of one policy. In Brussels the social policy and use of the MAS was supplemented by risk management and law enforcement approaches after the terrorist assaults in Paris and Brussels. This was inspired by the security policy developed by the Federal government, advised by the Coordinating Body for Threat Analysis (OCAD). Soldiers were deployed onto the streets and a set of anti-terrorist actions were planned.

This resulted in more disintegrated agenda setting in Brussels where there is less alignment between the security policies developed on a federal level and those developed within each of the 19 municipalities. The effect of the coordinating function of the new Brussels Prevention and Security Institute remains to be seen.

4 Conclusion and reflections

Nation-states often create regulations that leave large room for manoeuvre at the discretion of local authorities (Ponsaers et al., 2014). Compared to other European countries, the Belgian national level has an influence on the organisation of urban safety, but there is certainly room for local discretion. The institutional framework (as explained in section 2 of this chapter) determines the functioning of security policies and public policing, but local implementation may differ.

In Brussels and Antwerp we observe the same kind of 'public safety regime' as defined by Edwards and Hughes (2012). It can be characterised by a complex mixture of local and national police forces, steered by different policy agendas. Especially in Brussels we observe a complex mixture of local and national police forces, functioning according to different policy agendas on the territory of the same metropolitan area (Ponsaers & Devroe, 2015).

We can conclude that in Belgium certain steps are being taken towards 'convergence' (Edwards & Hughes, 2012). This is expressed through the emergence of several framework documents and security plans, but this tendency is impeded by the current Belgian State structure. The ongoing interference from the regions on the one hand, and the strong autonomy of the municipalities on the other are simultaneously causing greater 'divergence' (Edwards & Hughes, 2012). After all, local politics have a huge impact on local security plans and can differ widely from national policy.

The content of the local security policy has a strong 'political character' in Belgium. This is a double-edged sword: on the one hand, it generates involvement of the local administrators in the security policy for which they are responsible, while on the other, too much involvement can cause ideological and/or electoral motives to become both the security policy's starting point and the sole benchmark. This can pose a threat to the 'integral character' of the policy (Vermeersch et al., 2012). Devroe (2010) also mentions in her evaluation research '15 years of police and justice' that political policy decisions in Belgium vary greatly and are based on 'opinions', while a rational security policy should be based on scientific research. This raises the question of whether or not we actually want to live in an 'urban republic' where the mayor's political affiliation determines security policy (Devroe, 2013).

The observation of Ponsaers and Devroe (2015: 45) that 'politics in European metropolises is largely characterized by the competition of power between the national-state and metropolitan governance' is confirmed and further completed based on the Belgian case studies presented here. After all, in Belgium the level of the communities, the regions and the provinces are additional layers. Switching between the national, provincial, regional and local/urban administrative levels is a daily challenge of Belgian security policy. In the best-case scenario, the different levels adopt an attitude of partnership towards each other. Mutual coordination and adjustment puts high demands on the capacity and dedication of governments and various security actors. The urban security policy agendas in Antwerp and Brussels are clearly the result of a power struggle between the complex interplay of administrative levels, unique to Belgium.

At the city level, we have observed important differences. The city of Antwerp is led by one mayor steering one local police zone. The city is merging a focus on criminal justice and social justice in the 'Living Together' department. In the city of Brussels, part of a metropolitan area consisting of 19 municipalities, the focus is less obvious. The establishment of the Brussels Security and Prevention Institute is a first step to give the region more responsibility. The evolution towards an urban region is endorsed in the 2014–19 government policy statement of the Brussels government in which a single Regional Security Plan is advocated for, and in which greater cooperation is recommended between the different police zones with the objective of reaching one harmonised set of police regulations.

The European situation teaches us that metropolises are often equipped with robust police forces (such as the London Metropolitan Police), operating under the supervision of one mayor with the objective of guaranteeing adherence to the global city policy. Consider Berlin, where the prime minister of the Berlin sub-state also functions as mayor of the city and, for the most part, has control over the police force that is active within the metropolitan jurisdiction (Ponsaers, 2015). From this point of view one could argue that today there is still too much fragmentation in Brussels.

Furthermore, there are many other factors that are not connected to the administrative embedding of Antwerp and Brussels which are influencing the security agenda of these metropolises. The recent increase of the terrorist threat to level 3 (serious) and to level 4 (very serious) in Belgium and Brussels in particular caused a rearranging of the priorities on the national and urban agenda and a shift of the deployment of resources towards terrorism control as priority number one. At the same time, the increased terrorist alert put the challenges of the Belgian State structure to manage an efficient and effective security policy back on high alert. This was expressed in a flare-up of the discussion about the lack of one police force for Brussels and the differences in management by the 19 Brussels municipalities.

In the context of cutbacks (as described extensively in Part I of this book), the pressure of global/local challenges (such as terrorism and migration) on the administration is high, both at national and local levels, to establish forms of partnership within the public sector (between police and Army), as well as between the public and the private sectors (such as collaboration between private security and public police). Further research must demonstrate if and to what extent perspectives on the role of the police in Belgian society, imagined by administrators at different levels, play a role in the policy decisions that are made. These are choices that, in Belgium in any case, are always the result of negotiations and compromises because the political composition of the administrations differs at the various levels. More research is needed to find out the interactions between these perspectives, security policies, and the organisational and operational practices that they generate.

Notes

1 Circular letter of 6 November 2003, concerning the special work statute for long-term unemployed in a community guard function, BS, 13 December 2003. More information can be found on: www.werk.belgië.be
2 Non-police public actors execute police surveillance tasks in public space.
3 More information can be found on several websites. Council Agreement of the City of Antwerp: http://ocmw.antwerpen.be/sites/default/files/Bestuursakkoord_ %20Stad_Antwerpen_2013_2018.pdf; Council Agreement Brussels Capital Region: www.vgc.be/sites/www.vgc.be/files/download/bestuursakkoord_vgc_20142019_0.pdf; Security Plan of the Antwerp Police: www.pzantwerpen.be/zonaalveiligheidsplan; and the Security Plan of the Brussels Police: www.lokalepolitie.be/5339
4 A coalition of the Socialist Party (the Flemish SPA), the Liberal Party (the Flemish Open VLD), and Christian Democratic Party (the Flemish CD&V) in Antwerp; and a coalition of the Socialist Party (the Walloon PS) and the Christian Democratic Party (the Walloon CDh) in Brussels.
5 Royal Decree of 24 June 1988, New Communal Law, BS 3 September 1988, Act of May.
6 Belgian Law on the Integrated Police (07/12/1998).
7 The Incivility Act, 13 May 1999 (Municipal Administrative Sanctions Act – MAS), BS, 10 June 1999.
8 The approach of the liberal political party we refer to is a rejection of social and economic policy responses to problems of crime and civil unrest in favour of a more minimalist law enforcement state.

9 So called because the colours of the political parties are blue (Liberal Party) and yellow (Flemish National Party).
10 Royal Decree 8 November 2013 on Strategic Safety and Prevention Plans and Prevention Officers, BS, 29 November 2013.
11 Article 167, § 1, section 2, of the Constitution; the Law of 5 August 1992 on the office of the police (articles 7/5, 37 and 38); the Law of 20 May 1994 concerning the periods and positions of soldiers in the reserves as well as the employment and readiness of the Army; the Law on the integrated police force of 7 December 1998 (articles 43, 111 and 113); the programme law of 2 August 2002; the Royal Decree of 6 July 1994.
12 See Ordinance 28 May 2015 to establish a public service institution that centralises the management of the prevention and security policy in the Brussels-Capital Region, *Belgian Official Gazette*, 10 June 2015.
13 Ordinance, 28 May 2015 to establish a public service institution that centralises the management of the prevention and security policy in the Brussels-Capital Region, *Belgian Official Gazette*, 10 June 2015.
14 The Local Police are reinforced by the devolved Federal Police of Antwerp for execution of specialised police tasks (WGP, 1998).
15 The Local Police is divided into six departments that cover the nine districts. Those departments are working units under control of one zone.
16 Anderlecht, Brussels, Elsene, Etterbeek, Evere, Ganshoren, Jette, Koekelberg, Oudergem, Schaarbeek, Sint-Agatha-Berchem, Sint-Gillis, Sint-Jans-Molenbeek, Sint-Joost-Ten-Node, Sint-Lambrechts Woluwe, Sint-Pieters Woluwe, Ukkel, Vorst, and Watermaal-Bosvoorde.
17 Ordinance BBHR 9 July 2015 for the allocation of a general subsidy of €10,173,518.94 to the Brussels municipalities, in the framework of the Brussels prevention and neighbourhood policy for the first half of 2015.
18 http://brusselverkiezingen2012.irisnet.be/de-politiezone

Bibliography

Aden, H., De Pauw, E. (2014) 'Policing Berlin. From separation by the "iron curtain" to the new German capital and a globalised city', *European Journal of Policing Studies*, 2(1): 13–29.

ADS (Algemene Directie Statistiek – Statistics Belgium) (2015) 'Brussel, België 2015: 11.209.044 inwoners'. Via www.statistics.be (accessed 12 July 2015).

Bailly, N., Thiry, I., Francois, J., De Gendt, M., Siaens, M. (2015) *Brussels Observatorium voor Preventie en Veiligheid*, Verslag.

Bowling, B., Sheptycki, J. (2012) *Global Policing*, Sage.

Buurtmonitor Antwerpen (2015) 'De stad in cijfers'. Via www.antwerpen.be/destadincijfers (accessed 25 July 2015).

Council Agreement (2013–18) *Respect voor A. Stad*, Antwerpen.

Crawford, A. (1999) *The Local Governance of Crime: Appeals to Community and Partnerships*, Oxford: Oxford University Press.

Crawford, A. (2006) 'Networked governance and the post-regulatory state? Steering, rowing and anchoring the provision of policing and security', *Theoretical Criminology*, 10(4): 449–479.

De Pauw, E., De Pauw, K., Devroe, E., Dormaels, A., Gunst, J.C. (2012) 'Lokale integrale veiligheid op de terugweg?' *Orde van de dag*, 59: 5–13.

Devroe, E. (2010) 'Wetenschap voor beleid of beleid voor wetenschap? Een analyse van 15 jaar politie en justitie onderzoek in België', *Panopticon*, 31(3): 11–39.

Devroe, E. (2012) 'A swelling culture of control? De genese en toepassing van de wet op de gemeentelijke administratieve sancties in België', *Reeks politiestudies*, 2, Maklu, Antwerpen.

Devroe, E. (2013) 'Kiezen voor stadsrepublieken? Over administratieve afhandeling van overlast in de steden', *Tijdschrift voor Veiligheid*, 12–26.

Devroe, E. (2015) 'Purple vests. The origins of plural policing in Belgium', *European Journal of Policing Studies*, 2: 304–324.

Devroe, E., Ponsaers, P., De Pauw, E. (2014) 'Policing in Europese metropolen', *Orde van de dag*, 68: 2–7.

Edwards, A., Hughes, G. (2012) 'Public safety regimes: Negotiated orders and political analysis in criminology', *Criminology and Criminal Justice*, 12(4): 433–458.

Easton, M., Ponsaers, P. (2010) 'The view of the police on community policing in Belgian multicultural neighbourhoods' in M. Cools, B. De Ruyver, M. Easton, L. Pauwels, P. Pnsaers, T. Vander Beken, F. Vander Laenen, G. Vande Walle, G. Vynckier (eds), *Governance of Security Research Paper Series, Volume 3. New Empirical Data, Theories and Ananlyses on Safety, Societal Problems and Citiens Perceptions*. Antwerpen/Apeldoorn: Maklu, 161–182.

Edwards, A., Prins, R. (2014) 'Policing and crime in contemporary London. A developmental agenda?' in P. Ponsaers, A. Edwards, A. Verhage, A. Recasens i Brunet (eds), *European Journal of Policing Studies*, Special Issue Policing European Metropolises, Antwerpen/Apeldoorn: Maklu, 2: 61–93.

Flanders (2015) 'Organisatie van de Vlaamse Overheid'. Via www.vlaanderen.be (accessed 12 July 2015).

Gilleir, F., Easton, M., Ponsaers, P. (2010) 'Een U-Turn voor jongvolwassen veelplegers – Kanttekeningen bij een empirisch-begeleidend programma', *Panopticon*, 31(1): 5–19.

Government Policy Statement (2014) *Brussels Capital Region 2014–2019*.

Hebberecht, P. (2004) 'Het Belgische preventie-en veiligheidsbeleid', *Justitiële verkenningen*, 30(7): 81–94.

Jaarboek Lokale Politie Antwerpen (2014) Via www.politieantwerpen.be (accessed October 1, 2015).

Johnston, L., Shearing, C. (2003) 'Governing security', in *Explorations in Policing and Justice*, London.

Jones, T., Newburn, T. (2002) 'The transformation of policing? Understanding current trends in policing systems', *British Journal of Criminology*, 42(1): 129–146.

Jones, T., Newburn, T. (2006) 'Understanding plural policing', in *Plural Policing: A Comparative Perspective*, Sage.

Justaert, M., Vanhecke, N. (2015) 'Een jaar veiligheidsbeleid onder Michel I. Wat moet u onthouden?' *De Standaard*, October 5.

Loader, I. (2000) 'Plural policing and democratic governance', *Social & Legal Studies*, 9(3): 323–345.

Meerschout, K., De Hert, P. (2008) 'Het gebruik van de gemeentelijke administratieve sancties door de Brusselse gemeenten. Is er nood aan een regulerende rol voor het Brussels Hoofdstedelijk Gewest?' *Brussels Studies*, 18, May 18.

Meeuws, T. (2012) 'Veiligheid, lokaal verweven beleid. In De Pauw, E. ea. Lokaal Integraal Veiligheid revisited', *Orde van de dag*, 74–80.

Mincke, C., Smeets, C., Enhus, E. (2009) 'Staten-Generaal Brussel', *Veiligheid in Brussel, Synthesenota*, 2, January 9.
Ponsaers, P. (2015) 'De politie nog altijd uw vriend? Opinie'. Via www.deredactie.be (accessed December 9, 2015).
Ponsaers, P., Devroe, E. (2015) 'De toekomst van Europese Nationale Politiebestellen?' *De toekomstpolitie: Triggers voor een voldragen debat*, 10–45.
Ponsaers, P., Devroe, E., Meert, D. (2006) 'Kiezen voor een democratische politie: wat is dat?' *Orde van de dag*, 33: 7–14.
Ponsaers, P., Easton, M., Van den Broeck, T., Verhage, A., Bruggeman, W. (2014) 'Enkele markante bevindingen over "policing" in zeven Europese metropolen', *Orde van de dag*, 68: 80–85.
Reenaers, J. (2015) Personal communication, November 9, 2015.
Reiner, R. (2013) 'Who governs? Democracy, plutocracy, science and prophecy in policing', *Criminology and Criminal Justice*, 13(2): 161–180.
Shearing, C.D., Johnston, L. (2013) *Governing Security: Explorations of Policing and Justice*, London: Routledge.
Stenning, P. (2009) 'Governance and accountability in a plural policing environment – The story so far', *Policing*, 3(1): 22–33.
Vermeersch, H., De Pauw, E., Deprins, F. (2012) 'Integrale veiligheid, of de kunst van het haalbare ...', *Orde van de dag*, 59: 37–44.
WGP (1998) *Wet op de geïntegreerde politie* [Belgian Law on the Integrated Police], Belgisch Staatsblad, 7 December.
Zone Security Plan, Police Zone Antwerp (2013–17).
Zone Security Plan, Police Zone Brussels-Elsene (2013–17).

Chapter 11

The Netherlands
Local strategies for glocal challenges: Comparing policing agendas in Amsterdam and Rotterdam

Ruth Prins and Elke Devroe

1 Introduction

In this chapter we analyse the politics of policing, with a specific focus on policing agendas in the two largest cities in the Netherlands: Amsterdam and Rotterdam. Both metropolises are considered metropolises facing 'glocal' challenges related to multicultural populations in urban areas, social inequalities in terms of household income, international harbours, crime and disorder. The term 'glocal' refers to the interlinkages between global challenges and local communities. In order to get an understanding of the tendencies towards divergence and convergence in urban policing in the metropolises under study we start with a summary of general trends in policing in the Netherlands in the second section. In the third section national, regional and local governmental constitutional arrangements, discretionary powers and public police management are presented. The remainder of the chapter compares and contrasts policing agendas in Amsterdam and Rotterdam and concludes with an overview of their regimes and possible explanations for convergence and divergence in the politics of policing in these metropolises. The search for the regimes in the background of policing agendas in these two embedded case studies reveals both convergence towards the national agenda and divergence between the agendas in both metropolises. Possible explanations for these trends can be found in the political 'circuits of power' (Devroe, Edwards, Ponsaers, this volume) of the municipal ruling coalition and in wider institutional arrangements.

2 Trends in the politics of contemporary policing in the Netherlands

The Netherlands is a small country with approximately 17 million inhabitants in 2016. It contains a vital economy, a stable democratic system based on diplomacy, negotiation and consensus (Das et al., 2007) and, until recently, a tolerant permissiveness towards many vices, foreigner friendly and a tolerant penal climate. As in many other countries, tolerance changed after certain critical events as explained below (Downes & van Swaaningen, 2007). The Dutch policing and justice apparatus has traditionally been associated with pragmatism, tolerance and a sympathetic distaste for anything that feels like militarism (Wintle, 1996, in Andeweg & Irwin, 2002). This philosophy of policing, albeit altering significantly, fits well with the Dutch culture of consensus, equality and relative harmony (Andeweg & Irwin, 2002).

For a long time, the Netherlands has known its own peculiar social structure which was developed in order to permit all groups to be different but equal (Spruyt, 2006). This social structure was characterised by 'pillarisation'[1] and consisted of a four-fold, religiously inspired, division between a Protestant, a Roman-Catholic, a social democratic and a liberal pillar. The presence of an intermediate layer of ideologically based and pillarised organisations and institutions providing public resources for educational, social, cultural and even economic purposes, became a salient feature of the Dutch welfare state in the course of the 20th century (Spiecker & Sleutel, 2001). This rather unique societal arrangement rapidly declined after the 1970s. The so-called 'societal midfield',[2] constituted by the ensemble of pillarised associations and institutions, was transformed (Spiecker & Sleutel, 2001) into a multi-ethnic society with significant consequences for the policing of crime and disorder.

In the following sections we shed a light upon policing trends in the Netherlands in chronological order. Following the arguments of Edwards and Hughes (2012) in order to capture shifts in national security agendas and implementation processes, we define policing in terms of policy agendas arranged around the concerns of justice (differentiated further between those of 'criminal', 'restorative' and 'social' justice) and of 'risk management'. While these are not without their own limitations as sensitising concepts, they translate well in cross-cultural comparative criminological research into policy agendas. Using these concepts it is possible to identify three main phases in the contemporary politics of policing in the Netherlands, in which prevention, risk management and law enforcement have been privileged.

2.1 Policies aimed at the prevention (1983–93)

Until the 1970s crime and disorder were not a national concern nor as object of public policies in the Netherlands. This changed due to rising crime rates in the 1980s and the establishment of the Roethof Parliamentary Commission, named after its president (Commissie Kleine Criminaliteit, 1984). The committee identified a growing public concern with rising crime rates, a loss of trust in the government as protector of public and private interests, and the fear of a further erosion of norms and values within the population and in social control. The Roethof Commission argued the causes of crime were to be found in a weakened societal network of informal and formal control (Van Den Broeck, 2012), with the implication that external control had to be strengthened by formal and informal surveillance in public space (Jongman, 1988). Public programmes were created and aimed at restoring and intensifying social ties and inclusion in Dutch neighbourhoods (Van Dijk & De Waard, 2000).

In the aftermath of this Commission, national government opted for an 'integral security' policy entailing the involvement and cooperation of new actors in the prevention of crime besides the police. A few years later the larger cities in the Netherlands created 'Integral Security Policies'[3] prioritising incivilities and petty crime as policy priorities to be addressed by police in close collaboration with many partners from the public and private sectors. This led to a full-grown policy tradition of local governments formulating and coordinating policing in close collaboration with many partners from the public, voluntary and private sectors (Cachet & Prins, 2012). The Netherlands was internationally known for its permissive policy[4] towards crime and disorder. Political preferences to treat, for example, coffee shops selling cannabis and licensed prostitution permissively are widely known (Das et al., 2007). Moreover, 'community safety' and 'crime prevention' – policies that seek to increase public safety oriented to the social context in which crime emerges rather than to the punishment of offenders themselves (Van Swaaningen, 2005) – were the central concerns on which policing agendas were set during this period. Police officers were dedicated to lowering crime rates and enhancing (subjective) safety within a social justice framework.

2.2 Towards a risk management approach (1994–2010)

From the mid-1990s onwards the number of non-Western second-generation inhabitants grew by 62% to almost 1.5 million (Spiecker & Sleutel, 2001). The biggest ethnic groups in the Netherlands were the Surinamese, Moroccan, Turkish, Moluccan and Chinese communities, but lately the influx of (political) refugees, in particular from countries in the Middle East and Africa, has increased drastically. This large-scale arrival of people from non-Western countries created substantial demographic changes in the Netherlands (ibid.). The preventative approach, not leading to a visible decrease of crime numbers, combined with popular concerns over this immigration, have been acknowledged as key factors in the transformation of the policy agenda from a preventive and social policy orientation towards a preoccupation with identifying and controlling particular groups and behaviours thought to threaten the 'quality of life' in Dutch cities. This period is called 'risk management' because a narrative of risks and risk analysis was used to conceptualise problematic groups and behaviours for the purposes of their control (Terpstra, 2010).

It is argued that public feelings of insecurity and anxiety grew as many social problems were interpreted in terms of ethnic diversity and issues of urban security occupied a more prominent place in both national and local politics. Public debates about nuisance, youth gangs, terrorism and the misuse of social benefits became racialised (Van Swaaningen, 2005). The White Papers 'Security Policy'[5] (1995–98) and the 'Integral Security Programme' (1999)[6] launched debates on administrative sanctioning for offences and incivilities (Mein, 2005; Sackers, 2010). The papers called for more surveillance in the streets, more prison cells and more competences for the police (Devroe, 2012). Police capacity increased and wardens entered public space, reflecting a broader trend in which, it is argued, Western societies were increasingly being 'governed through crime' (Simon, 2007; Tonry, 2001). The urgency of tackling incivilities was thus strongly connected with public worries about immigration, ethnic minorities, and youngsters gathering in groups in public spaces. From 2000 onwards, politicians became increasingly critical of the police for inadequately fulfilling their duties for investigating crime and maintaining public order. This insight led to the establishment of supra-regional investigation teams and performance contracts with a strong focus on remittance notes and the performance management of detective work (Devroe, 2013).

In 2002 the right-wing politician Pim Fortuyn claimed to lead 'The Party of Law and Order' (Leefbaar Rotterdam), coining the term 'liveability'[7] as a buzzword on the political agenda (Van Swaaningen, 2005). His White Paper, 'Tackling Crime' (2001) argued for stricter and more severe controls on behaviour in public spaces. The notion of prevention through social justice diminished as greater emphasis was placed on a more repressive orientation to the maintenance of public order and an emphasis on criminal law enforcement. This can be called a focus event in turning Dutch tolerance towards more punitive policing. After the shocking assassination of Pim Fortuyn during the national election campaign on 6 May 2002, 'governing urban security' became a highly politicised issue in the Netherlands (Den Boer, 2007). After the murder, Fortuyn's party (LPF) gained seats in the national Parliament and entered the ruling coalition 'Balkenende I'.[8] LPF became part of the coalition with the Christian Democrats (CDA) and the Liberal Party (VVD). Jan Peter Balkenende (CDA) became prime minister and formalised one single policy document before the Cabinet collapsed due to internal conflicts after just 87 days in office. This policy was titled 'Towards a Safer Society'[9] and introduced the idea of administrative orders providing mayors with an instrument to sanction infringements on general police regulations (municipal code of prohibitions of certain behaviour). This policy resembled some core ideas of Pim Fortuyn by prioritising crime fighting, attention on maintaining public norms and values, more legal competences for the police and various incentives for police performance indicators.

The Dutch general elections in 2003 resulted in the cabinet Balkenende II, a coalition agreement with the CDA, VVD and Liberal Democrat Party D66.

One year later, the country was shocked again by the murder of art and film director Theo van Gogh (2004). Van Gogh launched a critical movie about Islam and was murdered by a radicalised Muslim three months later. The murder triggered a public debate on tolerance of religion and minorities in the Netherlands. Especially for Amsterdam, this was an important event, as it increased an 'us-against-them' mentality in the city (Verbeek, 2006). Afterwards, tensions in the city increased as radicalisation had become much more visible (Verbeek, 2006). In the summer of 2006 the Cabinet collapsed again, followed by the new Cabinet Balkenende IV. In these turbulent times, the policy 'Towards a Safer Society' remained the national security framework in the Netherlands until 2007. This policy called for a more repressive approach and a striking detail is that the word 'prevention' was completely absent in this document (Terpstra, 2007).

In 2009 the 'Act on Administrative Orders in Public Space' was passed, empowering local governments to sanction infringements on behaviour inserted in the 'Local Municipal Code' (mostly incivilities) by imposing fines (Mevis, 2004). The public police as well as wardens can report and sanction by means of fines labelled as 'administrative punishment'.[10] Meanwhile the Ministry of Justice's budget rose sensationally with injections of €70 million in 2003 and an expected €200 million in 2008, whilst police numbers grew from 40,000 to 50,000 officers in less than ten years (Das et al., 2007). During this period criminal justice was prioritised and the previous social prevention agenda marginalised (Pakes, 2005).

2.3 Law enforcement (2010–16)

This repressive agenda was further emphasised in the 'Law on Incivilities and Measures Against Football Hooliganism' (2010), which provides Dutch mayors with an extra set of tools against disorderly behaviour and incivilities in the cities. Mayors can, for example, impose a territorial ban,[11] a group ban[12] or a ban on particular individuals for disorderly behaviour, restricting their freedom of movement in particular places.

In 2010, a 'minority coalition' was formed consisting of the VVD and the CDA led by Prime Minister Mark Rutte in order to block the 'Party for Freedom' (PVV) led by Geert Wilders, who gained 24 out of 150 seats in the national Parliament. This party criticised the 'Islamification' of Dutch society and emphasised the law enforcement purposes of policing. Wilders advocated ending immigration from Muslim countries, supported banning the construction of new mosques and called for a hard line against what he called the 'street terror' exerted by minorities in Dutch cities. The electoral success of his populist party is thought to have shifted the policing agenda further away from the preventive approach that prevailed post-Roethof and towards an enforcement agenda.

The CDA and VVD formed a minority coalition as they did not want to rule with the PVV because of their different views on Islam and immigration. However, as this coalition had a minority of seats in Parliament they tried to negotiate with the PVV in order to be able to pass major reductions in public expenditure, worth millions of euros, in the context of the economic downturn that had followed the global financial crisis of 2008. The negotiations failed and new elections were called in 2012. This time Cabinet Rutte II was formed and consisted of a coalition between the VVD and the Labour Party (PvdA). Their governmental agreement 'Building Bridges' (2012–16) supplied an extra €105 million for the police each year, in order to have 'more blue on the streets and more capacity for investigation',[13] while a substantial budget cut was proposed for welfare, social insurance and the civil service.

Furthermore, debates about policing in the Netherlands in this period were also dominated by reorganisation of the Dutch police force from a regional to a national system. The Police Reform Act (2012) was proposed and installed by Minister of Security and Justice and former Mayor of Rotterdam Ivo Opstelten. This new national police organisation now shares the responsibility for setting policing agendas with local authorities and is consequently a significant factor in the evolving politics of metropolitan policing in the Netherlands (see section 3, below). The national agenda 2011–14 prioritised high-impact crimes such as burglaries and street robberies, youth gangs, organised crime such as human trafficking, the drugs trade and money laundering, animal abuse, cybercrime, environmental crime, illegal immigration, and urban safety on the street level.[14]

3 Governmental and constitutional arrangements

The Dutch system of public administration consists of three layers of government: national government, regional provinces, and local governments in almost 400 municipalities. Priorities, strategies and practices for urban policing in the Netherlands are heavily influenced by the circuits of power between this complex set of actors and their policing mandates.

At the national level, the Ministry of Internal Affairs and the Ministry of Justice were both responsible for internal security and criminal justice until 2010, when the new Ministry of Security and Justice integrated both tasks in one department. General crime policies are developed at the national level while community and citizen-based policing is negotiated at the local and regional levels, reflecting the Dutch tradition of legitimating policing policy through consultation and negotiation in localities (Tops, 1994). Local governments have formal responsibility for public safety within municipal boundaries, and this has been the case ever since the first Local Government Act in 1851. Local governments consist of three independent bodies: the mayor, having legal responsibility for public order and public safety within municipal boundaries;[15] the City Council; and the Board of Mayor and Aldermen. It is the mayor's individual responsibility to safeguard local order.[16] In order to do so, Dutch mayors may give orders to the police[17] and have been granted various powers to address specific threats to urban security over the past 20 years (Prins, 2014). Mayors of Dutch municipalities are not directly elected but are appointed by the Crown for a six-year term,[18] and are not consequently subject to the direct popular-democratic pressures that Belgian mayors (Devroe, 2013) or the police and crime commissioners in England and Wales are (Jones & Lister, 2015, Edwards et al., this volume). Dutch mayors apply for their position by responding to an official vacancy published by the Ministry of Interior Affairs. Once the commissioner of the king selects them as a potential candidate they then go through a formal procedure including interviews with a selection of Council members and finally appointment by the king.[19] Mayors are supposed to 'stand above' politics and guard the quality and outcome of local political and policy processes. Although they are usually affiliated with a political party, their job is not to be a politician but a professional administrator.

The Dutch police system[20] was, until recently, characterised by two types of dualism: a distinction between administrative policing (maintenance of public order and public safety) and law enforcement on the one hand, and between authority[21] and control[22] on the other (Cachet et al., 2009; Fijnaut, 2012; Naeyé, 2014). Authority refers to the ability to order police personnel to deploy a task in a specific area (operational policy). Control refers to taking care of the overarching organisational and financial aspects of the police organisation (organisational management). Control of the Dutch police has for the most part been in the hands of the national government, who kept the budgets and capacity division in their portfolio (Fyfe et al., 2013). When it came to the local level the police had two managers. Both the mayors and the public prosecutor were able to instruct the police on operational matters as well as influence some aspects of control. The mayor had the authority and some control on police personnel maintaining public order and safety (administrative policing). The public prosecutor held authority and some control over the criminal investigation activities carried out by the police (law enforcement). These matters were negotiated and harmonised as much as possible in the triangle concertation between the mayor, the public prosecutor and the police constable. However, the balance of powers over policing changed in 2012 when the national police system was introduced in the Netherlands. The critical implication of this was the abolition of the power of all mayors, in particular the 25 regional mayors, to exercise control over local police work.

This implies that Dutch mayors nowadays only have the ability to order police personnel to deploy a task in a specific local area (authority) and have lost their influence on the overarching organisational and financial aspects of the police organisation (control). As mayors have the statutory responsibility for local order and public safety they still hold a degree of discretion in setting local policy agendas. The minister of security and justice is seeking convergence between national policing priorities, as stipulated in the national security plan, and local policing priorities, as stipulated in local and regional security plans (Devroe & Ponsaers, 2013). However, this collaboration between local governments and the national police is subject to change as decisions about police core business have been shifted upwards to national level during the current reorganisation of the Dutch police system.

The shift towards centralisation grants the constitutional-legal authority to control all aspects of police work to the minister of security and justice, which has, in turn, provoked considerable controversy. Commentators have heavily criticised the new power balance between the minister and national police chief on the one hand and the increasingly limited power for mayors to steer local police work on the other (Terpstra & Gunther Moor, 2012; Fyfe et al., 2013; Cachet, 2015). They have argued that the consequence of the reform will be to push Dutch policing further away from involvement in preventive strategies in local neighbourhoods and maintaining public order and safety (administrative policing)[23] and towards law enforcement using a crime-fighting style of policing (like in France) instead of the former community-oriented policing style.

As a consequence of this constitutional arrangement, policy agendas for policing in Amsterdam and Rotterdam are the outcomes of a negotiation between many stakeholders with potentially rival mandates, including mayors and other local administrative bodies, the national minister of security and justice, the national police chief and the regional public prosecutors. Variegation in the policing agendas pursued in different cities can be understood as the outcome of these negotiation processes. In the remainder of this chapter this variegation is illustrated through reference to contemporary policing agendas in Amsterdam and Rotterdam. In the next section we will briefly expand on the methodological design for analysing those agendas.

4 Research questions and methods

The first sections of this chapter illustrated various phases in policing in the Netherlands as affected by the political landscape in the Netherlands and the constitutional setting of the police. Policing in metropolises will, by necessity, be subjected to these national spheres of influence. In the remainder of the chapter the contemporary policing agendas in Amsterdam and Rotterdam will be illustrated and compared. The key questions for comparative research to be answered are: *What are the general policing regimes in Amsterdam and Rotterdam? To what extent do agendas for urban policing diverge or converge between the two metropolises? How might tensions towards convergence and divergence on both local and national levels be explained?* The following section will present an analysis of the agendas for public policing in Amsterdam and Rotterdam during the past six years. The next sections present the findings of a qualitative analysis of policy agendas combined with academic studies on policing in Amsterdam and Rotterdam. The focus of the analysis is on the formulation of the policing agenda and limits the empirical findings to 'stated' goals (Kickert, 2002). Nevertheless, this allows us to unravel the policy agendas in an attempt to differentiate sub-national from national variation (Edwards & Prins, 2014; Recasens i Brunet & Ponsaers, 2014). Our analysis is based on Coalition Plans in which the Board of Mayor and Aldermen announces their overall plans for the city for the coming years (Amsterdam and Rotterdam) and related security plans available at city level.[24] For Amsterdam the Coalition Plan for Amsterdam city and the Regional Security Plan (covering six municipalities of which Amsterdam is the largest) was studied. This secondary source analysis was complemented with in-depth interviews with local representatives and police commissioners in Amsterdam. The city of Rotterdam works with Five-Year Action Plans in which priorities and strategies for public policing on a city level are announced. These were the main source for the analysis of this metropolis.

5 Urban Policing in Amsterdam

Amsterdam is the country's capital and largest city located in the western part of the Netherlands. Economically, Amsterdam has grown significantly since the expansion of its harbour in the past couple of decades and the ever increasing importance of Amsterdam's Schiphol Airport. Tourism in the city was at a peak in 2013 as Amsterdam hosted over 6 million tourists, the largest number ever recorded.[25] Amsterdam is known as one of the most diverse metropolises in the world, which is reflected in its demographics.

In 2015 Amsterdam counted 821,752 inhabitants, while the greater metropolitan area of Amsterdam has approximately 2,388,318 inhabitants.[26] Amsterdam is a fast growing city and it is expected that the population of the region will strongly increase in the coming years, due to the birth rate, further urbanisation and the expected influx of migrants.[27] More than half (51.1%) of the inhabitants have a non-Dutch background. Within this rate 16.4% have a European non-Dutch background and 34.7% a non-European one.[28] Most non-Western inhabitants are concentrated in particular districts, such as Amsterdam-North, Amsterdam Bijlmer and Zeeburg (WPR, 2016). Compared to other cities in the Netherlands, Amsterdam has relatively more ethnic minorities (De Poot & Meershoek, 2014). The colonial independence of Indonesia and Suriname triggered a large number of Indonesians and Surinamese individuals to move to Amsterdam. In the 1960s many from Italy, Morocco, Spain and Turkey emigrated to Amsterdam as guest workers. Furthermore, many (illegal) immigrants have come from Asian,

European, American and African countries.[29] The metropolis counts 176 different nationalities, which brands it as one of the most ethnically diverse capital cities in the world (WPR, 2016). This diverse demography helps to explain the development of policing strategy in the city.

There has been little government support for the social integration of this increasingly diverse city other than the recruitment of some Moroccan, Turkish and Surinamese social workers, who had the task of integrating foreign newcomers into the city (Vermeulen, 2008). Another interesting observation is the relatively young population of Amsterdam. Half of its population is younger than 35 years old, almost a quarter is between the age of 15 and 29 (De Poot & Meershoek, 2014). Amsterdam ranks fifth in the list of the strongest economic metropolises in Europe and is ranked 11th on Mercer's most habitable metropolises (Van Gent et al., 2014). In terms of income distribution, 51.8% of Amsterdam inhabitants had a low income, 32% a medium income, while only 16.2% had a high income in 2013[30] (Burgers & Van der Waal, 2007).

Before the police reform in 2013 Amsterdam region covered the same municipalities and was divided into five parts: North, South, East, West, and the City Centre of Amsterdam. Since the reorganisation, the new police unit has been split into only four districts, roughly geographically located in the north-western, north-eastern, south-western and south-eastern parts of Amsterdam. Each of those districts is furthermore divided into 'robust basic teams', operating only within a specific (broad) geographical area. The Regional Safety Plan labels 5,450 officers for the regional police unit of Amsterdam, and 215 as community officers, for the districts Centre-North, East, South and West (Regionaal Veiligheidsplan 2015–2018, 2014).[31] The local police officers are expected to spend 80% of their time in their assigned districts. According to a news item from the Amsterdam Police in 2015, community officers of Amsterdam are very focused on their core tasks like communication with citizens compared to community officers in other cities in the Netherlands (politie.nl, 2015). Amsterdam policing has always been one of an integral approach (Hulsebosch et al., 2008) where different actors both in law enforcement and outside law enforcement (health care, education, housing) work together on projects in order to decrease crime and social disorder.

5.1 Local politics and administration

The City Council is the highest governmental body in each metropolis in the Netherlands. Every four years municipal elections are held and local parties compete for the available 45 seats. This body controls the main policing directions set out by the Board of Mayor and Aldermen who create local security policies and steer policing on a daily basis. Amsterdam was for 65 years dominated by the PvdA, the Labour Party striving for a 'strong and social country'. Following a ghastly election season in both the local and national elections in 2014, the Labour Party in Amsterdam was overtaken by D66.

From 2001 until 2010 Job Cohen (PvdA) was the mayor of Amsterdam. He was a charismatic politician who greatly influenced urban policing. After the terrorist attacks in the United States on 11 September 2001, and the murder of Theo Van Gogh, Cohen reached out to all religious Moroccan and Muslim organisations in an attempt to get them out of isolation, trying to prevent the situation from escalating (Vermeulen, 2008). Before his mayoral position, Cohen had an academic career and held various functions in national politics, including secretaries of state on education as well as justice. After resigning as mayor of Amsterdam, he returned to the Dutch Parliament and became leader of the Labour Party. Mayor Van der Laan (PvdA), presiding over the Board of Mayor and Aldermen, took over and was installed in 2010. He remained mayor also after the 2014 elections, when the City Council consisted of eight different political parties, the D66 with 14 seats, the PvdA with ten seats, the VVD, Socialist Party (SP) and Green Left Wing Party (GL) all with six seats. Three months of negotiations after the 2014 election between the parties in this hung assembly produced a coalition. The new Board of Mayor and Aldermen in Amsterdam consists of the D66 (four aldermen), the VVD (two aldermen) and the SP (two aldermen), who together developed and signed the coalition plan 'Amsterdam Belongs to Everyone'. For the first time since World War II, the Labour Party is no longer part of the Board of Mayor and Aldermen in Amsterdam. Under Mayor Van der Laan many projects, plans and approaches for urban policing in Amsterdam were introduced with the so called 'Top 600' anti-crime approach as his brainchild (Nijmeijer & Van Dijk, 2014). Key to his philosophy is that if local government was to sanction Amsterdam nightlife when they overstepped their legal boundaries, they should also be rewarded when they adhered to their legal obligations (Blokker, 2015).

5.2 The Amsterdam agenda 2014–18

The Amsterdam agenda is noted in two important documents: the so-called coalition agreement 2014–18 with policy intentions of the Board of Mayor and Aldermen on the one hand and the Regional Safety Plan 2015–18 on the other. As the first is only applicable to the metropolises, the Regional Safety Plan covers the Amsterdam-Amstelland region including other smaller municipalities mentioned. We analyse both plans in our search for dispositions and indicate – if applicable – changes with former plans.

Coalition agreement 2014–18

The basic tone of this document is creating 'freedom' aiming at better housing, better regulation of space, better and more education for children, more job opportunities (fighting poverty) and less tax. The overall goal is a secure, social and liveable city for all Amsterdam inhabitants. Extra budget is foreseen for the fight against poverty, education, care, a green environment, and culture and art. The agreement is differentiated in different chapters with special attention given to problems of housing,[32] poverty, bad schooling, care for elderly and youngsters, and job creation.

Recent research (Van Steden & Broekhuizen, 2015) indicates that Amsterdam West is among the poorest boroughs of Amsterdam. The average total annual income lies approximately €5,200 below the mean of €30,600, and unemployment rates of non-Western migrants (circa 11.5%) are generally higher than elsewhere in the city (10.5%). The coalition agreement mentions an improvement in policing processes in chapters like 'simplifying' administration, less bureaucracy, fewer rules, less tax and an open dialogue with the City Council and the opposition; in short: 'more freedom' (the title of the agreement).

The coalition agreement foresees different offers of social care to citizens: 22 neighbourhoods are detected with a concentrated need for care. Budgets are also foreseen for asylum seekers who are refused, people in need of housing, medical and social attention and early youth care (in collaboration with schools). One of the top priorities is the fight against poverty, especially focused on children, striving for a decrease in Amsterdam families living in poverty before 2018. This issue needs, according to the plan, different preventive and social measures. A specific plan was developed to set up in detail the political agenda 'in the social domain'.[33]

When it comes to safety, stopping hate crimes and racism in the city is prioritised and the plan refers to the main stated goals of the Regional Safety Plan. The coalition mentions the desire for an increase in the Top 600 to Top 1,000, and a decrease in 'high-impact crimes' (HICs) as well as human trafficking in prostitution. As further explained in the following sections, the coalition plan demonstrates a combination of prevention, order maintenance and repression in an integrated way (with all partners). In the next section the current policing agenda from the Regional Safety Plan 2015–18 is analysed. As far as the stated goals differ from the 2012–14 plan, comments will be added.

The Regional Safety Plan 2015–18

The 'Regional Safety Plan 2015–18'[34] is an outcome of negotiations between the regional prosecutor and mayor, elected government and the Board of Mayor and Aldermen in Amsterdam, together with the different mayors, elected governments and boards of aldermen in each of the other five municipalities in the Amsterdam-Amstelland region. Amsterdam kept the independent position from national governance it has always had, and this regional plan does not need the approval of the national police commissioner. The plan sets out the overarching ambition of 'the improvement of the security within the area through the reduction of crime and opportunity', and is strongly based on the former regional plan[35] (2012–14), in which Mayor Cohen took the lead.[36] Its overall principle is the so-called 'integrated approach of crime and disorder', where all actors from different policy domains (care, welfare, education, housing, employment, crime law enforcement, justice, police) work together in networking governance arrangements and share information about possible offenders or places at risk. The plan is based on three principles. First of all, crime and insecurity are caused by people, so the policy has to focus primarily on the offenders and possible suspects. The focus of the regional plan lies in the causes of offending behaviour: 'police want to know the offenders, and offenders have to be aware that police are controlling them.'[37] Prevention consists – according to the plan – of monitoring potential offenders very closely (Van Steden et al., 2013; Boutellier et al., 2009) with observation techniques, preventive search (identity controls searching for illegal weapons) and other control activities like closed-circuit television (CCTV). The third principle is to intervene quickly by means of proportionate punishment immediately after the first offence ('quick justice'). This 'quick justice' and prompt punishment approach require close contact and collaboration between government, police and judges (as installed in Amsterdam).

The Regional Safety Plan 2015–18 mentions nine priorities, which cover the same priorities as those set by the former Mayor Job Cohen. The nine priorities are:

- Top 600/Top 1,000 and HICs
- Domestic and child abuse
- Intimidation in and around the living areas
- Discrimination including hate crimes
- Radicalisation and polarisation
- Prostitution (the 'red light district' is famous in Amsterdam)
- Abuse in human trafficking
- 'Undermining'[38]
- Surveillance and enforcement priorities (like taxis, housing, fraud in the catering industry, protests and events, scooters and incivilities)

On top of these main priorities, other local priorities can find a place, and some extra 'areas of attention' were added by Mayor Van der Laan – security themes that were not foreseen in the former Regional Safety Plan, namely 'return from custody', 'school safety', 'foreigners and refugees' and 'antisocial behavior by youngsters'.[39] The target groups are recidivist youngsters, offenders of domestic violence, addicts (who commit crime), illegal migrants and other recidivists. The public police aims to be close to the citizen (community-oriented policing) in order to detect and intervene in crime and incivility as early as possible. Furthermore, the plan focuses on specific hotspots (based on crime mapping) and certain neighbourhoods get extra police surveillance. The programme Amsterdam pioneered which is now spread around the Netherlands is the 'Top 600 strategy'. Because of the innovative aspect of this programme and because of its importance within Amsterdam priorities, we will elaborate further on this strategy.

Top 600

When reflecting on its history, Amsterdam has witnessed the cruel murder of filmmaker and writer Theo van Gogh by a young radicalised Muslim in 2004. This attack, along with an attack a few years before on Dutch politician Pim Fortuyn, acted as a wake-up call for Amsterdam regarding terrorism (Den Boer, 2007). It was also a trigger for the so-called Top 600 strategy which intensified the comprehensive and personalised approach towards finding offenders (De Poot & Meershoek, 2014). This Top 600/Top 1,000 programme became the flagship programme of Amsterdam and, related to this, the HICs – crimes with huge impact on the victim, the environment of the victim and the region as a whole. The focus lies on the offence itself as well as on the offender. Within the Top 600 strategy the offences of assault, street robbery, burglary in stores, serious and public violence and homicide/murder are qualified as high-impact crimes. Top 600 means the list of 600 offenders of HICs known to the police forces. The aim of the Regional Plan 2015–18 is to broaden this registration to 1,000 offenders. The programme itself not only holds these offenders accountable for the crimes they committed through punishment, but also prevents those close to them (family members, especially siblings) from following in their footsteps.[40] The Top 600 contains an intensive, integral and target-oriented approach aiming at changing behaviour of those listed. The programme objectives are surveillance, control, investigation, aftercare and communication of those involved in HICs. The programme consists of three steps (Top 600 Program Office, 2013):

- Tit-for-tat: those apprehended within the programme have an expedited court process, which should lead to a speed-up of the criminal justice process.
- Care: a thorough screening of not only the offender, but also their environment. By doing so, one finds out what the offender requires in order to prevent re-offending, whether this is psychological aid, employment needs or housing assistance.
- Tackling the 'pathways into crime', including the influence of other family members in promoting, encouraging and compelling offending behaviour: brothers and sisters are observed to ensure school attendance, preventing them from following in their family member's footsteps.

The priorities and Top 600 goals are to be accomplished not only through the 'Triangular Consultation' partners including local government, the public prosecutor and the public police, but also through the involvement of mental health institutions, schools, housing corporations, psychiatric institutions, childcare, the Salvation Army, rehabilitation and probation officers, prisons, drug and alcohol addiction self-help groups, and insurance companies, ensuring health insurance when needed. This collaboration is of utmost importance to the city and is emphasised by Mayor Van der Laan, who has always stressed the importance of citizen involvement in the well-being of society (Tonkens & Verhoeven, 2011). Over the years, the city has witnessed a diversification of providers of policing with a shift in focus from reactive measures (traditional law enforcement) to proactive and preventative work undertaken to stop those at risk from embarking upon criminal careers. Amsterdam has always been at the heart of urban policing in the Netherlands and considered one of the pioneers in this field. The 'Top 600' approach was copied by multiple big cities (Eindhoven, Utrecht and Rotterdam)[41] as well as municipalities of medium size.

Other priorities

In order to get a more complete picture of the Amsterdam disposition, we elaborate on additional priorities important to the metropolis. There is the priority of 'domestic and child abuse' based on different tracks: prevention and information of the citizen, investigation, intervening and public prosecution and aftercare. This approach requires long-term investment and a systemic integral approach from justice and health care workers, with attention to both offender and victim. Central to this multi-actor approach is the 'Safe Home' project, with a legal task to investigate reports and transfer dossiers to specialists and police and justice departments, if necessary. Information gathered in one focal point and disseminated to all actors is again essential. The third priority, 'intimidation in and around the living area', requires, according to the plan, a coordinated and integrated approach, combining criminal justice dispositions with civil procedural ones, administrative measures (competence of the mayor) and psychosocial interventions. In every neighbourhood 'information brokers' are appointed who gather all information on offenders intimidating other citizens, examining partner organisations such as housing corporations and the police. The problem of 'radicalisation and polarisation' became more important in Amsterdam after 2005. The approach here is 'risk-based', meaning focusing on youngsters at risk, aiming at early intervention programmes and monitoring, exchanging information with police, and intervention after an offence is committed. Programmes combine repression, care and prevention activities. Partners are, amongst others, the national coordinator of counter-terrorism and security, Security House,[42] street-corner work, youth protection and schools.

Even if not specified as a priority, the fight against vice and drugs markets is important, with the role of Amsterdam in transnational drug trafficking networks, importing narcotics into Europe and then redistributing them to other wholesale centres in other European metropolises (United Nations Office on Drugs and Crime, UNODC). In tackling drugs as well and other illegal activities of 'criminal' entrepreneurs an 'administrative law enforcement approach' was initiated by the city of Amsterdam over a decade ago and is still in place (Nelen & Huisman, 2008; Huisman et al., 2005). A frontrunner project was Emergo, launched in 2007, in which the city of Amsterdam collaborated with the police, the public prosecutor and several different government institutions to fight the drugs trade and human trafficking in and around the red light district (Spapens & Rijken, 2015). By excluding those expected to use legal facilities, services and subsidies for illegal activities, the infiltration of criminal networks in the legal and economic sectors of local society was hindered (Nelen & Huisman, 2008). Today, local authorities in Amsterdam as well as throughout the country still create barriers for illegal activities by means of local administrative laws. The Board of Mayor and Aldermen criminalises behaviour through 'municipal orders'[43] and once these are accepted by the City Council they can, for example, close down establishments, suspend licences and sanction certain offences with fines.

5.3 The Amsterdam regime

When analysing the stated goals and measures in both the Coalition Plan and the Regional Safety Plan, we see characteristics of mainly two types of policing regimes. First and foremost, we can discern a strong resemblance to a developmental regime which is known for leveraging greater corporate investment, like the public-private partnerships in the Top 600/Top 1,000 programme. The Regional Plan embraces a risk management approach by monitoring potential (young) offenders by means of information exchange between professionals, technical observation techniques such as CCTV, and quick justice – if needed – underlines this focus. Moreover, the Top 600 programme is all about managing the risks of offending careers, by prevention of the possible causes of crime in an integrated approach of all partners combined with quick criminal justice. Second, the Amsterdam agenda entails components of a transformative regime by seeking to transform classical law enforcement through the pursuit of social justice policy agendas entailing redistribution of income and creating equal welfare and housing possibilities in the struggle against poverty (Coalition Plan). Both plans illustrate an 'integrated approach' where social justice and welfare goals find a place (Coalition Plan) as the management of risky individuals (Top 600/ 1,000) elaborated on in the regional (police) plan. Programmes and extra budget for better education, more quality social housing, job opportunities for youngsters, programmes against hate crimes and racism in the city are oriented towards the socially disadvantaged, the weaker population of the metropolises and deployed to 'managing the opportunities of crime and disorder'. This is done by taking the so-called integral network approach between as many partners as possible oriented around the nine priorities. Information sharing is the key issue here, as well as working together to decrease problems and prevent crime. This is very interesting because it reasserts a criminal justice policy agenda and marginalises risk management (e.g. situational crime prevention) as well as social and restorative justice responses to crime and incivility.

6 Urban policing in Rotterdam

Rotterdam is the second largest city in the Netherlands located in the southwestern part of the country. The metropolis's history is strongly marked by the World War II bombings destroying the city centre as well as the importance of the harbour for local economy and employment. Today, the local economy has expanded with flourishing businesses and financial services as well. Rotterdam is a cultural and tourist hotspot in the Netherlands with modern architecture, iconic bridges and skyscrapers mostly located near the banks of the River Maas. The city housed exactly 624,815 inhabitants on 1 January 2015.[44] Nearly half of the population has a non-Dutch ethnic background and the overall division of income among the inhabitants of Rotterdam differs negatively from the national standard (Gemeente Rotterdam, 2015). Registered crime rates for Rotterdam show a slight drop during the past ten years, as in many European metropolises.[45]

6.1 Local politics and administration

As a blue-collar city, local politics in Rotterdam have been dominated by the PvdA since World War II. This changed when a new party called 'Liveable Rotterdam' (LR) participated in local elections for the first time and won 17 out of 45 Council seats in 2002, suddenly becoming the biggest party, and ending the traditional stable majority for the Labour Party in Rotterdam. Ever since, these two political parties have been flipping coins. Either the LR or the PvdA has won elections during the past ten years and formed a ruling coalition with the other parties participating in local elections, including the VVD, D66, CDA or GL.

The year 2002 was turbulent in both local and national politics. That year the front-runner of the new LR, Pim Fortuyn, formed a national party called 'Liveable Netherlands' and won seats in the national Parliament. Shortly after having political success in national elections as well, Fortuyn was murdered by an environmental activist. These events are considered a tipping point in national as well as local politics in Rotterdam.

The surprising election result of 2002 was understood as an expression of the Rotterdam people's dissatisfaction with a decrease in social cohesion due to crime, tensions caused by substantive migration and decreasing quality of life in the city's many neighbourhoods (Van Praag, 2003). The LR strategically embraced the public dissatisfaction during their election campaign and appointed crime and public safety as one of the five key topics in the 2002 coalition agreement titled 'The New Spirit of Rotterdam' (Van Ostaaijen, 2010). This can be seen as a defining moment when crime and urban safety became key topics in local politics and policies in the city. A period characterised by ad hoc projects addressing various issues popping up in the city came to an end and was replaced by a systematic approach aligning the mayor, the police and the public prosecutor with many professionals and citizens contributing to a safer city (Tops, 2007). More specifically, it led to the creation of long-term policies for urban policing named Five-Year Action Plans structuring urban policing in Rotterdam until today. These five-year programmes have a distinct and threefold policy strategy of: a) neighbourhood-oriented, b) person-oriented, and c) phenomenon-oriented policing, complemented by the overall ambition of structured and result-oriented policy steering with transparent and measurable outputs (Marks & van Sluis, 2012). In the next paragraphs we will further unravel the dispositions for urban policing of the current and previous Five-Year Action Plans in Rotterdam, 'Faith in the City' (2010–14) and 'Safe 010' (2014–18), as well as the overarching Coalition Plans in which the Board of Mayor and Aldermen set out their objectives and measures on all policy domains. Thereafter, in the concluding section, we will compare the Amsterdam and Rotterdam regimes.

6.2 The Rotterdam agenda 2010–14

In local elections in 2010 both the PvdA and LR won an equal number of seats in the City Council. After negotiations about the composition of the new ruling coalition the PvdA got in and LR ended up in the opposition. The new Board of Mayor and Aldermen consisted of the PvdA (three aldermen), the VVD (two aldermen), D66 (two aldermen) and the CDA (one alderman), and was presided over by Mayor Ahmed Aboutaleb (PvdA), who has been the mayor of Rotterdam since 2009. As explained later, shifts in the composition of the Board of Mayor and Aldermen affected fundamental aspects of urban policing in Rotterdam.

The same holds for the background, career paths and professional networks of the mayor. Mayor Aboutaleb is a Dutch citizen of Moroccan descent who held various positions in national and local police and administrations. Before he was installed as the mayor of Rotterdam in 2009 he was secretary of state dealing with social welfare and the labour market (2007–09), before which he was an alderman for the PvdA in Amsterdam.

Aboutaleb is often seen as the 'migrant face' of the PvdA and has strong ideas about the integration of migrants in Dutch society. As an alderman in Amsterdam he attempted to bring together clashing groups after the murder of Van Gogh, and proposed to abolish state allowances for females refusing to take off their burka during a job interview. As the mayor of Rotterdam he took a strong stance after the attacks in Paris in 2015 by stating that Islamic State must be eradicated, accompanied by the statement that those who do not respect the values and norms of Western society must leave and that Muslims must distance themselves from religious violence.

The Board of Mayor and Aldermen presided over by Mayor Aboutaleb from 2010–14 announced their overall plans for the years to come in a Coalition Plan titled 'Working on Talent and Entrepreneurship' (Gemeente Rotterdam, 2010a). The board declared investment in the talents of inhabitants by facilitating education, work and sports, as well as by boosting the local economy and entrepreneurship. In contrast to the previous ruling coalitions in Rotterdam, this one explicitly decided not to make urban safety a key priority. While they promised to continue previous investments and programmes in urban safety, the board opted for the labour market, economy and sustainability as key priorities for 2010–14. Nevertheless, the board acknowledged the importance of urban policing in their coalition programme by stating: 'the current level of urban safety is a result of a strict safety agenda during the past ten years. This agenda will be continued by implementing the Five-Year Action Plan 2010–2014' (Rotterdam, 2010: 23, translation R.P.). In order to make that happen, local priorities and strategies for urban safety were described in a separate Security Plan, titled 'Trust in Security' (Gemeente Rotterdam, 2010b). As explained below, this plan largely contained a mixture of law enforcement combined with investment in the social-economic sphere and physical environment.

Trust in security

The five-year action programme was titled 'Faith in the City', described the overall ambitions, priorities and strategies for the years 2010–14, and can be summarised in the bold objective that Rotterdam no longer has unsafe neighbourhoods by 2014. The plan was derived from a consultation round during which local authorities asked households, local entrepreneurs and professionals in urban policing about their wishes and demands. The plan was also shaped by the need to prioritise and make clear decisions due to limited resources during the economic crisis. This led to the following strategy in terms of *neighbourhood-, person- and phenomenon-oriented policing*.

First of all, the programme appoints several *neighbourhoods* scoring highest on crime and lowest on subjective safety to be addressed by a mixture of social-economic and infrastructural investments. By investing in the financial and intellectual capacity of their citizens the Board of Mayor and Aldermen explicitly addressed the fact that Rotterdam is a relatively 'poor metropolis', housing many people with a low income, a lower level of education, of whom many are unemployed. The board strongly believed in boosting knowledge and skills of specific groups of the Rotterdam population as a way to fundamentally invest in a safer city. Moreover, following the logic of broken windows (Wilson & Kelling, 1982), the board addressed the infrastructural quality of local neighbourhoods by investing in the quality of housing, public squares and cleaning up dark alleys. In some neighbourhoods these investments were partly financed by national government, who identified 23 neighbourhoods in the county, seven in Rotterdam, to be regenerated. The decision to opt for social-economic and infrastructural investments as means to increase local security have been made on a city level and within the policy domain of public order and safety. Further research is needed to explore whether or not these decisions are aligned with budgets and priorities in other policy domains (housing, welfare, labour market), and whether or not they have any criminogenic consequences as pointed out by the Copenhagen School.

Second, violence, nuisance and crimes undermining society were prioritised as key *phenomena* for urban policing between 2010 and 2014. Severe manifestations of drugs-related violence, domestic violence and hooliganism were addressed by administrative policing strategies as well as by law enforcement. Examples are temporary home restrictions given by the mayor to perpetrators of domestic violence, and sanctions by the prosecutor for individuals who violently attacked public providers of policing. However, the board hoped to use these rather repressive and reactive sanctions as a last resort and therefore deployed a wide variety of preventative interventions and programmes. These ranged from social interventions such as mediation between perpetrator and victim in order to prevent recidivism and more techno-situational measures such as installing surveillance cameras around soccer stadiums. The same holds for youth- and drugs-related nuisances in the public domain as a second phenomenon to be addressed. The plan revealed a range of repressive and preventative measures including public sanctions in order to lower the individual's street credibility as well as programmes aiming at keeping pupils in school. Also, the phenomenon of crimes undermining local society refers to illegal behaviour including money laundering, human trafficking and real estate fraud proven to disturb local society and undermining the integrity of local government. The board stated that it would systematically screen for and fight against these crimes by addressing at least one criminal network and clearing at least one drugs laboratory a year. Measures listed range from monitoring money transactions to tightening criteria for exploitation of soft drugs and enforcing these.

Third, but more implicitly, the five-year action plan mentioned specific *groups and individuals* as focal points in urban policing. These included youngsters or recidivists causing various forms of violence and nuisance as well as a specific group of people at risk of committing these crimes and disturbing public order. These individuals were addressed by means of personal programmes to alter behaviour including probation and internships. Especially youngsters from Moroccan and Antillean descent were screened for alarming behaviour, and were addressed by means of investments in their living environment, schooling and family.

The five-year action plan 2010-14 is characterised by a mixture of law enforcement and targeted investments in individuals and groups as well as boosting social, physical and economical spheres of the city. The latter are deemed necessary in order to get to the root causes of crime and disorder in the city. The board believed that a weighted combination of repressive reactions (when needed) and prevention by investing in quality of life (when possible) was the best strategy to maintain a safe city. Repressive measures included: increasing the number of local wardens with power to enforce administrative laws and the local adoption of new powers for Dutch mayors to carry out preventative measures, area restrictions and reporting duties. Preventative elements included: the personal and group programmes providing care and increasing skills (provided by, for example, social intervention teams and street coaches) focusing on youth and families.

6.3 The Rotterdam agenda 2014-18

The current Board of Mayor and Aldermen consists of Mayor Ahmed Aboutaleb (PvdA), three LR aldermen, two Social Democrat aldermen and one CDA alderman. This time the LR defeated the PvdA during local elections which clearly affected the priorities in the Coalition Plan and Local Security Plan. In their Coalition Plan titled 'Kendoe'[46] the board stated five core ambitions: a) a safe, joyful and green city; b) investing in the southern part of the city; c) creating opportunities in the labour market; d) boosting the economy and labour market in the harbour; and e) investing in social cohesion (Gemeente Rotterdam, 2014a). The current Coalition Plan can be distinguished from the previous one when it comes to the explicit prioritisation of urban policing. A safe city is the first key priority of the current board, who presented their agenda for urban policing in a separate five-year action plan titled 'Safe 010'. The striking return of urban safety as a key priority might be explained by the fact that the LR joined the Board of Mayor and Aldermen in 2014. This party always had a strong focus on urban safety and promoted a rather tough approach to law enforcement clearly mirrored in the new five-year action plan. Moreover, Mayor Aboutaleb left room for this as he partly shared his task of taking care of urban safety with an alderman representing the LR. This is an exceptional move as Mayor Aboutaleb is still individually held accountable by the City Council and public at large when it comes to urban policing. Dutch mayors are formally held responsible for public order and public safety and therefore usually do not wish to share policy actions in this area with others in order to keep urban safety policies completely under their control.

Safe 010

The current programme is titled 'Safe 010'[47] and is the fourth edition in a series of Five-Year Action Plans, and describes the overall ambitions, priorities and strategies for the years 2014–18. Within this programme the Board of Mayor and Aldermen formulated the straightforward ambition to make sure that 'Rotterdam has no unsafe neighbourhoods and that inhabitants, entrepreneurs and visitors feel safe' (Gemeente Rotterdam, 2014b: 5, translation R.P.). The current agenda was, again, derived from a consultation round during which local authorities asked inhabitants, local entrepreneurs, academics and professionals in urban policing about their priorities for the next five years. Mayor Aboutaleb described the strategy underlying the current agenda for urban policing as focusing on 'more than just crime', and 'providing help when possible and being tough when needed' (Gemeente Rotterdam, 2014b: 3, translation R.P.). The Board of Mayor and Aldermen explicitly chose to continue the strategy of *neighbourhood-oriented, person-oriented and phenomenon-oriented policing* as further explained in the following sections.

First of all, the board announced increased investment in specific *neighbourhoods* with relatively high scores on crime and social disorder. The board addressed these neighbourhoods by investing in social and physical aspects, this time combined with a strong emphasis on law enforcement. The emphasis lay on public wardens in neighbourhoods and public transport, who 'act fiercely if needed' (Gemeente Rotterdam, 2014a). The new alderman partly responsible for public safety introduced intervention teams fighting nuisance behaviour in residential areas and built container homes in a remote area near the local airport where inhabitants terrorising their neighbours could be forced to live temporarily. Furthermore, the local government attempted to take 'signals and complaints' from citizens as input when setting the agenda and explicitly activated representatives from local society to participate in daily practices of urban policing. This is, for example, supposed to happen during meetings in which the mayor, aldermen, police chief and public prosecutor engage in conversations with inhabitants and local entrepreneurs. Together they come to an agreement on how to deal with pressing problems which have to be solved by professionals and citizens before the next meeting. These programmes are called 'Neighbourhood Governs' and 'Neighbourhood Safety Steering Group', and mirror the involvement of citizens as agenda setters and co-producers of public policing.

Second, the Board of Mayor and Aldermen prioritised two types of current and unwanted *phenomena* in local society. These included so-called 'high-impact crimes' presumed to have a devastating impact on the lives of victims, such as burglary, robbery and theft from the person. The new strong focus on these phenomena might partially be explained by the fact that HICs are a key priority for the national police force and Mayor Aboutaleb is leading a national taskforce aiming to reduce the number of burglaries and street robberies since 2009. The local action plan on these topics described performance agreements between local government, police and the public prosecutor to solve at least 40% of all thefts from persons, raise the probability of catching those committing HICs by 37.5% and solve at least 15% of all burglaries (Gemeente Rotterdam, 2014b). These rather reactive measures were combined with home visits by civil servants, parole officers and police officers to roughly 600 perpetrators of HICs. These visits, partly similar to the strategy of the Amsterdam Top 600 approach, aimed to keep an eye on the perpetrators as well as on their siblings in order to prevent both from taking a criminal path.

Another prioritised phenomenon focuses on the somewhat invisible but illegal behaviour of 'undermining societal integrity'. This priority refers to illegal behaviour including money laundering, human trafficking, drugs trade and cybercrime, proven to disturb local societies and undermine the integrity of local government. Local government aims to prevent ties between legal and illegal infrastructures in local society to make sure they do not unintentionally facilitate illegal behaviour. A key instrument for addressing this type of crime for local government is the BIBOB[48] law allowing the screening for criminal records of applicants for permits and subsidies. Moreover, local government actively engaged in partnerships with the police, the public prosecutor and others to share information and pool manpower and instruments to prevent and sanction crimes undermining society.

Third, specific *individuals and groups* stand high on the current policy agenda for urban policing in Rotterdam. The current action plan strongly focuses on 'risk groups'. These are people considered to hold vulnerable positions in society, such as minorities, individuals suffering from mental health problems, labour immigrants from Central and Eastern Europe, and homeless people. Also individuals and groups engaged in all sorts of criminal behaviour were identified as risk groups targeted for public intervention, as well as individuals showing signs of radicalisation potentially leading to terrorist activities. It was the Board's ambition to disrupt and punish illegal behaviour, but their main focus lies in a preventative, networked approach to these individuals and groups. Local government aimed to activate and facilitate professionals, including the police, social workers and youth care, to pool information and resources in order to recognise these risk groups and deploy measures focused on changing behaviour and minimising factors stimulating criminal activities.

Overall, the action plan 2014–18 prioritised phenomena, persons and neighbourhoods to be addressed by means of a 'balanced mixture of prevention and repression' (Gemeente Rotterdam, 2014b: 5, translation R.P.). Again, a distinction was made between 'social measures' investing in the quality of life of individuals or groups in order to prevent unwanted behaviour, and 'physical measures' boosting the quality of public space inspired by the broken window thesis. Local government opted for such preventive measures investing in people and public space while promising to 'act fiercely' when rules are violated. The latter element of enforcing mostly administrative law is stronger in comparison to the previous action plan. Also the emphasis of identifying specific risk groups and making them a core action in public policing is much more explicit in this current programme. In terms of regime theory, Rotterdam's policy agenda for public policing could be qualified as a mixture of at least three regimes. The emphasis on enforcing administrative law mirrors a key component of a maintenance regime, while the plan also shows elements of a developmental regime due to the stronger focus on risk groups, and flirts with the idea of a transformative regime by making social and physical investments in the city a genuine part of urban policing. All in all, the local agenda leans most towards a maintenance regime as security reappeared on the coalition's list of priorities, the overall strategy of neighbourhood and phenomena, and individual- and group-oriented policing still characterised the local agenda, be it with a stronger emphasis enforcing administrative law instead of social-economic investments.

6.4 The Rotterdam regime

As indicated in the previous sections, the Rotterdam agenda for urban policing shows elements of a maintenance and transformative regime (2010–14 + 2014–18) as well as a developmental regime (2014–18). While both the current and previous boards upheld the policy tradition of designing agendas for public policing along the lines of *neighbourhood, person- and phenomena-oriented policing*, the previous action plan leant slightly more to a *transformative regime* whereas the current one leans a bit more to a *maintenance regime*. The main difference lies in the fact that the previous board deviated from its predecessor by not making local security a key priority in the Coalition Plan and focusing strongly on investing in social, economic and physical spheres in order to create a safer city, whereas the current Board of Mayor and Aldermen favours a more traditional approach marked by maintaining administrative laws as the primary response to crime and disorder which reappeared as a priority in the Coalition Plan.

We observed that local politics partly shaped the urban regimes for public policing in Rotterdam. It is the Board of Mayor and Aldermen who set the scene in their Coalition Plans and Five-Year Action Plans. Once the composition of the board had changed in terms of political affiliations, thus political stances on the urban policing regime changed as well. The fact that urban safety shifted from one of many points of interest in the years 2010–14 to a key priority between 2014–18 can partially be explained by the LR joining the Board of Mayor and Aldermen, pushing their core topic of safety back onto the agenda. In fact, the stronger emphasis on law enforcement promoted by the LR delivering an alderman responsible for safety, enforcement and public space clearly shifted the precarious balance from a dominant transformative to a maintenance regime. This resembles other studies demonstrating that the LR was indeed able to institutionalise their preferences on urban policing into policies and practices (Van Ostaaijen, 2010).

Apart from local politics there are many interlinkages to be observed between local and national circuits of power shaping the agenda for urban policing in Rotterdam. First of all, the current policy agenda for urban policing in Rotterdam, like in Amsterdam, addresses a mixture of nationally and locally defined issues. Roughly half of the local priorities stated in the current Five-Year Action Plan match national priorities for public policing,[49] namely youth, HICs, public safety in public spaces and crimes undermining society. Second, national government provided both money to tackle unsafe neighbourhoods as well as powers for Dutch mayors which were adopted in the Rotterdam agenda for public policing, thereby shaping local policy agendas. Third, Mayor Aboutaleb's predecessor Ivo Opstelten (1999–2008) became minister of safety and justice (2010–15) and installed the national police organisation replacing the regional police organisation. It is precisely this national police organisation that now reshuffles local policing structures and priorities in Rotterdam. These are the most striking observations when it comes to the connectedness of urban policing in Rotterdam with supra-local circuits of power.

7 Conclusion: convergence and divergence in Amsterdam and Rotterdam

As we detected in both metropolises a durable constellation of 'semi-autonomous' actors supporting and implementing a city-wide policing agenda, we can conclude that in both metropolises an urban regime (Stone, 1989, 2005; Mossberger, 2009; Mossberger & Stoker, 2001) is present. An in-depth analysis of policing agendas in both metropolises demonstrates that these *regimes* show elements of *divergence*. The current Amsterdam agenda primarily shows resemblance to the developmental and the transformative regimes, as the plans touch upon social justice dispositions as well as on public-private collaboration (Top 600/Top 1,000). The current Rotterdam agenda, however, can for a large part be qualified as a maintenance regime as it has a strong emphasis on enforcing administrative law. This is combined with a focus on risk groups and social and physical investments in the city as a genuine part of urban policing, adding a touch of a developmental and transformative regime to the mix.

A potential explanation for the divergence between the metropolises in terms of urban regimes may be that these regimes are partially shaped by political processes on the local and regional levels. In Rotterdam a change in the composition of the Board of Mayor and Aldermen led to the institutionalisation of alternative strategies for policing. The entrance of the LR in the Rotterdam Board of Mayor and Aldermen clearly led to a stronger focus on law enforcement resulting in a stronger emphasis on a maintenance regime.

Contrastingly, the policing agenda in Amsterdam remained more or less stable, also after the 2014 elections, when the composition of the local political coalition was slightly altered. Changes in the policing regime regarding the former coalition will, according to expert respondents, only become visible when analysing the actual implementation of the security plans, so-called 'policing in action'. This level of continuity in the formal policing agenda might be explained by the fact that the mayor of Amsterdam presided over both the previous and current Boards of Mayor and Aldermen and remained fully in charge of local security policies. In Rotterdam, the mayor also presided over two subsequent Boards, however he partially delegated some local security policies to an alderman responsible for safety, enforcement and public space, leading to some changes in local strategies for policing.

In the Netherlands, explanations for different regimes could thus be found in the interactions and negotiations between *all* parties in the political arena. This includes the mayors who, as we explained earlier, have a rather particular status when it comes to local policing. Although Dutch mayors have formal responsibilities and powers when it comes to urban policing, divergence of policing regimes cannot be solely explained by their political stance. Mayors Van der Laan (Amsterdam) and Aboutaleb (Rotterdam) are affiliated with the PvdA. Both had a career in local and national politics, making them rather experienced local leaders expected to be professional administrators in the Dutch political system of local governance. Their professional experience and networks on multiple levels make them influential in shaping local policy agendas as further indicated below.

Besides divergence, policing agendas in Amsterdam and Rotterdam partially show *convergence* in terms of policing priorities. Both metropolises listed HICs, forms of organised crime undermining society, as well as concerns regarding youth as key priorities in the security plans. This could be explained by institutional arrangements in place. The national police presented a list of national priorities which both cities adopted in their local security plans. The manifestation of convergence in terms of priorities for urban policing in both metropolises resembles half of the national priorities. Whether this can be explained as the outcome of an actual top-down mechanism of national government determining the content of local policy plans within the new framework of the national police is a subject for future research. Previous research shows that under the umbrella of the former regional police organisation local authorities only embraced national priorities if they were relevant for local priorities (Prins, 2014).

One way or another, Dutch arrangements for prioritising issues on the urban policing agenda tend to encourage convergence, both on local and national levels. This type of convergence could also be explained in terms of local leaders having close ties to other loci of power because of their flourishing careers at many levels of politics and administration in the Dutch system. The fact that mayors of both metropolises have ties to national government makes it easier to foster alignment between priorities and strategies for policing between national and local levels. This works both ways, as Mayor Aboutaleb is, for example, leading the national taskforce on HICs, so it is no surprise that this issue ended up in local security plans as well. The other way round, we saw local practices of Amsterdam authorities experimenting with administrative measures against the drugs trade and organised crime and elaborating the Top 600 programme, both of which have been embraced by national government and transferred as best practice to many other Dutch municipalities. A final explanatory factor for the fact that the metropolises under study are converging more than diverging in terms of priorities could be because in Europe public resources from central governments are often available for metropolitan development, fostering a similar focus on policing and lessening the need for reliance on private-sector finance (Mossberger, 2009)

In conclusion we are affirmative that the policing agendas leading to 'modes of governance' (Di Gaetano, 1999) in both metropolises under study can be called 'regimes' as they are characterised by pre-emptive power and enduring cooperation, recorded officially in the Coalitions Agreements and the Security Plans. Further research should indicate how these agendas are implemented and if these regimes stay stable over time within existing local political coalitions.

Notes

1 In Dutch: Verzuiling.
2 In Dutch: Maatschappelijk middenveld.
3 In Dutch: Integraal veiligheidsbeleid.
4 In Dutch: Gedoogbeleid.
5 Ministerie van Binnenlandse Zaken, Nota Veiligheidsbeleid 1995–1998, Kamerstukken 1994–1995, 24 225, nrs. 1 en 2.
6 Ministerie van Binnenlandse Zaken (1999). Integraal veiligheidsprogramma, Kamerstukken 1998–1999, 26 604, nr. 1.
7 In Dutch: Leefbaarheid.
8 This minister president led four governmental periods (Balkenende 1, 2, 3 and 4) until he resigned in 2007.
9 *Towards a Safer Society*, White Paper period 2002–06 (Ministry of Justice & Ministry of Interior Affairs, 2002).
10 In Dutch: Bestuurlijke strafbeschikking.

11 In Dutch: gebiedsverbod.
12 In Dutch: groepsverbod.
13 Coalition Agreement VVD – PvdA, 'Building bridges' (Bruggen slaan), Regeerakkoord VVD – PvdA – 29 oktober 2012.
14 www.rijksoverheid.nl/actueel/nieuws/2011/02/18/landelijke-prioriteiten-politie-voor-een-veiliger-nederland (last consulted on 4 April 2016).
15 This was set up in the first Local Government Act of 1851.
16 Local Government Act, section 172.
17 Police Act, 2012, section 11.2.
18 The appointment procedure in the Netherlands is a long-debated matter. In the early 2000s some political parties regarded the procedure as undemocratic and proposed a more direct election of the mayor either directly by the people or by the City Council. A constitutional change to allow this failed to pass the Senate in March 2005. Recently this matter has become a topic of political debate again as Parliament took the first legal step towards a potential change in the constitutional law describing the procedure for appointing Dutch mayors.
19 www.rijksoverheid.nl/onderwerpen/gemeenten/inhoud/burgemeesters/benoeming-vacatures-en-ontslag (last consulted on 6 April 2016).
20 For an in-depth understanding of the Dutch police system, we refer to Devroe et al., this volume.
21 In Dutch: Gezag.
22 In Dutch: Beheer.
23 To be clear, 'administrative policing' in this context means the maintenance of public order (as contrasted with the enforcement of the criminal law).
24 In Rotterdam the Security Plan covers solely the metropolis. In Amsterdam the Security Plan covers the metropolis is Amsterdam as well as five other (smaller) municipalities.
25 www.ois.amsterdam.nl/media/Amsterdam%20in%20cijfers%202014/#21/z (accessed on 4 April 2016).
26 www.ois.amsterdam.nl (last consulted 2015).
27 www.metropoolregioamsterdam.nl (last consulted 2016).
28 http://statline.cbs.nl/Statweb/publication/?DM=SLNLandPA=70072NEDandD1=0-88andD2=126andD3=landVW=T (last consulted on 4 April 2016).
29 www.idfwpr2016.org
30 www.ois.amsterdam.nl/feiten-en-cijfers/ (last consulted on 4 April 2016).
31 *Regionaal Veiligheidsplan 2015–2018*, www.amsterdam.nl/wonen-leefomgeving/veiligheid/openbare-orde/bibliotheek/downloads/r/regionaal-2/ (last consulted in 2014).
32 In Amsterdam 187,000 households have the right to the 'social housing' projects, because they earn less than €34,700 each year, so at least 187,000 social houses have to be offered by the housing companies.
33 Concept Meerjarenbeleidsplan Sociaal Domein 2015–2018, 'Alle Amsterdammers doen mee' Cluster Sociaal, 16.09.2014.
34 www.amsterdam.nl/wonen-leefomgeving/veiligheid/openbare-orde/veiligheid-cijfers/regionaal/ (last consulted on December 24, 2015)
35 The first Regional Security Plan was elaborated in 2012 (period 2012–14).
36 The only difference from the former plan is the fact that in the Regional Plan 2015–18 the rural metropolises around Amsterdam negotiated to include a specific priority that is important to them, namely the fight against the production of drugs (cannabis) in rural areas.
37 Conference 'Veiligheid in Amsterdam: van gevoel naar feiten' (Security in Amsterdam: from feelings to facts), on 20 November 2003. www.ois.amsterdam.nl/pdf/2004_veiligheid_in_amsterdam.pdf (last consulted on 9 January 2016).

38 Which is a generic term to indicate all types of crime that 'undermine' the integrity of local government and the quality of life in neighbourhoods.
39 www.amsterdam.nl/wonen-leefomgeving/veiligheid/openbare-orde/veiligheid-cijfers/regionaal/
40 www.amsterdam.nl/wonen-leefomgeving/veiligheid/openbare-orde/aanpak-top600/top600/top600/ (last consulted on 6 April 2016).
41 The city of The Hague evaluated the Top 600 as too stigmatising and believes more in direct social contact with the inhabitants of the neighbourhood by 'community officers'. See: http://toezine.nl/artikel/13/top-x-aanpak-is-sexy-maar-werkt-het-ook/ (last consulted on 6 January 2016).
42 In Dutch: veiligheidshuis.
43 In Dutch: Algemene Plaatselijke Verordeningen.
44 http://statline.cbs.nl/statweb/?LA=nl (last consulted December 2015).
45 http://ec.europa.eu/eurostat/statistics-explained/index.php/Crime_statistics (accessed 6 January 2016).
46 'Kendoe' is slang for 'can do'.
47 010 is the telephone area code for Rotterdam and is often used as a symbol promoting the city.
48 Wet bevordering integriteitsbeoordelingen door het openbaar bestuur.
49 www.rijksoverheid.nl/actueel/nieuws/2011/02/18/landelijke-prioriteiten-politie-voor-een-veiliger-nederland (last consulted on 4 April 2016).

Bibliography

Andeweg, R.B., Irwin, G.A. (2002) *Governance and Politics of the Netherlands*, Houndmills and New York: Palgrave Macmillan.
Blokker, B. (2015, September 19). *De burgemeester wil altijd winnen*, NRC.
Boutellier, H., Scholte, D.S., Heijnen, M. (2009) 'Criminogeniteit in Amsterdam. Een nieuw concept, een monitor en een index', *Tijdschrift voor Veiligheid*, 8(3): 30–51.
Burgers, J., Van der Waal, J. (2007) 'Het "global city"-debat over sociale ongelijkheid ontrafeld. Een analyse van loonverschillen op bedrijfsniveau in Amsterdam en Rotterdam', *Sociologie*, 3(4): 427–448.
Cachet, L. (2015) 'Verantwoordelijk en verantwoord. Nationale politie en veranderende lokale verantwoording in Nederland', *Cahiers Politiestudies*, 4(37): 17–40.
Cachet, A., Prins, R.S. (2012) 'Ontwikkeling van het lokaal veiligheidsbeleid', in E. Muller (ed.), *Veiligheid en veiligheidsbeeld in Nederland*, Kluwer, 447–459.
Cachet, A., van Sluis, A. et al. (2009) 'Het betwiste politiebestel', *Politie en Wetenschap*, 49. Amsterdam/Apeldoorn.
Commissie Kleine Criminaliteit (Commissie Roethof) (1984) *Interim rapport*.
Das, P., Huberts, L., van Steden, R. (2007) 'The changing "soul" of Dutch policing: Responses to new security demands and the relationship with Dutch tradition', *Policing. An International Journal of Police Strategies & Management*, 30(3): 518–532.
Den Boer, M. (2007) 'Wake-up call for the lowlands: Dutch counterterrorism from a comparative perspective', *Cambridge Review of International Affairs*, 20(2): 285–302.
De Poot, C., Meershoek, G. (2014) 'Veiligheidszorg in Amsterdam', in E. Devroe, P. Ponsaers, W. Bruggeman, E. De Pauw, M. Easton (eds), *Policing in Europese metropolen*, Orde van de Dag, 4(68): 69–79.
Devroe, E. (2013) 'Local political leadership and the governance of urban security in Belgium and the Netherlands', *European Journal of Criminology*, 10(3): 314–325.

Devroe, E., Ponsaers, P. (2013) 'Reforming the Belgian police system between central and local', in N.R. Fyfe, J. Terpstra, P. Tops (eds), *Centralizing Forces? Comparative Perspectives on Contemporary Police Reform in Northern and Western Europe*, Boom Legal Publishers/Eleven, 77–98.

Di Gaetano, A. (1999) *Power and City Governance: Comparative Perspectives on Urban Development*, University of Minnesota Press.

Di Gaetano, A., Klemanski, J.S. (1993) 'Urban regimes in comparative perspective: The politics of urban development in Britain', *Urban Affairs Review*, 29(1): 54–83.

Downes, D., van Swaaningen, R. (2007) 'The road to dystopia? Changes in the penal climate of the Netherlands', *Crime and Justice*, 35: 31–72.

Edwards, A., Hughes, G. (2012) 'Public safety regimes: Negotiated orders and political analysis in criminology', *Criminology and Criminal Justice*, 12(4): 433–458.

Edwards, A., Prins, R. (2014) 'Policing and crime in contemporary London. A developmental agenda?' in P. Ponsaers, A. Edwards, A. Verhage, A. Recasens i Brunet (eds), Policing European Metropolises, *European Journal on Policing Studies*, 2(2): 61–93.

Fijnaut, C. (2012) *Het nationale politiekorps – achtergronden, controversies en toekomstplannen*, Amsterdam: Uitgeverij Bert Bakker.

Fyfe, N.R., Terpstra, J.B., Tops, P. (2013) *Centralizing Forces? Comparative Perspectives on Contemporary Police Reform in Northern and Western Europe*, The Hague: Eleven International Publishing.

Gemeente Rotterdam (2010a). *Collegewerkprogramma 2010–2014. Werken aan talent en ondernemen*.

Gemeente Rotterdam (2010b). *Vertrouwen in Veiligheid. Meedoen in de stad. Vijfjarenactieprogramma 2010–2014*.

Gemeente Rotterdam (2014a). *#Kendoe. Collegeprogramma 2014–2018*.

Gemeente Rotterdam (2014b). *#Veilig010. Programma Veiligheid 2014–2018*.

Gemeente Rotterdam (2015) *Feitenkaart Inkomensgegevens Rotterdam en regio* (second edn).

Huisman, W., Huikeshoven, M., Nelen, H., van de Bunt, H., Struiksma, J. (2005) *Het Van Traa project, Evaluatie van de bestuurlijke aanpak van georganiseerde criminaliteit in Amsterdam*, Den Haag: WODC.

Hulsebosch, A., Beijers, G., Elffers, H., Bijleveld, C. (2008) *Integraal veiligheidsbeleid in Amsterdam ZuidOost. Een beknopte evaluatie van het beleid, de samenwerking tussen partners en de communicatie met burgers*, VU Amsterdam, Faculteit der Rechtsgeleerdheid.

Jones, T. (1995) *Policing and Democracy in the Netherlands*, London: Police Studies Institute.

Jones, T., Lister, S. (2015) 'The policing of public space: Recent development in plural policing in England & Wales', *European Journal of Policing Studies*, 2(3): 245–267.

Jones, T., van Steden, R. (2013) 'Democratic police governance in comparative perspective: Reflections from England & Wales and the Netherlands', *Policing: An International Journal*, 36(3): 561–576.

Jongman, R. (1988) 'Over macht en onmacht van de sociale controle', *Tijdschrift voor criminologie*, 1: 4–31.

Kickert, W.J.M. (2002) 'Public governance in small European states', *International Journal of Public Administration*, 25(12): 1475–1495.

Marks, P., van Sluis, A. (2012) *Tussen richting en rekenschap. Tien jaar werken aan een veiliger Rotterdam*, Boom Lemma Uitgevers: Den Haag.

Mein, A.G. (2005) 'Wet bestuurlijke boete: recht doen aan gemeentelijke autonomie', *Justitiële verkenningen*, 31(6): 35–43.

Mevis, P.A.M. (2004) 'Strafbeschikking openbaar ministerie, WAHV en kleine ergernissen', *Delikt en Delinquent*, 353–368.

Ministry of Justice and Ministry of Interior Affairs (2002) *Naar een veiliger samenleving, veiligheidsprogramma voor de periode 2002–2006* (Towards a safer society, White Paper period 2002–2006), Den Haag.

Mossberger, K. (2009) 'Urban regime analysis', in J.S. Davies, D.L. Imbroscio (eds), *Theories of Urban Politics*, Padstow: TJ International, 40–54.

Mossberger, K., Stoker, G. (2001) 'The evolution of urban regime theory: The challenge of conceptualization', *Urban Affairs Review*, 36(6): 810–835.

Naeyé, J. (2014) *De organisatie van de nationale politie*, Deventer: Kluwer, a Wolters Kluwer Business.

Nelen, H., Huisman, W. (2008) 'Breaking the power of organized crime? The administrative approach in Amsterdam', in D. Siegel, H. Nelen (eds), *Organised Crime, Culture, Markets and Politics*, New York: Springer.

Nijmeijer, P., van Dijk, C. (2014) 'Hoe een integrale aanpak echt van de grond kan komen: de Top600 in Amsterdam', *Cahiers Politiestudies*, 30: 11–27.

Pakes, F. (2005) 'De Britse aanpak van antisociaal gedrag', *Tijdschrift voor Criminologie*, 47(3): 284–289.

Prins, R.S. (2014) *Safety First. How Local Processes of Securitization have Affected the Position and Role of Dutch Mayors*, The Hague: Eleven International Publishing.

Recasens i Brunet, A., Ponsaers, P. (2014) 'Policing Barcelona', in P. Ponsaers, A. Edwards, A. Verhage, A. Recasens i Brunet (eds), *European Journal of Policing Studies, Special Issue Policing European Metropolises*, 2(1): 452–470.

Sackers, H.J.B. (2010) *Herder, hoeder en handhaver. De burgemeester en het bestuurlijk sanctierecht*, Inaugurele rede van 15 januari 2010, Radboud Universiteit Nijmegen.

Simon, J. (2007) *Governing Through Crime*, Oxford: Oxford University Press.

Spapens, T., Rijken, C. (2015) 'The fight against human trafficking in the Amsterdam red light district', *International Journal of Comparative and Applied Criminal Justice*, 39(2): 155–168.

Spiecker, B., Sleutel, J. (2001) 'Multiculturalism, pillarization and liberal civic education in the Netherlands', *International Journal of Educational Research*, 35(3): 293–304.

Spruyt, B.J. (2006) 'De verdediging van het Westen. Leo Strauss, Amerikaans neoconservatisme en de kansen in Nederland', in H. Pellikaan, S. van der Lubben (ed.), *Ruimte op rechts? Conservatieve onderstroom in de Lage Landen*, Utrecht: Spectrum, 278–298.

Stone, C.N. (1989) *Regime Politics: Governing Atlanta, 1946–1988*, Lawrence: University Press of Kansas.

Stone, C.N. (2005) 'Looking back to look forward: Reflections on urban regime analysis', *Urban Affairs Review*, 40(3): 309–341.

Terpstra, J.B. (2007) 'Regulering van de publieke ruimte in Nederland', in P. Ponsaers, E. Devroe (eds), *Publieke ruimte*, IV-Cahier, 113–138.

Terpstra, J.B. (2010) *Het veiligheidscomplex. Ontwikkelingen, strategieën en verantwoordelijkheden in de veiligheidszorg*, Den Haag: Boom Lemma Uitgevers.

Terpstra, J.B., Fyfe, N. (2015) 'Mind the implementation gap. Police reform and local policing in the Netherlands and Scotland', *Criminology and Criminal Justice*, 15(5): 527–544.
Terpstra, J.B., Gunther Moor, L. (2012) 'Nationale politie. Kanttekeningen tegen de stroom', *Nederlands Juristenblad*, 87(7): 451–457.
Tonkens, E., Verhoeven, I. (2011) *Bewonersinitiatieven: proeftuin voor partnerschap tussen burgers en overheid. Een onderzoek naar bewonersinitiatieven in de Amsterdamse Wijkaanpak*, Amsterdam: Universiteit van Amsterdam/AISSR.
Tonry, M. (2001) 'Symbol, substance and severity in Western penal policies', *Punishment and Society*, 3(4): 517–536.
Top 600 Programme Office (2013) *Top 600*, flyer, Amsterdam: Amsterdam City Council.
Tops, P. (1994) *Moderne regenten: over lokale democratie*, Amsterdam: Atlas.
Tops, P. (2007) *Regimeverandering in Rotterdam. Hoe een stadsbestuur zich opnieuw uitvond*, Amsterdam/Antwerpen: Atlas.
Van Den Broeck, T. (2012) *Formalisering/informalisering van sociale controleprocessen. 20 jaar politie- en veiligheidsbeleid in perspectief*, Amsterdam: Groene Gras, Boom Juridische uitgevers.
Van Dijk, F., De Waard, J. (2000) *Legal Infrastructure of the Netherlands in International Perspective. Crime Control*, Ministry of Justice the Netherlands, Directorate for Strategy Development.
Van Gent, W., Musterd, S., Veldhuizen, E. (2014) 'De ongedeelde stad onder druk. De veranderende geografie van armoede in Amsterdam', in L. Michon, J. Slot (ed.), *Armoede in Amsterdam. Een stadsbrede aanpak van hardnekkige armoede*. Amsterdam: Bureau Onderzoek en Statistiek.
Van Ostaaijen, J. (2010) *Aversion and Accommodation. Political Change and Urban Regime Analysis in Dutch Local Government: Rotterdam 1998–2008*, Delft: Eburon Academic Publishers.
Van Praag, P. (2003) 'The winners and losers in a turbulent year', *Acta Politica International Journal of Political Science*, 38(1): 5–22.
Van Steden, R., Boutellier, H., Scholte, R.D., Heijnen, M. (2013) 'Beyond crime statistics: The construction and application of a criminogenity monitor in Amsterdam', *European Journal of Criminal Policy and Research*, 19: 47–62.
Van Steden, R., Broekhuizen, J. (2015) 'Many disorderly youth, few serious incidents: Patrol officers, community officers, and their interactions with ethnic minorities in Amsterdam', *Police Journal: Theory, Practice and Principles*, 88(2): 106–122.
Van Swaaningen, R. (2005) 'Public safety and the management of fear', *Theoretical Criminology*, 9(3): 289–305.
Verbeek, A. (2006) 'Een jaar later: Verschuivende journalistieke taakopvattingen na de moord op Theo van Gogh'. www.denieuwereporter.nl/2007/09/een-jaar-later-verschuivende-journalistieke-taakopvattingen-na-de-moord-op-theo-van-gogh/ (accessed March 22, 2006).
Vermeulen, F. (2008) *Diversiteit in uitvoering. Lokaal beleid voor werkloze migrantenjongeren in Amsterdam en Berlijn*, Institute for Migration and Ethnic Studies (VU Amsterdam).
Wilson, J.Q., Kelling, G.L. (1982) 'Broken windows: The police and neighborhood safety', *The Atlantic*.
Wintle, M. (1996) *Culture and Identity in Europe*, London: Avebury.

Part IV

Conclusion

Chapter 12

The European world of metropolitan policing

Interpreting patterns of governance, policy and politics

Adam Edwards, Elke Devroe and Paul Ponsaers

I Introduction: the metropolis as an object of policing governance, policy and politics

It is presumed in the Policing European Metropolises Project (PEMP) that the metropolitan area is an increasingly important object of policing governance, given the transnational challenges encountered by European nation-states, including the movement of capital, labour, goods and services enabled by the Treaty on European Union: the 'Amsterdam Settlement.' In this sense, metropolitan policing is, in part, an artefact of the Amsterdam Settlement and the four freedoms that facilitate mobility across national territories and, in doing so, create new internal security fields. This is a principal insight of the concept of multiple, overlapping, internal security fields introduced in Chapter 1 of this collection. Illicit, as well as licit, capital, labour, goods and services move from particular localities to others and, especially, to the metropolises in which the markets for these are concentrated. This can be understood as a specific European instance of the broader process of 'glocalisation', a concept coined by social scientists to characterise greater transnational mobility and how this privileges certain localities that are able to project their political, economic and cultural power, acting as 'command points' (Sassen, 2001; Massey, 2007) in emerging global markets, whilst subordinating those localities that struggle to adapt to these global forces (Swyngedouw, 1997). The basic assumption behind the PEMP is that this process is producing a significant and uneven development of security problems and responses that need to be registered at the level of the metropolis, given that city-regions have different trajectories in the import and export of security problems. Contributors to this edited collection were invited to reflect on the particular significance of metropolitan policing in different nation-state contexts, as registered through reference to particular governing arrangements and policy agendas, in order to test and to adapt this proposition (see Chapter 1, this volume).

Contributions to Parts II and III of this book reflect on different trajectories for nation-states in Europe and their implications for metropolitan policing, contrasting those nation-states in which there has been an explicit attempt to create city-regions with metropolitan-specific policing plans or 'metropolitan-centred metropolitan agendas', as in Belgium (De Pauw and Easton, this volume), Britain (Edwards et al., this volume), Italy (Calaresu and Selmini, this volume), Germany (Aden and Frevel, this volume) and the Netherlands (Prins and Devroe, this volume), with those in which national policing strategies are predominant, or 'national-centred metropolitan agendas', produced by, *inter alia*, the defence of French republicanism (de Maillard and Mouhanna, this volume), the transition from dictatorship in Portugal (Cardoso and Castro, this volume), the defence of Nordic social democracies (Virta and Taponen, this volume), or the transition from communism in Eastern and Central Europe (Modic et al., this volume). In Spain the reconciliation of regional conflicts between Catalonia and the Basque Country on the one hand, and the Castilian State on the other, produces a series of quasi-national police agendas driven by each of these regional powers (Recasens i Brunet & Ponsaers, 2014).

In interpreting the various contributions to Parts II and III of the book, we argue here that it is possible to identify the existence of a 'European world of metropolitan policing' characterised by a significant diversity of metropolitan policing agendas. To elicit theoretical propositions from these contributions that are in turn capable of building explanations of this diversity, we revisit the conceptual framework for comparing metropolitan policing that was introduced in Chapter 1, specifically the circuits of causal, dispositional and facilitative power that constitute multiple, overlapping, internal security fields.

The concept of a European world of metropolitan policing captures the particularity and urgency of the challenges currently confronting the politics of security in European city-regions better than the conventional framing of security issues as problems of inter*national* relations. Most obviously, this concept is better placed to grasp the rapid and mass migration of populations around Europe, as European Union (EU) citizens with the freedom to relocate from more economically depressed regions in the South and East of the Union move into the more buoyant labour markets of the North and West, and as there is an intensification in refugees and economic migrants fleeing civil war and poverty in the Middle East and Africa. This mobility can generate major challenges to internal security, including pressures on social cohesion arising out of the unplanned and significant demands for housing, labour, health and educational services, and the cultural adaptation between settled residential populations and new arrivals, including, for example, sexual mores and expectations.[1]

At the same time, the recent history of terrorist attacks on particular metropolises has evolved from 'home-grown' assaults on the public transport systems of Madrid (2004) and London (2005), into paramilitary assaults undertaken by transnational networks such as Islamic State, as in the attacks on Paris in January and November 2015, then on Brussels airport and the subway station at Maalbeek in March 2016, as well as the earlier attempted assault on the Thalys international train service from Brussels to Paris in August 2015 and the shooting in the Jewish Museum of Belgium, in Brussels, in May 2014. Again, these emphasise the inadequacy of framing internal security threats as either solely national or European-wide problems. Rather, these threats, as with the longer-standing concern with 'transnational organised crime', are a consequence of asymmetrical networks that traverse nation-states and in which particular metropolises are the key nodes.

Another cause of the metropolis as a distinctive object of policing governance in this European world is the unfolding consequences of the financial crisis of 2008, the subsequent sovereign debt crises, and their highly uneven impact. The city-regions in the South and East of the Union, including Rome and Milan (see Calaresu and Selmini, this volume), that are amongst the initial destinations for refugees, are the very locations most under pressure from austerity measures and whose governing capacity has been so degraded by these measures. In turn, pressure on public services in the Northern and Western metropolises that are the ultimate target destination of these migrants has been identified as a key factor in the rise of national-populist political movements and anti-EU sentiment, epitomised in the 'Brexit' result of the UK referendum on EU membership held in June 2016 (Tilford, 2016; Edwards et al., this volume).

This concluding chapter offers an interpretation of the key patterns of governance, policy and politics arising out of this European world by distinguishing different types of metropolitan policing 'regime'. Section two presents a diagnostic tool for distinguishing between regimes that seek to maintain, develop, reform or transform conventional criminal justice and public order agendas on the basis of the 'rules of meaning and membership' that integrate various policing actors into governing arrangements. These rules concern a regime's orientation towards particular kinds of offenders, victims and environments, their privileging of particular populations, 'at-risk' groups and individual offenders and victims known to the authorities, and finally the balance of their objectives for reducing crime, maintaining public order and/or enhancing social cohesion. It is argued that these rules have both the dispositional power to integrate various actors into metropolitan policing regimes but also the liability of generating contradictions that threaten their stabilisation and further reproduction. Section three applies this diagnostic tool to case studies of metropolitan policing presented in this edited volume and, in section four, their contradictions and 'policing dialectics' are discussed in terms of future scenarios and further implications for the comparative analysis of metropolitan policing.

2 Understanding the European world of metropolitan policing

To characterise metropolitan policing agendas within this European world, we draw upon one of the predicates of comparative analysis introduced in Chapter 1: that of 'disposition', which can be understood as a type of power, more specifically, the 'rules of meaning and membership' that organise social actors, admitting those willing and able to adhere to these rules into membership of the organisation in question, whilst excluding those neither able nor willing to adhere to these rules (Clegg, 1989). In turn, dispositions can be distinguished from our other predicates of comparative analysis: the 'causal' power and agency of particular actors (strategic policy makers such as elected mayors, chiefs of police, national ministers of the interior), and the 'facilitative' power of various technologies of production and discipline that can disorganise governing coalitions and shift their policy agendas (for example, the external shock of economic crises, incidents of terrorism and mass migrations of people, the invention of disruptive technologies such as digital communications and surveillance or political scandals such as the corruption of public officials). By contrast, dispositional power acts as a means of social integration, binding social actors together through rules of meaning and membership such that any one actor could not participate in an organisation, including governing coalitions responsible for metropolitan policing, if they did not adhere to these rules – rules that predate the involvement of particular actors and are not reducible to their causal agency. For the purposes of this analysis, the concept of *dispositional power* can be used to characterise the rules of meaning and membership in rival metropolitan policing agendas. In applying this concept, we have developed a framework for diagnosing policing dispositions, summarised in Table 12.1.

This framework draws upon two intellectual traditions. First, the rules of meaning and membership in policing dispositions are defined in terms of arguments over the different orientations, populations and objectives of policing (Graham & Bowling, 1995; Crawford, 1998; Reiner, 2010). Second, these rules are related to different concepts of justice and risk management, which are prevalent across Europe (Edwards & Hughes, 2012; Edwards et al., 2013). These can be summarised in the following terms:

- *Orientations*: the classical and positivist traditions of criminological thought orientate policing towards *offenders* or those deviating from social norms, whereas the victimology movement, which gathered pace in North America and Western Europe in the 1970s, privileges a focus on *victims* and their vulnerability to further victimisation. A longer-standing tradition, epitomised in the work of the Chicago School, privileges a research and policy focus on the *environments*, especially within cities, which are thought to generate problems of offending and victimisation.

Table 12.1 Diagnostic tool of metropolitan policing dispositions: orientations, populations and objectives

| Dispositions | Rules of meaning and membership ||||||||
| | Orientations ||| Populations ||| Objectives ||
	Offender	Victim	Environment	Primary	Secondary	Tertiary	Social service	Public order	Crime reduction
Criminal justice	X					X		X	X
Restorative justice	X	X	X			X		X	X
Social justice			X	X	X		X	X	X
Managing the risks of opportunities for crime and disorder		X	X	X	X	X		X	X
Managing the risks of offending crimes	X		X		X	X		X	X

- *Populations*: another way of conceptualising competing priorities for policing agendas is to consider the different kinds of population that can be prioritised by alternative agendas. Here criminological thought draws upon a distinction found in epidemiology and public health policy between *primary* populations of interest, that is to say the entire population, *secondary* populations or particular social groups who are thought to be particularly 'at risk' of being victimised or of engaging in offending behaviour, and finally, *tertiary* populations of actual victims and offenders known to the authorities, especially as a consequence of their multiple and repeated victimisation and/or their prolific offending.
- *Objectives*: a final set of concepts for diagnosing policing agendas draws upon the well-established literature on the alternative objectives of policing, to reduce *crime*, to maintain *public order* and to provide various social *services*.

These concepts help to define the necessary rules of meaning and membership in policy agendas in ways which, we contend, translate across different political and cultural contexts of policing governance whilst providing insight into the contingent political competition to formulate policing agendas within specific contexts. In this way this analytical dimension of the diagnostic tool addresses the basic problem of comparative research in defining concepts that translate across cultural contexts without inhibiting contextualised insight.

This concern with reconciling the cross-contextual translation of concepts with context-specific insight is also behind our use of a second intellectual tradition to define metropolitan policing dispositions. This contrasts theories of justice with an increasing interest in the pre-judicial, precautionary management of 'risks' and 'risky actors'. Again we contend that concepts of criminal, restorative and social justice, along with concepts of risk management, are now global in their scope of applicability and consequently translate across the different contexts of metropolitan policing found in Europe. More specifically, these global policing dispositions can be distinguished as follows:

- *Criminal justice*: metropolitan policing is about the enforcement of criminal law by supporting the prosecution and sanctioning of offences against this law. As such, policing is limited to a reaction to offences already committed and is thus essentially reactive.
- *Restorative justice*: metropolitan policing is accomplished through the negotiation of reparations between offenders and victims and through a deliberate attempt to circumvent the criminal justice process, and can be considered as a means of diversion. It is also concerned with the role of non-state actors, such as churches and other faith organisations, in the reintegration of offenders.

- *Social justice*: metropolitan policing is accomplished through the use of social and economic policies to address problems of the social and political exclusion of citizens that are, in turn, believed to cause social conflicts including criminal victimisation and civil unrest. A social justice agenda seeks to extend the entitlements of citizens to improved education, training, employment, housing, health, leisure and family support, and to address inequalities in access to these entitlements by means of wealth redistribution. Such a disposition is in essence aetiological in its concern with the root, social,causes of crime.
- *Managing the risks of opportunities for crime and disorder*: metropolitan policing anticipates risks through such measures as reducing the situational opportunities for crime and prudential advice and inducements enabling citizens to take responsibility for reducing their own risk. It is in essence an anti-aetiological and proactive disposition.
- *Managing the risks of criminal careers*: early interventions with groups 'at risk' of embarking on offending careers and desistance programmes for prolific and priority offenders. It is a proactive disposition but one premised on aetiological thinking and informed by the insights of innovations in longitudinal studies of criminal careers.

In defining these dispositions, we have been careful to use concepts that are in use by policy makers as well as social scientists, although, of course, it is important for social scientists to retain their ability to place their own interpretation on what these concepts actually signify in practice if they are to maintain an important critical distance from policy makers. As such, these dispositions provide an initial means of diagnosing the often complex and contradictory admixture of dispositions that can be found in any one particular metropolitan policing agenda, often as a consequence of the bargaining and exchange relationships that occur in specific 'assemblages' of policing governance, policy and politics.

The concept of 'governing assemblage' (Bevir, 2013) alerts us to the bargaining and exchange relationships that are central to governing in liberal democracies where mandates to govern do not of themselves equip elected administrations with the financial, organisational and informational resources to translate their policy agendas into practice, and where powerful organisations also need to legitimate their public authority. As a consequence of these bargaining relationships there is always the possibility of governance 'failure' and 'drift' in which a governing coalition cannot be stabilised long enough to deliver on its policy agenda. An assemblage still exists, in the sense that minority administrations stumble on, keeping the everyday machinery of public administration going but failing to advance the objectives of their policy agendas. Where, however, governing coalitions are stabilised long enough to implement their policy agendas or at least their key policy priorities, it is possible to diagnose the existence of a governing 'regime' (Stone, 1989, 2009; Stone, 2002; Edwards & Hughes, 2012).

Using this differentiation of policing dispositions it is possible to define the following types of governing assemblage:

- *Maintenance regimes*: in which the criminal justice disposition, the oldest and most familiar, ever-present, policing disposition is maintained, even in the face of severe criticism about the limits to this form of 'punitive display' (Garland, 1997), in which a policy agenda is stabilised around the following rules: an orientation around offenders rather than victims or environments, that are already known to the authorities for predicate offences against criminal and public order laws (Nagin, 1998; Pogarski, 2002).
- *Developmental regimes*: in which a criminal justice agenda is augmented by forms of risk management that are oriented around those known or suspected by the authorities of embarking upon offending careers and/or reducing the opportunities for victimisation that can include particular criminogenic environments and be targeted at whole populations as well as 'at-risk' groups of repeat victims and prolific offenders.
- *Reformist regimes*: in which a criminal justice agenda is reformed to place a greater emphasis on the diversion of offenders and victims away from the criminal justice and penal process towards civil remedies such as reparation schemes and other forms of restorative justice.
- *Transformative regimes*: in which a criminal justice agenda is transformed from a core to a peripheral concern and replaced by a focus on social as well as restorative justice objectives. These entail reducing crime and reordering public safety through policies oriented towards the environmental conditions that produce offending, victimisation and civil unrest, in particular, gross social and economic inequalities and the exclusion of social groups from effective political participation.
- *Failed regimes*: in which rival agendas cancel each other out and effectively preclude the stabilisation of a governing regime.

3 Contemporary metropolitan policing regimes in Europe

It is suggested that this conceptual scheme for diagnosing and comparing metropolitan policing encompasses the breadth of possible arrangements and agendas that seek to maintain, develop, reform or transform criminal justice agendas for policing or which can be characterised as failing to do so.

3.1 Maintenance regimes: the consolidation of criminal justice dispositions

Policing has been as, if not more, concerned with maintaining public order as it has with reducing crime, but in its modern form policing became associated with the use of criminal and administrative sanctions against particular offenders known to the authorities for predicate offences (Bittner, 1970). Whilst this disposition continues, we argue it is possible to differentiate those metropolitan policing regimes that have retained this core mission from others which have acknowledged its limitations and have sought either to develop, reform or transform it (van Dijk et al., 2015). In these terms, a maintenance regime can be diagnosed as one which continues to reduce the policy agenda for policing to a concern with:

- offenders
- already known to the authorities; and
- subject to tertiary interventions for reducing crime and maintaining order amongst prolific and priority offenders, be these individuals concerned with particular kinds of offence and/or engaged in behaviour labelled 'anti-social'.

In these terms, there may not be a public policy agenda explicitly stated as such, just an expectation that authorities responsible for enforcing laws on criminality and public disorder simply execute this role. This is the implication of studies of metropolitan policing in the context of Eastern and Central European countries in transition from former communist regimes (Devroe & Petrov, 2014; Meško et al., 2013; Meško & Lobnikar, 2005; Modic et al., this volume). This disposition can also characterise the direction that metropolitan policing has taken in France since the administration of President Sarkozy (de Maillard and Mouhanna, this volume), and in the strong continuity of the policing agenda in Finland, where high public confidence in established policing regimes has provided little stimulus for reform (Virta and Taponen, this volume). There are different kinds of maintenance regime that share particular orientations, populations of concern and objectives, but are nonetheless grounded in very diverse governing arrangements and histories.

In European countries with a Napoleonic tradition, as in France, Belgium and the Netherlands, police officers execute two different *maintenance* mandates: a) they execute judicial police tasks guided by the public prosecutor ('crime fighting', compliance with the criminal code), with the objective of bringing criminal cases to court; and b) they execute administrative police tasks, under the supervision of an administrative authority, mostly the local mayor, who has important competences in this domain.

In the Napoleonic tradition, administrative police competences can be very broad, reflecting the autonomy and discretion of the mayor to set municipal policing agendas about the maintenance of public tranquillity, security and health. Under the auspices of this mandate, police officers have essentially a preventive and service function (surveillance, patrolling, oversight during mass events including football matches and political demonstrations), but they also have the function of maintaining and restoring public order in the event of civil unrest. Interventions made under the auspices of the administrative police mandate are bound to specific regulations (administrative arrest, administrative search and frisk, use of force in the framework of public disorderly behaviour, administrative fines, administrative identity controls, administrative information gathering), which are different from those in the framework of judicial (criminal) police tasks. Administrative functions are considered in Napoleonic countries as the core business of police forces, while the judicial mandate accounts for only a marginal part of the police role.[2]

By contrast, in the governing arrangements for public policing in England and Wales the role of elected officials, such as mayors and police and crime commissioners (PCCs), is limited by the 'doctrine of Constabulary Independence'. This grants unelected police chiefs, 'chief constables', autonomy over matters of the operational deployment and conduct of police officers in their constabulary. Whilst PCCs and, in London, the elected mayor, have the right to formulate the strategic goals of a constabulary (for example, to prioritise certain kinds of crime and anti-social behaviour and even to aim to reduce their incidence by a specified percentage over the course of a PCC's or mayor's elected term of office), they cannot instruct police chiefs, much less particular officers, on the operational details of how such goals are to be accomplished. This distinction between policing operations and policing strategy is regarded as an important means of insulating mundane policing from corruption. Further checks and balances exist in the execution of operational police powers beyond the enforcement of the criminal law, which is left to the discretion of individual constables, and for the maintenance of public order. There now exist a number of civil injunctions for controlling 'anti-social behaviour' between individual complainants such as household neighbours, 'Community Protection Orders' that control the behaviour of particular individuals deemed to be damaging to the environment or local population, and 'Public Space Protection Orders' that impose restrictions on collective behaviour in public places, such as group consumption of alcohol. In each instance, however, an application for an order or civil injunction needs to be made by the police (but can also be made by other 'responsible authorities' in multi-agency policing partnerships, including local authorities and environmental agencies) to the magistrates' court for approval before it can be enforced.

It is clear that mayors in countries with a Napoleonic tradition of public administration have much more discretionary power and direct control over municipal policing than in common law countries. Notwithstanding these significant variations in governing arrangements for maintenance regimes, however, they share a policy agenda that privileges the enforcement of criminal laws and civil/administrative sanctions over other methods of regulating public behaviour. Maintenance regimes thus start from the conviction that sanctions have a preventative effect on future behaviour.

3.2 Developmental regimes: augmenting criminal justice with risk management

At the time maintenance regimes first encountered a major challenge, in the early 1980s, it was possible to identify a basic split between rival agendas that sought to develop these regimes and those that sought to reform or transform them (see sections 3.3 and 3.4, respectively, below). Whilst it is possible to distinguish different kinds of developmental regime, it is suggested here that they all share the following rules:

- an orientation towards victims and environments as well as offenders;
- a focus on entire populations or 'at-risk' groups as well as individuals already known to the authorities; and
- in ways that augment criminal justice and public order agendas with policing strategies aimed at managing the risks of victimisation and/or offending careers.

In turn, it is possible to distinguish different kinds of developmental regimes in terms of their *privileging* of offender, victim or environmentally oriented policing, of primary, secondary or tertiary interventions, and of crime reduction and/or public order objectives. Amongst the case studies reported in the book, we think it is possible to identify three basic variants of the developmental regime in metropolitan policing.

Offender-oriented tertiary strategies targeting prolific and priority offenders to expedite their desistance from criminal careers.

This variant of the developmental regime is exemplified in the Regional Safety Plans of Amsterdam (2010–14, 2014–18), Rotterdam (2010–14, 2014–18) and Antwerp (2003–17), which are premised on the increasing research and policy interest in crime and the 'life course', in particular the idea that it is possible to identify common patterns in the onset and reproduction of offending behaviour amongst prolific 'career' criminals and, on the basis of this, to engineer desistance.

Allied to this interest is the belief that prolific criminals are responsible for the overwhelming majority of offences in a locality, the policing implication being that substantial reductions in crime and disorder can be accomplished quickly and can be sustained if these particular individual offenders can be identified and subject to intensive supervision, surveillance and rehabilitation. This conception of policing is neatly captured in the concept of the 'Top 600' programme that is the centrepiece of the Amsterdam and Rotterdam plans, and the U-Turn project in Antwerp. These plans commit substantial resources to the involvement of a wide range of agencies in the intensive supervision, surveillance and rehabilitation of prolific offenders including their schools or employers, their families, friends and extended kinship networks, as well as a breadth of relevant municipal agencies including social workers, teachers, housing and health authorities, as well as the police and probation services.

Offender-oriented secondary strategies targeting 'risky' groups on the basis of suspect profiles such as age, gender, ethnicity and residential status

In stark contrast to the research-driven agenda of developmental regimes concerned with the desistance of prolific offenders, another kind of developmental regime is premised on the punitive-populist concern with 'outsider', 'suspect' groups, in particular migrants and refugees, homeless street populations and, more generally, young street populations. These regimes are oriented around offenders but employ secondary interventions against whole social groups, rather than particular individuals, whose members are thought to be 'at risk' of offending because of their demographic profiles. Although such (ethnic) 'profiling' is now proscribed by article 14 of the European Convention on Human Rights and the related case law of the European Court of Justice, it nonetheless persists, explicitly in some metropolitan policing agendas in Europe, notably the security pacts signed between the Italian minister of the interior and successive mayors of Rome from 2008 onwards, and in the use of the administrative orders passed by these mayors, targeting 'nomad populations', street vendors and unauthorised camps of 'Roma' (see Selmini, this volume; Calaresu and Selmini, this volume).

The policing implication of this targeting is to employ aggressive, militarised street patrolling to disperse and 'move on' street populations, to disrupt street vice and narcotics markets and tackle 'incivilities' or 'antisocial behaviour'. It is precisely through this shift from criminal justice to risk management that metropolitan policing in certain cities has witnessed an exponential increase in the innovative and highly discretionary use of administrative rather than criminal law to regulate citizens' freedoms of movement, assembly and speech.

Victim-oriented and environment-oriented primary, secondary and tertiary strategies aimed at reducing the opportunities for crime and disorder.

By contrast again, a third variant of the developmental regime can be identified, which has been driven both by populist demands for more immediate security than possible through criminal justice and penal processes and by key innovations in applied criminological research in the British Home Office and subsequently in the research wings of other European ministries of the interior. The key innovation, as articulated by one of the principal researchers behind this thinking, is to shift policing from a concern with the dispositions[3] of offenders to the opportunities for victimisation, in particular those opportunities afforded by, and remediable through, highly situational factors (Clarke, 1983). This approach has found particular favour in the UK, in some sense the 'home' of situational crime prevention given the amount of investment in the research and development of this agenda, and more recently can be discerned in Mayor Johnson's Police and Crime Plan for London (Edwards et al., this volume). Part of the political appeal and success of opportunity reduction is the perceived economy and effectiveness of sustaining quick reductions in victimisation and/or deflecting the harmful impact of victimisation from particularly vulnerable groups to more resilient populations.

This agenda seeks to facilitate 'security for all' by embedding the reduction of opportunities for crime and disorder into the routines of everyday life and accomplishes this, again, through innovative applications of administrative not just criminal law to increase the effort of commissioning offences, reduce the rewards and increase the risks of apprehension (Cohen & Felson, 1979; Clarke, 1980). For example, improved surveillance, both natural and electronic, of particular victims (those repeatedly and multiply victimised), 'at-risk' groups (e.g. users of car parks) and populations (e.g. all users of public highways). Of particular importance in the impetus behind the agenda of opportunity reduction has been the use of intelligence and data for analysing 'crime patterns' (Ekblom, 1988; Ekblom & Pease, 2005; Sherman et al., 1997; Leeuw, 2005) and the identification of concentrations of crime and disorder in 'hot spots' and at 'hot times' which provide a logic for targeting policing, often used within the framework of problem-oriented policing strategies (Spelman & Eck, 1987; Tilley, 2003).

This logic is currently being developed further through 'smart policing', meaning the insights into patterns of crime and disorder that can be gleaned from so called 'big data' arising out of developments in the computation of digital communications, including social media as well as digitalised administrative data sets that include police, educational, health, employment and housing records. This intelligence-driven approach is also behind one of the most dramatic developments in metropolitan policing and that is the rise of 'predictive' modelling in such programmes as the US National Institute of Justice PredPol (predictive policing) and the UK Institute of Crime Science ProMap programmes (Edwards, 2017).

The rapid development of smart policing has, in turn, provoked a dispute over the conceptual and political assumptions that are being fed into the modelling of policing problems using big data. A basic argument exists between advocates of the 'contagion thesis' and the 'immunisation thesis'. Contagion understands, and now seeks to predict, the distribution of crime and disorder in terms of its frequency in particular places (hot spots) and at particular times (hot times) (Braga, 2001; Braga & Bond, 2008). Critics of the contagion thesis argue that a preoccupation with the frequency of crime and disorder ignores inter-relationships with the distribution of non-victims. Once Bayesian analyses of how patterns of victimisation are related to patterns of non-victimisation are taken into account, new logics of policing and security emerge. A key example of this is the analysis of victimisation and non-victimisation for high-volume personal and property crimes in the UK (Hope, 2000, 2009a, 2009b). This identifies an 80:20 distribution in which it is estimated that 80% of the residential population experience only 20% of crime (and most of the population experience no crime at all), whilst 20% of this population are chronically victimised, experiencing 80% of all personal and property crime as indicated through self-report studies such as the British Crime Survey. Moreover, there is an interrelationship between populations of non-victims, able to better 'immunise' themselves against victimisation through access to private security goods (especially mobility in the housing market and the consequent capacity to exit high-crime neighbourhoods), and chronically victimised populations whose vulnerability to victimisation is increased precisely by their lack of access to private security and their dependence on limited public services. As discussed below (see section 3.4), this 'immunisation thesis' implies a very different policing agenda, one that self-consciously uses social and economic policies to redistribute access to security, particularly for chronically victimised and vulnerable populations.

Risk management agendas share a concern with anticipating various 'risks' or 'risky groups' for the purposes of 'early intervention' to reduce, if not completely prevent, the actual realisation of these risks and their associated harms. In turn, this generates a key strategic dilemma for metropolitan policing agendas: how to reconcile due process in criminal justice, prosecuting particular suspects on the basis of predicate offences and on the 'facts' of the cases to establish guilt 'beyond all reasonable doubt' prior to any executive action to punish or 'correct' this behaviour, with the anticipatory and extra-judicial logic of risk management.

A further dilemma for reconciling security and justice arises out of the alleged displacement effects of risk management regimes in which targeted, extra-judicial, action on particular individuals, groups or places increases the vulnerability of the non-targeted individuals, groups or places. This is a distinctively different complaint from that of the 'deflection' argument which uses concepts of 'distributional justice' (Wiles & Pease, 2001) to justify the redistribution of offending and victimisation from more to less vulnerable populations (as in the example of using risk management strategies to deliberately deflect street vice from residential to deserted business districts). Rather, the dilemma here is that focusing intervention on prolific or priority offenders or 'high-crime neighbourhoods' or multiple and repeat victims necessarily removes security from those who offend or are victimised but at less prolific rates or who live in areas of *significant* but not 'high' rates of crime and disorder. In these terms risk management regimes may enhance security but at certain costs to freedom of movement and/or equality before the law, including the right to equal protection by state authorities, a problem exacerbated by the enrolment of commercial security agencies into risk management regimes whose primary duty is to their clients, not to the broader citizenry.

Within this shared disposition, however, an important distinction exists between risk management agendas that are oriented towards reducing the opportunities for victimisation and those oriented towards the promotion of desistance amongst prolific and priority offenders. This distinction can be registered in the contrasting developmental regimes found in London Mayor Johnson's Police and Crime Plan, which invested a significant amount in opportunity reduction, and in Amsterdam and Rotterdam, which have prioritised investment in managing the 'Top 600' prolific career offenders. In turn, this reflects another strategic dilemma and focus for political competition around metropolitan policing agendas: whether to pursue a highly targeted, tertiary policing strategy in the belief that targeting the Top 600 offenders will produce a much greater impact on the volume and concentration of crime and disorder problems, or whether to privilege secondary policing strategies aimed at those groups 'at risk' of embarking upon prolific offending careers or of becoming multiple and repeat victims, or else to privilege strategies that address offending and victimisation amongst the whole population. This dilemma is represented most clearly in the use of administrative orders and security pacts in Rome, since 2008, to manage the perceived risks associated with 'nomad settlements' and 'mobile populations', in particular robbery, inter-personal violence, drug use and prostitution.

A key impetus behind the rise of developmental regimes since the 1980s and since the explicit invitation of a plurality of governmental actors to participate in metropolitan policing strategies, is the increasing recognition amongst municipal authorities of their ability to formulate their own policing agendas through the use of the administrative laws and sanctions under their control. The key analytical point here is that municipal authorities have negligible powers to set policing agendas in maintenance regimes but can develop these regimes through the use of the broad repertoire of administrative sanctions that are at their disposal.

We might identify a number of possible drivers behind the rise of developmental regimes, including: the saturation and increasing incapacity of criminal justice systems to cope with the demands being placed upon them; evidence questioning the efficacy of criminal justice sanctioning for accomplishing sustainable reductions in volume crimes; the political and economic appeal of risk management policies promising substantial, sustainable and cost-effective reductions in crime and disorder; and the increasing interest of municipal authorities in using their powers in pursuit of this promise and for electoral gain. The promise of risk management becomes even more attractive to those municipal authorities under particular pressure from the 'perfect storm' of 'austerity', including severe reductions in public expenditure for policing, combined with the concentration of victimisation on those cohorts of the population who are most dependant on public services and least able to 'immunise' themselves through access to private security.

3.3 Reformist regimes: recognising the victim and the shift from criminal to restorative justice

Yet other kinds of regime can be distinguished in terms of their primary concern with reforming rather than maintaining or augmenting criminal justice and penal processes. The principal example of this in contemporary criminology is the global movement in restorative justice popularised in the action research of John Braithwaite (1989, 2002, 2003), the distinguishing qualities of which are:

- an orientation towards repairing the inter-relationship of victims and offenders in the context of the familial and communal environments they inhabit;
- the use of tertiary strategies to divert disputes between victims and offenders from criminal justice and penal processes and into reparations agreed directly between particular victims and offenders; and
- repairing the harms experienced by victims whilst enabling the reintegrative, rather than stigmatic, shaming of offenders.

In terms of the case studies of metropolitan policing agendas reported in Part III, this reformist regime can be most clearly identified in Cardiff and Edinburgh, reflecting, in part, the commitment of the Welsh and Scottish governments, post-devolution, to a rights-based agenda particularly for youth justice (Edwards et al., this volume). A clear expression of this can be found in the Welsh government's All Wales Youth Offending Strategy, and the Child Hearings system in Scotland, which both express a policy commitment to diverting young offenders from the juvenile justice system and limiting the detrimental effects of early and deep contact with this system. Restorative justice approaches are, in this context, promoted as a means of diverting young offenders whilst recognising and repairing the harms experienced by their victims (McAra & McVie, 2005). Such is the political priority accorded to this diversionary strategy, that Cardiff explicitly portrays itself as a 'restorative city' (Cardiff Partnership, 2010). Another aspect of Cardiff as a restorative city has been its support for the street pastors movement and their role in repairing conflict in the night-time economy, in particular their role in reducing alcohol-related inter-personal violence. In principle, the priorities of reformist regimes can also be found in relation to corporate as well as volume personal and property crimes (Braithwaite & Ayres, 1992), although, as yet, this is less discernible in the particular metropolitan policing agendas considered in the second phase of the PEMP.

A major limitation on the diffusion of reformist regimes in metropolitan policing in Europe, however, is its labour-intensive and thus costly implications, particularly in the context of austerity and major pressures on public expenditure. Whilst Top 600-style programmes are labour intensive, they are highly selective, whilst reformist regimes are extensive in replacing prosecution with reparation for high-volume crime and disorder.

3.4 Transformative regimes: recognising environmental conditions, the shift from criminal to social justice

Further types of regime can be distinguished insofar as they seek not just to reform but to transform criminal justice agendas, in accordance with principles of social justice, to recognise gross inequalities in the experience of offending and victimisation within and between specific city-regions and to redistribute security accordingly. In contemporary criminology, this transformative agenda is most obviously related to preventive strategies that are:

- oriented towards the environments that generate unequal distributions of offending and victimisation;
- undertake remedial action to reduce the concentration of offending and victimisation in high-crime environments; and
- use social and economic policies to reduce criminogenic inequalities of wealth and opportunity throughout a social formation.

In relation to the case studies reported in Parts II and III of the book, it is possible to identify two distinctive social justice agendas for policing. The first transforms criminal justice agendas by reorienting the focus from street crimes to 'crimes of the powerful' (Pearce, 1976; Verhage & Ponsaers, 2009), as in Mayor Pisapia's agenda for policing in Milan (Calaresu and Selmini, this volume). This prioritises the policing of corruption amongst public officials and various corporate crimes, including the health and safety of their workforces, an issue that has become increasingly prominent in criminological studies of the failure to enforce protection in the workplace (Croall, 1989; Tombs & Whyte, 2009).

The second type of social justice agenda has a much longer provenance in criminology and in public policy agendas, although one thought to have been 'eclipsed' in 'late-modern strategies of crime control' by the combination of 'punitive display' and the risk management agendas discussed above (Garland, 1997, 2001). This agenda locates problems of crime and disorder as problems, primarily, of social and economic policy rather than of criminal justice and public order policing (Crawford, 2002, 1998). Indeed, a logical implication of this agenda is to challenge the very idea of crime and disorder as objects of 'policing', other than in the very broadest sense of this term as equivalent to 'government' (Pasquino, 1991), and to reframe them as objects of 'social crime prevention' (Hope & Karstedt, 2003), 'community safety' (Hughes, 2007; Hughes & Rowe, 2007), 'integral security' (Devroe, 2013) or as 'urban security' (EFUS, 2012; Edwards et al., 2013).

This latter sense of social justice can also be detected in Pisapia's agenda for Milan (2011–16) (Calaresu and Selmini, this volume), in which problems of 'street' crime and disorder, such as prostitution and young people's use of public space for leisure and entertainment, are reframed as issues of social and economic inclusion rather than as 'risks' to be controlled through aggressive, militarised, street policing and/or managed through forms of opportunity reduction or the targeting of prolific offenders. In Pisapia's agenda these are issues to be addressed by interventions in the social and economic environments of Milan's housing and labour markets and its educational and leisure services, promoting the social integration of hitherto excluded street populations.

Still another example of a social justice agenda is that pursued by the current 'centre-left' regional government in Brussels (De Pauw and Easton, this volume). This regional government is responsible for allocating funding for social policy to the 19 municipalities under its administration, and has used its control of this funding to privilege the use of social and economic policy responses to problems of crime and civil unrest in these municipalities. This, however, is in tension with the current Federal government agenda for policing in Belgium which seeks to maintain and further enhance criminal justice and penal policy responses. It is suggested that the relative power of the regional government in advancing its social justice agenda has, however, been disrupted by the series of terrorist incidents that have either occurred in Brussels, such as the attack on Brussels airport in March 2016, or that commenced in Brussels, in particular the use of the municipality of Molenbeek as a base by those undertaking the attack on Paris in November 2015 (De Pauw and Easton, this volume). These attacks have been used by the Federal government and its supporters to discredit the social justice agenda of the regional government for failing to tackle the threat of terrorism and to reassert the case for a more punitive agenda.

The cases of Berlin and Cologne reveal other important challenges confronting social justice regimes as a consequence of the particular conditions of the post-war constitutional settlement in West Germany and, following reunification, in the Federal Republic (Aden and Frevel, this volume). As part of de-Nazification, policing governance was distributed between the Federal police (Bundeskriminalamt) and the state police (Landeskriminalamt). This, in addition to the devolution of social and economic policy making to the Länder, has created the opportunity for social justice agendas on crime and security, particularly in those Länder dominated by the centre-left Social

Democratic Party (SPD). When considered as a political and cultural and not just as a constitutional process, de-Nazification has also placed certain significant constraints on the adoption of pre-judicial 'risk management' agendas, most notably on the kind of extensive deployment of closed-circuit television (CCTV) surveillance experienced in British city-regions. Such agendas run counter to the 'Rechtsstaat' principle of a state that adheres to due process in the rule of law and limits blanket surveillance of populations. This political and cultural anxiety over prejudicial and extra-judicial interventions has resulted in a 'path dependency' for metropolitan policing agendas in Germany that constrains divergence in these agendas to varieties of criminal and social justice and helps to explain the relatively limited uptake of restorative justice and risk management, a phenomenon described as 'unity in diversity' (Aden and Frevel, this volume).

In considering the strategic dilemmas associated with social justice regimes it is useful to refer to criminological work that explicitly seeks to shift the policy response to crime and disorder in this direction. As noted in the discussion of the dilemmas associated with opportunity reduction (see section 3.2, above), an alternative to targeting policing on hot spots and times that are indicative of the 'contagion' of crime and disorder within a city is a concern with the political economy of 'immunising' particularly vulnerable populations against the risk of victimisation. This entails an appreciation of the immunity that the majority of the metropolitan population already have against crime as a consequence of their access to the 'private club goods' of security, especially their ability to move away from high-crime neighbourhoods through their access to alternative accommodation in urban housing markets and/or to better secure their accommodation through access to commercial security (Hope, 2000, 2009a, 2009b). Those unable to access these private club goods are left dependent on residual public services (including state policing and crime prevention measures) which, in many metropolises, have been degraded through austerity programmes imposing severe public expenditure cuts, thereby intensifying their lack of immunity. In countering the concentration of victimisation on already vulnerable communities, a gross inequality that is often masked by reference to nationally aggregated trends indicating an alleged 'crime drop' in many Western societies over the past two decades, social justice agendas seek to enhance the collective efficacy of urban populations and thus their immunisation against problems of volume crime and disorder (Sampson & Raudenbush, 1999; Morenoff et al., 2001).

However, a major dilemma encountered by social justice agendas *for policing* is the criticism from libertarians that it 'criminalises social policy' and further fuels the 'securitisation' of everyday life in cities (Van Swaaningen, 2005; Hebberecht, 2002). From this perspective, the dilemma encountered by social justice agendas is the subordination of (negative) freedoms (*from* authoritarian welfare state intervention in citizens' lives) to forms of collective security. More recently, however, advocates of social justice agendas in security advance a positive concept of the *freedom to be* an effective citizen, empowered by state social and economic policies (Schuilenburg, 2015). This positive concept of security can, for example, be detected in the post-war experience of Finland and in the social democratic programmes of other Scandinavian governing arrangements, even though this has been eroded by the influence of the EU's Area of Freedom, Security and Justice and by the broader struggle of Nordic social democracy to adapt to the increased mobility of capital, labour, goods and services arising out of European integration (Virta and Taponen, this volume).

3.5 Regime failure: inchoate and contradictory policing agendas

A final diagnosis of metropolitan policing implied by the conceptual framework advanced here, is the absence of, or failure to stabilise, regimes as a consequence of governing arrangements and political competition. An example of this is the case of policing in Rome during Mayor Marino's administration, in which his political weakness and failure to form a stable governing coalition resulted in direct rule from national government (Calaresu and Selmini, this volume).

It has also been suggested that Cardiff is an example of regime failure in that its agenda for restorative and socially just policy responses to problems of crime and disorder in the city were effectively subverted by the severe reductions in public expenditure it had to accommodate as part of the British government's broader austerity programme (Edwards et al., this volume). In such cases the dilemmas generated by competing programmes of freedom, security and justice destabilise rules of meaning and membership in metropolitan policing. Such a condition of governing 'drift' might, arguably, become a central tendency in metropolitan policing given basic disputes over reconciling the competing, in some instances mutually exclusive, conceptions of freedom, security and justice present in Europe (see section 4.5., below).

4 Future scenarios in the European world of metropolitan policing: 'policing dialectics'

Given the strategic dilemmas encountered by maintenance, developmental, reformist and transformative regimes, it is possible to envisage a number of unfolding scenarios. The anticipation of these is a necessary prerequisite of the kind of role that criminology and political analysis needs to play in continuing to constructively criticise metropolitan policing agendas, especially those prioritising pre-emptive interventions against threats yet to be realised over due process in prosecuting offences that have actually occurred. Proactive policing strategies cannot be adequately criticised by retrospective social science. If social science is to avoid being reduced to a backward-facing narrative of success or failure, always one step behind its subject matter, then it needs to acquire its own capacity for anticipation. In terms of the conceptual framework adopted in this chapter, it is possible to engage in a number of thought experiments about policing futures which reflect upon the dialectical relations driving maintenance and other regimes and which may generate an increasing tendency toward regime failure in metropolitan policing. In promoting the concept of 'policing dialectics', the focus of analysis shifts to the contradictions inherent in each regime and their political-economic conditions for reproduction or failure. By way of conclusion, these scenarios also imply further questions for comparative research.

4.1 A renewed commitment to maintenance regimes?

Notwithstanding the substantial criticism encountered by policing agendas premised on criminal justice objectives, contributions to this book provide a number of reasons for expecting the persistence, even predominance, of maintenance regimes in particular national contexts. As noted above, maintenance regimes privilege a concern with due process, a 'path-dependent' commitment to the rule of law and an antipathy towards pre-judicial and extra-judicial policing. In this context, it is plausible, even likely, that political choices will be made to subordinate the promise of greater security through risk management to the 'Rechtsstaat' tradition. If such maintenance regimes leave metropolitan populations more vulnerable to various security threats then this is a price worth paying to maintain the rule of law and constrain the proliferation of extra-judicial and pre-judicial interventions in processes of 'securitisation' (Buzan et al., 1998).

The political calculation to subordinate such pre-emptive security to the rule of law, in which individuals are prosecuted for predicate offences on the facts and only after these facts is, however, likely to come under a number of considerable pressures. Specifically, a growing sense of injustice and popular frustration with criminal justice systems already saturated in terms of the demands placed upon them, the slow throughput of cases in the courts, and their incapacity to deliver 'quick justice' or at least timely justice for aggrieved victims. Second, the political, as well as technical, feasibility of maintenance regimes is likely to be challenged by the realisation of further catastrophic security incidents, such as the paramilitary assault on the civilian population in Paris in November 2015. It is precisely in relation to such 'existential' threats that commentators identify processes of 'securitisation' in European policing, in which normal democratic oversight and scrutiny is continuously suspended in favour of expediting executive actions capable of reducing the severity of such threats (Buzan et al., 1998). Other existential threats might be identified such as the vulnerability of critical infrastructures to being crippled by cyber-attacks as well as the vulnerability of civilian populations to other kinds of viral assaults including chemical warfare and the use of 'dirty bombs'. In this climate, it is predictable that processes of securitisation cease to be time-limited and exceptional moments in the governance of metropolitan policing and segue into a permanent state. In this context, of the possible technical and political exhaustion of the criminal justice disposition in policing, a key question for further research arises, particularly in those metropolises, such as Paris or Cologne, in which maintenance regimes can be diagnosed: can maintenance regimes adapt to pressures for pre-emptive interventions without undermining their own conditions of existence?

4.2 The proliferation of developmental regimes?

Partly as a consequence of the perceived exhaustion of maintenance regimes, it is plausible to forecast the further proliferation of developmental regimes premised on variants of risk management. The prospective appeal of developmental regimes is enhanced by the political agency they grant to municipal authorities to define their own policing agendas particularly in national and broader European contexts which frustrate the formulation of more immediate and responsive security strategies in response to the demands of metropolitan electorates. The opportunities for such 'metropolitan-driven metropolitan agendas' are enabled through a broadening of policing agendas beyond the use and enforcement of criminal law to innovations in the application of civil laws and the administrative regulations that are available to municipal authorities. Extra-judicial and pre-judicial methods of risk management also enable a greater role for commercial and non-governmental organisations in metropolitan policing and thus offer opportunities for 'leveraging' increased investment in a context of austerity and substantial reductions in expenditure on public services.

As noted, however, the dialectics of developmental regimes include threats to due process, in particular the imposition of major constraints on the freedom of movement, assembly and speech placed on entire populations as well as those targeted on particular groups believed to be 'at risk' of offending or victimisation. These are the concrete, practical, consequences of securitisation through risk management, elsewhere anticipated as the shift towards the 'society of control' (Deleuze, 1995) or, more provocatively, the advent of 'micro-Fascism' (Hallsworth & Lea, 2011) and increasingly used to refer to the forensic management of everyday life and citizens' mundane routines. In addition, targeting can generate miscarriages of justice and other harms associated with the arbitrary exercise of policing discretion, the 'Obrigkeitsstaat' tendency against which the commitment to maintaining the rule of law, the 'Rechsttaat' tradition, was defined in post-war de-Nazified Germany. Precisely because risk management regimes enable municipal authorities to better define their own policing agendas, they can also be seen as existential threats to national political ideals aimed at protecting an equal guarantee of freedoms for all citizens within the national polity, as in French republicanism or Scandinavian social democracy. In this scenario local discretion is regarded as a major threat to a (national) concept of democracy rather than as an unproblematic enhancement of local democracy. Again, the dialectics of developmental regimes provoke a further question for research, particularly in those cases of metropolitan policing, in Amsterdam, Antwerp, London, Rome and Rotterdam, that have pursued risk management agendas: can developmental regimes sustain pre-emptive policing in ways that do not undermine the very conditions of the liberal democracies they aim to secure?

4.3 The shift to civil society and prospects for reformist regimes?

Amongst the metropolitan policing agendas considered thus far in the Policing European Metropolises Project, regimes concerned to reform criminal justice agendas through reference to alternative and restorative concepts of justice have been peripheral. Even so, it is possible to identify episodic experiments in victim-offender conferencing, particularly in policies aimed at diverting juvenile offenders from the penal estate given well-established criminological research findings on the harmful effects of (criminal justice) 'system contact' on the stigmatic shaming of offenders and their subsequent recidivism (Braithwaite, 1989; McAra & McVie, 2005). There is the political attraction of augmenting metropolitan policing agendas with civil society-based conflict resolution, facilitating self-regulation amongst, and direct reparations between, offenders and victims, in ways that are less threatening to the freedom of movement, assembly and speech of other citizens not directly involved in these 'private' conflicts. In these terms, the more specific targeting of policing on the immediate parties of a conflict liberates other citizens to go about their business without the kinds of controls placed on their freedom by primary risk management strategies. Public authorities are envisaged as having a role in facilitating civil society-based policing and, within this enabling role, municipal authorities are provided with another means of defining their own policing agendas, a mission often expressed in the claim of some metropolises to be 'restorative cities' (see Edwards et al., this volume).

However, as conflicts between offenders and victims are effectively shifted from public criminal justice into private conferencing, from the state and into civil society, due process in their resolution is threatened. If risk management threatens the rule of law through the enhancement of forms of arbitrary state and commercial power, then restorative justice threatens it through the development of a kind of arbitrary private power to resolve conflicts (Ashworth, 1993, 2007; Ashworth & Zedner, 2014). Moreover, reformist regimes necessarily undermine the collective symbolic power of public policing as conflict resolution is reduced from an issue of public interest to one of private troubles between individual offenders, victims and their immediate kin. These dialectics provoke the question: can reformist regimes establish forms of self-regulation and private conflict resolution without undermining the public interest in policing?

4.4 The prospects for socially just policing?

Advocates of social justice claim that whilst rival regimes entail trade-offs between citizens' freedoms, security and access to justice, their transformative agenda for metropolitan governing arrangements can better reconcile these different aspects of citizenship. The claim to prioritise intervention in the generative causes of insecurity distinguishes transformative policing regimes from the alternatives considered here. The claim is that through a focus on generative causes there is the possibility of accomplishing more secure and just metropolises without undermining the freedoms of the general population.

This claim, however, recalls Offe's (1984) criticisms of the 'contradictions of the welfare state' and the argument that attempts to accomplish social justice in one country, much less one city, encounter crises of rationality. One such crisis refers to the sheer magnitude of the governing programme envisaged in social justice regimes, entailing simultaneous action on generative causes of policing problems such as labour market conditions, access to education and training, housing conditions and the cultivation of social cohesion through multi-cultural awareness programmes. In turn, such agendas can encounter a lack of clarity about the direction of causality between these 'distal' conditions and specific, 'proximal', security threats (Clarke, 2004). A second type of rationality crisis refers to the problems of collective action encountered by social justice agendas, in particular the redistributive costs of investing in socially just regimes requiring high-tax localities provoking, in turn, the flight of corporate and other taxpayers to other, lower-tax, city-regions. In pursuing the 'larger purposes' of social justice agendas, through necessary tax and spending programmes, transformative regimes can undermine their own conditions of existence (Stone, 2005, 2006). An antidote to this problem of the 'competitive dumping' of social justice agendas is to restrict the freedom of movement for capital, labour, goods and services, but this fundamentally challenges the idea of a European Area of Freedom, Security and Justice. The attempt to pursue these larger purposes of metropolitan policing, for example in the cases of Milan and Brussels and more generally in the social democratic conditions of 'Nordic criminology', but without taking the British option of exiting the EU, its Single Market and its Area of Freedom, Security and Justice, provokes a further question for research: how can socially just regimes be reproduced given the rationality crises they encounter in the European world of metropolitan policing without undermining the freedom of movement of capital, labour, goods and services that constitute this European world?

4.5 Prospects for regime failure?

Further reflection on these policing dialectics suggests another scenario in which metropolitan policing becomes increasingly stymied, if not 'ungovernable', as a consequence of the contradictions encountered by each of the regime types considered above. If social justice goals cannot be reconciled with the 'four freedoms' of the Amsterdam Settlement, if restorative justice cannot deliver common, equal access to justice for the same kinds of victimisation, if the prejudicial threats of risk management are politically unpalatable and if criminal justice responses cannot adapt to the frequency and/or the severity of the case load confronting them, then what could constitute regime success? 'Failure', however, is a relative concept that provokes further reflection and argument: what, in the context of the contradictions encountered by metropolitan policing regimes, can constitute relative success or failure?

Ultimately, we return to the core refrain of PEMP, that comprehending and intervening in these various scenarios necessitates a sociology of translation: *literally*, in terms of a common language of argument about freedom, security and justice; *conceptually*, in terms of some agreement over the terms of this argument, encompassing rather than precluding the breadth of debates about the orientation, populations of interest and possible objectives of metropolitan policing agendas and evaluative criteria for their success and failure; and *methodologically*, in terms of collaborative and deliberative methods that can combine extensive comparisons with contextualised insight. The contention of the Project is that in a European world of metropolitan policing, the metropolis will continue to be a key object of policing governance, policy and politics, whether or not this is self-consciously acknowledged by national- and European-level policy makers, indeed especially where it is not acknowledged as this obscures an understanding of the experience of policing problems in the key, city-regional markets for illicit as well as licit capital, labour, goods and services in which these problems are concentrated.

Notes

1 Celebrations of the New Year 2016 in Cologne and Malmo were marred by reports of a series of sexual assaults on females by recently arrived migrants. It was claimed these and other assaults had initially been covered up by the authorities for fear of exacerbating anti-immigrant sentiments. Subsequently, these assaults were attributed to a basic cultural misunderstanding over the presentation of self by Western women and perceptions of their sexual availability on behalf of the migrants. See www.theguardian.com/world/2016/jan/11/swedish-police-accused-cover-up-sex-attacks-refugees-festival (accessed on 10 August 2016).

2 For example, the functional division of labour in Belgium requires the local police to invest 7% to 10% of their funding in criminal investigation. See the Law on the Police Function of 07.12.1998.
3 Not to be confused with the dispositions of policing *policy responses* considered here.

Bibliography

Ashworth, A. (1993) 'Some doubts about restorative justice', *Criminal Law Forum*, 4 (2): 277–299.
Ashworth, A. (2007) 'Security, terrorism and the value of human rights', in B.J. Goold, L. Lazarus, *Security and Human Rights*, Oxford: Hart Publishing, 203–207.
Ashworth, A., Zedner, L. (2014) *Preventive Justice*, Oxford Monographs on Criminal Law and Justice, Oxford University Press.
Bevir, M. (2013) *A Theory of Governance*, Berkeley, CA: University of California Press.
Bittner, E. (1970) *The Functions of the Police in Modern Society*, Maryland: National Institute for Mental Health, Centre for Studies of Crime and Delinquency.
Braga, A. (2001) 'The effects of hot spot policing on crime', *The Annals of the American Academy of Political and Social Science*, 578(1): 104–125.
Braga, A., Bond, B.J. (2008) 'Policing crime and disorder hot spots: A randomized controlled trial', *Criminology*, 46(3): 577–607.
Braithwaite, J. (1989) *Crime, Shame and Re-integration*, Cambridge: Cambridge University Press.
Braithwaite, J. (2002) 'The new regulatory state and the transformation of criminology', *British Journal of Criminology*, 40: 222–238.
Braithwaite, J. (2003) 'What's wrong with the sociology of punishment?', *Theoretical Criminology*, 7(1): 5–28.
Braithwaite, J., Ayres, I. (1992) *Responsive Regulation*, New York: Oxford University Press.
Buzan, B., Waever, O., De Wilde, J. (1998) *Security: A New Framework for Analysis*, Lynne Rienner Publishers.
Cardiff Partnership (2010) *Cardiff: What Matters 2010:2020 – The Ten Year Strategy*, Cardiff: The Proud Capital Secretariat, www.cardiffpartnership.co.uk/wp-content/uploads/What-Matters-June-2011.pdf (accessed 28 August 2016).
Clarke, R.V. (1980) '"Situational" crime prevention: Theory and practice', *British Journal of Criminology*, 20(2): 136–147.
Clarke, R.V. (1983) 'Situational crime prevention', in M. Tonry, N. Morris (eds), *Crime and Justice, an Annual Review of Research*, 4, Chicago, IL and London: The University of Chicago Press, 225–256.
Clarke, R.V. (2004) 'Technology, criminology and crime science', *European Journal on Criminal Policy Research*, 10(1): 55–63.
Clegg, S. (1989) *Frameworks of Power*, London: Sage.
Cohen, L.E., Felson, M. (1979) 'Social change and crime rate trends: A routine activities approach', *American Sociological Review Albany*, 44(4): 588–608.
Crawford, A. (1998) *Crime Prevention and Community Safety: Politics, Policies and Practices*, Harlow: Longman.
Crawford, A. (ed.) (2002) *Crime and Insecurity: The Governance of Safety in Europe*, Cullompton: Willan.

Croall, H. (1989). 'Who is the white-collar criminal?', *British Journal of Criminology*, 29(2): 157–175.
Deleuze, G. (1995) 'Postscript on control societies', *Negotiations: 1972–1990*, 177–182.
Devroe, E. (2013) 'Local political leadership and the governance of urban security in Belgium and the Netherlands', *European Journal of Criminology*, 10(3): 314–325.
Devroe, E., Petrov, M. (2014) 'Policing in Sofia. From centralisation to decentralisation', *European Journal of Policing Studies*, 2(1): 372–403.
Edwards, A. (2017) 'Big data, predictive machines and security: The minority report', in M. McGuire (ed.), *Routledge Handbook of Technology, Crime and Justice*, London: Routledge.
Edwards, A., Hughes, G. (2012) 'Public safety regimes: Negotiated orders and political analysis in criminology', *Criminology and Criminal Justice*, 12(4): 433–458.
Edwards, A., Hughes, G., Lord, N. (2013) 'Urban security in Europe: Translating a concept in public criminology', *European Journal of Criminology*, 10(3): 260–283.
EFUS (European Forum for Urban Security) (2012) *Security, Democracy and Cities: The Aubervilliers and Saint-Denis Manifesto*, Paris: EFUS.
Ekblom, P. (1988) *Getting the Best Out of Crime Analysis*, Crime prevention paper 10, London: Home Office Crime Prevention Unit.
Ekblom, P., Pease, K. (2005) 'Evaluating crime prevention', *Crime and Justice*, 19: 585–662.
Felson, M. (1979) *Crime and Everyday Life*, London: Sage.
Garland, D. (1997) 'Governmentality and the problem of crime. Foucault, criminology, sociology', *Theoretical Criminology*, 1(2): 173–214.
Garland, D. (2001) *The Culture of Control. Crime and Social Order in Contemporary Society*, Oxford: Oxford University Press.
Graham, J., Bowling, B. (1995) *Young People and Crime*, Home Office Research Study145, London: Home Office.
Hallsworth, S., Lea, J. (2011) 'Reconstructing Leviathan: Emerging contours of the security state', *Theoretical Criminology*, 15(2): 141–157.
Hebberecht, P., Duprez, D. (2002) *The Prevention and Security Policies in Europe*, Brussels: VUB University Press.
Hope, T. (2000) 'Inequality and the clubbing of private security', in T. Hope, R. Sparks, *Crime, Risk and Insecurity: Law and Order in Everyday Life and Political Discourse*, London: Routledge, 83–106.
Hope, T. (2009a). 'The political evolution of situational crime prevention in England and Wales', in A. Crawford (ed.), *Crime Prevention Policies in Comparative Perspective*, Cullompton: Willan Publishing, 38–62.
Hope, T. (2009b). 'The illusion of control: A response to Professor Sherman', *Criminology and Criminal Justice*, 9(2): 125–134.
Hope, T., Karstedt, S. (2003) 'Towards a new social crime prevention', in H. Kury, J. Obergfell-Fuchs (eds), *Crime Prevention: New Approaches*, Mainz: Weisse Ring Verlag, 461–489.
Hughes, G. (2007) 'Community cohesion, asylum seeking and the question of the stranger', *Cultural Studies*, 21(6): 931–951.
Hughes, G., Rowe, M. (2007) 'Neighbourhood policing and community safety. Researching the instabilities of the local governance of crime, disorder and security in contemporary UK', *Criminology and Criminal Justice Systems*, 7(4): 317–346.

Leeuw, F. (2005) 'Trends and developments in program evaluation in general and criminal justice programs in particular', *European Journal on Criminal Policy and Research*, 11(3): 233–258.

Massey, D. (2007) *World City*, Cambridge: Polity.

McAra, L., McVie, S. (2005) 'The usual suspects? Street-life, young people and the police', *Criminology and Criminal Justice*, 5(1): 5–36.

Meško, G., Fields, Ch., Lobnikar, B., Sotlar, A. (eds) (2013) *Handbook on Policing in Central and Eastern Europe*, New York: Springer.

Meško, G., Lobnikar, B. (2005) 'The contribution of local safety councils to local responsibility in crime prevention and provision of safety', *Policing: An International Journal of Police Strategies & Management*, 28(2): 353–373.

Morenoff, J., Sampson, R., Raudenbush, S. (2001) 'Neighborhood inequality, collective efficacy, and the spatial dynamics of urban violence', *Criminology*, 39(3): 517–558.

Nagin, D.S. (1998) 'Criminal deterrence research at the outset of the twenty-first century', *Crime and Justice*, 23: 1–42.

Offe, C. (1984) *Contradictions of the Welfare State*, London: Hutchinson.

Pasquino, P. (1991) 'Theatrum politicum: The genealogy of capital – Police and the state of prosperity', in G. Burchell, C. Gordon, P. Miller (eds), *The Foucault Effect: Studies in Governmentality*, Chicago, IL: University of Chicago Press.

Pearce, F. (1976) *Crimes of the Powerful: Marxism, Crime and Deviance*, London: Pluto.

Pogarski, G. (2002) 'Identifying "deterrable" offenders: Implications for research on deterrence', *Justice Quarterly*, 19(3): 431–452.

Recasens i Brunet, A., Ponsaers, P. (2014) 'Policing Barcelona', *European Journal of Policing Studies*, 2(1): 452–470.

Reiner, R. (2010) *The Politics of the Police*, fourth edition, Oxford: Oxford University Press.

Sampson, R., Raudenbush, S. (1999) 'Systematic social observation of public spaces: A new look at disorder in urban neighborhoods', *American Journal of Sociology*, 105(3): 603–651.

Sassen, S. (2001) *The Global City: New York, London, Tokyo*, Princeton, NJ: Princeton University Press.

Schuilenburg, M. (2015) 'Behave or be banned? Banning orders and selective exclusion from public space', *Crime, Law and Social Change*, 64(4): 277–289.

Sherman, L.W., Gottfredsson, D., MacKenzie, D., Eck, J., Reuter, P., Bushway, S. (1997) *Preventing Crime: What Works, What Doesn't, What's Promising, Report to the U.S. Congress*, Washington, DC: US Department of Justice.

Spelman, W., Eck, J.E. (1987) *Problem Oriented Policing*, Washington, DC: National Institute of Justice.

Stenson, K. (2012). 'The state, sovereignty and advanced marginality in the city', in P. Squires, J. Lea (eds), *Criminalisation and Advanced Marginality, Critically Exploring the Work of Loic Wacquant*, Bristol: The Policy Press.

Stone, C.N. (1989) *Regime Politics: Governing Atlanta*, Lawrence, KS: University Press of Kansas.

Stone, C.N. (2005) 'Looking back to look forward. Reflections on urban regime analysis', *Urban Affairs Review*, 40(3): 309–342.

Stone, C.N. (2006) 'Power, reform, and urban regime analysis', *City and Community*, 5(1): 23–38.

Stone, C.N. (2009) 'Who is governed? Local citizens and the political order of cities', in J.S. Davies, D.L. Imbroscio (eds), *Theories of Urban Politics*, London: Sage, 257–273.

Stone, D. (2002) *Policy Paradox: The Art of Political Decision Making*, New York: Norton.

Swyngedouw, E. (1997) 'Neither global nor local: "Glocalization" and the politics of scale', in E. Swyngedouw (ed.), *Spaces of Globalization: Reasserting the Power of the Local*, London: Longman.

Tilford, S. (2016) 'Britain, immigration and Brexit', *CER Bulletin*, 105, December 2015–January 2016, Centre for European Reform, see: www.cer.org.uk/sites/defa ult/files/bulletin_105_st_article1.pdf (accessed 22 August 2016).

Tilley, N.J. (2003) 'Community policing, problem-oriented policing and intelligence-led policing', in T. Newburn (ed.), *Handbook of Policing*, Cullompton: Willan, 311–339.

Tombs, S., Whyte, D. (2009) 'The state and corporate crime', in R. Coleman, J. Sim, S. Tombs, D. Whyte (eds), *State, Power, Crime*, London: Sage, 103–115.

van Dijk, A., Hoogewoning, F., Punch, M. (2015) *What Matters in Policing?: Change, Values and Leadership in Turbulent Times*, Bristol: The Policy Press.

Van Swaaningen, R. (2005) 'Public safety and the management of fear', *Theoretical Criminology*, 9(3): 289–305.

Verhage, A., Ponsaers, P. (2009) 'Power-seeking crime? The professional thief versus the professional launderer', *Crime, Law and Social Change*, 51(3–4): 399–412.

Wiles, P., Pease, K. (2001) 'Distributive justice and crime', in R. Matthews, J. Pitts (eds), *Crime, Disorder and Community Safety: A New Agenda*, London: Routledge.

Index

accountability, 36, 42, 59, 117, 144, 146, 147, 177, 205
activating state, 18, 245
Adam Edwards, 3, 4, 6, 7, 8, 10, 11, 13, 14, 15, 17, 19, 40, 42, 43, 64, 79, 96, 115, 157, 168, 182, 183, 201, 204, 205, 206, 208, 209, 211, 212, 215, 216, 217, 218, 223, 224, 249, 251, 260, 262, 268, 269, 274, 276, 303, 304, 305, 306, 310, 315, 318, 320, 322, 325
administrative orders, 171, 172, 173, 174, 176, 186, 188, 191, 271, 314
administrative police, 35, 311, 312
agency, 4, 31, 109, 136, 169, 202, 203, 210, 220, 222, 306, 312, 324
agenda setting, 11, 18, 75, 83, 183, 188, 189, 190, 193, 210, 250, 251, 256, 258, 259, 261, 262
agreement, 45, 70, 127, 134, 185, 191, 235, 237, 243, 254, 257, 258, 271, 273, 278, 279, 285, 289, 327
Alistair Henry, 17, 201, 206
Amsterdam, 19, 64, 217, 268, 272, 275, 276, 277, 278, 279, 280, 281, 282, 283, 285, 286, 290, 292, 293, 294, 303, 313, 317, 325, 327
analytical tool, 24
Andrej Sotlar, 16, 144, 147, 148, 149, 151, 153, 158
anti-social, 108, 211, 217, 223, 255, 257, 259, 311, 312
Antwerp, 18, 249, 250, 251, 253, 255, 256, 257, 258, 259, 260, 261, 262, 263, 313, 325
Area of Freedom, Security and Justice, 3, 138, 322, 326
Army, 31, 41, 46, 54, 56, 70, 62, 176, 254, 264, 282

assemblage, 309, 310
asylum, 35, 129, 136, 137, 279
asymmetric, 12, 17, 84
asymmetrical networks, 305
at risk, 189, 280, 282, 288, 308, 309, 314, 317, 324
austerity, 9, 16, 101, 102, 109, 115, 117, 129, 178, 183, 205, 212, 214, 215, 222, 223, 224, 305, 318, 319, 321, 322, 324
Austria, 27, 40, 50, 147, 150, 157
autonomy, 16, 18, 24, 39, 44, 48, 50, 56, 70, 71, 63, 90, 106, 158, 170, 192, 193, 230, 243, 249, 250, 251, 252, 255, 259, 262, 311, 312

Barcelona, 8, 37, 39, 63, 65, 183
Basque Country, 37, 39, 50, 304
Belfast, 56, 70
Belgium, 8, 18, 19, 39, 40, 47, 48, 49, 50, 249, 250, 251, 252, 253, 254, 255, 256, 258, 261, 262, 263, 264, 304, 305, 311, 320
Berlin, 18, 45, 63, 64, 65, 144, 148, 229, 230, 232, 233, 234, 235, 236, 237, 238, 241, 242, 243, 244, 245, 258, 260, 263, 320
Bern, 45
Bernarda Tominc, 16, 144, 151
Bonaparte, 28, 30
Bonnemaison, 15, 77, 78, 81
border police, 44, 45, 232
borough, 40, 43, 205, 279
Branko Lobnikar, 16
Brexit, 6, 12, 17, 201, 202, 203, 204, 209, 224, 305
Bristol, 12, 201, 202, 205, 206, 207, 209, 212, 213, 214, 215, 216, 221, 222, 223, 224

Britain, 8, 17, 56, 169, 201, 204, 207, 211, 216, 221, 222, 224, 304
Brixton, 42, 218
Brussels, 18, 19, 47, 249, 250, 251, 252, 253, 254, 255, 256, 258, 259, 260, 261, 262, 263, 264, 305, 320, 326
Bulgaria, 8, 157
Bundesgendarmerie, 27
Bundeskriminalamt, 44, 45, 233, 320
Bundespolizei, 44, 45

cantonal police, 46
Carabinieri, 27, 30, 31, 32, 37, 175, 176, 190
Cardiff, 12, 201, 202, 205, 206, 207, 208, 209, 210, 212, 213, 214, 215, 216, 221, 223, 224, 318, 322
Carla Cardoso, 15, 95
Carnation Revolution, 33, 97
case studies, 11, 79, 104, 204, 206, 221, 222, 223, 263, 268, 313, 318, 319
case study, 8, 183, 201, 205, 210, 214
Catalonia, 37, 39, 50, 60, 63, 304
Catholics, 56
causes of crime, 108, 269, 283, 288, 309
Central and Eastern Europe, 144, 145, 146, 148, 149, 150, 290
central government, 36, 37, 40, 41, 63, 77, 78, 80, 107, 108, 109, 110, 116, 117, 169, 174, 176
central services, 59, 60
central state, 38, 45, 52, 71, 63, 96, 100, 101, 108, 115, 116, 169, 176
centralisation, 30, 77, 116, 117, 138, 139, 168, 172, 173, 175, 176, 177, 182, 183, 184, 185, 192, 194, 195, 204, 208, 221, 258, 260, 275
centralised state, 16, 36, 130, 157
centrality, 12, 63
Chicago School, 306
chief constable, 41, 42, 70, 212, 220
chief superintendent, 70, 207
Christian Mouhanna, 15, 29, 30, 77, 79, 80, 253, 304, 311
circuits of power, 4, 11, 14, 203, 211, 221, 223, 268, 273, 292
citta sicura, 5
city guards, 24, 71
city-regions, 4, 16, 19, 165, 183, 201, 202, 204, 208, 221, 222, 223, 224, 303, 304, 305, 319, 321
city-state, 18, 63, 229, 230, 232, 241, 244, 258

Civil Guard, 35, 36, 148
civil society, 18, 63, 110, 144, 146, 169, 177, 241, 245, 325
civil unrest, 6, 17, 202, 213, 218, 253, 309, 310, 312
civil war, 70, 304
coalition, 17, 79, 183, 189, 191, 192, 193, 195, 205, 207, 230, 235, 237, 241, 250, 254, 255, 257, 258, 259, 268, 271, 272, 273, 278, 279, 284, 285, 286, 291, 293, 309, 322
collaboration, 34, 46, 53, 55, 65, 88, 111, 238, 256, 264, 270, 275, 279, 280, 282, 292
collaborative approach, 7, 8
Cologne, 18, 229, 230, 232, 233, 234, 237, 238, 239, 240, 241, 242, 243, 244, 245, 320, 324
communism, 33, 145
Communist, 38
community policing, 6, 32, 35, 48, 62, 90, 104, 110, 112, 128, 130, 131, 133, 135, 138, 146, 151, 152, 170, 175, 194, 252
community safety, 9, 139, 167, 203, 213, 214, 215, 216, 222, 270, 320
comparative analysis, 9, 10, 11, 116, 173, 212, 306
comparative perspective, 167, 168, 174
comparative research, 4, 122, 129, 183, 207, 211, 308
competition, 7, 18, 30, 86, 129, 175, 183, 211, 214, 224, 234, 263, 308, 322
complaints, 42, 71, 157, 158, 289
compliance, 107, 208, 311
compromise, 56, 203
conservatives, 81
constable, 42, 70, 274
constitution, 4, 14, 15, 40, 203
constitutional arrangements, 19, 268, 273
Constitutional Law, 34, 103
constitutional mandate, 17
constitutional monarchy, 34, 39
constitutional reform, 175, 209
constitutional-legal powers, 11, 211
constructionism, 7
consultation, 32, 52, 53, 54, 55, 104, 210, 216, 219, 273, 286, 289
contract, 43, 79, 81, 82, 83, 131, 135, 156, 242
convergence, 3, 4, 11, 12, 14, 16, 18, 19, 149, 150, 157, 168, 182, 183, 189, 192,

209, 210, 212, 214, 222, 231, 232, 242, 243, 244, 249, 255, 262, 268, 275, 292, 293, 294
convergent, 168, 193, 204, 231
cooperation, 18, 25, 34, 42, 65, 82, 87, 98, 99, 103, 105, 108, 111, 114, 121, 122, 123, 125, 127, 129, 131, 132, 134, 135, 136, 137, 138, 139, 147, 149, 155, 156, 158, 173, 174, 176, 185, 189, 191, 194, 195, 201, 231, 243, 244, 245, 258, 270, 294
cooperative federalism, 18, 229, 230, 242, 244
Copenhagen, 52, 122, 126, 287
corruption, 32, 140, 170, 192, 195, 306, 312, 319
crime prevention, 5, 32, 44, 78, 81, 85, 86, 87, 88, 96, 97, 98, 99, 100, 101, 106, 108, 113, 114, 123, 132, 133, 134, 136, 137, 139, 151, 157, 167, 170, 171, 176, 177, 184, 211, 230, 234, 237, 241, 245, 270, 284, 320, 321
criminal investigation, 24, 28, 103, 114, 136, 238, 274
criminal justice, 7, 11, 14, 17, 39, 100, 102, 103, 110, 113, 124, 145, 146, 157, 170, 186, 203, 211, 212, 214, 215, 223, 253, 263, 272, 273, 281, 282, 283, 284, 305, 308, 310, 313, 314, 316, 317, 318, 319, 320, 323, 324, 325, 327
criminal law, 186, 191, 231, 271, 314, 315
criminal police, 34, 44, 230, 232

decentralisation, 27, 79, 100, 115, 144, 146, 147, 168, 172, 177, 183, 204, 207, 208, 231, 260
de-concentration, 27
demilitarisation, 31, 62, 146
democratisation, 38, 146
demonstrations, 80, 97, 137, 194, 217, 229, 236, 241, 242, 244
Denmark, 51, 53, 60, 61, 122, 125, 126, 127, 130
dependency, 117, 128, 230, 321
Derry, 70
desistance, 309, 313, 314, 317
developmental regime, 81, 215, 219, 283, 291, 313, 314
diagnostic tool, 305, 308
dictatorship, 3, 15, 33, 34, 36, 37, 97, 98, 99, 115, 169, 304

discretion, 4, 15, 16, 17, 18, 63, 186, 203, 222, 238, 262, 275, 311, 312, 324
discretionary powers, 312
disorder, 19, 32, 78, 98, 102, 108, 111, 170, 171, 172, 173, 176, 194, 208, 218, 220, 223, 268, 269, 270, 277, 280, 284, 288, 289, 291, 307, 309, 311, 313, 314, 315, 316, 317, 319, 320, 321, 322
disposition, 16, 215, 218, 282, 306, 309, 310, 311, 317, 324
dispositional power, 220, 222, 305, 306
districts, 40, 52, 53, 54, 70, 80, 81, 90, 131, 216, 233, 237, 256, 280, 283
divergence, 3, 4, 11, 12, 14, 18, 19, 182, 183, 192, 207, 209, 211, 212, 221, 222, 231, 249, 255, 268, 275, 292, 293, 321
divergent, 6, 17, 182, 195, 202, 203, 204, 206, 208, 221, 223, 224
diversion, 308, 310
diversity, 4, 16, 145, 150, 230, 231, 258, 259, 271, 304, 321
divisions, 47, 70, 59, 60, 89, 103, 130, 167
dominance, 12, 15, 18, 23, 24, 40, 56, 70, 63, 64, 75, 93, 116, 183
dominant position, 15, 78, 92
double hermeneutic, 7
drift, 17, 309, 322

Edinburgh, 12, 59, 201, 202, 207, 212, 216, 219, 220, 221, 318
Elke Devroe, 3, 10, 15, 19, 23, 50, 63, 175, 183, 184, 223, 249, 250, 251, 253, 256, 262, 263, 268, 271, 274, 275, 303, 304, 311, 320
England, 8, 17, 39, 40, 42, 43, 49, 50, 54, 71, 59, 202, 203, 204, 205, 206, 207, 208, 210, 212, 214, 224, 274, 312
environment, 19, 85, 109, 121, 122, 123, 124, 134, 139, 140, 153, 159, 219, 221, 222, 244, 252, 281, 286, 288, 314
Ertzainza, 37, 39
ethnic minority, 42
EU, 3, 5, 6, 9, 12, 17, 27, 45, 100, 102, 116, 121, 122, 123, 124, 129, 131, 132, 137, 138, 140, 149, 150, 187, 201, 202, 209, 222, 224, 231, 304, 305, 322, 326
Eurojust, 5
Europe, 3, 4, 5, 7, 12, 13, 15, 17, 26, 27, 33, 40, 51, 59, 61, 62, 63, 115, 116, 122, 144, 145, 147, 148, 150, 173, 182, 187, 201, 202, 212, 216, 231, 258, 277,

283, 294, 303, 304, 306, 308, 310, 314, 319, 322
European Society of Criminology, 8, 11
European Sourcebook, 29, 30, 33, 35, 37, 43, 45, 47, 49, 53, 55, 59
European Union, 3, 4, 9, 11, 17, 27, 100, 121, 149, 187, 201, 209, 231, 303
Europeanisation, 3, 5, 146, 149
Europol, 5, 25, 138, 149
Eurostat, 30, 33, 35, 37, 43, 45, 47, 49, 53, 55, 71, 59, 104
Evelien De Pauw, 18, 45, 230, 249, 253, 258, 260, 304, 320
exclusion, 99, 106, 108, 133, 136, 218, 253, 259, 309, 310
external border, 5

facilitative powers, 11, 219
fascism, 38
federal government, 18, 46, 64, 234
federal police, 27, 44, 147, 230, 232, 235, 242, 252
federal republic, 44, 45, 50, 62, 150, 229, 320
federal state, 40, 44, 50, 252
federalism, 49, 230, 231, 241, 244
federation, 36, 229
feudalism, 49, 50
financial crisis, 9, 11, 17, 101, 115, 172, 187, 212, 221, 273
Finland, 8, 30, 60, 121, 122, 123, 125, 126, 127, 129, 130, 131, 132, 133, 134, 135, 137, 139, 311, 322
Flanders, 18, 253, 255, 256
Fouché, 28
four freedoms, 4, 5, 303, 327
fragmentation, 17, 85, 86, 88, 89, 92, 95, 147, 173, 177, 202, 263
France, 8, 15, 27, 28, 29, 30, 32, 37, 39, 47, 77, 87, 88, 90, 104, 92, 175, 230, 245, 253, 275, 311
Franco, 35
freedom of movement, 4, 16, 209, 272, 317, 324, 325, 326, 327
French Revolution, 28
Frontex, 25, 149
functional integrated, 49
functional integration, 39
functionally integrated, 29, 32, 39, 60
Future scenarios, 322

gendarmerie, 25, 27, 30, 36, 37, 46, 54, 144, 150
German Democratic Republic, 44, 146
Germany, 8, 18, 33, 39, 40, 44, 45, 49, 51, 62, 63, 229, 230, 231, 232, 237, 242, 243, 245, 304, 320, 321, 324
Glasgow, 71, 59
globalisation, 4, 92, 96
glocal, 19, 249, 268, 279
glocalisation, 4, 5, 201, 202, 224, 303
Gorazd Meško, 16, 144
governance, 8, 15, 17, 18, 19, 23, 32, 37, 63, 64, 78, 83, 95, 96, 101, 103, 107, 108, 110, 114, 115, 116, 121, 125, 129, 130, 131, 132, 137, 139, 140, 148, 149, 157, 168, 171, 173, 174, 175, 176, 177, 183, 202, 205, 206, 207, 212, 214, 220, 223, 224, 249, 251, 255, 256, 258, 263, 279, 280, 293, 294, 303, 308, 309, 320, 327
governance by consent, 63
governing, 4, 7, 63, 110, 129, 183, 186, 201, 202, 203, 205, 206, 207, 210, 211, 212, 213, 215, 231, 235, 238, 250, 251, 255, 271, 303, 305, 306, 309, 310, 311, 312, 322, 326
governing arrangements, 207
governmentalities, 7
Greece, 27, 101, 102
Guardia Civil, 35, 36, 37
Guardia di Finanza, 31, 39, 190
Guardia Nazionale, 31
Guardia Urbana, 37

Hartmut Aden, 18, 44, 45, 63, 229, 230, 231, 232, 234, 236, 245, 248, 258, 260, 304, 320, 321
Helsinki, 121, 126, 129, 131, 132, 134, 135, 136, 137
hierarchical integration, 39, 59
Historical diverse police systems, 27
Home Office, 39, 40, 41, 42, 43, 50

ideology, 65, 124, 127, 145, 182, 193
immigration, 5, 35, 99, 103, 107, 124, 129, 132, 138, 253, 270, 272, 273
in action, 11, 14, 145, 183, 223, 293
independence, 17, 47, 50, 71, 60, 63, 126, 130, 146, 150, 202, 203, 204, 276
inductive, 8, 9
inequalities, 19, 124, 208, 218, 224, 268, 309, 310, 319

integral security, 5, 55, 252, 270, 320
integrale veiligheid, 5
Integrated Police, 48, 252
integration, 5, 6, 9, 28, 46, 97, 100, 101, 111, 116, 128, 137, 174, 241, 253, 257, 261, 277, 286, 306, 320, 322
intelligence, 11, 14, 24, 29, 45, 52, 80, 136, 138, 211, 232, 315
internal security, 3, 5, 6, 11, 12, 13, 14, 15, 16, 34, 96, 101, 103, 104, 113, 114, 122, 132, 133, 139, 170, 201, 204, 208, 209, 235, 252, 273, 303, 304, 305
Interpol, 25
investigation, 24, 28, 48, 51, 52, 54, 126, 189, 273, 281, 282
IRA, 56, 70
Ireland, 39, 40, 50, 55, 56, 70, 71, 101, 202, 204
Irish Republican Army, 217
Islamic State, 14, 139, 286, 305
Italy, 8, 9, 16, 17, 27, 30, 31, 32, 33, 37, 38, 39, 63, 150, 167, 169, 170, 172, 173, 175, 176, 177, 182, 184, 186, 187, 190, 191, 192, 194, 195, 276, 304

Jacques de Maillard, 15, 77, 79, 80, 253, 311
Jari Taponen, 12, 16, 121, 304, 311, 322
Josefina Castro, 15, 95, 104, 304

known to the authorities, 305, 308, 310, 311, 313
Koninklijke Marechaussee, 27
Kriminalpolizei, 44, 46, 238

Landeskriminalamt, 44, 237, 245, 320
Landespolizei, 44, 49
law and order, 17, 194, 195, 258
law enforcement, 24, 31, 32, 81, 97, 103, 115, 130, 193, 194, 220, 221, 231, 250, 261, 262, 269, 272, 274, 275, 277, 282, 283, 286, 288, 289, 292, 293
leadership, 26, 29, 39, 49, 50, 51, 53, 54, 59, 131, 195, 205, 206, 215, 222, 235, 241
Leviathan, 23, 211
liberalism, 33
Liberals, 237
Lisbon, 15, 33, 34, 35, 39, 96, 97, 98, 99, 102, 103, 106, 107, 108, 109, 112
Ljubljana, 16, 146, 150, 152, 153, 154, 155, 156, 157, 159

local police, 3, 16, 30, 31, 37, 39, 40, 41, 42, 43, 48, 49, 52, 53, 89, 129, 130, 131, 132, 133, 134, 144, 147, 153, 156, 159, 219, 221, 230, 236, 238, 241, 252, 256, 257, 258, 260, 263, 274, 275, 277, 285
local policing, 3, 42, 123, 131, 135, 138, 139, 140, 150, 157, 158, 170, 172, 184, 185, 189, 207, 212, 220, 221, 260, 275, 292, 293
local politics, 121, 262, 271, 284, 285, 291, 292
local states, 17
Local strategies, 19, 268
localisation, 144, 146, 149
London, 8, 10, 12, 13, 14, 40, 41, 42, 43, 70, 64, 80, 201, 202, 204, 205, 206, 207, 209, 211, 212, 213, 214, 215, 216, 217, 218, 219, 220, 221, 222, 223, 224, 260, 263, 304, 312, 315, 317, 325
Luxembourg, 27
Lyon, 78, 79, 80, 81, 83, 85, 87, 104

Madrid, 5, 36, 39, 63, 304
maintenance regimes, 304, 312, 313, 317, 323, 324
Maja Modic, 16, 144, 147, 304, 311
major events, 241, 242, 243, 244
management, 130, 131, 149, 244
Marco Calaresu, 32, 174, 182, 185, 186, 190, 191, 192, 193, 304, 305, 314, 319, 320, 322
Maribor, 16, 146, 152, 153, 154, 155, 156, 157, 159
Marleen Easton, 18, 29, 79, 249, 252, 304, 320
mass events, 105, 311
mayors, 10, 18, 35, 53, 54, 63, 79, 80, 81, 82, 83, 84, 85, 87, 88, 104, 107, 108, 147, 152, 158, 167, 175, 188, 189, 191, 192, 193, 194, 195, 204, 205, 206, 211, 215, 216, 218, 222, 235, 237, 238, 240, 244, 251, 256, 257, 258, 259, 260, 261, 263, 273, 274, 278, 279, 282, 285, 286, 287, 289, 293, 311, 312
membership, 14, 17, 201, 209, 211, 222, 305, 306, 307, 322
metropolisation, 15, 77, 92
Metropolitan Police, 40, 41, 43, 55, 206, 215, 220, 263
metropolitan policing, 8, 9, 11, 12, 15, 17, 18, 19, 23, 63, 79, 92, 122, 127,

Index

137, 139, 149, 150, 159, 185, 186, 187, 192, 193, 194, 195, 201, 202, 203, 204, 207, 209, 210, 211, 212, 213, 219, 221, 222, 251, 254, 259, 273, 303, 304, 305, 306, 307, 308, 309, 310, 311, 314, 315, 316, 317, 318, 319, 322, 324, 325, 327
Middle East, 5, 270, 304
migrants, 137, 235, 237, 240, 276, 279, 280, 286, 304, 305, 314
migration, 11, 107, 209, 212, 237, 256, 264, 285, 304
Milan, 17, 182, 183, 185, 186, 187, 188, 189, 190, 191, 192, 193, 194, 195, 305, 319, 320, 326
minister of security and justice, 273
minister of the interior, 44, 125, 171, 188, 191, 194, 314
Molenbeek, 260, 320
money laundering, 43, 46, 273, 287, 290
monopoly of legal violence, 64
Mossos d'Esquadra, 37, 39
multiple-embedded case study design, 8
municipal, 16, 18, 19, 26, 28, 29, 32, 35, 39, 44, 46, 47, 48, 49, 50, 52, 53, 54, 71, 59, 60, 77, 78, 79, 80, 81, 82, 83, 84, 85, 86, 87, 88, 89, 90, 104, 92, 107, 108, 109, 112, 113, 115, 116, 129, 134, 135, 139, 140, 144, 147, 148, 151, 152, 153, 155, 156, 157, 158, 159, 170, 171, 172, 174, 175, 176, 184, 186, 189, 191, 192, 194, 195, 205, 210, 211, 214, 221, 249, 250, 251, 252, 254, 255, 259, 268, 271, 273, 274, 277, 283, 311, 312, 314, 317, 318, 324, 325
municipal authorities, 35, 107, 108, 158, 317
municipal forces, 29, 46, 71
municipal police, 29, 32, 35, 46, 47, 54, 81, 82, 83, 84, 107, 108, 112, 148, 170, 175, 176, 186
municipal wardens, 148, 153, 155, 158, 159
municipality, 19, 29, 32, 40, 53, 54, 55, 80, 81, 82, 83, 104, 107, 109, 134, 147, 151, 152, 153, 155, 159, 175, 189, 194, 241, 243, 245, 260, 261, 320
Mussolini, 31

Napoleonic, 30, 36, 37, 38, 47, 311, 312
national borders, 4, 16
national boundaries, 25
National Crime Agency, 217

National Crime Squad, 43
national police, 9, 15, 18, 23, 24, 25, 28, 30, 31, 37, 39, 40, 43, 50, 51, 52, 53, 54, 55, 70, 59, 60, 62, 63, 64, 97, 103, 105, 108, 110, 111, 113, 115, 116, 129, 131, 144, 147, 148, 149, 157, 168, 170, 175, 176, 190, 194, 220, 221, 262, 273, 274, 275, 279, 290, 292,☒306, 304
national policy, 18
national sovereignty, 203, 224
national state, 5, 15, 17, 18, 126, 167, 170, 172, 174, 183, 184, 201, 250
national territory, 24, 29, 34, 36, 49, 60
nationalists, 6, 201, 204
nation-state, 4, 6, 8, 15, 16, 17, 23, 25, 44, 50, 56, 63, 85, 95, 96, 183, 201, 202, 203, 303
negotiation, 70, 83, 84, 92, 108, 173, 176, 177, 211, 233, 244, 268, 273, 275, 308
neighbourhood, 24, 64, 106, 177, 253, 255, 289
neo-liberal, 16, 96, 117, 140, 254
network, 3, 8, 24, 65, 79, 80, 96, 99, 115, 231, 238, 243, 269, 284, 287
New Labour, 17, 207, 210
new localism, 17, 207, 223
NGOs, 151, 157, 230, 234, 237, 241, 244, 245
Nick Fyfe, 17, 52, 55, 59, 138, 201, 206, 207, 274, 275
nodal points, 4
nodes, 305
non-governmental organisations, 44, 111, 151, 216, 230
Nordic countries, 16, 121, 122, 123, 124, 125, 126, 127, 128, 129, 130, 137, 138, 139, 140
Nordic states, 12, 16
North Rhine-Westphalia, 18, 229, 233, 239, 242, 244
Northern Ireland, 17, 39, 40, 50, 51, 55, 56, 70, 71, 60, 61, 62, 202, 203, 204, 217
Norway, 60, 122, 123, 125, 126, 127, 138, 139

objectives, 42, 77, 84, 100, 108, 109, 110, 111, 113, 114, 132, 133, 135, 136, 138, 195, 215, 223, 256, 257, 259, 281, 285, 305, 306, 307, 308, 310, 311, 313, 323, 327
Octopus Agreement, 48

338 Index

Offender-oriented secondary strategies, 314
offender-oriented tertiary strategies, 257
offenders, 100, 112, 153, 156, 194, 203, 240, 242, 257, 270, 280, 281, 282, 283, 305, 306, 308, 309, 310, 311, 313, 314, 315, 316, 317, 318, 320, 325, 326
organised crime, 5, 43, 46, 99, 101, 102, 103, 124, 132, 135, 184, 189, 192, 202, 233, 273, 293, 305
outsourcing, 64, 101, 124, 147

Paris, 14, 15, 19, 28, 29, 39, 63, 64, 78, 79, 80, 83, 88, 90, 183, 212, 250, 254, 260, 262, 286, 305, 320, 323, 324
participation, 63, 96, 104, 109, 111, 113, 116, 140, 144, 146, 217, 310
patrolling, 123, 147, 148, 176, 185, 311, 314
Patten Report, 70
Paul Ponsaers, 3, 6, 8, 15, 19, 23, 25, 37, 48, 50, 54, 63, 147, 157, 175, 183, 184, 223, 249, 250, 252, 258, 260, 262, 263, 268, 275, 303, 304, 319
performance, 42, 52, 84, 130, 131, 132, 133, 135, 158, 175, 187, 210, 221, 222, 271, 290
plural policing, 3, 10, 24, 65, 96, 103, 144, 147, 148, 149, 157, 174, 175, 242, 249, 258
pluralisation, 32, 63, 64, 96, 110, 115, 126, 129, 137, 144, 146, 149, 168, 172, 175, 176, 177, 230, 244
plurality, 49, 64, 240, 243, 317
police academy, 54, 55, 59
Police and Crime Commissioners, 18, 202
Police and Crime Plan, 8, 204, 205, 215, 216, 218, 315, 317
police apparatus, 24
police authority, 41, 42, 105, 127, 240
police capacity, 27, 30, 33, 35, 37, 43, 61
police chief, 52, 54, 136, 289
police function, 24, 45, 64, 126
police models, 25
police reform, 27, 48, 64, 145, 219, 277
police system, 18, 24, 25, 26, 27, 28, 30, 31, 32, 33, 36, 39, 40, 41, 43, 44, 45, 46, 47, 49, 50, 51, 53, 54, 55, 70, 71, 59, 60, 62, 230, 243, 244, 274
policing agendas, 4, 6, 11, 15, 16, 17, 18, 19, 165, 182, 183, 186, 190, 201, 202, 203, 204, 205, 207, 209, 210, 211, 212, 221, 222, 223, 268, 270, 273, 275, 292, 293, 294, 304, 306, 308, 311, 314, 317, 323, 324, 325, 327
policing dialectics, 305, 322, 323, 327
policing strategy, 13, 16, 17, 133, 137, 177, 220, 277, 312, 317
policy agenda, 18, 109, 133, 170, 182, 192, 251, 253, 254, 270, 284, 290, 291, 292, 309, 310, 311, 312
policy formulation, 3, 11, 14, 25, 210, 211
political power, 31, 38, 63, 64, 96, 97, 158
polizia giudiziaria, 32
polizia sicurezza, 32
Porto, 11, 15, 34, 35, 39, 96, 98, 99, 102, 103, 106, 107, 108, 109
Portugal, 8, 15, 27, 33, 34, 35, 37, 38, 39, 95, 96, 97, 99, 100, 101, 102, 103, 104, 106, 107, 108, 115, 116, 117, 304
post-socialist, 16, 144, 145, 146, 148, 149, 157, 159
predicates, 9, 10, 11, 25, 209, 211, 221, 306
Préfecture de Police, 29
prevention, 24, 34, 35, 59, 77, 78, 79, 80, 81, 82, 84, 86, 87, 88, 104, 92, 93, 97, 99, 100, 102, 103, 104, 105, 106, 108, 109, 110, 112, 114, 116, 126, 132, 133, 134, 136, 137, 151, 174, 184, 190, 192, 230, 235, 237, 245, 253, 254, 256, 257, 258, 259, 269, 270, 271, 272, 279, 282, 288, 291, 315
primary populations, 308
priority, 185, 216, 220, 237, 238, 244, 254, 257, 259, 264, 282, 283, 286, 288, 290, 291, 292, 309, 311, 313, 316, 317, 318
privatisation, 117, 124, 146, 147, 149, 176, 254, 255
proactive, 70, 109, 174, 175, 177, 282, 309
problem-oriented, 25, 112, 315
professionalism, 71, 116
prosecution, 51, 52, 111, 114, 126, 155, 251, 308, 319
prosecutor, 32, 47, 48, 53, 54, 79, 87, 114, 156, 157, 240, 251, 256, 274, 279, 282, 283, 285, 287, 289, 290, 311
protection, 106, 123, 312
Protestants, 56

provinces, 49, 63, 186, 190, 249, 251, 263, 273
public order, 6, 24, 28, 31, 32, 34, 35, 51, 53, 97, 103, 108, 126, 127, 134, 138, 139, 147, 153, 155, 167, 170, 184, 242, 243, 249, 251, 252, 256, 271, 273, 274, 275, 287, 288, 305, 308, 310, 312, 313, 319
public space, 35, 78, 82, 113, 256, 270, 271, 291, 292, 293, 320
punitive display, 319
punitive turn, 102, 171

Rechtstaat, 18, 130
redistribution, 32, 147, 168, 172, 283, 309, 316
referendum, 6, 12, 17, 71, 106, 201, 202, 204, 305
reform, 17, 27, 28, 31, 40, 47, 48, 49, 54, 55, 60, 62, 82, 85, 101, 110, 113, 114, 117, 130, 135, 176, 186, 206, 209, 212, 219, 220, 235, 238, 251, 252, 259, 275, 305, 310, 311, 313, 319, 325
reformist regime, 318
regime failure, 322, 323, 327
regime theory, 291
regional, 15, 16, 17, 18, 19, 24, 26, 35, 36, 37, 39, 43, 50, 54, 60, 63, 64, 77, 78, 84, 116, 127, 130, 131, 133, 140, 150, 151, 167, 169, 170, 171, 175, 177, 184, 189, 190, 202, 203, 205, 206, 210, 213, 216, 217, 222, 223, 224, 229, 233, 237, 238, 250, 252, 253, 267, 255, 256, 258, 259, 260, 263, 268, 271, 273, 274, 275, 277, 279, 280, 283, 292, 293, 294, 304, 320, 327
regional forces, 37, 54
regions, 4, 18, 32, 39, 40, 45, 50, 63, 106, 107, 145, 167, 170, 172, 173, 176, 184, 185, 186, 190, 202, 206, 224, 234, 249, 251, 252, 254, 255, 262, 263, 304, 326
reintegration, 99, 224, 308
reorganisation, 4, 59, 89, 97, 98, 101, 190, 252, 273, 275, 277
reparation, 310, 319
republic, 28, 34, 45, 263
research strategy, 8
resilience, 6, 132, 139, 219
resistance, 63, 89, 109, 182, 194, 195, 222
restorative justice, 14, 223, 284, 310, 318, 321, 325, 327
Rigspolitiet, 52

Rijkspolitie, 54
riots, 42, 139, 140, 167, 218
risk management, 11, 14, 17, 78, 81, 115, 186, 194, 206, 211, 212, 223, 250, 257, 261, 262, 269, 270, 283, 284, 306, 308, 310, 313, 314, 316, 317, 319, 321, 323, 324, 325, 327
Rome, 17, 39, 63, 64, 167, 173, 182, 183, 185, 186, 187, 188, 189, 190, 191, 192, 193, 194, 195, 305, 314, 317, 322, 325
Rossella Selmini, 9, 17, 32, 167, 172, 173, 175, 176, 182, 184, 185, 186, 191, 192, 304, 305, 314, 319, 320, 322
Rotterdam, 19, 167, 268, 271, 275, 276, 282, 284, 285, 286, 287, 288, 289, 290, 291, 292, 293, 313, 317, 325
Royal Irish Constabulary, 55
Royal Ulster Constabulary, 55
rules of meaning and membership, 306
Ruth Prins, 8, 10, 13, 19, 40, 42, 43, 54, 65, 115, 182, 183, 204, 205, 209, 211, 215, 216, 217, 218, 249, 251, 260, 268, 270, 274, 276, 294, 304

safety, 5, 70, 64, 79, 96, 108, 109, 110, 123, 131, 132, 133, 134, 136, 137, 139, 140, 148, 151, 152, 153, 155, 171, 186, 192, 194, 213, 214, 215, 223, 229, 238, 241, 243, 249, 251, 256, 257, 262, 270, 273, 274, 275, 279, 280, 285, 286, 287, 288, 289, 292, 293, 310, 319
Salazar, 15, 33
Sarkozy, 311
Scandinavia, 124
Scarman, 42
scenario, 170, 224, 263, 325, 327
Schengen, 3, 6, 12, 44, 127, 138, 209, 232
Schutzpolizei, 44, 238
Scotland, 8, 39, 40, 50, 51, 71, 59, 60, 61, 62, 202, 203, 204, 206, 207, 208, 209, 219, 220, 221, 222, 318
secret police, 33, 146
securitisation, 3, 7, 321, 323, 324
Securitrans, 46
security, 3, 4, 5, 6, 7, 9, 10, 12, 13, 14, 15, 16, 17, 18, 23, 29, 31, 32, 33, 34, 35, 36, 37, 38, 44, 45, 52, 54, 70, 64, 65, 77, 78, 79, 80, 81, 82, 83, 84, 85, 86, 87, 88, 89, 90, 104, 92, 93, 95, 96, 97, 98, 99, 100, 101, 102, 103, 104, 105, 106, 107, 108, 109, 110, 111, 112, 113, 114, 115, 116, 117, 121, 122, 123,

124, 125, 126, 128, 129, 130, 131, 132, 133, 134, 135, 136, 137, 138, 139, 140, 141, 144, 147, 148, 149, 150, 151, 152, 155, 156, 157, 158, 159, 167, 168, 169, 170, 171, 172, 173, 174, 175, 176, 177, 182, 184, 185, 188, 189, 190, 191, 192, 194, 201, 202, 206, 208, 209, 217, 218, 219, 222, 223, 224, 229, 230, 231, 232, 234, 235, 236, 237, 238, 240, 241, 242, 243, 244, 245, 249, 250, 251, 252, 253, 254, 255, 256, 257, 258, 259, 260, 262, 263, 264, 269, 271, 272, 274, 275, 276, 277, 280, 282, 286, 287, 291, 293, 294, 303, 304, 311, 314, 315, 316, 317, 318, 319, 320, 321, 322, 323, 324, 326, 327
security threats, 13, 323
Seirbheis Phoilis na h-Alba, 59
separatists, 56
serious crime, 135, 170, 208, 233, 238
Serviço de Estrangeiros e Fronteiras, 34, 35, 103
Sicherheitspolizei, 46
Sinn Féin, 56
Sirpa Virta, 12, 16, 121, 125, 128, 130, 131, 132, 133, 134, 138, 139, 304, 311, 322
Slovenia, 144, 145, 146, 148, 150, 151, 152, 153, 154, 155, 156, 157
smart policing, 11, 315
social cohesion, 96, 100, 110, 202, 215, 253, 285, 288, 304, 305, 326
social democratic, 16, 122, 130, 224, 269, 322, 326
social integration, 253
social justice, 11, 14, 115, 208, 211, 214, 215, 218, 219, 222, 223, 263, 270, 271, 283, 292, 308, 319, 320, 321, 322, 326, 327
social unrest, 31
socialism, 33
socialist, 28, 79, 145, 146, 256
sociology of policing, 10
soldiers, 71, 149
Sophie Chambers, 17, 201, 214
sovereign state, 24, 71, 115, 117, 169, 174, 176, 177, 184
sovereignty, 5, 24, 117, 150, 168, 169, 170, 172, 177, 201
Spain, 8, 15, 27, 32, 35, 36, 37, 38, 39, 60, 61, 97, 175, 276, 304
standing conditions, 11, 14, 23, 209, 211, 212, 214, 219, 221, 222

state, 3, 5, 6, 7, 10, 16, 17, 18, 23, 24, 28, 30, 31, 32, 34, 36, 37, 38, 39, 40, 44, 45, 50, 51, 71, 63, 79, 80, 81, 83, 92, 95, 96, 97, 98, 100, 101, 102, 105, 106, 110, 111, 112, 113, 114, 115, 116, 117, 121, 122, 123, 124, 125, 127, 128, 129, 130, 146, 137, 138, 139, 140, 144, 145, 147, 148, 150, 151, 157, 158, 159, 167, 168, 169, 170, 172, 173, 174, 176, 177, 183, 185, 186, 188, 201, 202, 203, 204, 208, 210, 213, 222, 224, 229, 230, 231, 232, 233, 234, 235, 236, 237, 238, 241, 242, 244, 245, 249, 251, 252, 258, 263, 269, 278, 285, 286, 308, 317, 320, 321, 322, 324, 325, 326
state police, 232
Stockholm programme, 5, 9
Strasbourg, 15, 78, 79, 81, 82, 83, 85, 87
sub-national policing, 3, 8, 12, 204
subordination, 12, 321
surveillance, 6, 28, 35, 55, 64, 78, 82, 87, 105, 107, 108, 112, 137, 185, 190, 235, 242, 258, 270, 271, 281, 287, 306, 311, 313, 315, 321
Sweden, 60, 122, 123, 125, 126, 127, 139
Switzerland, 39, 40, 45, 46, 47, 49, 50

Tampere, 5, 126, 131, 134
territorial, 24, 26, 27, 28, 40, 42, 49, 50, 51, 59, 60, 61, 62, 63, 89, 92, 98, 101, 103, 107, 112, 130, 168, 175, 193, 204, 272
territorial competences, 26
territorial divided forces, 59
territorial forces, 40, 50
territorial police, 42, 51, 59, 60
territorially divided police systems, 15, 62
territorially divided systems, 62
terrorism, 5, 19, 35, 45, 46, 80, 98, 101, 102, 123, 124, 131, 132, 137, 138, 170, 202, 208, 231, 264, 271, 282, 306, 320
terrorist attacks, 123, 260, 278, 304
tertiary populations, 308
the Hague programme, 5
the Netherlands, 19, 27, 51, 53, 55, 60, 61, 268, 269, 270, 271, 272, 273, 274, 275, 276, 277, 281, 284, 293, 304, 311
The Troubles, 56
Top 600, 278, 279, 280, 281, 282, 283, 290, 292, 294, 313, 317, 319
Toulouse, 15, 78, 79, 82, 83, 84, 85, 87, 90

transformations, 95, 96, 97, 145, 150
transformative regimes, 292, 322, 326
transition, 3, 15, 16, 38, 52, 56, 97, 99, 116, 121, 138, 144, 145, 146, 149, 218, 234, 244, 254, 304, 311
translation, 4, 6, 7, 10, 286, 289, 291, 308
transnational, 3, 4, 5, 6, 12, 15, 16, 23, 127, 183, 201, 208, 212, 217, 218, 222, 224, 283, 303, 305
transnational threats, 5
transnationalisation thesis, 6
trust, 98, 121, 125, 128, 130, 133, 138, 139, 140, 149, 208, 223, 269
types of police, 26, 27, 30, 37, 48, 61
typology, 15, 24, 62

UK, 6, 12, 17, 39, 40, 43, 50, 56, 201, 202, 203, 204, 205, 206, 207, 208, 209, 212, 214, 215, 217, 219, 222, 223, 224, 242, 245, 305, 315, 316
Ulster Special Constabulary, 56
Ulster Volunteer Force, 56
uniformed service, 41, 52
urban, 4, 5, 6, 9, 10, 13, 17, 18, 19, 32, 34, 35, 36, 37, 38, 70, 77, 78, 80, 81, 85, 87, 88, 90, 104, 95, 96, 97, 99, 100, 102, 103, 105, 106, 108, 109, 110, 113, 115, 144, 167, 168, 169, 170, 171, 172, 173, 174, 176, 177, 182, 184, 185, 186, 187, 189, 190, 191, 192, 194, 206, 207, 230, 237, 238, 249, 251, 253, 255, 256, 257, 259, 260, 261, 262, 263, 264, 268, 271, 273, 274, 275, 278, 282, 285, 286, 287, 288, 289, 290, 291, 292, 293, 294, 320, 321
urban areas, 108
urban policing, 19, 185, 285, 288, 289, 291, 292
urban security, 96, 190, 263

variegation, 8, 12, 201, 202, 275
victimisation, 100, 111, 215, 218, 306, 308, 309, 310, 313, 315, 316, 317, 318, 319, 321, 324, 327
victim-oriented, 112
victims, 81, 82, 100, 109, 111, 194, 241, 290, 305, 306, 308, 310, 313, 315, 316, 317, 318, 323, 325, 326
vigilantes, 71

Wales, 8, 17, 39, 40, 41, 42, 43, 49, 50, 54, 71, 59, 202, 203, 204, 205, 206, 208, 210, 211, 212, 213, 214, 223, 274, 312, 318
Wallonia, 18, 252, 255
web of policing, 65
welfare state, 112, 117
Wiesbaden, 45, 232
working classes, 41

zonal, 40, 49, 50, 250
zones, 48, 49, 250, 252, 255, 260, 263

eBooks
from Taylor & Francis
Helping you to choose the right eBooks for your Library

Add to your library's digital collection today with Taylor & Francis eBooks. We have over 50,000 eBooks in the Humanities, Social Sciences, Behavioural Sciences, Built Environment and Law, from leading imprints, including Routledge, Focal Press and Psychology Press.

Free Trials Available

We offer free trials to qualifying academic, corporate and government customers.

Choose from a range of subject packages or create your own!

Benefits for you
- Free MARC records
- COUNTER-compliant usage statistics
- Flexible purchase and pricing options
- 70% approx of our eBooks are now DRM-free.

Benefits for your user
- Off-site, anytime access via Athens or referring URL
- Print or copy pages or chapters
- Full content search
- Bookmark, highlight and annotate text
- Access to thousands of pages of quality research at the click of a button.

eCollections
Choose from 20 different subject eCollections, including:
- Asian Studies
- Economics
- Health Studies
- Law
- Middle East Studies

eFocus
We have 16 cutting-edge interdisciplinary collections, including:
- Development Studies
- The Environment
- Islam
- Korea
- Urban Studies

For more information, pricing enquiries or to order a free trial, please contact your local sales team:

UK/Rest of World: **online.sales@tandf.co.uk**
USA/Canada/Latin America: **e-reference@taylorandfrancis.com**
East/Southeast Asia: **martin.jack@tandf.com.sg**
India: **journalsales@tandfindia.com**

www.tandfebooks.com